and **Deviance**

Social Control

and Deviance
Social Control

THIRD EDITION

Linda B. Deutschmann
University College of the Cariboo

NELSON

━━━━✦━━━━ ™

THOMSON LEARNING

Australia • Canada • Mexico • Singapore • Spain • United Kingdom • United States

NELSON

™

THOMSON LEARNING

Deviance and Social Control
Third Edition

by Linda B. Deutschmann

Editorial Director and Publisher:
Evelyn Veitch

Executive Editor:
Joanna Cotton

Marketing Manager:
Cara Yarzab

Developmental Editor:
Su Mei Ku

Production Editor:
Bob Kohlmeier

Production Coordinator:
Hedy Sellers

Copy Editor:
Dawn Hunter

Creative Director:
Angela Cluer

Proofreader:
Claudia Kutchukian

Interior Design:
Linda Neale and Katherine Strain

Cover Design:
Linda Neale and Katherine Strain

Cover Image:
EyeWire

Compositors:
W.G. Graphics and Alicja Jamorski

Indexer:
Edwin Durbin

Printer:
Webcom

National Library of Canada Cataloguing in Publication Data

Deutschmann, Linda Bell, 1943–
Deviance and social control

3rd ed.
Includes bibliographical references and index.
ISBN 0-17-616906-7

1. Deviant behavior. 2. Social control. I. Title.

HM291.D47 2001   302.5'42
C2001-900885-6

CONTENTS

CHAPTER 4 CLASSICAL THEORIES OF DEVIANCE AND THEIR INFLUENCE ON MODERN JURISPRUDENCE 105

CHAPTER 5 BIOLOGICAL AND PHYSIOLOGICAL EXPLANATIONS OF DEVIANCE 133

PREFACE

Unlike most other deviance textbooks, this one is organized to introduce the topic of deviance in a sequence that does not force students to grapple with concepts, names, and explanations that have not been introduced, that are explained a chapter or two later, or that are called different names without any explanation for the variation.

Three possible approaches can be used in the organization of a deviance text. The one chosen here has theory as its central theme and uses specific forms of behaviour as examples to illustrate these theories. It focuses on explanations and principles of analysis, and the way in which traditional approaches persist despite the arrival of newer orthodoxies. Unlike many other texts, each theory is presented in a serious and respectful way. This presentation allows the instructor to update the material quickly and adapt it to his or her interests simply by providing more examples or detail.

An alternative approach is to present each form of deviance in a separate chapter and attempt to include all relevant theories as applied to each form, and all the most contemporary data on its incidence and prevalence. Such a book might have a chapter on drug addiction and others on homosexuality and prostitution. This alternative is cumbersome, repetitive, likely to become outdated, and may offend some students who do not agree that a particular behaviour should be labelled deviant. It also allows the instructor little flexibility.

Another alternative is to present most theories as inadequate, while touting the universal applicability of the author's approach. This means that students are repeatedly asked to learn about a theory, only to be told that what they have just digested is useless or pernicious. The favoured theory gets uncritical attention. Thus, students are not given the evidence they need to make up their own minds about the validity and utility of each theory. When they go on to higher studies, they may find that what they have learned needs to be revised.

DEFINING DEVIANCE

This book takes a broad view of the nature of deviance, seeing it as both a constructed reality and as a phenomenon in society that has real causes and real consequences, and that often involves real behaviour. The connections between deviance and freedom, fun, and chaos are emphasized as much as its connection with social disapproval. This approach avoids both the extreme assumption that deviance is real and wrongful behaviour, and the more fashionable but also untenable idea that deviance is nothing but a label put on people by others.

METHODOLOGY

A grounding in "how we know what we know" underlies the material in all chapters of this book, not just Chapter 2, which deals specifically with methods. This approach permits students to be self-educating. Whenever possible, the book attempts to demonstrate how theoretically guided research enables us to see connections that were not obvious before. Students take away an enhanced understanding of how ideas about the nature of deviance and social control are related to the social circumstances in which they developed, and why there are so many competing voices in the field.

PRESCIENTIFIC THEORIES

Most texts spend little or no time on the perspectives of deviance that preceded the Renaissance. Nonetheless, these perspectives are still part of modern life and are important to a full understanding of the phenomena associated with deviance. The witchcraft craze, in particular, provides a paradigm for the analysis of what is real and what is constructed about deviance.

NONSOCIOLOGICAL THEORIES

Unlike most sociologically oriented texts, this one carefully considers alternative approaches—in particular, biological and psychological ones. Students are exposed to these ideas daily in the news and in literature. They have a right to know how these explanations "stack up" against sociological ones, and how these explanations might fit in with sociological ones.

SOCIOLOGICAL APPROACHES

Sociological approaches are presented in roughly the order in which they achieved popularity in the field, without ignoring the fact that most of them have roots in the late 1800s or earlier. In each case, the theories are presented in the context that made them popular, and with concern for the way in which their ideas continue to influence the field. The structure of the text allows instructors to increase or modify the coverage of these theories (particularly the later ones, where controversy still reigns) without confusing students.

WOMEN AND DEVIANCE

Most textbooks on deviance have assumed, without explicitly saying so, that women's deviance is not a separate issue from men's, or is not interesting enough, except with respect to prostitution, to discuss. This text attempts to "bring women back in" in a real sense, noting when and how theorists have distorted the images of women, and when and how these lacunae are being met in modern approaches such as power-control, conflict, and feminist theories, as well as postmodern and postfeminist theories.

READABILITY AND INTEREST

Every effort has been made to make this text the kind of book that can be read without a great deal of instructional assistance, but also without "writing down" to the reader. Wherever possible, theorists have been presented as real people whose personalities and social contexts matter. Throughout, examples have been chosen that typically represent the central interests of the relevant theorists, and that also have interest for today's students and instructors.

ACKNOWLEDGMENTS

I owe a debt of gratitude to my husband, Karl, and children, Michael and Audrey, for making space for me to work on this. I'd like to thank my sister and brother-in law, Sheila and George Hervey, for very tangible support and encouragement. I would particularly like to thank Doug Campbell and Marion Blute at the University of Toronto for the help they provided with the first edition, and Nan McBlane, Dawn Farough, John Cleveland, David MacLennan, and Julianna Momirov, at the University College of the Cariboo, for putting up with me during the process of this edition.

I also wish to thank all those who have helped transform this work from its untidy proposal, to overlong manuscript, all the way to finished book. Reviewers helped to make an unwieldy manuscript clearer and more accurate. I would particularly like to thank the following: Ingrid Connidis, University of Western Ontario; John Manzo, University of Toronto; Doug Skoog, University of Winnipeg; and Terry Willett, Queen's University.

Thanks also to the reviewers of the second edition, and thanks to all at Nelson Thomson Learning. Su Mei Ku performed brilliantly in pruning excess verbiage and generally making the product more readable. I am grateful to Joanna Cotton for her strong leadership and organization, and especially for her help in bridging the gap between the second edition and this one. My thanks also to those who helped make the earlier editions a good basis for this one. All of this effort resulted in a better book.

Linda B. Deutschmann
University College of the Cariboo

ISSUES IN THE STUDY OF DEVIANCE

This book is about sin, violence, road rage, sexualities, adultery, "bad seed" children, drug trafficking, insanity, alcoholism, treason and terrorism, nudism, obesity, and being rude. It is about any behaviour or characteristic that is improper, illegal, weird, bizarre, immoral, or contaminating. It is also about the rule makers and enforcers of all kinds—the moral majority, the boycotters, ostracizers, gossips, "old ladies in tennis shoes," and (sometimes) best friends. This book is about all kinds of deviance and about social control, which is an inseparable part of these things.

Deviant activities are usually at least partially hidden and frequently misrepresented; they invite us to become detectives who uncover, describe, and explain them. Some deviant activities can be fascinating and (at least in part) not much different from their media images. The drug trafficker may take breathtaking risks—making jungle runway landings in the middle of civil wars, risking violent intervention by underworld rivals and possible long-term incarceration at home or in foreign prisons, and relying heavily on dangerous and unpredictable people (Andreas, 2000). Trafficking also offers a chance at a life of luxury: jet-setting parties, celebrity connections, and a certain kind of respect (Dorn, Murji, & South, 1992; Rice, 1989; Sabbag, 1976/1990). Even lower-level traffickers may have flashy cars and expensive clothes, making them powerful role models for youths (Boyd, 1991; Malarek, 1989). However, much deviance (mental disorders, street prostitution, drug dependence) is, or can be, part of lives that are ugly and banal, full of despair, and potentially much less interesting than their media representations.

Some deviant activities (or deviant characteristics) are openly bizarre or "freakish." For example, people who have dramatic types of acquired or inherited disorders, people who mutilate themselves, and people who defecate in public are just not like the rest of us, even if a great deal of their difference is developed in response to the way in which they are treated. Other kinds of deviance, such as taking a few pens home from work or being less than truthful to customs officers, are often treated as almost normal. Still other kinds of deviance, such as treason or corporate crime, can be conspiratorial and subversive, either undermining the fundamental beliefs, values, and rules of a society or forcing us to defend what we value. Whatever shape they take, deviance and its control are central aspects of social life, and understanding them can make us more aware of our surroundings.

WHY STUDY DEVIANCE?

When you choose to study deviance, you should be aware of your own motives. These motives will influence which topics will interest you, the methods you will select to find out about the deviance, and the kinds of answers that will satisfy you. Typical reasons for studying deviance are discussed below, along with some indication of how each motive can affect the enterprise of understanding deviance.

VICARIOUS EXPERIENCE

We can enrich our lives vicariously by living (in our heads) the apparently more exciting or interesting lives of others—or by investigating them and discovering that our own lives are preferable. Psychiatrists tell us that fascination with deviance can be a way of dealing with disowned parts of ourselves. It can be an indirect way of coping with the forbidden urges that most of us suppress as we grow up. Even for the most conforming of us, certain "moral and sensual attractions of evil" (Katz, 1988) exist. These attractions seduce some people into deviance, entice some into voyeurism, and inspire others to seek increased understanding through careful research.

Vicarious living is a habit that our culture reinforces. Media moguls know, and program ratings prove, that watching sneaky conniving people treat each other badly is much more interesting to most of us than watching pleasant orderly people be good, responsible citizens. Vicariously, we can experience the thrill, without taking the risks, of deviance.

Vicarious experience as a research motivation, however, can distort our understanding of deviance. It leads us to study the rare specimens of deviance (such as homosexual-necrophiliac-cannibal-serial killer Jeffrey Dahmer). The result is a concentration on violent, sexual, and crazy deviance and a lack of interest in the more frequent but less dramatic forms of deviance such as cheating, exploiting, and living on the edge. This disparity increases the commonsense errors of seeing the dividing line between normal and deviant as much clearer than it really is and of seeing the deviants as much more reprehensible than most of them (most of us?) really are.

REFORM

Sometimes an interest in reform is personal. Living in a district plagued by prostitution and drug use can cause daily aggravations and sharpen a person's interest in understanding street deviance and its control. Similarly, personal knowledge of the devastation of drug dependence, rape, murder, or drunk driving may provoke the desire to know more about their causes and cures.

Box 1.1   Deviance as a Means of Literary Inspiration

Great literature often has as its theme sin, crime, or disorder and treats it as a central aspect of the human condition. Writers have been criticized for glamorizing or glorifying deviance in their works and sometimes for even addressing it at all. In authors as diverse as Sophocles, Dickens, Dostoyevsky, and Shakespeare are common themes of transgression, punishment, remorse, and revenge. Other literary figures have written about adultery, incest, and homosexuality (Lawrence Durrell, Jean Genet, William S. Burroughs); about drug intoxication (Samuel Taylor Coleridge, Thomas de Quincey, Aldous Huxley, Malcolm Lowry); about pacts with evil or with the devil (Joseph Conrad, Bram Stoker, Robert Louis Stevenson); and about being an "outsider" (Camus).

Many well-known authors themselves lived on the fringes of acceptability and used their experiences in deviance as literary themes. The Beat Generation, exemplified by such writers as William S. Burroughs and Jack Kerouac, actively pursued deviant sexual and drug experiences as a way of shaping their public personas and inspiring their literary efforts (Morgan, 1988). Malcolm Lowry used his alcoholic dreams to fuel his writing, as did Aldous Huxley with his mescaline-induced visions. Coleridge's "Kubla Khan" resulted from a dream inspired by the poet's use of laudanum, a form of opium. The French recognize a whole school of "criminal writers," including Jean Genet, a homosexual-pederast thief who did much of his writing in prison. The British, somewhat less extreme, produced the "Angry Young Men" writers who revolted against good taste, the prevailing mores, and class distinctions during the 1950s.

Other writers may have owed their creativity to various forms of mental or physical illness (Gutin, 1996). William Blake, John Keats, Edgar Allan Poe, Mary Shelley, and Robert Louis Stevenson, for example, were very likely manic-depressives. Dostoyevsky suffered from epileptic seizures. Even syphilis and tuberculosis have been credited with creative inspiration (Gutin, 1996).

The actual creative benefits to be accrued from illnesses or from perilous lifestyles are debatable. Perhaps these writers might have been even more creative had they not been afflicted or lived such dissolute lives.

Sometimes the interest is more abstract and professional but still oriented toward changing something. Some of us study deviance because we recognize that knowing how (and whether) to do something about deviance has value. Being the expert who knows how to make hyperactive children happy in the classroom, how to identify stalkers, or how to set up the most effective parole system is very satisfying. Discovering the real dimensions of hidden abuses such as family violence or the problems of assisted suicide among AIDS patients can lead to better policies (DeKeseredy & Hinch, 1991; Ogden, 1994). Revealing that some fears about deviance are unnecessary and exaggerated (for example, most fears about people with mental illnesses) is also satisfying, especially when it eventually allows for the liberation of people who are just a bit different (in choices, in appearance, or in abilities) and for their inclusion as part of an enriched community.

Reform as a research motivation has its own dangers. There are three main ones. First, our search for reform policies sometimes outruns our tested knowledge. For example, the currently popular assumption that lack of self-esteem causes delinquent behaviour can result in programs that produce proud delinquents rather than ex-delinquents. The idea that criminals lack social skills can mean programs that produce more highly skilled criminals (Weisman, 1993). Examples of such programs, which were based on improperly tested theories, abound, as do examples of procedures such as hysterectomy or sex therapy for female unhappiness and stress (Maines, 1999).

Second, the belief that understanding means excusing is often part of the reform motivation, and this belief may hinder us. Criminal profilers, for example, have learned that they can be more successful if they set their own discomfort aside and "think like the predator" (Douglas & Olshaker, 2000; Jackson & Bekerian, 1997; Michaud, 2000). The good detective is not afraid of understanding the subject matter.

Third, reform impulse also ignores the fact that many kinds of deviance are not as harmful as they are made out to be. The historical record shows us that many things that were deviant a generation ago (such as women going to medical schools) are now seen as precursors of social change and signs of the growth and adaptation of society to new conditions.

SELF-PROTECTION AND SOPHISTICATION

Something is inherently appealing about knowing what goes on behind the facades of social life. Being knowledgeable about the tactics of cult recruiters, drug pushers, muggers, terrorists, and con artists can make us feel wiser and safer (though researching these tactics can be dangerous and difficult). Equally valuable, though, is the ability to recognize that some deviants are not as harmful as their demonized reputations imply so that we do not become caught up in moral panics about things that are better left alone.

UNDERSTANDING ONESELF AND OTHERS

Some people enjoy having a deviant image, even if they can indulge in it only on Saturday night; others seek a more permanent identification with deviant lifestyles and images. They cultivate a style that wins them respect in unconventional milieus. They may use tattoos, clothing styles, or body language to symbolize their "otherness."

We see a different cultivation of deviant identity in popular and fringe artists and performers. Some choose names associated with evil and chaos and carry this theme through to their CD covers, stage performances, and lyrics. Many adopt lifestyles

Box 1.2   Deviance and the Media

Deviance, especially bizarre or criminal deviance, is the bread and butter of modern journalism. This phenomenon is not new. In the supposedly prudish Victorian era, newspapers teemed with sensationalist accounts of murder, suicide, child battering, and social disorder. As Boyle (1989) recounts,

> *The Times* of January 3, 1857, lay open before me. It featured an account of "The Double Murder of Children in Newington," a lead article on "Robberies and Personal Violence," an extended rendition of "A Week of Horror." Having consumed these tid-bits, I decided to move on to something I assumed would be quite different. *The Miner and Workman's Advocate*—the other end of the journalistic social scale from the august *Times*—featured, on page 3 alone of the January 7, 1865, edition, "The Poisoning of Five Persons at Gresford," "Extraordinary Outrage in Ireland," "Horrible Murder at Aldershot by a Madman," "Steamer Runs Down and Four Men Drowned on the Clyde," "Shocking Child Murder," and "Horrible Death by Fire." (pp. 3–4)

The contemporary mass media give even greater attention to themes of deviance (especially violence and sex), which resonate with people's anxieties about their personal safety and about threats to the social order. A brief look at the front pages of almost any newspaper will confirm that deviance is a major part of the messages we receive each day. Television also carries these images. Since the latter part of the 1980s, we have seen an exponential increase in true-crime and simulated-crime programs (Kappeler & Blumberg, 1996, p. 11). In the news, "if it bleeds, it leads"(Kerbel, 2000). As for commercial films, in Medved's words (1991, p. 40): "Indescribable gore drenches the modern screen, even in movies allegedly made for families. And the most perverted forms of sexuality—loveless, decadent, brutal and sometimes incestuous—are showing regularly at a theatre near you."

The media do not merely reflect true stories: they create legends that construct our perception of reality and have a heavy impact on what we fear and how we behave as a result.

that cross the normal bounds of polite society, and in the process, they attract media (if not police) attention. Learning about the choices of others can make our own choices clearer.

INTELLECTUAL CURIOSITY

A very important reason for studying deviance is pure, disinterested curiosity. An investigation of the role of the pimp in prostitution may be conducted either with an interest in controlling pimps (reform motivation) or with a *disinterested* agenda of simply finding out who pimps are, how they become pimps, what they actually do, and how they leave the role, if they do. Ironically, the second approach is sometimes more practical than the first.

Wanting to know how things work, without worrying about the consequences, has a respectable history in the hard sciences such as chemistry and physics (despite their connection to pollutants and bombs). It has had a more troubled history in the social sciences, where the demand for immediate practical results has usually been more pressing, less easily evaded, and more clearly political. Those who study deviance are often pressured to share common value judgments about it and to provide solutions for controlling it. Although disinterested research may ultimately change social values, and may have policy implications, this is not its primary purpose.

Whatever our initial motives in researching deviance, we will find it a challenging endeavour. Many kinds of deviance are either totally hidden or presented to us only in distorted images. When authorities want to seem effective, they may hide evidence of deviance, but when they want to justify new or greater controls, they may maximize or even invent deviance. Deviants often develop camouflages to avoid detection, to make others afraid of them, or to create social space in which they can operate undisturbed. Such hidden activity becomes fertile ground for illusions and misunderstandings, which are not easily corrected without extensive, controlled, and repeated research. The final truth is always a bit out of reach. But good research is rigorous and honest in its approach to deviance, and it seeks to discover what lies behind the facades maintained by deviants and authorities alike.

PERSPECTIVES ON DEVIANCE

People do not always agree about which behaviours are deviant or about how deviant they are. This is particularly true when people have different backgrounds or standpoints with respect to the behaviour. The standpoint of rapper musician Eminem (accused of believing the messages of his racist, homophobic, and theatrically obnoxious songs) will have little in common with that of advice columnist Miss Manners (Martin, 1997). Your own standpoint on a subject such as cheating or speeding may well vary by whether the perpetrator is an insider or an outsider, friend or stranger. Context is also important. For example, acceptable behaviour in the classroom will likely show much less variation than acceptable normal behaviour at a sports event. But within the same context, this range of tolerance varies by social class, gender, ethnic and cultural background, age, and political power of the actors involved, and it changes over time. Many current icons (saints) were deviants in their own times.

STUDENT VIEWS ON DEVIANCE

In a classroom exercise carried out in the 1980s, Erich Goode asked 230 undergraduates to write down examples of what they regarded as deviant behaviour (1990). Most commonly mentioned were murder (50 percent) and rape (37 percent). Among the 80 examples unique to individual students were "pretending you are a bird" and "wearing shorts when it snows." Students cited homosexuality and robbery with equal frequency (23 percent) (Goode, 1990, p. 2). Does this mean that murder and sexual variation are seen as equally serious forms of deviance? Probably not.

A less formal 1991 classroom survey of nearly 300 Canadian university students uncovered the following nominations for deviant status: murderers, rapists, child molesters, flashers, delinquents, junkies, drug sellers, "mental cases," prostitutes, pimps, the morbidly obese, idiots, freaks, nymphomaniacs, pyromaniacs (and other maniacs), drag queens, nerds, cheats, clowns, boors, lawyers, politicians, and a wide variety of people judged to be nasty, sneaky, vile, evil, corrupt, sick, twisted, violent, dangerous, decadent, perverted, bizarre, eccentric, outlandish, or simply annoying (Deutschmann, 1991). Campus living produced some special categories of deviance that might not have been mentioned as often outside a university setting. These included freeloading, getting drunk and throwing up, smoking in bed, keeping watermelons in the refrigerator, indulging in loud tasteless music, and being a "gross slob." Among nominations were people who were "too good" to be normal, including "browners," drudges, (obvious) virgins, tattletales, and religious or political do-gooders.

Students in another Canadian deviance class were asked to "do something deviant for six weeks, without explaining to others that it is a class assignment, and then write a report on this experience." Complaints about the assignment resulted in regulation by an administratively appointed committee. The committee demanded student proposals concerning the deviance they would commit and decided which proposals were "acceptable." Students, at first alarmed that they were being asked to commit serious offences and ruin their reputations and then mystified by the challenge of finding "acceptable deviance," finally settled into behaviour such as wearing dark glasses all the time or bringing a two-year-old to their classes. One Toronto student, who painted each of her nails a different colour, actually started a new, but brief, fad.

Stuart Henry, a professor at Eastern Michigan University, ran a similar project. He reports:

> The high trust between myself and the students brought some very worrisome problems, including a planned burglary with dates, times, places and method of entry, and a proposal from two students who wanted to steal a car in order to "get into the deviant action scene"! Both proposals, of course, were signed by the students and contained enough evidence to guarantee a criminal conviction for us all. (Henry & Eaton 1999, p. ix)

Henry's class produced papers on erotic activities, restaurant (and other workplace) scams, sports deceptions, drug use, self-mutilation, alternative lifestyles, and coping with the involuntary deviance of alcoholism, hyperactivity, and chronic illness.

PUBLIC OPINIONS ABOUT DEVIANCE

In the 1960s, J. L. Simmons reported that a sample of 180 persons, varying in age, sex, education, religion, ethnicity, and locale, cited 152 distinct acts and persons as deviant (Simmons, 1969, p. 3). Most subjects reported criminal behaviour and sexual variants as deviant. Less common nominations included suburbanites, "straights," executives, "smart-aleck" students, and "know-it-all" professors.

One way of measuring the seriousness attributed to deviance is to ask respondents to rate the seriousness in a vignette or story (Byers, 1993) or to rank different types of deviance (Mentor & Dorne, 1998). Repeatedly, and across various nationalities, we find that people rate similar acts as "criminal" and tend to rate these criminal acts as more serious than "immoral or disgusting" deviant acts. Examination of the penalties for particular offences suggests that we tend to take disloyalty (especially treason) more seriously than most other infractions, even violent ones.

Nonetheless, significant variations occur in the views of people with differing religious beliefs and social backgrounds, and waves of concern (moral panics) over particular kinds of infractions are discernable over the course of history (Jenkins, 1998; Mentor & Dorne, 1998; Thompson, 1998). Little work has been done at a general level to isolate the situations or contexts in which various kinds of deviance will be taken seriously, but we can observe wide variations in people's responses to real-life situations. For example, many celebrities engage in behaviour that, if indulged in by the rest of us, would lead to arrest or committal for psychiatric observation. What is tolerated and rewarded (if not approved) for them is out of bounds for us.

ACADEMIC VIEWS OF DEVIANCE

Before the 1960s, academics studying deviance tended to focus on "outsiders"—addicts, strippers, prostitutes, and people with mental illnesses—and treated them as exotic specimens in the "deviance zoo" (Polsky, 1967). Apart from Edwin Sutherland's heavily censored criminological work, little interest was manifested in the behaviour of powerful and "respectable" white-collar criminals and cheats. Textbooks included chapters on sexual perversions ("nuts, sluts, and perverts") (Liazos, 1972). Deviance was treated as *absolute;* that is, it was treated as something real in itself rather than something that depended on the attitudes of others.

The increasing popularity of sociological conflict theories in the 1960s helped to expose this imbalance. There was increased activism on the part of formerly marginalized "deviant" populations (for example, homosexuals) who resisted the double deviantization of being treated as outsiders by academics as well as the public. The idea that deviance was relative to the situation and the observers became more commonly accepted.

Sometimes, however, academics have attempted to establish their own absolute standards. Marxian and humanist writers in particular have maintained that deviance is found whenever human actions are exploitative or threaten the dignity and quality of life of others (Platt, 1985; Schwendinger & Schwendinger, 1983; Simon & Eitzen, 1993). Here, it is the researcher who decides what is (or ought to be) deviant, and studies it even if it turns out to be the most common and most accepted way of doing things.

DEFINING DEVIANCE

Many attempts have been made to establish a definition of deviance. Most of these attempts are seriously flawed, as will be shown below. A definition is neither right nor wrong, it is merely more or less useful. A useful definition is usually one that is objective, basic, noncircular, and distinctive.

OBJECTIVE CHARACTERISTICS

A purely objective definition points to empirical features of the subject, to what is physically present and can be seen, heard, and measured. It does not involve moralistic or emotional evaluations. The achievement of such value neutrality is neither easy nor always possible. Values slip into our choice of subject matter, our division of fields of study, and our language. Social science must frequently work with (or find ways around) concepts like "slum," "pervert," or "bastard," all of which contain negative emotional and moral evaluations.

One way around this problem is to translate value-laden statements into statements that have empirical referents. Thus, value statements such as "these boys are delinquent" can be translated into statements such as "these boys damage other people's property," or "these boys have juvenile court convictions"—statements that can be shown to be correct or incorrect by recording the boys' observed behaviour or by examining court records. Such translation increases the chances that different researchers will classify "these boys" in the same way, thus allowing for meaningful discussion and the accumulation of information.

The main problem with objective approaches to deviance is that the actual assignment of deviance labels by society is never purely objective. Deviance carries a negative moral evaluation as an intrinsic part of its popular meaning, and the label of "deviant" is sometimes applied to people based on very flimsy or even manufactured evidence.

A BASIC DEFINITION (NO ASSUMPTIONS)

A basic definition points to the phenomena that we want to study without making any unnecessary assumptions about them. Some definitions of deviance include the assumption that deviance is sickness or political protest (e.g., the thief is working out psychological problems or protesting the institution of private property). Such assumptions are premature. A useful rule to remember is not to assume what you may want to investigate.

Useful definitions are *noncircular*. An example of circularity would be defining a violation of the rules as something you can be arrested for, and then defining something you can be arrested for as a violation of the rules. When a definition goes in circles like this, it is essentially meaningless. The challenge of deviance studies is to find ways of identifying deviance without falling into the trap of circularity.

One way of evading circularity is to find something *distinctive* about deviance, something that is present in every case of deviance and that distinguishes deviance from other kinds of behaviour (Gibbs, 1981, p. x). Many false starts have been made in the effort to find something objective that distinguishes deviance, some of which are outlined below.

Statistical Rarity

Deviance is often equated with atypicality or deviation from a common centre. This conception is represented in the *bell curve* or *normal* distribution (see Figure 1.1). Characteristics that are counted as most common are deemed normal, while behaviour that varies from this norm (often measured in standard deviations) is held to be deviant. Data on many characteristics, such as alcohol consumption (abstainer, casual drinker, alcoholic), intelligence (below average, average, genius), driving speed (far below the limit, at the limit, far above the limit), and moral development (degenerate scum, slightly imperfect, saint) seem to fit this pattern.

Although heavy drinkers, people with below average intelligence, and extremely fast drivers are likely to be deviant in both the statistical and the social sense of the term, the connection is not always so close. Not all curves in society are normal

Figure 1.1   The Normal Curve and Alcohol Use

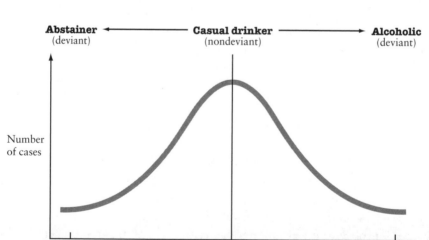

curves. For example, a deviance class may consist of two groups of students: those who are taking the course because it sounded more interesting than anything else that would fit their last-minute timetable, and those who are acquiring a highly desired credit that will help them gain access to a competitive program, such as law. In such a case, the grades curve may very well be bimodal, with a lower central tendency for the slight interest students, and a higher one for the competitive ones. What is normal in the one subgroup may be deviant with respect to the other. In addition, neither group will be called or think of itself as deviant.

Another type of curve often found in social life is the J-curve of institutional conformity (see Figure 1.2), which applies to behaviour such as arriving on time, getting back to your car before the meter runs out, filing your income tax return before the deadline, and stopping your car behind or just over the line at intersections (Allport, 1934, p. 167; Katz & Schanck, 1938). In the normal case, not as many people will arrive half an hour late as will arrive half an hour early for an appointment. The assumption that curves are, or should be, normal (or J-shaped) has occasionally distorted conclusions about whether a behaviour differs from the norm and is deviant.

An even more important risk in the use of statistical measures of deviance is the fact that many kinds of disreputable behaviour are hidden rather than rare. The normal behaviour may only seem to be the most common form. Kinsey's studies of human sexuality shocked North Americans in the 1940s and 1950s not only by revealing the pervasiveness of extramarital relationships but also that more than half of the men studied had had "at least some homosexual experience to the point of orgasm" (Gathorne-Hardy, 2000; Kinsey, Pomeroy, & Martin, 1948). Similarly,

Figure 1.2   The J-Curve of Institutional Conformity

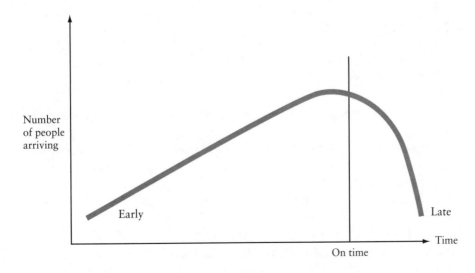

behaviour that is regarded as bad and even criminal (e.g., the use of illegal drugs or certain sexual practices) may be statistically normal or at least quite common. Consider the following people; are they statistically deviant, socially deviant, both, or neither: Politicians who deceive, former hippies who smoke marijuana, people who eat rattlesnake steaks, adults who attend church more than once a week, skydivers, students who love to study? The statistical method is simple and apparently objective, but it is not a reliable way of distinguishing deviance.

Harmfulness

It is often supposed that deviance is distinctively harmful. Terrorists may threaten us directly when they blow up a plane and indirectly when their activities lead to airports becoming so regulated that they are almost impassable. Corporate criminals pollute our environment, steal our money, allow unsafe workplaces, or sell us dangerous products. Pedophiles steal children's innocence and, because of them, pats on the back and supportive hugs have become off-limits in the classroom and on the playing field.

The harms that people associate with deviance are usually physical (bodily harm), functional (harm to the working of the system), and ontological (disruption of faith in the system, fears of chaos or disorder). Physical harm is the easiest to demonstrate. Almost every action or inaction carries some risk, and when an act is deemed deviant, the perpetrator risks the additional consequences of social disapproval. Thus, even if you are among those who regard a bit of marijuana as harmless in itself, you know that possessing it can get you into trouble. Functional harm occurs when deviance has a negative effect on the way that a particular system works. Consider the case of a man who buys products in one city and sells them at a higher price in another. Is he deviant? Not in a capitalist country, where he is simply fulfilling the expected role of the entrepreneur and helping the system to run at maximum efficiency. In a country with a government-controlled economic system, however, he might well be disturbing the central plan for the distribution of goods and earning himself a prison term. The least easy to explain is ontological harm. Giordano Bruno was among the first to claim that the earth is not the centre of the universe. This belief (now confirmed) undermined the cosmology of Church teachings in his time and threatened the order that was based on these beliefs. Bruno was executed by burning, and others like him were silenced by their fear of the same fate. Bruno's ideas not only threatened the working of the system but also undermined things that made the medieval world meaningful. The fact that Bruno contributed to chaos and disorder seemed much more important, at the time, than the evidence that he was correct.

For at least three reasons, harmfulness does not distinguish or define deviance. First, the evidence that deviance is harmful is often exaggerated or even entirely invented by those who, for whatever reasons, want to control it. Although heroin, marijuana, and cocaine undoubtedly present real dangers, all these drugs have been subject to grossly inflated claims concerning the speed, totality, and inevitability of their destructive effects. Marijuana, for example, was once blamed for sudden outbursts of violent insanity, for provoking the murder of families, and even for contributing to mental retardation and interracial sex (Murphy, 1922/1973). These exaggerated claims were spread by government agencies and asserted by respected people such as judges. This dissemination helped fuel public support for legislation that was in turn used to increase the regulation of those deemed likely to be users: a variety of "outsiders" such as jazz musicians, sailors, Mexicans, and Chinese immigrants (Blackwell & Erickson, 1988; Boyd, 1991). Politically effective in the 1930s, these claims are now thoroughly discredited. They have left a credibility gap that continues to plague drug and safe sex information programs more than 70 years later.

Second, in many cases the greatest harm of deviance lies in the cost of its suppression. In some countries, political deviants are tortured and killed, and citizens' lives are circumscribed by fear of denunciation. In many places, consensual adult sexual activity is punished, even when there is no direct victim. And over and over again, incorrect allegations of deviant behaviour cause innocent people to be harmed. The policing of deviance typically results in increasing restrictions on social freedom. For example, stores must protect their goods from thieves, shoplifters, and internal shrinkage at the hands of employees, which not only increases the cost of goods but also gives rise to the invasion of privacy by secret shoppers, hidden cameras, and other forms of technology. Wiretapping, opening mail, and keeping files on a wide range of citizens and organizations arise out of fears of terrorism and subversion. In turn, our fears sometimes induce us to accept control by powers that can be abused. When those entrusted with the control of deviance are themselves corrupted, or just ignorant, society loses twice.

Third, many kinds of deviance are demonstrably less harmful—physically or emotionally—than other things that are not so labelled. As Pfohl (1985) notes, "The executive who manipulates prices, who builds unsafe vehicles, and refuses to allow his wife to have interests of her own may do more harm than the thief, the embezzler or the rapist." The ideas of Galileo, like those of Bruno, so deviant in their time, are now celebrated as breakthroughs to a better society. Thus, despite the fact that claims about its distinctive rarity or harmfulness almost always accompany claims that an act or appearance is deviant, we cannot use this as a reliable defining characteristic of what deviance is.

Normative Violation

If rarity and harmfulness do not work consistently to define deviance, what might be a more reliable defining characteristic? Current definitions of deviance tend to agree with Robert Merton (1961), who says that deviant behaviour "refers to conduct that departs significantly from the norms set for people in their social statuses" (pp. 723–724). That is, there is a right and respectable (normative) way to be a professor, a student, an officer of a bank, or a priest, and a wrong or deviant way to behave in these status positions.

One way of looking at the normative definition of deviance is to look for the normative standard that governs the behaviour. For each form of deviance, at least one standard is being violated. For example, in terms of gender roles, the normative standards invoked in Box 1.3 establish heterosexual males as the standard and those who differ from them as deviants. Similarly, the normative dominance of capitalist forms of enterprise over alternative forms has often meant that people who prefer to involve themselves in noncompetitive, nonprofit, environmentally conscious types of enterprise have, at least until recently, been subjected to deviance labels.

It would appear, at first glance, that normative violation *should* be a good way of defining deviance. (It is certainly more defensible than rarity or harmfulness.) We will first look at how well it fits, and then deal with its limits. Normative violation lies closer to the way in which social groups formulate and identify deviations than does the statistical or harmfulness measure. As human beings, we can do anything that our size, strength, intelligence, and coordination permit. Nevertheless, most of us act within a far more limited range than potentially allowed by our physical nature. Consider, for example, how human clothing varies from the enveloping black or white robes favoured in the desert to the nude or nearly nude beach fashions. The sand and temperature may be the same, but the adaptation to it is not. The overall style is not left to the individual in either place but is enforced through norms that are expressed in rules and customs.

Many motivations for conformity exist. We conform because we want respect, because we respect those who teach us what is right and wrong, because we fear to do otherwise, or because we cannot imagine doing things differently. The rules that inform this behaviour may not be recognized as external ones. Often they seem like the only right way to do things or simply like the way things are done, without any accompanying rationale. Even if we break the rules, we are likely to do so in ways suggested by them, following the distinctive patterns of our society (Cancian, 1975; Sagarin, 1977, p. 431).

Box 1.3　Normative Standards and Definitions of Deviance

Deviant Category	*Normative Standard*
Heretic	Religious orthodoxy, violated beliefs
Sinner	Religious regulation, acts
Traitor	Loyalty
Homosexual	Gender roles, opposite-gender cathexis
Transvestite	Gender-role signification
Promiscuous woman	Gender-specific regulations
Dangerous driver	Highway Traffic Act
Robber	Criminal Code
Alcoholic	Self-control, reliability
Welfare recipient	Work ethic

There are, however, several problems with defining deviance this way. First, although all deviance violates standards, not all violations of standards are treated as deviance, even when a rule is unambiguously present. This is true even when the rule is doubly reinforced by being legislated as a law. For example, smuggling goods across borders is usually illegal, but in many communities it is a subject of humour and pride, not censure. In many sports, the actual norms of the participants differ significantly from the written rules of the game. James Naismith, who founded the game of basketball in 1891, for example, was dismayed by the transformation of basketball he saw in this century. His rules excluded body contact between players, yet players, coaches, and officials over time collectively determined that "shoving, elbowing, holding and clawing" are part of the game. An attempt to enforce Naismith's rules "would bring the game to a standstill" (Jimerson, 1996, p. 359).

Although some people who violate the rules may be called deviant, others may be ignored, tolerated, or even admired. Baseball players sometimes brag about getting an edge by cheating (Gutman, 1990). The deviant may even be identified by an overly rigid and robotic adherence to regulations. In addition, behaviour that violates rules is not deviant if the individual is not subject to these particular rules. Police may carry weapons or use violence in ways forbidden to civilians; psychiatrists may ask highly personal questions that would not be permitted in a job interview; soldiers in combat situations may obtain equipment through means that would be called theft or fraud in any other context. Similarly, behaviour that violates rules may not be deviant if the situation has been set apart from the usual rules. European wine festivals held in the fall, New Year's celebrations, and the masked carnival of Mardi Gras are events during which behaviour that is normally treated as deviant is encouraged.

A second problem with the normative violation definition is that being deviant does not mean one escapes from all demands concerning the behaviour. In fact, the moderately conforming citizen probably has more freedom than do many deviants or criminals, who must deal not only with the forces of law and order but also with the often brutal social controls of the subculture or underworld. In prisons, for example, sex offenders and police informants often need special protection from the general prison population, which is dominated by the inmate code enforced by the armed robbers and drug kingpins. The protected prisoners are deviants within a deviant community, doubly isolated and despised.

A third problem with the use of normative standards to define deviance is that objectively visible regulations are not always the most powerful codes of behaviour operative in a particular situation. Some norms are high etiquette ideals known only to the elite. An example of this is the rule against applause between the movements of a symphony. Some norms enjoy widespread, active cultural support, while others are regularly ignored. Norms and rules routinely contradict each other. Students, for example, typically juggle the contrary demands of family and friends, school and work, and religious and secular values. A member of a jury, asked to rule on whether

Box 1.4   Which Norms Really Count? *Hamilton vs. Burr*

Most countries have laws against duelling as a private settling of accounts between citizens, and the practice has become quite rare. But duelling persisted long after the passing of legislation against it. The contradiction between custom and criminal law is exemplified by the 1804 duel between Alexander Hamilton and Aaron Burr. Hamilton, a founding father of the United States, was known and respected as a diplomat of greater than average intelligence, courage, and moral integrity. He died as a result of a duel in which he had resolved not to fire at his challenger on the first round (and possibly even the second).

About a week before the duel, Hamilton wrote a letter to his wife in which he explained why he felt compelled to participate in this "interview" with Burr. The first part of the letter outlines his arguments *against* taking up Burr's challenge.

1. Hamilton's religious and moral principles were strongly opposed to the practice of duelling.
2. Duelling was illegal in his home state, New York, because of a law that he had helped to create.
3. He understood his importance to his wife and seven children.
4. He was concerned about his creditors, to whom he had obligations.
5. He felt (or claimed) no personal ill will toward Burr, only political opposition.

In Hamilton's calculations, the norms that required a man to defend his honour, or else lose respect and influence, were more powerful than the combined weight of criminal law, religious and moral principles, and his responsibilities as a father, husband, and public figure. Without this respect, Hamilton thought it would be impossible to influence others to do good or to prevent harm (Mitchell, 1957, p. 159).

particular materials are obscene, may find it difficult to admit, for the public record (as opposed to actual viewing choices), that he or she finds nothing wrong with them.

The written rules, religious precepts, and even laws of the land do not always represent the effective "common values" of society. For example, in Egypt, new laws prohibit the practice of female genital mutilation (FGM). These laws, however, have so far proven to be unenforceable in the face of entrenched cultural resistance. In other cases, the written law lags behind changing customs. For example, "blue laws" (named for the colour of early law books) are usually aimed at people's sexual behaviour or at the availability of intoxicants. These maintain normative standards that no longer reflect the will of all citizens. They tend to be enforced selectively, if at all. Thus, although all deviance violates some normative standard, violating norms is not enough to establish that deviance has occurred.

Social Reaction

Deviance is sometimes defined in terms of the social response it evokes. For example, if being cross-eyed produces negative reactions from others, we could (at some risk of

Box 1.5   Crime and Deviance

A democratic country's Criminal Code is a set of rules mandated by its elected legislature. These rules tell citizens what actions the state prohibits, what defences protect them against convictions, and what punishments may be imposed if guilt is determined. In the abstract, it would seem that crime is much easier to define than deviance, because the rules (which parallel the social regulation of deviance) seem to be much clearer (Scheider & Florence, 2000). In fact, however, defining crime is just as difficult as defining deviance. What, for example, is pornography? Canadians seem to have a lot of trouble defining just what this means, and so do the courts. An example of this is the saga of the Little Sister's Book and Art Emporium's efforts to stop Canada Customs from seizing gay and lesbian materials ordered for the store. This battle covered more than a decade in the courts, ultimately reaching the Supreme Court of Canada. The Supreme Court confirmed that the previous court decisions to the effect that Customs officials had "wrongly delayed, damaged, prohibited, or misclassified Little Sister's materials in a systematic targeting of the store's importations" (*Little Sisters v. Canada*, 2000).

Justice Ian Binnie noted that

> Seizure included ... works by internationally acclaimed authors such as *The Man Sitting in the Corridor* by Marguerite Dumas and *Querelle* by Jean Genet. Also seized were the award-winning novels *Trash* by Dorothy Allison and *The Young in One Another's Arms* by Jane Rule. Frequently AIDS/HIV safe-sex education literature was classified as prohibited. (*Little Sisters v. Canada*, 2000, para. 9)

In a complex judgment, which you can find at <www.legal-rights.org/rulings/littlesisters.html>, the Court strongly suggested the need for a more workable definition of unacceptable material. Canada Customs can continue to inspect and (temporarily) detain material at the border, but the onus is now on the government (Customs) to show that this material is obscene if it is to be prohibited or seized, rather than on the importer (the bookstore) to show that it is not.

Even if a definition of what is unacceptable is eventually agreed on, the issue of who can have it, where, and when is destined to continue to be controversial.

circularity) define this condition as deviant. We can look at the issue of response under four headings: negative response, tolerant response, denial, and romanticization.

Negative Response

If a particular behaviour typically elicits criticism or punishment, it is deviant in the eyes of those who respond this way. Deviants can be identified by the ridicule, scorn, exclusion, punishment, discrimination, fear, disgust, anger, hate, gossip, arrest, fines, confinement, or other negative reactions that they experience because of being labelled deviant.

According to the negative response view, any person who is called deviant, whether a Clifford Olson (serial killer) or a Copernicus (scientific pioneer), will be subject to rejection, treatment to induce change, or punishment. This way of establishing deviance is probabilistic: it holds that an act or characteristic is deviant if the probability of punishment on discovery is high, but recognizes that punishment may not be found in each and every case (Goode, 1978, p. 24).

Tolerant Response

Not only may society define some deviancy as reasonable, it may also congratulate itself for its tolerance in doing so. Canadians, for example, pride themselves on showing greater tolerance in many areas than they believe is shown by the people of other nations. When Kim Campbell and Jean Charest, as candidates for the leadership of the Progressive Conservative party in early 1993, admitted they had tried marijuana, they were compared favourably with U.S. President Bill Clinton, who had admitted to marijuana use but denied having inhaled. Canadian snowboarders whose blood samples revealed a bit too much inhaled product received more backslapping than real censure, at least from the Canadian public (Vogel, 1998).

Many rules are "honoured in the breach," and breaking them simply establishes one's claim to a normal level of mischief or flexibility. Thus, children often shun a playmate who follows adult rules too well. Many adults are quite pleased with themselves for successful income tax "avoidance," or getting a little drunk now and then. How much one can get away with before tolerance ends varies. One episode of bad humour will not matter much; one episode of murder may result in a complete rewriting of our moral history. Most of us occasionally test limits only to find that the deviance label is not automatically conferred on us. A great deal depends on the circumstances surrounding the offence and its discovery. Behaviour that touches on the highest values of a culture is more likely to be labelled deviant than is behaviour that is less central. In a society in which bank buildings are higher than the spires and towers of religious buildings, economic heresy will get you into more trouble than will religious heresy.

Denial

Another element that comes between an individual's behaviour and society's response to it is denial. When we do not want others to be deviant (e.g., we may like or depend on them) and, especially when acknowledging the abnormality of their behaviour frightens us, we may attempt to normalize their behaviour. We may deny the reality of their deviance until alternative explanations are exhausted. Thus, in one study, wives of men with mental illnesses preferred to deny their husbands' abnormal behaviour by interpreting it as tiredness, strain, or eccentricity. They accepted the diagnosis of mental illness only slowly and unwillingly (Yarrow et al., 1987). In contrast, if a person or group is already unpopular, the connection between odd behaviour and punitive response may be made more quickly.

Romanticization

In the absence of hard evidence, the deviant may become an imagined moral monster (Dracula), a romantic hero (Robin Hood), or a combination of both (Blackbeard the Pirate). In Milton's *Paradise Lost*, the demonic character of Satan is presented as something magnificent and positive. When the deviant is one who challenges the status quo, fights back against the ever-present regulation of life, or demonstrates a better way of doing things, many people may come to admire his or her courage and audacity.

Box 1.6   The Robin Hood Myth

Although an outlaw in the eyes of the Sheriff of Nottingham, the mythical Robin Hood was a respected insider among his merry men and local supporters. (Actual highwaymen were not nearly so well liked.) The Robin Hood myth colours society's response to many deviants, especially those who can lay claim to being skillful, daring, cunning, and tough. The myth is particularly well supported if the heroic deviant appears to harm only anonymous, unpopular institutions or oppressive, conniving individuals. In the film *Butch Cassidy and the Sundance Kid,* the audience cheers for the bank robbers, not the wooden, vicious, or simpleminded bank and railroad representatives. A Canadian equivalent, profiled in Greg Weston's *The Stopwatch Gang,* concerns "three affable Canadians who stormed America's banks and drove the FBI crazy" (Weston, 1992). Canadian criminal heroes have also included a large number of smugglers (Hunt, 1988). "Supercrooks" often develop a status not unlike that of movie stars or popular athletes.

Similarly, the jailed environmental protester is a deviant in the eyes of the logging company or developer but a hero to groups that are committed to environmental and humanistic values.

The outsider–hero paradox reflects our ambivalence toward the demands of conformity that make society work but that also force us to give up many forms of gratification and self-expression.

> Even as we put down the deviant, he sparks our desires to be free and wild, to chafe at our moral restraints. The world seems to love its outlaws even while it hangs them. For example the Spaniards have traditionally alternated between purging the gypsies and singing romantic ballads about them. (Simmons, 1969, p. 22)

Teen rebellion is usually portrayed as deviant, while teens themselves often regard standing up to their parents as normal or even as a badge of belonging. The film *Ferris Bueller's Day Off* is the story of one such youth. The humour in this film works only if you accept the rights of the teenaged hero to get back at venal school officials and imbecilic parents for subjecting him to classroom boredom and excluding him from the moneyed world of good restaurants and fancy cars. Even in the teen groups, however, some kinds of rebellion go too far and are not accepted.

An interesting variation on the phenomenon of deviant as celebrity occurs when people who have been convicted of atrocities are pursued by admirers. For example, men convicted of serious offences against women often attract a following of women who visit them in prison and are even willing to marry them. Ted Bundy, a serial killer of women, was able to marry and father a child while awaiting execution. Rarely if ever does this minority approval cause either the justice system or the public to reverse its verdict on the deviant status of these offenders.

STIGMATIZING LABELS

Another way of addressing the problem of identifying and defining deviance is to focus on the process of naming or labelling deviance. Deviants are those people identified by names or images that mark (stigmatize) them as being less worthy than other people. These labels designate characteristics that the deviant is presumed to have, just as a label on a can supposedly tells us what is inside. Although labels of deviance are wide ranging, all of them identify someone who is a likely subject of correction or avoidance, at least by decent people.

Defining deviance as a matter of label or category allows us to see that deviance is not a simple matter of actual behaviour. Deviance is sometimes attributed to people who are not responsible for their behaviour or appearance and even to people who have not actually done anything but are accused anyway. In our society, stigma inheres as much (or more) in the schizophrenic as in the calculating thief, even though diagnosis of schizophrenia is notoriously loose. Moreover, false accusations of wrongdoing are frequently implicit in deviant labels. In Canada during both world wars, many Japanese, Germans, Italians, Ukrainians, Slavs, Jews, radicals, trade union leaders, and pacifists were labelled "enemy aliens," which meant that they could be interned in camps and have their property confiscated (Koch, 1980). In the Cold War period, some of the same Canadians were blacklisted as suspected "Communist subversives" (Scher, 1992). In all cases, little or no hard evidence existed to justify their exclusion, confinement, or loss of employment. Apology or compensation for their mistreatment has been very slow in coming. Even when a deviant label contains some truth, it usually stereotypes and exaggerates the negative aspects of the person being labelled.

PULLING IT ALL TOGETHER: COMMON GROUND

We have demonstrated how difficult it is to define deviance according to the standards of objectivity, noncircularity, and distinctiveness while avoiding unnecessary assumptions. How can we forge a path through all the definitional pitfalls and arrive at some useful general definition of deviance? The approach outlined in the following pages takes a great deal from theories that define deviance as a socially constructed category of behaviour or being. From this perspective, a behaviour, act, or condition is deviant if enough important people (people with influence) say it is.

In the most general formulation, deviance is a descriptive name or label used to exclude people who—in the view of influential others—should not be allowed as regular members in a particular social setting or group context, even if they may be included and even celebrated in a different one. It is a form of moral exclusion, sometimes reaching the point at which the very humanity of the deviant is denied—the deviant is not one of us, he does not need to be accorded the rights and protections that are basic human rights (Opotow, 1990, p. 1).

This perspective compels us to focus as much on the people who are *definers* of deviance as on the deviants themselves and on the *role of power* in the process. For a definition of deviance to be arrived at, we must have four things:

1. *Motivated observers* who maintain that deviant acts have taken place, whether or not they have personally observed them, and who call attention to the observed "deviants."

   Observer reaction is not automatic. Even people paid to detect wrongdoing will sometimes let things pass, while polite inattention shelters other slips. Some observations are falsely made. Some individuals act as moral entrepreneurs in the area of rule making and rule enforcement. They gain access to the rule-making processes, whether in the legislature, the company standards committee, the board of directors, or the media. In this capacity, they help to create definitions of deviance. Then, they gain profit or prestige from being experts at applying them to others.

2. *The observed* who are rightly or wrongly accused of committing acts or having certain characteristics.

   Accusation, by itself, is not enough. The accused may be able to reject the designation. ("I'm not an alcoholic. I'm a sociologist doing participant observation of bar culture.")

3. *Cultural standards* that can be used to define these acts or characteristics as immoral, disturbing, or illegal.

   Such standards vary over time and place and are not applied automatically.

4. *Social control*: application of the standards to particular people in particular settings.

   The mere existence of cultural standards does not amount to deviance designation. Someone, or some people, must make an active effort to apply them.

A UNIVERSAL DEFINITION

Throughout history, then, we find that whatever the form of deviance, the deviance designations have been used to describe (1) *presumed behaviour* that (2) *defies social expectations* that (3) are made and *enforced by people with influence (power)* and (4) have been applied to *particular people or groups in particular situations*. This defining set of universally valid characteristics helps us to distinguish deviance from other phenomena. Deviance is the *outcome* of a particular social process; it does not exist apart from that process.

Witches, for example, were presumed to be consorting with the devil and bringing death and disaster to their communities. The rules they were supposedly breaking were made by church authorities, supported by religious beliefs and a variety of superstitions, enforced through a combination of sacred and secular authorities, and applied to particular kinds of people (mainly women) in particular circumstances such as drought, war, or plague.

From this perspective, the actual characteristics of deviants hardly matter. Deviants are chosen because they lack the power to protect their own image. As scapegoats, they can be made to represent any problem. It is much easier to blame witches, Communists, or drug traffickers than it is to grasp the real causes of natural disasters, economic recessions, and urban civil disorder.

Whatever the form of deviance, it is important to look at the characteristics of the labellers as well as the characteristics of those labelled. Deviants represent the losing side of a moral argument. They include members of cults, extremists at the far right or far left of the political spectrum, and people who support a country that is at war with their own country. The categories of the morally excluded change over time. Tobacco smokers, wearers of fur coats, and people who make sexist comments are, for example, increasingly finding themselves on the receiving end of deviant designations.

CHARACTERISTICS OF DEVIANCE

As part of almost every introduction to the study of deviance, the reality of deviance is proven by its *universality,* and then qualified out of existence by its *relativity* and *situationality.* In the following sections, we examine these three important dimensions of deviance.

DEVIANCE AS A UNIVERSAL PHENOMENON

In the sense that every social grouping generates deviant designations and rules for their application, the deviance process is universal. As noted by Durkheim, even a community of saints will include members who fail to live up to the expected standards of saintliness (1965, pp. 68–69). In communal groups that maintain highly restrictive standards of conduct, deviant status may result from using the wrong kind of buttons on clothes (Hutterites) or from showing greater interest in one's own children than in the group's offspring as a whole (early Israeli kibbutzim). In some groups, having private property is deviant, whereas in others communism is considered deviant. Deviant communities such as outlaw biker gangs include their own deviants, who may be expelled if their behaviour is insufficiently in tune with what the group requires.

DEVIANCE AS A RELATIVE PHENOMENON

If a visitor from another era, civilization, or galaxy were to ask why users of illicit drugs face possible expulsion from positions of responsibility, the response might be that the behaviour is wrong, immoral, unnatural, and intolerable—in short, deviant. The same sort of answer might have been given several generations ago to someone who questioned the lack of human rights for slaves, or two generations ago to someone asking why women were not allowed to vote. What was once obviously deviant is no longer seen that way. Alternatively, things once seen as quite acceptable, even heroic, are now considered deviant.

In earlier studies on deviance, the fact that something was deviant was often accepted as an absolute attribute or condition. The role of culture and observers in making deviance was ignored. This absolute view is rarely expressed in modern academic writing. (It has, in fact, become a deviant perspective on deviance.) Are you a "rate buster" (a worker who ignores group norms and works too hard) or a "slacker" (lazy student)? The degree of your deviation from the norm of student life depends on who is doing the evaluation and on what standards they believe apply to you. Your friends, fellow students, instructors, and parents may not agree about whether you belong in one of these deviant categories. Your placement will thus be *relative to their standards* rather than inherent in the amount of work you do.

The observer's point of view is usually *culturally defined*. What the observer feels is right or wrong and acceptable or unacceptable is strongly influenced by the dictates of the surrounding culture. In this sense, deviance is said to be "culturally relative." In a heterogeneous society, deviance has multiple sources of definition. A deviant or outsider in one context may enjoy insider status in another. Indeed, most people who are called deviants are excluded only from some groups, not all. To be seen as deviant by the mainstream may even be a subcultural goal. ("If the teacher hates me, then I'll qualify to join the gang.")

The passage of time can result in re-evaluations of the deviance of long-dead men and women. Executed as a traitor in 1885, Métis leader Louis Riel has since become a powerful symbol of French-Canadian and Aboriginal aspirations. His passage from traitor to Father of Confederation shows the potential for designations to change over time (Winsor, 1989). Examples of this kind of elevation from deviant status are numerous and include Jesus (crucified) and Socrates (forced to take poison) (Proietto & Porter, 1996). Sometimes the change comes within the lifetime of the deviant: the Irgun terrorists in Palestine became the new government of Israel; and South African President Nelson Mandela was still listed by the U.S. State Department as "an international terrorist" when he travelled to the United States following his release from prison. *The New York Times*, in the space of about a week (in 1988), transformed the Tamil Tigers of Sri Lanka "from 'terrorists,' to 'guerrillas,' to 'freedom fighters' as the priorities of U.S. foreign policy shifted" (Allen, 1996, p. 8). The Tigers did not change, but their position as deviants did.

Within the past few decades, activities once considered socially acceptable have started to take on deviant designations. Cigarette smoking, for example, is gradually assuming deviant status through a drawn-out process of medical lobbying, public pressure, legislation, and changing expectations (Corelli, 1997; Troyer & Markle, 1983). In a reversal of this process, divorce and common-law relationships have lost their former stigma in much of Western society. Similarly, nudism, certain forms of sexual expression, and a wide range of clothing alternatives, all of which would once have produced outrage, have gained wide social acceptance.

DEVIANCE AS A SITUATIONAL PHENOMENON

Definitions of deviance are more than just a reflection of broad cultural standards. They also emerge from our individual experiences and from our understanding of the situations in which the behaviour occurs.

Deviance is always relative to the situation, to the leadership that prevails there, and to the beliefs and expectations of the observer. Imagine that you have just started watching a film already in progress. One character is gunning down other characters: blood is everywhere. Are you supposed to be cheering for the gunman, or is he a villain? You are suddenly aware of the relativity of the situation. You missed the setup that enables the audience to judge whether this is Rambo-like heroism or an act of depravity. If you watch long enough, however, the situational clues allow you to figure it out.

The observer's judgment concerning the degree of deviance in a situation will depend on context, knowledge of the biography and positions of those involved, and assumptions about their motives. If a stranger on a city street is behaving eccentrically, it may be because she has just experienced some traumatic event such as a mugging or a bad reaction to medication. Just how deviant the observer judges the behaviour to be will depend on the observer's assessment of these situational factors, as well as on the actual, observed behaviour.

APPLYING CHARACTERISTICS OF DEVIANCE TO SPECIFIC BEHAVIOURS

The idea that deviance is relative to a cultural or situational perspective rather than inherent in the act or appearance is not always easy to accept. Although we understand that clothing, food, and music choices may be culturally relative, and usually legitimately left up to the individual, we have difficulty thinking the same of other practices. With human sacrifice or cannibalism, for example, deviance *seems* to be an intrinsic quality, just as real or objective as the weight or height of objects.

Cannibalism

Eating human flesh violates a strong taboo in our time and society. It results in immediate deviant status for those accused of it. It has been used by writers and filmmakers to create moral monsters, like Hannibal Lector in *The Silence of the Lambs* or the many vampires who jolt us into shivers of horror or nervous laughter. Even under extreme conditions (e.g., survivors facing starvation following an airplane crash in a wilderness area opting to save themselves by eating the flesh of the crash's victims), cannibalism is only very reluctantly tolerated in modern Western society (Askenasy, 1994). The perpetrators are likely to face criminal charges of murder or of committing an indignity to a human body. Even if acquitted on the grounds of necessity, "cannibals" may be seen as somehow polluted by their experience (Harris, 1978; Simpson, 1984; Visser, 1991).

Despite its current taboo status, the apparent objective deviance of cannibalism is an illusion. In different times and places, the cannibalization of defeated enemies, even of recently deceased relatives, has been accepted (*New Encyclopaedia Britannica*, 1984, p. 512) or treated as an unpleasant necessity (Simpson, 1984). Anthropologists have established that some cannibalistic cultures even had rules covering the niceties of the practice: who (and what parts) could be eaten, by whom, and when (Visser, 1991). Thus, although we may feel that certain activities, especially those with a powerful taboo attached to them, are intrinsically and objectively bad, wrong, and deviant, it is important to recognize that we are judging them based on rules that exist merely in one particular society at one particular time.

Murder

Murder is the *wrongful* taking of human life, not *all* taking of human life. Although murder is always and universally condemned, different societies—and even different subcultures within a society—may disagree as to what kinds of killing qualify as murder. Some situations, such as combat, legitimize killing. Indeed, soldiers can be court-martialled (treated as deviant) for failing to kill. Those who must kill frequently resort to phrases such as "wasted" and "acted with extreme prejudice" to avoid calling the action murder. Similarly, police may kill in the line of duty, and, as long as proper procedures have been followed, not be charged with murder.

In some countries, the killing of adulterous wives and their lovers is considered either acceptable or treated as a minor indiscretion. Brothers have killed their sisters in so-called honour killings intended to preserve the family honour from the sister's unchaperoned behaviour. In Canada, women who kill their abusive husbands are now less likely to be charged with murder than they were a decade ago (Johnson, 1996, pp. 191–192) and, since May 1991, have been able to use, under very limited circumstances, battery as a defence for killing an abusive spouse.

In ancient Greece and Rome, human sacrifice was not treated as murder but rather as an annual ritual the purpose of which was to unload the burden of sins and omissions that had accumulated over the year. Human sacrifice has also been part of rituals undertaken to ward off drought, plague, famine, and other misfortunes or even to satisfy bloodthirsty gods. Around the same time as such activities as cannibalism and collecting human heads as trophies were taking place in Africa, witches, heretics, and dissenters were being burned at the stake in Europe. Each culture would likely have regarded the other's behaviour as barbaric.

Indirect killing has rarely been treated as murder. When the hunting and fishing economies of Indigenous North American populations were destroyed by economic exploitation and land pressure (the restriction of land use through reservations, game laws, and population increases within the restricted areas), death rates in Indian and Inuit communities increased. Homicide, suicide, and infant mortality rates also rose (Shkilnyk, 1985). These deaths were not considered murders, at least not by the legal system. Similarly, many preventable deaths in industry are called accidents, not murders. The production of cars, medicines, and other consumer goods that are unsafe costs lives, as does pollution. Is this murder or just business as usual? Avoidable but non-criminal deaths and injuries far exceed those that are crime related (Brown, 1986, pp. 34–42; Simon & Eitzen, 1993; Snider, 1992, pp. 317–319).

Sometimes the line between justifiable or excusable killing and murder is so unclear the courts must decide the issue. Can a storekeeper shoot a would-be burglar? Can parents who rely on herbal remedies or faith healers be held accountable if their children die (Molony, 1991)?

Suicide

Taking one's own life is generally regarded as deviant in Western society. At one time, suicide, whether attempted or successful, drew penalties in both ecclesiastical and criminal courts. Typical punishment involved the confiscation of the suicide's property, burial in unsanctified ground, and mutilation of the corpse. Although suicide is no longer a criminal offence, some social stigma is still attached to it.

In contrast, ritual suicide in Japan has historically been an accepted, sometimes required, response to many situations in which face has been lost or one's social position has been hopelessly compromised. Japanese children still learn the story of the 47 *ronin* (samurai warriors), which allegedly took place in Tokyo in the early eighteenth century. By killing an unjust overlord, the master of the 47 left the master's followers in a situation in which their only honourable choice was to commit ritual suicide. This drama has been the subject of many popular Japanese plays and books. However, the acceptance of ritual suicide is no longer as strong as it once was. In 1970, the three-time Nobel Prize–nominated Japanese writer Yukio Mishima ended his life in a dramatic ritual (*seppuku*) as a protest against Japanese society's loss of its spiritual way. The mildly critical Japanese media response to this showed that this form of maintaining face is no longer a major force within Japanese culture (Mishima, 1970, 1958/1988; Pinguet, 1993).

Most societies honour those who lay down their lives for others, for a worthy cause, or for their country. During World War II, selected Japanese bombers (*kamikaze*) deliberately flew their planes into Allied ships. Suicide by students and by Buddhist monks has been a recurrent form of political protest in the Far East. Suicide by working too hard, "working oneself to death" (called *karoshi* in Japan), however, is regarded as pathological in Western society and a social problem in the East (Makihara, 1991, p. 41).

Starving oneself to death is usually seen as pathological and given medical labels such as anorexia nervosa. In the Middle Ages, however, holy mystics such as Catherine of Siena, Veronica Giuliani, and the Daughters of God practised "holy anorexia" as a form of self-abnegation and piety. According to Bell (1985), half of the 42 women in Italy who were recognized as saints in the fourteenth century exhibited anorexic behaviour, and many of them died of starvation. In this period, denial of the body for the sake of the soul was considered saintly. At a later period, such exceptional self-control was opposed by the church as a form of willfulness.

Addiction

The use of addictive substances for pleasure or religious enlightenment, rather than for medical purposes, is sometimes accepted and sometimes condemned. Most societies regulate some forms of drugs, but not always the same ones. Muslim societies have a low tolerance for alcohol, but some have a considerable social acceptance of other drugs, such as marijuana. In North American society, alcohol is not only tolerated but also hard to avoid, while marijuana use is criminalized. In Japan, amphetamine use—often by workers trying to increase their productivity—routinely brings two-year prison sentences. In North America, however, amphetamines are frequently prescribed by doctors and treated as a serious issue only when used by "speed freaks" and outlaw bikers, whose lifestyles are already disreputable.

The prohibition of a particular drug corresponds less to the physiological danger it poses than to the degree to which the groups that are believed to use it are accepted in society. Opiates and their derivatives were accepted—if not admired—until they became associated with outsider ethnic, racial, and occupational groups. Outlawing these drugs criminalized the undesirable groups that used (or misused) them, allowing for increased surveillance of users and increased stigmatization of their identities (Blackwell & Erickson, 1988; Cook, 1969). Yet, tobacco kills far more North Americans each year than heroin does, even if we control for the number of people using each drug (Addiction Research Foundation, 1980; Brown, Esbensen, & Geis, 1991, p. 18; Clark, 1988; Markle & Markle, 1983; Trebach, 1982). Many (though by no means all) of the undesirable effects attributed to illegal drugs derive from the way these substances are regulated. The involvement of organized crime and its attendant violence, inflated prices that provoke users to theft and corruption, and an absence of control over drug purity are just a few of the unwelcome consequences of making certain drugs illegal.

Child Abuse

All societies impose limits on the ways adults may treat children. What is considered abnormal, unnecessary, and unacceptable childrearing varies over time and place. Many cultures expect parents to expose their children to hardships to prepare and strengthen them for adult life. Other cultures practise painful procedures that are deemed necessary to increase the child's attractiveness to prospective mates; these include tattooing, tooth-filing, and genital surgery (without anesthetic).

A free, multicultural society is challenged to define child abuse in a way that respects subcultures while also protecting children. In Sweden, hitting children is illegal, and the state may take children into its care if their parents use disciplinary tactics that are quite common elsewhere. In many other countries, parents who *refuse* to discipline their children risk losing them to social welfare agencies. In Canada, many Native children have been seized by the Children's Aid authorities primarily because the Native cultural prohibition against telling children what to do is judged negligent rather than just different (Ross, 1992). Although normative in many parts of the world, child marriage is treated as child abuse in the industrialized West. In England in 1986, the public was outraged over the report that an Iranian had been allowed to bring his 12-year-old wife into Britain. Changes in immigration regulations were demanded. The husband protested that he had done nothing wrong and had not been warned that his actions would offend "British sensibilities" (West, 1987, p. 2).

The need to distinguish between legitimate cultural activities and child abuse becomes even more urgent with respect to such practices as genital mutilation—the ritual or medical circumcision of boys or the much more drastic clitoridectomy and infibulation of girls. The Western doctor who is asked to perform such operations may either comply or else report the parents as child abusers. In Canada some regulating bodies (such as the Ontario College of Physicians and Surgeons) prohibit doctors from performing female circumcision.

Homosexuality

Same-gender sexual behaviour may be perceived as shocking, as required, or as something in between, depending on the rules of the society or subculture. The anthropological literature shows that societies with at least some institutionalized male–male relations (often surrounding male puberty) outnumber those without. Many of these societies believe that boys must receive sperm from adult males in order to become men themselves. Sapphic (lesbian) female–female relationships have been less institutionalized but have long been tolerated or ignored in many societies (Schur, 1984, pp. 118–132; Stone, 1990).

The Christian church has traditionally condemned all forms of sexual expression that are not heterosexual ("missionary position") relations carried out for the purpose of procreation (Maines, 1999; Masters, Johnson, & Kolodoy, 1985; West, 1987, p. 1). Islamic law also condemns homosexual behaviour. In many countries throughout the world, Christian and Islamic influences are found in laws that prohibit and punish homosexual relations. In Canada, homosexual behaviour (buggery) engaged in by not more than two consenting adults in private is legal, but the amount of disapproval, tolerance, or acceptance it meets varies considerably (Kinsman, 1987; Nelson, 1992; Salamon, 1988; West, 1987).

CORE ISSUES IN THE SOCIOLOGICAL STUDY OF DEVIANCE

Three core issues in the sociological study of deviance reflect the definitional concerns discussed above.

1. *The behaviour of people called deviant*—who does what? Before any reasonable explanation of deviance can be invoked, we need clear and accurate descriptions of what deviants actually do (if anything) as opposed to the images that are held about them. For example, people called witches rarely did the things for which they were tried and condemned. It should not surprise us too much that most persons found guilty of an offence do not readily fit into the standard cultural image of that kind of person. These people, as Pfohl (1985, p. 3) puts it, are "Losers ... trapped within the vision of others," and, therefore, part of our role as researchers and students is to discover other views of the deviant.

2. *The rules or standards that define deviance*—made by whom, why, and with what effect? What are the social constructions of deviance that become labels for those called deviant? What effect do they have on those trapped in these definitions? What effect do they have on society as a whole? If a society is judged by the way it treats its least-valued citizens, then the study of deviance has important moral dimensions.

3. *The methodology of deviance research*—how we go about investigating deviance. Why do we use one methodology rather than another?

SUMMARY

Reasons for studying deviance include vicarious experience, a reforming impulse, self-protection and sophistication, understanding oneself and others, and intellectual curiosity. Each plays a role in the social scientist's approach to deviance. Various perspectives on deviance—student, public, and academic—have little in common when it comes to identifying deviant behaviours, beyond, that is, an agreement that most criminal behaviour is deviant. These perspectives reveal the diversity of ideas about deviance but do not help us define it.

Defining deviance in a way that accommodates people with different cultural standards and political beliefs is difficult. A useful definition is one that meets the standards of objectivity, minimal assumptions, noncircularity, and distinctiveness. Most definitions of deviance, whether popular or academic, fail to live up to these standards and may involve the criteria of rarity, harmfulness, and violation of normative standards, which are insufficient measures by themselves.

Deviance is best identified as a process in which a stigmatizing label is placed on people by influential others who claim (and usually believe) they are just enforcing social rules. This definition can be used by supporters and opponents of the stigmatization. It allows us to investigate not only the deviant but also the definers; that is, those who create and apply the labels of deviance. Deviance can be characterized by its universality, relativity, and situationality. These characteristics can be applied to specific behaviours, including cannibalism, murder, suicide, addiction, child abuse, and homosexuality.

STUDY QUESTIONS

1. Look at the reasons for studying deviance outlined in this chapter. What is your own motivation or combination of motivations? Select a topic you might like to investigate further, and consider how your motivation might be affecting the way that you would approach this investigation. How may your motivation affect your findings?

2. Consider the issue of deviance as an inspiration for film, literature, or pop culture. Is being deviant important to the work of creative people? Explain.

3. How does deviance in your environment differ from the things called deviant by the students discussed in the text?

4. How do you feel about the student assignment to "do something deviant for six weeks and record the experience"? What would these students learn that they would not likely learn from a text? What would they *not* learn from this experience?

5. How have academic views of deviance changed since the 1950s?

6. Find a definition of deviance in another book, or work with one suggested by your instructor. Critique the definition, indicating in what ways it may not live up to the standards listed in the text.

7. Explain why deviance cannot be defined purely in terms of its rarity or its harmfulness.

8. What are the different kinds of harm associated with many kinds of deviance?

9. Is deviance sometimes a good thing? Explain.

10. Select a form of deviance and, using the discussion of cannibalism as a model, indicate the constructed nature of the deviant qualities of this behaviour.

REFERENCES

Addiction Research Foundation. (1980). *Facts about ... Tobacco*. Toronto: Addiction Research Foundation.

Allen, B. (1996). Talking "Terrorism": Ideologies and Paradigms in a Postmodern World. *Syracuse Journal of International Law, 22*(7), 7–12.

Allport, F. H. (1934). The J-Curve Hypothesis of Conforming Behavior. *Journal of Social Psychology, 5*, 141–183.

Andreas, P. (2000). *Border Games: Policing the U.S.–Mexico Divide*. Ithaca, NY: Cornell University Press.

Askenasy, H. (1994). *Cannibalism*. New York: Prometheus.

Bell, R. (1985). *Holy Anorexia*. Chicago: University of Chicago Press.

Blackwell, J. C., & Erickson, P. G. (Eds.). (1988). *Illicit Drugs in Canada: A Risky Business*. Scarborough, ON: Nelson Canada.

Boyd, N. (1991). *High Society: Legal and Illegal Drugs in Canada*. Toronto: Key Porter.

Boyle, T. (1989). *Black Swine in the Sewers of Hampstead: Beneath the Surface of Victorian Sensationalism*. New York: Penguin.

Brown, S. E. (1986). The Reconceptualization of Violence in Criminal Justice Education Programs. *Criminal Justice Review, 11*, 34–42.

Brown, S. E., Esbensen, F.-A., & Geis, G. (1991). *Criminology: Explaining Crime and Its Context*. Cincinnati, OH: Anderson.

Byers, B. (1993). Teaching about Judgement of Crime Seriousness. *Teaching Sociology, 21*(1), 33–41.

Cancian, F. (1975). *What Are Norms? A Study of Beliefs and Action in a Maya Community*. New York: Cambridge University Press.

Clark, M. (1988, May 30). Getting Hooked on Tobacco: Is Nicotine as Addicting as Cocaine or Heroin? *Newsweek*, p. 56.

Cook, S. (1969). Canadian Narcotics Legislation: A Conflict Model Interpretation. *Canadian Review of Sociology and Anthropology, 6*(1), 34–46.

Corelli, R. (1997). The New Outlaws. *Maclean's, 110*(15), pp. 44–47.

DeKeseredy, W., & Hinch, R. (1991). *Woman Abuse: Sociological Perspectives*. Toronto: Thompson Educational.

Deutschmann, L. B. (1991). Unpublished informal survey, University College of the Cariboo, Kamloops, BC.

Dorn, N., Murji, K., & South, S. N. (1992). *Traffickers: Drug Markets and Law Enforcement*. London, UK: Routledge.

Douglas, J. E., & Olshaker, M. (2000). *The Anatomy of Motive: The FBI's Legendary Mindhunter Explores the Key to Understanding and Catching Violent Criminals*. New York: Simon & Schuster.

Durkheim, É. (1965). *The Rules of the Sociological Method*. New York: Free Press.

Gathorne-Hardy, J. (2000). *Sex, The Measure of All Things: A Life of Alfred C. Kinsey*. Bloomington, IN: Indiana University Press.

Gibbs, J. (1981). *Norms, Deviance and Social Control: Conceptual Matters.* New York: Elsevier.

Goode, E. (1978). *Deviant Behavior.* Englewood Cliffs, NJ: Prentice-Hall.

———. (1990). *Deviant Behavior* (3rd ed.). Englewood Cliffs, NJ: Prentice-Hall.

Gutin, J. A. C. (1996). That Fine Madness. *Discover, 17*(10), 75–82.

Gutman, D. (1990). *It Ain't Cheatin' If You Don't Get Caught: Scuffing, Corking, Spitting, Gunking, Razzing and Other Fundamentals of Our National Pastime.* New York: Penguin.

Harris, M. (1978). *Cannibals and Kings: The Origins of Cultures.* New York: Random House Vintage.

Henry, S., & Eaton, R. (Eds.). (1999). *Degrees of Deviance: Students Accounts of Their Deviant Behavior.* Salem, WI: Sheffield.

Hunt, C. W. (1988). *Booze, Boats and Billions Smuggling Liquid Gold.* Toronto: McClelland and Stewart.

Jackson, J. L., & Bekerian, D. A. (1997). *Offender Profiling: Theory, Research, and Practice.* Wiley Series in Psychology of Crime, Policing, and Law. New York: Wiley and Sons.

Jenkins, P. (1998). *Moral Panics: Changing Conceptions of the Child Molester in Modern America.* New Haven, CT: Yale University Press.

Jimerson, J. B. (1996). Good Times and Good Games. *Journal of Contemporary Ethnography, 25*(3), 353–371.

Johnson, H. (1996). *Dangerous Domains: Violence against Women in Canada.* Toronto: Nelson Canada.

Kappeler, V. E., & Blumberg, M. (1996). *The Methodology of Crime and Criminal Justice* (2nd ed.). Prospect Heights, IL: Waveland Press.

Katz, D., & Schanck, R. L. (1938). *Social Psychology.* New York: Wiley.

Katz, J. (1988). *Seductions of Crime: Moral and Sensual Attractions in Doing Evil.* New York: Basic Books.

Kerbel, M. R. (2000). *If It Bleeds, It Leads: An Anatomy of Television News.* Boulder, CO: Westview Press.

Kinsey, A. C., Pomeroy, W. B., & Martin, C.E. (1948). *Sexual Behavior in the Human Male.* Philadelphia, PA: W. B. Saunders.

Kinsman, G. (1987). *The Regulation of Desire: Sexuality in Canada.* Montreal: Black Rose.

Koch, E. (1980). *Deemed Suspect: A Wartime Blunder.* Toronto: Methuen.

Liazos, A. (1972). The Poverty of the Sociology of Deviance: Nuts, Sluts, and Perverts. *Social Problems, 20,* 103–120.

Little Sisters Book and Art Emporium v. Canada (Minister of Justice), 2000 SCC 69. File No. 26858.

Maines, R. P. (1999). *Technology of Orgasm: "Hysteria," the Vibrator, and Women's Sexual Satisfaction.* Johns Hopkins Studies in the History of Technology, New Series 24, Baltimore, MD: Johns Hopkins University Press.

Makihara, K. (1991, May/June). Death of a Salaryman. *Health,* 41–50.

Malarek, V. (1989). *Merchants of Misery: Inside Canada's Illegal Drug Scene.* Toronto: Macmillan Canada.

NTL

Markle, R. J., & Markle, G. E. (1983). *Cigarettes: The Battle over Smoking*. New Brunswick, NJ: Rutgers University Press.

Martin, J. (1997). *Miss Manners Guide to Excruciatingly Correct Behavior: The Ultimate Handbook on Modern Etiquette*. New York: Budget Book Services.

Masters, W. H., Johnson, V. E., & Kolodoy, R. C. (1985). *Human Sexuality* (2nd ed.). Toronto: Little, Brown.

Medved, M. (1991). Popular Culture and the War against Standards. *New Dimensions: The Psychology behind the News* (June), 38–42.

Mentor, K., & Dorne, C. K. (1998). The Association between Right-Wing Authoritarianism and the Perceived Seriousness of Deviant Acts: A Research Note. *Deviant Behavior 19*(1), 73–87.

Merton, R. (1961). *Social Theory and Social Structure* (rev. ed.). Glencoe, IL: Free Press.

Michaud, S. G. (2000). *The Evil That Men Do*. New York: St. Martin's.

Mishima, Y. (1970). *Sun and Steel: Personal Reflections on Art and Action*. Tokyo: Kodansha International.

———. (1988). *Confessions of a Mask*. London, UK: Collins. (Original work published in 1958)

Mitchell, B. (1957). Hamilton's Motives in Meeting Burr. In M. Broadus (Ed.), *Heritage from Hamilton*. New York: Columbia University.

Molony, P. (1991, July 19). Third Trial Expected over Girl's Starvation. *The Toronto Star*, p. 19.

Morgan, T. (1988). *Literary Outlaw: The Life and Times of William S. Burroughs*. New York: Avon Books.

Murphy, Judge E. F. (1973). *The Black Candle*. Toronto: Coles. (Original work published in 1922)

Nelson, E. D. (1992). Homosexuality: Sexual Stigma. In V. Sacco (Ed.), *Deviance: Conformity and Control in Canadian Society* (2nd ed.). Scarborough, ON: Prentice-Hall Canada.

New Encyclopaedia Britannica. (1984). Macropaedia: Vol. 2. Chicago: Benton.

Ogden, R. (1994). *Euthanasia: Assisted Suicide and AIDS*. New Westminster, BC: Peroglyphics.

Opotow, S. (1990). Moral Exclusion and Injustice: An Introduction. *Journal of Social Issues, 46*(1), 1–20.

Pfohl, S. (1985). *Images of Deviance and Social Control: A Sociological History*. New York: McGraw-Hill.

Pinguet, M. (1993). *Voluntary Death in Japan*. Cambridge, UK: Cambridge University Press.

Platt, A. M. (1985). Criminology in the 1980s: Progressive Alternatives to "Law and Order." *Crime and Social Justice, 21–22*, 1–11.

Polsky, N. (1967). *Hustlers, Beats and Others*. Chicago: Aldine.

Proietto, R., & Porter, J. N. (1996). Socrates: A Sociological Understanding of the Production of an Outcast. *Economy and Society, 25*(1), 1–35.

Rice, B. (1989). *Trafficking: The Boom and Bust of the Air America Cocaine Ring*. New York: Scribners.

Ross, R. (1992). *Dancing with a Ghost: Exploring Indian Reality*. Markham, ON: Octopus.

Sabbag, R. (1990). *Snowblind: A Brief Career in the Cocaine Trade.* New York: Random House. (Original work published in 1976)

Sagarin, E. (1977). Sex and Deviance. In E. Sagarin & F. Monanino (Eds.), *Deviants: Voluntary Actors in a Hostile World.* Glenview, IL: Scott Foresman.

Salamon, E. D. (1988). Homosexuality: Sexual Stigma. In V. Sacco (Ed.), *Deviance, Conformity and Control.* Scarborough, ON: Prentice-Hall Canada.

Scheider, M. C., & Florence, J. M. (2000). Are We Explaining Different Things? The Failure to Specify the Dependent Variable in Criminology. *Deviant Behavior 21*(3), 245–269.

Scher, L. (1992). *The Un-Canadians: True Stories of the Blacklist Era.* Toronto: Lester.

Schur, E. M. (1984). *Labelling Women Deviant: Gender, Stigma, and Social Control.* Philadelphia, PA: Temple University Press.

Schwendinger, J., & Schwendinger, H. (1983). *Rape and Inequality.* Beverley Hills, CA: Sage.

Shkilnyk, A. (1985). *A Poison Stronger than Love: The Destruction of an Ojibwa Community.* New Haven, CT: Yale University Press.

Simmons, J. L. (1969). *Deviants.* Berkeley, CA: Glendessary Press.

Simon, D. R., & Eitzen, D. S. (1993). *Elite Deviance* (4th ed.). Boston: Allyn and Bacon.

Simpson, B. A. W. (1984). *Cannibalism and the Common Law.* Chicago: University of Chicago Press.

Snider, L. (1992). Commercial Crime. In V. Sacco (ed.), *Deviance: Conformity and Control in Canadian Society* (2nd ed.). Scarborough, ON: Prentice-Hall Canada.

Stone, S. (Ed.). (1990). *Lesbians in Canada.* Toronto: Between the Lines.

Thompson, K. (1998). *Moral Panics.* London, UK: Routledge.

Trebach, A. S. (1982). *The Heroin Solution.* New Haven, CT: Yale University Press.

Troyer, R. J., & Markle, G. E. (1983). *Cigarettes: The Battle over Smoking.* New Brunswick, NJ: Rutgers University Press.

Visser, M. (1991). *The Rituals of Dinner: The Origins, Evolution, Eccentricities and Meaning of Table Manners.* Toronto: HarperCollins.

Vogel, B. (1998). Warning: This Is Not a Performance-Enhancing Column by Any Means. *Student Publications.* [On-line]. Available: <http://collegian.ksu.edu/issues/v102/sp/n099/sports/spt-col-vogel.html>.

Weisman, R. (1993, June). *Reflections on the Oak Ridge Experiment with Psychiatric Offenders, 1965–1968.* Paper presented at the annual meeting of the Canadian Sociology and Anthropology Association, Ottawa, ON (copies available from Professor Weisman, Glendon College, York University).

West, D. J. (1987). *Sexual Crimes and Confrontations: A Study of Victims and Offenders.* Cambridge Studies in Criminology. Aldershot, UK, Brookfield, VT: Gower.

Weston, G. (1992). *The Stopwatch Gang.* Toronto: Macmillan Canada.

Winsor, H. (1989, August 18). Tories Urged to Recognize Riel as a Father of Confederation. *The Globe and Mail.*

Yarrow, M. R., Green Schwartz, C., Murphy, H. S., & Calhoun Deasy, L. (1987). The Psychological Meaning of Mental Illness in the Family. In E. Rubington & M. S. Weinberg (Eds.), *Deviance: The Interactionist Perspective* (5th ed.). New York: Macmillan. Originally published in 1955 in the *Journal of Social Issues, 11*(4), 12–24.

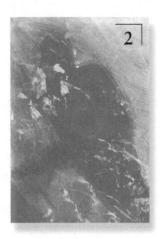

UNDERSTANDING AND TESTING THEORIES OF DEVIANCE

In every society, some people do things defined as deviant, and some people are accused of deviance. Hardly anyone just observes that this is true; most of us have some explanations (theories) as to *why* it happens. Unfortunately, most of these commonsense theories are inconsistent with each other and suffer from serious logical flaws (Hagan, 2000). In this chapter we consider what kinds of evidence can properly support (or refute) our beliefs and opinions about why deviance occurs.

MANY PATHS: MANY THEORIES?

Periodically, a popular book or enthusiastic researcher bursts on the scene with the claim that the one real cause of deviance has been found. Whether it is junk food, working mothers, the decline of religious observance, a disturbance of the genetic code, or even the contradictions of capitalism, the single explanation has appeal in that it holds out the possibility of a quick fix. Unfortunately, no single cause can effectively explain all kinds of deviant designations and deviant actions. No single theory has managed to stake out a monopoly on truth.

If deviance is a destination, many paths lead to it, some more heavily used than others (Nettler, 1982a, p. 6). Consider, for example, the many paths that might lead to someone committing arson. One path is marked by psychopathy (some people are pyromaniacs). Another is fraud (a person burning property to claim insurance money). Yet another path is organized crime (using arson in extortion rackets). Fires may be set by jilted lovers or mischievous children. Taking yet another path, the Sons of Freedom Doukhobors for many years had a reputation for burning not only their own property but also that of Orthodox Doukhobors to "help" free them from materialism. Some paths to deviance, such as psychopathy, are mainly motivated by the deviant, while others (e.g., scapegoating) are more strongly associated with the motivation of those in authority. As long as there are many paths, we are unlikely to develop a single (one-size-fits-all) theory that explains every kind of deviance.

THEORY AS EXPLANATION

Explanations have been described as "the stories we tell each other in attempts to produce some order in our lives" (Nettler, 1970, p. 175). Explanations outline the paths that lead to particular outcomes. They allow us to feel as if we know why something happened and under what conditions it is likely to occur again. Suppose that a professor notices that a large number of students in her class are half asleep. She may choose from a wide variety of explanations the one that appears to make the most sense. She may decide that the students should go to bed sooner or that the air in the classroom is too stuffy. If she is honest enough to take a reflexive approach, she may conclude her lecturing style is soporific. Such *ad hoc* theories suffice for everyday life, but they are often either self-serving or incorrect. They are not developed into consistent models of reality or tested by appropriate and controlled observations. In the study of deviance within the social science disciplines, this same explanatory process occurs, but, when properly done, it is more systematic, comprehensive, and self-conscious (Tittle & Paternoster, 2000).

Theories can be classified in many ways. For our purposes, one of the most important distinctions is among theories that are empathetic, scientific, or ideological, or some combination of the three (Nettler, 1970).

EMPATHETIC EXPLANATIONS

As the philosopher Alfred Schütz noted, "I am able to understand other people's acts only if I can imagine that I myself would perform analogous acts if I were in the same situation" (Schütz, 1960). When we hear of a woman who has killed her husband, we may be quite satisfied with the explanation that he was abusive to her or threatened her children. The empathetic explanation, because it includes much of the subjective as well as the objective reality of the event being explained, often seems more complete, and thus more satisfying, than a totally objective explanation.

Empathy, however, has limits. Most of us cannot imagine any circumstances in which we would, if not already infected with AIDS, seek out a partner with AIDS for unprotected high-risk sex, yet this kind of "bug chasing" does occur (Gauthier & Forsyth, 1998). We cannot easily empathize with someone who has hunted and killed other human beings, much less someone who eats his victims, and yet that happens too (Askenasy, 1994).

In deviance studies, the subjective, empathetic approach is the one most keyed to understanding the actor's point of view and the actor's decisions. This approach is found mainly in the so-called interpretive or interactive theories (the subject of Chapter 10).

SCIENTIFIC EXPLANATIONS

Scientific explanations make use of the scientific method or adaptations of it. This method, first developed in the study of the physical world, provides techniques for developing models of how the world works, as well as hypotheses about the connectedness of things. The scientific method works best with inorganic and nonsocial realities and does not handle human agency—the capacity to think and act creatively—very well. We sometimes enclose the word "scientific" in quotation marks to indicate that, for studies of deviance, science is an ideal, not an achieved reality, and we use the term "positivism" to indicate work that may be extreme in its refusal to give *any* importance to human feelings, understandings, and choices.

Social data differ from physical data, and the difference is important. For example, we can understand objectively and dispassionately why a person with a chest cold sometimes coughs, but to understand coughing when it is used as an act of social communication is a different matter. Similarly, we can understand why people who are addicted to nicotine, smoke; more difficult to explain is why they take up smoking in the first place and why they later try to quit.

The scientific method provides for controlling observations so that the knowledge gained will be tested and cumulative. In deviance studies, the scientific approach has been most fully developed in the area of biological explanations. Early biological positivists abused the approach and produced many invalid studies. The scientific method has been applied much more successfully in later biological and psychological research (see Chapter 6).

IDEOLOGICAL EXPLANATIONS

Ideological explanations are based on systems of ideas that are held as irrefutable doctrine. They are not just tentatively proposed, in the manner of scientific hypotheses, but rather are often a matter of passionate belief (Nettler, 1970, p. 178). Ideologies are almost impervious to new information or alternative interpretations. If the data do not fit, ideologues think something is wrong either with the data or with the way in which they were collected.

In deviance studies, ideological explanations are found most openly in the writings of prescientific religious authorities (see Chapter 3) and in the work of some radical conflict theorists (see Chapters 12 and 13). At the same time, they may be implicit (present but not so obviously present) in other works. It is important to recognize that ideological positions that are not acknowledged may affect the attainment of knowledge as much as—if not more than—acknowledged doctrines.

THE FORMULATION OF THEORY

Consider the following cases:

1. J., age 16, lives in a rent-subsidized housing project where few recreational facilities or opportunities for unskilled, legal employment exist. J. is arrested for attempting to sell cocaine to an undercover police officer. (*Social disorganization*)

2. When S. is diagnosed as an alcoholic, it is pointed out that many members of her family have been "drunkards." (*Socialization, biological inheritance*)

3. H., a middle-aged male, comes from a culture in which playfully pinching unescorted females is considered normal masculine behaviour. In downtown Vancouver, he is arrested for sexual assault. Unable to speak English well enough to explain himself, or even to understand what the fuss is about, he is sent to a psychiatric hospital. When the hospital acquires a doctor who speaks his language and knows his culture, he is released. (*Culture conflict*)

4. A., a high-school student, feels tired. She feels that she cannot live up to the expectations of family, friends, school, and work. Just living requires great effort. (*Depression; illness*)

5. Joe, Jamal, and Jack are suspects in the case of a violent act. Joe is fat and looks slow. Jamal is skinny, has a high-pitched voice, and wears glasses. Jack is wiry and athletic. Which of these suspects will be charged, found guilty, and sent to training school? (*Somatotypes; labelling*)

6. T.'s father is a successful, hard-driven businessperson who admires only material success. T. escapes into drugs and alcohol. (*Stress*)

7. R. dreads the day her friends find out that her family takes holidays at a nearby nudist camp. (*Role conflict; labelling*)

8. G., a conscientious government-employed meat inspector, looks at the rulebook and knows that if he follows all the procedures required by law, he will be fired for being too slow. He skips some of the less important rules, is caught, and faces criminal charges. (*Role strain*)

Each case above suggests an explanation—you can tentatively understand these scenarios. In each case, a condition or circumstance precedes the deviance, without which the deviance probably would not have occurred. In Case 1, J.'s delinquent behaviour is preceded by environmental conditions that may have caused or may have potentiated the delinquency. In Case 6, T.'s escape into drugs and alcohol is preceded by his father's rigid demands.

But have we missed the real variables (the actual causes) entirely? In each of the cases, a single causal variable was proposed. In real life, however, many events may precede (and seem to have some role in producing) the behaviour we are studying. Theory helps us to select events worth investigating. A neurological theory may make sense when the case involves people whose behaviour has changed dramatically after a brain injury; a sociological theory may seem more promising when the actions we want to explain occur among groups of youths living in ghetto conditions.

Theories are generally developed through alternating processes of inductive and deductive logic. In an *inductive approach,* we look at many specific cases and then make generalizations about them. For example, DeAnn Gauthier and Craig Forsyth (2000) studied "buckle bunnies," females who seek sexual encounters with successful rodeo riders (i.e., men who wear the buckles that show they have won a rodeo contest). Buckle bunnies initiate public sex with a sequence of partners, and they engage in a frank and open utilitarian rating of these partners (p. 362). Gauthier and Forsyth did not test the ideas of an existing theory; they used interviews to develop tentative generalizations about this subculture.

In *deductive approaches,* we derive specific expectations from general ones that have been suggested either by previous research or by the logical relations of an existing theory. For example, over the years it has been observed that the age of first deviance seems to be connected with the length and seriousness of a deviant career. Thomas, Reifman, Barnes, and Farrell (2000) deduced two hypotheses from this: (1) "the later the age of first drunkenness, the lesser the likelihood of increased alcohol misuse in later adolescence," and (2) "the later adolescents initiate sexual intercourse, the less likely they will be to increase their sexual risk-taking in later adolescence" (p. 189). They found that early onset was important with respect to future alcohol abuse but not for later sexual risk-taking. They were able to develop a theory about the developmental pathways of alcohol abuse and sexual behaviour that has strong empirical support.

Over the years, we have weighed and tested many explanations. A great deal of information about deviance has been accumulated. Whether this represents progress is debatable, since the perfection of one kind of theory may be irrelevant to those who favour a different theory (Kuhn, 1970). Nonetheless, within each branch of theory, we can plot a trajectory of work that shows an increase in both logical consistency and amounts of supporting evidence, leading us to believe that we have increased our understanding of the facts about deviance.

THE COMPONENTS OF THEORY

Whether an explanation is empathetic, ideological, or scientific, it will require the use of concepts and variables and statements of connections among them.

SENSITIZING CONCEPTS

A sensitizing concept symbolizes aspects of reality that we particularly want to think about. For example, police may use a concept such as "suspiciousness" when describing a particular kind of behaviour. A psychiatrist (or a spouse) might very well use a different concept for the same behaviour. Using one set of concepts rather than another has a clear impact on what we are able to see. Examples of concepts used in future chapters of this book are *relative deprivation, marginalization, disidentifier, secondary deviance,* and *white-collar crime.*

Relative Deprivation

This concept refers to the state of discontent felt by people who, even if they have enough to get by on (they are not absolutely deprived), feel that they are not getting as much as they deserve. For example, a student who receives a high mark on a test will be pleased until she discovers that less able and hardworking people achieved even higher marks. Relative deprivation has often been cited as a motive for actions such as cheating and rioting.

Marginalization

The concept of marginalization highlights the fact that some people are not fully included in the society in which they exist. In some societies, people who are not part of the dominant racial group are marginalized. Women may be marginalized when they try to participate in activities that are traditionally designated as part of the men's world. Ex-offenders, addicts, and others must overcome marginalization to achieve a respected place within society.

Disidentifier

Erving Goffman (1963) developed the disidentifier concept to designate the symbols that people use to contradict or counteract the impression that they unintentionally (or unwillingly) convey. For example, defence lawyers often counsel their clients to cover tattoos, wear clean clothes, and get a haircut to disidentify with the common image of a criminal.

Secondary Deviance

This concept was introduced by Edwin Lemert (1951) to call attention to the importance of societal reaction in creating and shaping deviance. Secondary deviance refers to deviance that occurs because the deviant has acquired a deviant label and finds it easier to conform to the label than to try to change it. For example, the youth who is treated as the class dummy may well prefer to play this up rather than fight it.

White-Collar Crime

White-collar crime is "crime committed by a person of high social status in the course of his [or her] occupation" (Sutherland, 1949, p. 9). Sometimes called "suite crime" (rather than "street crime"), these offences are committed by people who have an established base of trust and respectability. They may embezzle money or commit homicide by putting profit and their career ahead of safety on the job or, perhaps, the safety of products. This type of harm is not always treated as crime or even deviance, and such people very rarely spend much time in prison (Hills, 1987).

VARIABLES

A variable is a concept that can be operationalized by being counted or measured. Age (for example, age of first drunkenness) can be an important variable in many kinds of deviance. Beauty is usually treated as a *qualitative* (nonnumerical) variable. People can be ranked as more or less beautiful, but the idea of measuring someone's looks on a scale of 1 to 10 is (mostly) taken humorously. Some evidence, however, suggests that less attractive people are more likely to be accused of wrongdoing and more likely to be convicted if they are accused.

HYPOTHESES

The relationship between variables is usually expressed as a tentative statement or hypothesis. It asserts that particular variables are regularly related to each other under specified conditions. Normally, we conceive of one variable (or set of variables) as the causal or *independent variable,* while the outcome we seek to explain is the *dependent variable.* Other variables in the causal chain are known as intervening variables (see Figure 2.1). If the hypothesis is correct, when one variable changes, the other will change in the predicted way, as long as the intervening conditions remain the same. The selection of which hypothesis to test is normally guided by a theory. A biological theory might stress variables such as genetic inheritance or blood-sugar levels; a psychological theory might stress differences in temperament and personality; and a sociological theory of delinquency would likely emphasize aspects of the social environment.

Figure 2.1   The Elemental Form of Theory

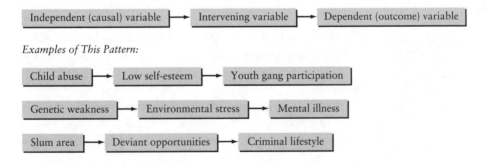

METHODS AND MEASURES FOR TESTING THEORY
AND ITS COMPONENTS

Unlike journalists or fiction writers, social scientists must test and evaluate, using established rules of research, the extent to which their findings either support or challenge competing theoretical explanations. Each discipline continually adjusts or eliminates ideas that are not supported by evidence and by doing so refines methods that produced research errors or ambiguities.

TESTS OF HYPOTHESES

The idea that beautiful theories are killed by ugly facts is highly misleading. A theory can survive many incompatible results. For example, the hypothesis that the size of the brain is correlated with criminal behaviour has been thoroughly tested and, apart from some ideologically suspect work, rejected. However, the theory from which that hypothesis came—that genetic inheritance might have something to do with deviance—is still very much alive. Thus, a theory is never entirely discredited, no matter how many facts refute it. By the same token, a theory is never entirely proven, no matter how many times the facts support it (Chafetz, 1978, p. 3). The most we can say is that it is "strongly supported."

THE CLASSICAL EXPERIMENTAL DESIGN

The classical experimental design has evolved as the ideal type of research in science, the norm against which most research designs are evaluated. Very few, if any, studies in the field of deviance fully meet all the criteria of this design, but it remains an important model for our work.

Four steps or stages are followed in the primary model of experimental research. Step 1 involves the selection of at least two groups that are equivalent, particularly with respect to the dependent variable. For example, the two groups might be two neighbourhoods with almost identical rates of crime and fear of criminals. One neighbourhood is designated the *experimental group*, while the other is called the *control group*.

In Step 2, the experimental group is exposed to the independent variable, which might be a community policing program. The control group is treated in the same way except that it is not exposed to the independent variable. It continues to receive the usual kind of policing.

At Step 3 both groups are measured on the dependent variable. At this stage (sometimes known as "time two"), the two groups will likely no longer be identical.

In Step 4, the difference between time one and time two (vis-à-vis the measure of the dependent variable) is computed for the control group and the experimental group. In the case of the two neighbourhoods, it will likely be found that crime rates have not changed in either neighbourhood but that fear of crime in the experimental neighbourhood has been substantially reduced (National Institute of Justice Research, 1994). Any significant (greater than chance) difference between the districts can be attributed to the effect of the independent variable, and we can use the research to help guide our policy decisions.

Box 2.1   Developing a Hypothesis: Durkheim's Theory of Suicide

Émile Durkheim's (1897/1951) study of suicide provides a model of the deductive method of theory development. In this study, the independent variables were the integration and regulation of group membership; the dependent variable was the rate of suicide. *Integration* refers to the degree to which a person belongs in a group. In well-integrated groups, people tend to have similar values and to care about each other. If a group has too little integration, the individual is permitted to become egoistic and may not let group values restrain a personal decision to die. In groups characterized by too much integration, individual members may develop a selfless altruism that divests them of any sense of autonomous, personal value apart from the group. Soldiers who sacrifice their lives on behalf of their buddies are committing a form of *altruistic suicide*.

Regulation refers to the degree to which a person's life is subject to the rules of the group. If the group is unregulated, the individual is in a state of *anomie* or normlessness. *Anomic suicide* results from the breakdown of common rules for behaviour. In contrast, if there is too much regulation, the individual may give up trying to live an independent life and choose death. *Fatalistic suicide* tends to occur in prisons and other highly regulated settings.

According to Durkheim, conditions in modern Western society favour egoistic and anomic suicide, while societies characterized by higher integration and regulation, such as traditional Japan, were more likely to record fatalistic and altruistic suicides. Despite the crudeness of the information about suicide that was available in the late nineteenth century, Durkheim correctly predicted, across a wide variety of situations, the relationship between suicide and group membership. Clearly, suicide is not just a matter of great unhappiness or despair: the social system also plays a role in people's decisions about their lives.

MEASURING CONNECTEDNESS:

CORRELATION COEFFICIENTS

The correlation coefficient is a statistical measure that tells us to what extent, and in what ways, two variables are related to each other (Chafetz, 1978, p. 15). Its size helps us to decide whether a difference is statistically significant. A direct or positive relationship is one in which both variables change in the same direction. If one increases, the other increases; if one decreases, the other decreases. For example, illiteracy and street crime, or poverty and child neglect, are positively related. A negative or inverse relationship, in contrast, occurs when increases in one variable are regularly associated with decreases in the other. Supervision and cheating, celibacy and pregnancy, employment and homelessness are likely to be negatively related.

Correlations range from a potential +1.00 (perfect positive correlation) to –1.00 (perfect negative correlation). A correlation of +.85 is a high positive correlation indicating that two variables consistently co-vary, such that when one increases the other also increases (although not necessarily to the same degree). This correlation might be found, for instance, between a student's declared liking for a school subject and the grades he or she receives in that subject. A correlation of –.80 indicates that the variables are strongly, but inversely, related. Such a correlation might be found between hard drug use and the size of the police force and might be used as support for increasing the size of the force. A correlation of +.32 indicates a much less predictable relationship, while a correlation of 0 would mean that knowing the change in measure of one variable would not be enough to enable the researcher to predict change in the other at all.

A strong correlation does not always mean a causal relationship exists between the two variables. It says only that they change together, which may be caused by a third variable that we have not considered. The number of storks and the number of babies may be correlated, but the causal variable may be rural residence rather than the stork delivery service (Cole, 1980, p. 48).

A positive correlation exists between the number of privately owned handguns in an area and its rate of gun crime. Does this mean that guns cause crime?

CAUSALITY

Causality is a complex subject in both philosophy and science. Causality is considered strongly supported when three conditions are met. First, when one variable changes, the others change in predictable ways. For example, we might find a positive relationship between the criminal records of adults and the delinquency of their children. Second, we must show that the variable deemed to be the independent (causal) variable occurs, or changes, *before* the variable that is deemed to be caused undergoes change. For example, the behaviour of parents normally precedes the delinquent behaviour of their children.

Third (and this is a really difficult one) we must be able to rule out other variables that emerge as candidates for causal status. If police statistics show a high correlation between low-income neighbourhoods and crime, is this because more crime is committed there or because that is where police look for crime? If we find that a high inverse correlation exists between hours spent in videogame arcades and school grades received, we might want to interpret this as proof of the theory that videogames turn the brain to mush. But other variables may account for both game playing and low school marks. Perhaps the kind of parents who permit their children to spend long hours in video arcades are also the kind of parents who fail to reward or encourage academic success, quite apart from any effects of the games themselves. If so, the causal variable is parenting, not excessive game playing.

If we were to take every variable in a study and test its relationship to every other variable (a dubious practice made possible by computers), many relationships would appear, some of which would be meaningless. For example, a single study might reveal a correlation of +.66 between moving onto a street that begins with the letter A and cheating on income tax returns. If this correlation has not been predicted based on a guiding theory, it is probably meaningless. We place more trust in our findings when they support ideas that have been drawn from theory and that are consistent with other data of a similar kind.

REPRESENTATIVENESS

A major goal of research is to find data that are meaningful and that can be generalized beyond one study. We may find, however, that nudists on Wreck Beach in British Columbia have little in common with nudists in holiday camps in Ontario. Compounding the problem of representativeness in deviance research is the fact that much deviance is hidden from view. For example, most studies of drug addicts have been based on small samples of individuals who are undergoing some form of rehabilitation; such persons may not be representative of other addicts (i.e., those who have not sought or been forced into therapeutic settings). The untreated users may well have a less dependent relationship to the drugs they use than is found among those in treatment (Blackwell & Erickson, 1988, pp. 63–68). In addition, our perceptions of deviance and crime are often distorted by the way we learn about them. Media accounts tend to be distorted when they are written for newsworthiness or even "info-tainment" (Barak, 1999).

The problem of representativeness can be illustrated by the crime funnel (see Figure 2.2), which expresses the relationship between the total number of crimes that occur and the number of crimes that are represented by people who are at various stages in the criminal justice process.

The top of the funnel represents the unknowable number of all crime, whether detected or undetected. A very large part of this, sometimes called the "dark figure of crime," remains unrecorded. A broken window may be evidence of a windstorm, a neighbourhood baseball game, vandalism, or an attempted break-in. A missing wallet may be evidence of carelessness or a pickpocket. A punch to the shoulder may or may not be an assault.

The middle part of the funnel depicts all crimes reported to, or otherwise discovered by, the police. In 1941, German criminologist Kurt Meyer suggested that for every reported homicide, between three and five went unreported (Meyer, 1941). Even recent studies have shown that many of those who die in accidents may well have been murdered (Nettler, 1982b).

If the police believe that an act took place and that it was a crime, it is considered "founded" (confirmed), and it becomes part of the official statistical record. Robberies are more likely to be considered founded than are reports of sexual assault, partly because the evidence is less susceptible to subjective interpretation. If the offence seems trivial or if the victim does not cooperate with the police or is perceived

Figure 2.2   The Crime Funnel

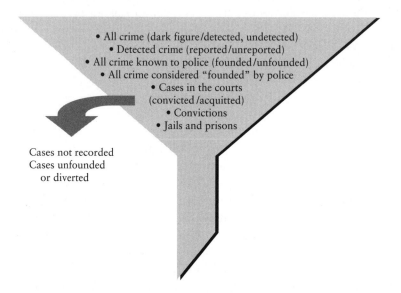

• All crime (dark figure/detected, undetected)
• Detected crime (reported/unreported)
• All crime known to police (founded/unfounded)
• All crime considered "founded" by police
• Cases in the courts
(convicted/acquitted)
• Convictions
• Jails and prisons

Cases not recorded
Cases unfounded
or diverted

Source: Statistics Canada, *Juristat Service Bulletin, 10,* July 1990. Reproduced by authority of the Minister of Industry, 2000.

as being undeserving of help, the offence may be treated as unfounded and be uncounted.

At the bottom of the crime funnel are those individuals who are incarcerated in a regular prison instead of diverted into community service, psychiatric care, or back to their families. Those who remain in the system may have a great deal in common with one another but not so much in common with those criminals who are not caught or processed by the system.

At the bottom of the funnel, we have a considerable amount of information about a few unrepresentative cases (i.e., persons who were accused, convicted, and incarcerated), while at the top we find virtually no information about a great many cases (Hood & Sparks, 1970, pp. 3–37).

RELIABILITY

Reliable measures are consistent measures that presumably reflect a regularity that occurs in nature. We may find in the course of one study that second-born children are more likely to be risk takers than are first-born children. (Risk taking tends to be associated with many forms of deviance.) To find out whether this is a reliable finding, we have to do further research under the same methodological conditions as existed in the earlier study. Achieving the same results will give us test–retest reliability. When replication fails (i.e., test–retest reliability is low), we place less faith in the original findings.

Durkheim's research permitted him to generalize about the relationship between group membership and suicide. Since he followed the rules of the scientific method as much as possible, other researchers have been able to replicate his work and show the reliability of his findings in additional settings. This replication adds support to the belief that Durkheim's hypothesis was, and continues to be, a reliable one.

VALIDITY

Validity raises the question, "Are we measuring what we think we are measuring?" Measures can be accurate and consistent but irrelevant. For example, activations of residential burglar alarms produce what are thought to be highly accurate statistics, and these numbers are sometimes used as indicators of crime attempts; in some jurisdictions, however, more than 90 percent of activated alarms are false alarms produced by family pets, high winds, or careless owners. Thus, alarm records are statistically accurate but are not valid measures of break-in attempts. Similarly, in the Middle Ages, warts and other bodily marks were seen as indications that the people who had them were involved with the devil. The validity of this indicator was not effectively challenged until the eighteenth century.

Invalid indicators are quite commonly used. For example, decisions about granting parole often rest on measures of how well the convict has adapted to institutional life. Parole boards consider whether the applicant is respectful of authority and expresses a convincing amount of remorse for past offences. These characteristics are, in fact, very poor indicators of that person's ability to stay out of trouble *outside* the prison. Similarly, many programs that aim to rehabilitate juvenile delinquents regard such qualities as neatness and orderliness as indications of effective reform. Little evidence exists, however, to suggest that the teen who has acquired bed-making skills will no longer seek out drugs at the earliest opportunity.

THE VALIDITY OF STATISTICS

Numerical measures allow us to be more precise and rigorous than is possible with descriptive adjectives. It is often assumed that numerical data are more valid than qualitative data, but precision is not always the same thing as validity. Changes in the statistical rates of crime are sometimes due more to shifts in policing policies than to changes in the numbers of criminals or their activities. Prostitution arrests may increase immediately before a major tourist-attracting event, as the police act to clean up the neighbourhood; conversely, arrests may decline if police attention is directed elsewhere.

Box 2.2   Validity of Information

In his research on an organized crime family, Ianni (1972, pp. 188–189) developed a scale of validity for the data he gathered. From highest to lowest, the assumed trustworthiness was ranked as follows:

1. data gathered by Ianni's team through personal observation
2. data gathered through the personal observations of participants, who, though not members of Ianni's team, were trusted on the basis of their past accuracy
3. interview information that could be checked against documented sources (e.g., records of arrest or business ownership)
4. data corroborated by more than one informant
5. data from only one source

Source: Francis A. Ianni (1972), "The Lupollo Family." In Francis A. Ianni, *A Family Business: Kinship and Social Control in Organized Crime.* New York: Russell Sage. Reprinted with permission of the Russell Sage Foundation.

Furthermore, statistics can reflect attempts to deceive as well as to report real events. Insurance companies suspect that as many as one in five car thefts reported to police in Canada has been arranged by the owners as a form of insurance fraud (Picard, 1990).

Social statistics have the following components:

1. *Real figure.* The real figure represents the actual number of people who engage in a particular kind of deviance, or the total number of deviant acts that occur in a specified time and place.

2. *Error component.* The error component is caused by over- or underreporting. Overreporting can be used to sell a book or to justify police budget increases. Underreporting may occur for several reasons. The victim may be too embarrassed to admit having been taken in by the criminal (e.g., consumer fraud) or, as is typical of rape victims, may be unwilling to undergo further suffering, this time at the hands of the criminal justice system. Finally, reporting may be seen as just not worth the effort.

3. *Random errors.* Random errors are generally accidental and self-cancelling: the honest but overworked cashier's errors may favour the customer as often as they favour the company. Random errors can creep into many parts of the counting process. Coders of interview data, for example, may make errors of judgment in classifying respondents' answers, and these, in turn, may produce errors in the final counts that are used to test theories.

4. *Systematic errors.* Systematic errors do not cancel each other out, and they may create cumulative distortions in the data. The tendency to suspect people based on

such factors as age or occupation may create systematic biases in the collection of deviance data.

Social policies, too, may distort the recording of empirical realities. For example, in our society, all babies are recorded as either male or female shortly after birth. When anomalous cases occur (i.e., some babies are born with both male and female physical characteristics), surgery is performed to clarify the sex of the baby one way or the other; doctors and families do not demand that a third category be created for the child (Kessler, 1990). Adults who find standard male or female gender choices too restrictive may simply invent their own, but they do so at great risk of being treated as deviants. Social policies also influence how many people are recorded as Black, White, Indigenous, or "other." The individual who has Black, White, Indigenous, and Asian forebears could be classified as belonging to any of these groups, depending on such factors as place of residence, colour of skin, economic position, or self-definition. Using ethnicity as a criterion for collecting statistics on crime and deviance thus poses problems.

Validity can be improved if we have multiple measures. For example, in establishing a valid assault rate estimate, we might consult official police records and hospital reports and compare these sources with others, such as interview data. When estimates based on several of these methods agree, we are inclined to accept their validity; when they disagree, we are alerted to possible sources of error.

OBSERVATION AND THE PROBLEM OF ACCURACY

A particularly acute problem in deviance studies is the failure to obtain an accurate description of the thing to be explained (the dependent variable). All too often it is assumed that what is going on is already known. The impressions we receive from common knowledge may lead us to explain realities that exist only in our minds. For example, many Canadians believe that pedophiles are predominantly homosexual. In fact, most child molesters are heterosexual males (Miethe & McCorkle, 1998, p. 72). Another example of inaccurate assumptions is the "mindless crowd" concept. For years collective behaviour specialists tried to devise theories about why people in crowds lost their individuality and became parts of a primitive, headless monster given to committing violent and senseless acts. But this perspective changed with the arrival of handheld cameras, participant-observation techniques, and less prejudiced observers, all of which allowed for a proper investigation of what people in crowds were actually doing, and what they said to each other as they decided how to act. In most crowds, it was discovered, individuals do not behave uniformly, and the violent acts they commit are purposive, not mindless (McPhail, 1991). When sociologists had a better description and conceptualization of the "what"—the dependent variable— their answers to why crowds do what they do became more accurate. We can see the same process occurring with respect to studies of urban youths. Only when researchers freed themselves from the sensationalist accounts of drugs, violence, and the spread of gangs from major centres to smaller ones could they see that most gangs are local and that most are only marginally criminal (Klein, 1995; Shelden, Tracy, & Brown, 1997).

DATA COLLECTION AS A SOCIAL ACTIVITY

An important consideration in all research is that the collection of data is itself a social activity. Social values intrude at every point in the research process. They affect decisions about which problems to investigate, which research tactics to use, and which research to publish. The social organization of research activity can introduce distortions that may have undesirable consequences. For example, it is generally much easier to obtain research money to investigate alcoholism as a disease rather than as a learned behaviour. This has implications for the findings that will emerge from alcoholism research and for the cures that will be proposed and funded based on these findings.

MAJOR SOURCES OF DATA ON DEVIANCE

To make and test meaningful hypotheses, we need to gather information about deviance. The major sources of data on this subject are

- self-report data and victimization surveys
- field observation
- secondary analysis of statistical data
- secondary analysis of biographical materials
- simulations
- journalistic accounts

SELF-REPORT DATA (SRD)

Self-report surveys and interviews have been used mainly to ask people what kinds of deviance they have participated in. This method allows us access to information about uncaught or unrecorded deviance.

Self-Report Questionnaires

A common form of SRD is the survey questionnaire, which consists of a series of questions answered by respondents, who are usually assured of anonymity. The questionnaire may be mailed to respondents, administered in a group situation such as a high-school classroom or prison cafeteria, or circulated at work or school. Although this is convenient for both parties, it has the drawback of removing the subject from

Box 2.3   Self-Report Survey Questions

Please indicate (as accurately as you can) how often in the past six months you did each of the following:

	Never	1 time	2 times	3 times	4 times	5 or more times
Told a lie to get something you wanted	—	—	—	—	—	—
Drank enough alcohol to become drunk	—	—	—	—	—	—
Sold an illegal drug	—	—	—	—	—	—
Told a racist or sexist joke	—	—	—	—	—	—
Dyed your hair an unnatural colour	—	—	—	—	—	—
Used a weapon to threaten another person	—	—	—	—	—	—

the setting in which the deviance occurs. "Asking people about their behavior is a poor way of observing it," according to Gwynn Nettler (1978, p. 107)

When Austin Porterfield conducted a self-report study in 1943, one of his findings was that 77 percent of males admitted to throwing spitballs (Porterfield, 1943), while very few females admitted to this. Most of the early surveys dealt with minor delinquency. For example, Ivan Nye's (1958) survey asked respondents if they had ever openly defied their parents; skipped school without a legitimate excuse; bought or drunk beer, wine, or liquor; or purposely damaged or destroyed public or private property. In this and later studies, middle-class teens admitted to far more delinquent behaviour than was ever recorded in the official statistics or recognized by the public. These findings challenged the theory that such delinquency was primarily caused by poverty or other aspects of low socioeconomic status.

The early studies were often criticized for their sampling (they used available samples of high-school students rather than random samples from the population as a whole); for their trivial nature (they rarely looked at the most serious forms of delinquency, and they had no provision for reporting how often an offence occurred); for their lack of reliability testing (they were rarely repeated to ascertain test–retest reliability); and for their failure to check for dishonest reporting or distorted recall.

By the late 1960s, however, many of these criticisms were met by better designs. The National Survey of Youth (NSY)—begun in 1967 by the Institute for Social Research at the University of Michigan—used probability samples of 847 boys and girls between 13 and 16 years of age. Among the behaviours addressed in this study were serious offences such as assault, violent gang activities, taking a car, and carrying a weapon. Every person in the sample admitted to at least one chargeable offence over a three-year period; a minority admitted to more than one (Williams & Gold, 1972, p. 213). Newer surveys typically include lie scales to detect deception. They have been used to investigate vandalism, drug use, prostitution, and other forms of socially undesirable behaviour that are difficult to study in any other way (Adlaf, Smart, & Walsh, 1994; Coleman & Moynihan, 1996; Lowman, 1992). Canadian studies, like the earlier American ones, found that boys report more delinquency than girls, that social status is not an important difference between offenders and nonoffenders (at least with minor offences), and that the self-reporting strategy uncovered far more delinquency than was reflected in official statistics (Gomme, Morton, & West, 1984; LeBlanc & Ferchette, 1989). This method has only recently been used for international comparisons (Junger-Tas, Terloun, & Klein, 1994).

Self-report studies are increasingly used by researchers in the career criminal area of research, where the studies fuel the argument over how much crime is prevented by incarceration of known offenders (Greenberg, 1996; Shover, 1996). Does locking up the three-time offender for a very long time protect us enough to be worth the cost?

Interviews

Another form of SRD is the interview, which may be structured (following a set pattern for each respondent interviewed) or unstructured (exploratory). Although most early interview work was done in connection with case studies of individuals or families, the Kinsey studies of human sexuality pioneered the technique of combining individual interviews with survey forms.

Kinsey and his colleagues attempted to maximize interview effectiveness by canvassing the community in question for ideal interview candidates. Thus, if the community was a prison population, the researchers would attempt to interview "the oldest-timer, the leading wolf, the kingpin in the inmate commonwealth, or the girl who is the chief troublemaker for the administration" (Kinsey, Pomeroy, & Martin, 1948, p. 39).

Kinsey used three trained interviewers (four, including himself). He provided them with an exhaustive list of sexual activities and instructed them to ask subjects about their participation in each of them. "It is important to look the subject squarely in the eye," Kinsey advised, "while giving only a minimum of attention to the record that is being made" (Kinsey et al., 1948, p. 48). Kinsey's interviewers were also taught to not be evasive: they never used euphemisms, nor did they avoid words like "masturbation" and "climax." Had they done so, Kinsey explained, the interviewee would have answered in kind, picking up on the message that it was not all right to admit to such things. Kinsey was very concerned with reducing the probability of deliberate deceit and willful or unconscious exaggeration (Bullough, 1994, p. 173).

Interviewers were, Kinsey wrote, to "begin by asking *when* [their subjects] first engaged in such activity. This places a heavier burden on the individual who is inclined to deny his experience; and since it becomes apparent from the form of our question that we would not be surprised if he had had such experience, there seems to be less reason for denying it" (Kinsey et al., 1948, p. 53). Finally, interviewers were advised to use rapid-fire questioning, not only because it would enable them to cover the maximum amount of material in a single interview but also because it would encourage spontaneous responses (Kinsey et al., 1948, p. 54).

Kinsey's goal was to secure 100 000 sex histories. At the time of his death, some 18 000 interviews had been completed, 8000 of them recorded by Kinsey himself (Bullough, 1994, p. 173). Partly because of the expense, most interview studies involve far fewer respondents than Kinsey's did, and most do not incorporate the techniques Kinsey's researchers used to build rapport and undermine evasion. It is hardly surprising that later attempts to duplicate Kinsey's work done by researchers less determined to elicit openness have generally found lower rates of participation in deviant forms of sexuality.

Victimization Surveys

Interviews and questionnaires have been used in victimization surveys to obtain information from people who have been raped, robbed, cheated, injured, threatened, or deceived. The first major victimization studies, initiated in the United States in the 1960s, were based on nationally representative samples that involved contacting thousands of households by telephone. The technique, although it has been criticized for underreporting such categories of victimization as family violence, suggests generally much higher rates of victimization than are indicated by police statistics. In a typical study of this kind, the victimization rate for rape is eight times higher than official figures based on police reports (Brown, Esbensen, & Geis, 1991, p. 153).

Canadian victimization data come from three main sources: international efforts such as the International Crime Survey (Van Dijk, Mayhew, & Killias, 1990), Statistics Canada's General Social Survey (Canadian Centre for Justice Statistics [CCJS], 1998), and the Solicitor General's Canadian Urban Victimization Survey. All these studies suggest that many serious and violent offences are not reported to police (see Figure 2.3).

The first Violence Against Women Survey (VAWS), conducted by Statistics Canada in 1993, illustrates just how controversial victim survey research can be. This survey involved more than 12 000 respondents and was conducted according to the dominant standards of survey research (Johnson, 1996). Its findings—that women report experiencing violence mainly from men that they know, and that women are often afraid to be out after dark—produced an outcry that protested the lack of males in the study and its failure to ask women about violence perpetrated by women. Editorials denounced a general anti-male bias in the questions, the analysis, and the conclusions of the research. Protesters decried the study as "sub-science" and accused

Figure 2.3   Victimization Data versus Uniform Crime Reporting (Police) Data

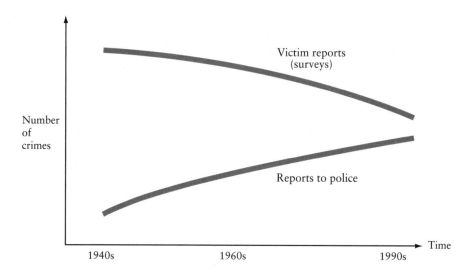

Note: Until recently, police reports showed increases while victim surveys showed declines. In the 1990s, the curves began to become more alike. Still, much crime goes unreported to the police. The curves are unlikely to cross each other. Police statistics are beginning to decline.

Statistics Canada of support for a "violence against women industry" (Fekete, 1995; Mercer, 1999, p. A28).

Problems encountered in victimization studies parallel those found in other kinds of questionnaire material. Findings can be distorted by poorly worded questions, selective or faulty memory, deliberate deception, and reluctance to report. In addition, unavailability or lack of interest on the part of some respondents may lead to unbalanced, nonrandom interviewing (e.g., more homemakers than commuters). Another important consideration is that the subject's notion of being victimized may not correspond, in any simple way, to the formal or legal definitions of crime or deviance as understood by the researcher.

FIELD OBSERVATION

Evidence about deviance may also be gathered through *participant observation* (joining in the activities of the people being studied), through *nonparticipant field research* (taking notes and asking questions but remaining an outsider), or through *staged activity analysis* (in which subjects are asked to "reconstruct and simulate" their past deviant activities as closely as possible, thus allowing the researchers to "participate" in the re-enactment) (Cromwell, Olson, & Avary, 1991, pp. 15–16). Arguing on behalf of observation techniques, Polsky (1967) likens studying criminals in prisons to studying animals in the zoo: neither is nearly as valuable as watching subjects in their natural habitat. In Polsky's words,

> data gathered from caught criminals … are not only very partial but partially suspect. These are data that are much too heavily retrospective; data from people who aren't really free to put you down; data often involving the kind of "cooperativeness" in which you get told what the criminal wants you to hear so you will get off his back or maybe do him some good with the judge or parole board; data from someone who is not behaving as he normally would in his normal life-situations; and, above all, data that you cannot supplement with, or interpret in the light of, your own direct observation of the criminal's natural behaviour in his natural environment.

> To put the argument another way: Animal behaviour has a narrower range of determinants than human behaviour, [and is therefore] much less complex and variable. And yet, in recent years, animal ecologists have demonstrated that when you undertake a "free ranging" study of an animal in his natural habitat, you discover important things about him that are simply not discoverable when he is behind bars. (pp. 115–116)

An interesting study by Prus and Irini (1980) employed participant observation to produce an ethnographic description of the hotel and bar community in a Canadian city. The study documented the supportive relationships among prostitutes, strippers, underworld hustlers, bellhops, hotel desk clerks, security personnel, bartenders, performers, waitresses, taxi drivers, and many others who form an interdependent deviant community that is within, but generally invisible to, the community at large.

Participant observation can be *overt* (open) or *covert* (hidden). In an overt study, the observer announces his or her research intentions. A study of people who collect tattoos, for example, was not hard to do, even though some of the participants had tattoos in very personal places or over their entire bodies (Vail, 1999). Daniel Wolf (1991) in his ethnography of a Canadian outlaw biker club tells us that informing the bikers that he wanted to study them proved a delicate matter.

A covert study of deviance is sometimes more possible than an overt one in that people who are unaware that their actions are being recorded will behave more naturally. However, this kind of study can be dangerous; we resort to it when we think people will change or hide their actions under observation, and this is most likely to be the case when they have a great deal invested in privacy from outsiders. Studying people who are breaking the law can be dangerous—especially if the police mistake you for one of the gang (Wright & Decker, 1997). Also, covert tactics are ethically questionable. Consider the example of Humphreys (1970), who assumed the role of "watchqueen" (lookout) to study the behaviour of men who went to public washrooms ("tearooms") for quick, impersonal sexual encounters with other anonymous men. Humphreys kept records of the washroom activities and, having changed his appearance to avoid recognition, later interviewed some of the men involved (located through their licence plate numbers). He found that most were married and living with their wives. They did not think of themselves as homosexual and did not participate in the gay subculture. They tended to be above average in their performance of home and community duties, often playing the role of the perfect neighbour with the immaculate lawn and the regularly washed car. Their participation in the tearoom trade, so drastically at odds with their public identity, was a matter of the greatest secrecy. Such men are likely to become suicidal if arrested and exposed (Deroches, 1991, p. 19). A particular concern here is how much damage might have been done had Humphreys' notes fallen into the hands of others. The controversy over this almost resulted in revocation of Humphreys' Ph.D. and threatened his continued employment. The second edition of *Tearoom Trade,* Humphreys' book on the study, included a 65-page "Retrospect on Ethical Issues."

Researchers who use participant observation techniques are normally highly alert to the issue of objectivity: they try to avoid "going native" (identifying with, and taking sides with, the people being studied) or its opposite, developing so much disgust at the norms of the group that it is no longer possible to be rational in discussing them.

SECONDARY ANALYSIS OF STATISTICAL DATA

Most official data used in studies of deviance and criminality come from various agencies of control, including police, courts, prisons, social agencies, and various government ministries at the municipal, provincial, and federal levels. Sir William Petty, known as the father of English "political arithmetic," argued as early as 1670 that prisoner statistics should be collected and used as a measure of "vice and sin" in the nation, in roughly the same way that public health could be gauged by the number of deaths from contagious disease (Sellin & Wolfgang, cited in Gatrell, Lenman, & Parker, 1980).

Statistics Canada collects data through the Uniform Crime Reporting (UCR) system (Statistics Canada, 1995). The UCR system contains information only on crimes that are known to police and reported monthly by them (see Figure 2.4). Until recently, UCR data have been limited by the fact that detailed information about specific incidents was lost when it was coded in aggregate fashion for the report. For example, if four nonviolent offences occurred at the same time, the counting rule meant that only the most serious of them (usually the one with the longest possible prison sentence under the Criminal Code) was recorded. If two violent offences (murder and rape, for example) involved only one victim, only one crime would be

Figure 2.4   An Example of the Use of Uniform Crime Reporting Data in Combination with Other Sources of Information

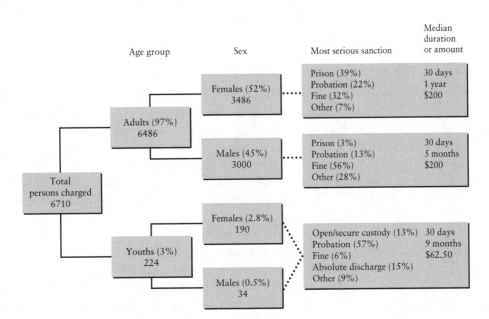

Source: Statistics Canada, "Uniform Crime Reporting Survey," from CANSIM database, Matrix No. 3302; "Youth Courts Survey," from CANSIM database, Matrix No. 3309; "Sentencing in Adult Provincial Courts: A Study of Nine Jurisdictions, 1993–94," Cat. No. 85-513. Reprinted by permission.

reported. For each victim, only the most serious offence is counted. If a murder and a rape occurred, the rape would be lost from the record.

A new version of the UCR has been launched, while the old one continues. The newer version (UCR2) takes an incident-based approach that allows researchers to access multiple aspects of the criminal event, including both accused and victim characteristics such as "age, sex, alcohol consumption, relationship, level of injury and weapon causing injury," as well as characteristics of the incident such as its location and secondary violations that may have occurred at the same time (Statistics Canada, 1995, p. 2). UCR2 promises to be a much more useful research tool once all police departments are participants.

Not all statistical data pertinent to deviance research come from the criminal justice system. Researchers have also made use of data collected by agencies such as hospitals (on injuries and death), schools (truancy and vandalism), coroner's offices (causes of death), and social welfare workers (drug abuse, family breakdown).

Insurance data, although rarely directly available, are also useful for some kinds of research. The rates insurance companies are charging for different kinds of protection, for example, reflect evidence collected by the companies concerning either the deviance of the insured—drivers, boat owners, householders, and others—or the amount of harm that was perpetrated against them.

SECONDARY ANALYSIS OF BIOGRAPHICAL MATERIALS

Biographical material is often used in conjunction with other kinds of evidence as a way of seeing how real-life cases correspond to the models developed in the research process. We might, for example, read Jack Henry Abbott's autobiographical *In the Belly of the Beast* (1981) to see how Abbott's perceptions of his violent life flesh out or contradict the understandings that have been gained through other kinds of research. Or we might read a biography, such as Catherine Dunphy's *Morgenthaler: A Difficult Hero* (1996), to increase our understanding of those involved in Canada's explosive abortion debate.

In the case study, biographical data predominate. Case studies are usually in-depth qualitative accounts of one or more illustrative individuals, families, or communities. They typically make use of personal documents (letters, diaries, autobiographies), as well as interviews with the subject or with people who know the subject. Even though a particular case study may have some unique features, it is usually presented as being representative of many other cases of the same sort. For example, Sutherland (1937) presents what he calls the autobiography of Chic Conwell along with a running commentary that places Conwell's life in the context of what was then known about professional thieves. A different sort of case study is provided in Jane Balin's *A Neighborhood Divided* (1999), which describes the reaction of a neighbourhood to a proposed AIDS care facility. The "not in my back yard" response of many of the neighbours resembles that found in many communities in Canada and the United States and reflects the common urge to exclude people who are perceived as deviant.

Although some autobiographies are highly reliable and reasonably objective, some accounts are self-serving, selective, or fanciful and should be approached with considerable caution. Micky McArthur's *I'd Rather Be Wanted Than Had* (1990), Roger Caron's *Go-Boy!* (1978), and Dwight Pichette's *The Diary of a Bank Robber* (1988) all show considerable commitment to underworld social values, even while professing a change of heart. A very different kind of quasi-autobiographical work is Malcolm Lowry's *Under the Volcano* (1947), which describes the experiences of an alcoholic diplomat living in Mexico. This book has inspired many other writers, among them Michel Foucault (Miller, 1993, pp. 197, 250, 355), whose work is discussed in Chapter 12.

Although biographies tend to be less self-serving than personal accounts, they are also further removed from the reality of their subjects. Like autobiographies, they vary considerably in their usefulness to the social scientist. Literally hundreds of biographies are published every year, usually about people who are well known in the political, literary, artistic, or entertainment worlds. Almost without exception, they reveal aspects of their subjects' lives that might be regarded as deviant. They can, therefore, be useful as illustrations of the way in which deviance is understood by the subjects and those around them. At the same time, they reveal how deviance of certain kinds, and by certain people, may result in repression, notoriety, or celebration. The biography of cult leader and prophet Brother Twelve is a fascinating account of a man who attracted thousands of followers to an island in British Columbia and created a saga of occult beliefs and unusual sexual practices (Oliphant, 1991). The biography of hockey player John Kordic reveals many of the factors that encourage some players, even those with a profound desire to be respected, to go beyond the rules of the game and to live violent lives both on and off the ice (Zwolinski, 1995). Biographies of many creative people also reveal how deviance is a way of going beyond society's limits to feed the imagination, as is clearly shown in Miller's (1993) biography of Michel Foucault, a social philosopher who sought the "limit-experience" in sex and politics as a means of freeing himself from the mundane rigidities of normal thought, so that he could experience something beyond.

CONTENT ANALYSIS

Content analysis is any systematic procedure used to analyze materials such as documents, films, audio recordings, and video presentations. Content analysis may involve simply measuring the amount of column space devoted to an issue in newspaper accounts or, in the visual media, the amount of time allocated to a particular subject. Content analysis of this kind shows us that violent street crimes and horrific accidents have always been given disproportionately greater amounts of space in the front pages of the newspapers than do other kinds of news. Films can be content analyzed for their portrayal of kinds of people and kinds of social roles. An example is the woman's role in "psycho-femme" thrillers such as *Single White Female* (1992), which depend heavily on violations of the way in which women are supposed to act (Thompson, 1998, p. 211)

Even suicide notes have been subjected to content analysis for the light they shed on motivations for suicide (Schneidman, 1976, p. 280). One study used on-line accounts by pedophiles participating in a Usenet discussion group to provide insight on how uncaught pedophiles justify their deviant thoughts and actions (Durkin and Bryant, 1999). Official documents, sometimes released under freedom of information regulations, provide useful information about the treatment of "deviant" populations. Kinsman's (1993) report, based on his analysis of the Canadian security force's internal memoranda, shows how the homosexual-as-security-risk idea was constructed out of partial facts (and a good deal of prejudice) and led to a purge of homosexuals from positions of power and responsibility in the Canadian federal civil service.

A unique form of content analysis is the study of people's garbage—"garbology" or "the archaeology of us" (Rathje, 1996, p. 158). This research exposes many unsuspected truths previously hidden behind our social fronts. Few people tell interviewers the truth about how much alcohol or how many cigarettes they consume, or how much they spend on adult video rentals and magazines. Most of us report food spending that conforms with our notions of a balanced diet and do not bother to mention such behaviours as recent binges on high-fat meats or desserts (Rathje, 1996, p. 169). The results of this research further underline the fact that when people are interviewed, they often underreport any behaviour that might be viewed negatively (Rathje, 1996, p. 166). Garbology is sometimes used by law-enforcement agencies to find out about people under surveillance. For example, as part of an FBI investigation, the home garbage of mobster Joseph ("Joe Bananas") Bonanno was collected for years. It showed that Bonanno was working on a revealing autobiographical manuscript. This was sufficient to convince a judge to permit a raid in which evidence of crime was seized.

Michel Foucault's techniques, which are described in his *Archaeology of Knowledge* (1972), are a form of content analysis that involves a very different conception of what knowledge means. Foucault's is a highly personalized form of social philosophy that makes use of archival documents to discover the forms of power and knowledge in the past and in the modern world. We will be looking at this work in Chapter 12.

SIMULATIONS

Simulations can be made with people (dramatizations and games) or with computers that are programmed to produce games or virtual reality scenarios (Halpin, 1999; Hamburger, 1979; Sanders, 1988). Researchers have posed as both thieves and victims to find out what happens among passers-by when an offence occurs (Stewart & Cannon, 1977). Mock trials have helped us to understand how a jury arrives at a verdict (Haney, Banks, & Zimbardo, 1973) and to clarify such issues as plea bargaining and sentencing. Many studies in the 1970s were aimed at understanding why good people might sometimes do evil things, just by obeying the instructions, even suggestions, of people in authority. One particularly well-known study was Stanley Milgram's obedience study in which volunteers were willing to give high levels of shock to others, apparently because they respected the researcher's authority (Milgram, 1974). Another famous (or infamous) study of this kind was Zimbardo's simulation of a prison setting. The experiment had to be terminated when the "guards" got out of hand (Zimbardo, 1972, 1973). Simulations have also been used to explore control and compliance patterns in organizations (Patrick, 1995).

JOURNALISTIC ACCOUNTS

Investigative journalists have played an important role in uncovering evidence that has changed social theories. Many social scientists are made uneasy by the fact that journalists are not held to the same standards of proof and method as their academic counterparts and are sometimes a good deal less committed to respectability and value neutrality. But these reasons are often precisely why journalists can provide data not otherwise available to academics.

Muckraking in journalism has a long tradition (Eksterowicz, Roberts, & Clark, 1998). One of the best-known muckrakers was Lincoln Steffens, who exposed the shameful and seamy underside of American government and business in the early twentieth century (Kaplan, 1974). Journalistic accounts have helped us to develop a better knowledge of the inner workings of organized crime, outlaw motorcycle clubs, drug trafficking, and the laundering of illegally obtained money (Dubro, 1985), as in Mick Lowe's *Conspiracy of Brothers* (1988), Victor Malarek's *Merchants of Misery: Inside Canada's Illegal Drug Scene* (1989), and Jeffrey Robinson's *The Laundrymen: Inside the World's Third-Largest Business* (1994). Journalists have also provided an insider perspective on several cases in which people convicted of homicide were later exonerated (e.g., Harris's 1986 account of the Donald Marshall case) and have written controversial accounts of the way in which the justice system works with respect to criminals and victims alike (Birnie, 1990; 1992; Marshall & Barrett, 1990; Stroud, 1993). David Cruise and Alison Griffiths (1997) exposed a painful saga of incest and abuse in their account of "the Goler clan" of Nova Scotia.

Sometimes journalism and biography overlap, as in Vernon Oickle's *Jane Hurshman-Corkum: Life and Death after Billy* (1993) and Anne Kershaw and Mary Lasovich's *Rock-a-Bye Baby: A Death behind Bars* (1991). In a different vein, Diane Francis's *Contrepreneurs* (1988) provided a nonacademic perspective on stock market fraud, money laundering, and white-collar crime in Canada. And Marlene Webber's *Street Kids: The Tragedy of Canada's Runaways* (1991) is an excellent and well-documented survey of her topic. Thus, although journalists may not use the same methodology as social scientists, their very separation from the need for academic respectability allows them to raise valuable questions. In addition, they sometimes provide the social scientist with evidence that can be used in conjunction with data from other sources.

SUMMARY

This chapter introduced the elements of theoretical thinking, some of the ways in which theories are tested, and the principal sources of information on deviance. Much of the chapter dealt with issues that have emerged from attempts to conduct the study of deviance according to the standards of science. At the same time, recognition was given to the possibility of learning about deviance through alternative approaches and methods such as participant observation.

Throughout, the central issue has been "How do we know?" To assess the work of others and to ensure the validity of our own, it is important that we understand issues relating to concept formation, the development of hypotheses, and the nature of correlation and causation, and that we know which kinds of evidence will best test or illustrate our ideas.

STUDY QUESTIONS

1. What is the difference between a common sense (*ad hoc*) explanation and a disciplined explanation? Which is easier? Which is most likely to be correct?

2. Select a kind of deviance that interests you. Write its name in the middle of a page. Then draw lines toward it indicating the different possible and likely paths to that kind of deviance. How many paths can you identify? Draw the common paths with a thicker line.

3. Empathetic explanations are usually more humanly satisfying. Why do many social scientists distrust them?

4. Which kind of reasoning do you use most often, inductive or deductive? Why do ideological thinkers usually use deductive reasoning?

5. Invent a hypothesis (for example, concerning the causes of child abuse). Identify your concepts, and indicate how you can operationalize these concepts as variables. Identify which variables are independent and which are being treated as dependent in your hypothesis.

6. What is the difference between a correlation and a cause? A high correlation exists between drinking alcohol and smoking. Does drinking alcohol cause smoking?

7. Can we study homosexuality by studying people who are being treated for homosexuality by psychiatrists? What's wrong with this approach?

8. What does the crime funnel show us about the representativeness of federal prison inmates as a sample of people who commit crimes?

9. Many of you have consistent grades in your courses. Are your grades *reliable*? What does this tell us about how *valid* they are?

10. The text observes that data collection is a *social activity*. What does this mean? How can this affect the data that is collected?

11. How does the work of a sociologist or anthropologist studying a phenomenon such as biker gangs differ from a journalist covering the same material? How is it the same?

12. Select one form of study (self-report, victim survey, analysis of official data) and indicate its strengths and potential weaknesses.

REFERENCES

Abbott, J. H. (1981). *In the Belly of the Beast*. New York: Random House.

Adlaf, E. M., Smart, R. G., & Walsh, G. W. (1994). *Ontario Student Drug Use Survey*. Toronto: Addiction Research Foundation.

Askenasy, H. (1994). *Cannibalism: From Sacrifice to Survival*. Amherst, NY: Prometheus.

Balin, J. (1999). *A Neighborhood Divided: Community Resistance to an AIDS Care Facility*. Ithaca, NY: Cornell University Press.

Barak, G. (1999). Constituting O.J.: Mass Mediated Trials and Newsmaking Criminology. In S. Henry & D. Milovanovic (Eds.), *Constitutive Criminology at Work: Applications of Crime and Justice*. Albany, NY: State University of New York.

Birnie, L. H. (1990). *A Rock and a Hard Place: Inside Canada's Parole Board*. Toronto: Macmillan Canada.

———. (1992). *Such a Good Boy: How a Pampered Son's Greed Led to Murder*. Toronto: Macmillan Canada.

Blackwell, J. C., & Erickson, P. G. (1988). *Illicit Drugs in Canada: A Risky Business*. Toronto: Nelson Canada.

Brown, S. E., Esbensen, F.-A., & Geis, G. (1991). *Criminology: Explaining Crime and Its Context*. Cincinnati, OH: Anderson.

Bullough, V. L. (1994). *Science in the Bedroom: A History of Sex Research*. New York: Basic/Harper Collins.

Canadian Centre for Justice Statistics (CCJS). (1998). *Victim Survey* (Vol. 18[6]). Ottawa: Statistics Canada.

Chafetz, J. S. (1978). *A Primer on the Construction and Testing of Theories in Sociology*. Itasca, IL: Peacock.

Cole, S. (1980). *The Sociological Method: An Introduction to the Science of Sociology* (3rd ed.). Chicago: Rand McNally.

Coleman, C., & Moynihan, J. (1996). Self-Report Studies: True Confessions? In C. Coleman & J. Moynihan (Eds.), *Understanding Crime Data*. Buckingham, UK: Open University Press.

Cromwell, P. F., Olson, J. N., & Avary, D. A. W. (1991). *Breaking and Entering: An Ethnographic Analysis of Burglary* (Vol. 8). Newbury Park, CA: Sage.

Cruise, D., & Griffiths, A. (1997). *On South Mountain: The Dark Secrets of the Goler Clan*. Toronto: Penguin Books Canada.

Deroches, F. (1991). Tearoom Trade: A Law Enforcement Problem. *Canadian Journal of Criminology* (January), 1–21.

Dubro, J. (1985). *Mob Rule: Inside the Canadian Mafia*. Toronto: Totem Books.

Dunphy, C. (1996). *Morgenthaler: A Difficult Hero*. Toronto: Random House.

Durkheim, É. (1951). *Suicide*. New York: Free Press. (Original work published in 1897)

Durkin, K., & Bryant, C. D. (1999). Propagandizing Pederasty: A Thematic Analysis of the On-Line Exculpatory Accounts of Unrepentant Pedophiles. *Deviant Behavior: An Interdisciplinary Journal, 20*(2), 103–127.

Eksterowicz, A., Roberts, R., & Clark, A. (1998). Public Journalism and Public Knowledge. *Harvard International Journal of Press Politics 3*(2), 74–96.

Fekete, J. (1995). *Moral Panic: Biopolitics Rising (Food for Thought)* (2nd ed.). Montreal: Robert Davies.

Foucault, M. (1972). *Archaeology of Knowledge and the Discourse on Language* (A. M. Sheridan Smith, Trans.). New York: Pantheon.

Gatrell, V. A. C., Lenman, B., & Parker, G. (Eds.). (1980). *Crime and the Law: The Social History of Crime in Western Europe since 1500.* London, UK: Europa.

Gauthier, D. K., & Forsyth, C. J. (1998). Bareback Sex, Bug Chasers, and the Gift of Sex. *Deviant Behavior: An Interdisciplinary Journal, 20*(1), 85–100.

———. (2000). Buckle Bunnies: Groupies of the Rodeo Circuit. *Deviant Behavior: An Interdisciplinary Journal, 21*(4), 349–365.

Goffman, E. (1963). *Stigma: Notes on the Management of Spoiled Identity.* Englewood Cliffs, NJ: Prentice-Hall.

Gomme, I., Morton, M. E., & West, W. G. (1984). Rates, Types and Patterns of Male and Female Delinquency in an Ontario Community. *Canadian Journal of Criminology, 26*(3), 313–323.

Greenberg, D. F. (1996). *Criminal Careers* (Vol. 1). Brookfield, VT: Dartmouth.

Hagan, F. E. (2000). *Research Methods in Criminal Justice and Criminology* (5th ed.). Boston: Allyn & Bacon.

Halpin, B. (1999). Simulation in Sociology. *American Behavioral Scientist 42*(10), 1488–1509.

Hamburger, H. (1979). *Games as Models of Social Phenomena.* San Francisco, CA: Freeman.

Haney, C., Banks, W. C., & Zimbardo, P. G. (1973). Interpersonal Dynamics in a Simulated Prison. *International Journal of Criminology and Penology, 1,* 69–77.

Harris, M. (1986). *Justice Denied: The Law versus Donald Marshall.* Toronto: Macmillan Canada.

Hills, S. L. (1987). *Corporate Violence: Injury and Death for Profit.* Totowa, NJ: Rowman and Littlefield.

Hood, R., & Sparks, R. (1970). *Key Issues in Criminology.* London, UK: Weidenfeld and Nicholson.

Humphreys, L. (1970). *Tearoom Trade: Impersonal Sex in Public Places.* Chicago: Aldine.

Ianni, F. A. (1972). The Lupollo Family. In F. A. Ianni, *A Family Business: Kinship and Social Control in Organized Crime.* New York: Russell Sage.

Johnson, H. (1996). Violent Crime in Canada. *Juristat Service Bulletin* (Vol. 15), p. 5.

Junger-Tas, J., Terloun, G. J., & Klein, M. (1994). *Delinquent Behaviour among Youth in the Western World: First Results of the International Self-Report Delinquency Study.* Amsterdam: Kugler.

Kaplan, J. (1974). *Lincoln Steffens: A Biography.* New York: Simon & Schuster.

Kessler, S. J. (1990). The Medical Construction of Gender: Case Management of Intersexed Infants. *Signs: The Journal of Women in Culture and Society, 16*(11), 3–26.

Kinsey, A. C., Pomeroy, W. B., & Martin, C. E. (1948). *Sexual Behavior in the Human Male.* Philadelphia, PA: W. B. Saunders.

Kinsman, G. (1993). *"Character Weaknesses" and "Fruit Machines": Towards an Analysis of the Social Organization of the Anti-Homosexual Purge Campaign in the Canadian Federal Civil Service, 1959–1964.* Paper presented at the annual meeting of the Canadian Sociology and Anthropology Association, Ottawa, ON.

Klein, M. W. (1995). *The American Street Gang: Its Nature, Prevalence, and Control.* New York: Oxford University Press.

Kuhn, T. (1970). *The Structure of Scientific Revolutions* (2nd ed.). Chicago: University of Chicago Press.

LeBlanc, M., & Ferchette, M. (1989). *Male Criminal Activity from Childhood through Youth: Multilevel and Developmental Perspectives.* New York: Springer Verlag.

Lemert, E. (1951). *Social Pathology.* New York: McGraw-Hill.

Lowman, J. (1992). Street Prostitution. In V. Sacco (Ed.), *Deviance: Conformity and Control in Canadian Society.* Scarborough, ON: Prentice-Hall Canada.

Marshall, W. L., & Barrett, S. (1990). *Criminal Neglect: Why Sex Offenders Go Free.* Toronto: Doubleday.

McPhail, C. (1991). *The Myth of the Madding Crowd.* New York: Aldine de Gruyter.

Mercer, I. (1999). Sub-Science Bolsters Violence-Against-Women Claims. [On-Line]. Available: <http://www.calgaryherald.com>. *Calgary Herald,* p. A28.

Meyer, K. (1941). *Die Unbestraften Verbrechen (Unpublished Crimes).* Leipzig, Germany: G. Thieme.

Miethe, T. D., & McCorkle, R. (1998). *Crime Profiles: The Anatomy of Dangerous Persons, Places and Situations.* Los Angeles: Roxbury.

Milgram, S. (1974). *Obedience to Authority: An Experimental View.* New York: Harper.

Miller, J. (1993). *The Passion of Michel Foucault.* New York: Simon & Schuster.

National Institute of Justice Research. (1994). Update on NIJ-Sponsored Research: Six New Reports. *National Institute of Justice Research in Brief* (April).

Nettler, G. (1970). *Explanations.* New York: McGraw-Hill.

———. (1978). *Explaining Crime* (2nd ed.). New York: McGraw-Hill.

———. (1982a). *Explaining Criminals* (Vol. 1). Cincinnati, OH: Anderson.

———. (1982b). *Killing One Another.* Cincinnati, OH: Anderson.

Nye, F. I. (1958). *Family Relationships and Delinquent Behavior.* New York: John Wiley.

Oliphant, J. (1991). *Brother Twelve: The Incredible Story of Canada's False Prophet and His Doomed Cult of Gold, Sex and Black Magic.* Toronto: McClelland and Stewart.

Patrick, S. (1995). The Dynamic Simulation of Control and Compliance Processes in Material Organizations. *Sociological Perspectives* 38(4), 497–519.

Picard, A. (1990, January 22). Many Car Thefts Arranged by Their Owners. *The Globe and Mail.*

Polsky, N. (1967). *Hustlers, Beats and Others.* Chicago: Aldine.

Porterfield, A. L. (1943). Delinquency and Its Outcome in Court and College. *American Journal of Sociology,* 49, 199–208.

Prus, R., & S. Irini. (1980). *Hookers, Rounders and Desk Clerks: The Social Organization of the Hotel Community.* Toronto: Gage.

Rathje, W. L. (1996). The Archaeology of Us. *Science and the Future: 1997 Year Book* (pp. 158–176). Chicago: Encyclopaedia Britannica.

Sanders, T. R. (1988). *Virtual Law II: Virtual Law in the Courtroom.* [On-Line]. Available: <http://www.vremag.com/vr/features/virtuallaw/virtuallaw11/html>.

Schneidman, E. S. (Ed.). (1976). *Suicidology: Contemporary Developments.* New York: Grune & Stratton.

Schütz, A. (1960). The Social World and the Theory of Social Action. *Social Research, 27*(Summer), 203–221.

Shelden, R., G., Tracy, S. K., & Brown, W. B. (1997). *Youth Gangs in America.* Belmont, CA: Wadsworth.

Shover, N. (1996). *Great Pretenders: Pursuits and Careers of Persistent Thieves.* Boulder, CO: Westview/HarperCollins.

Statistics Canada. (1995). *Canadian Crime Statistics 1994.* Ottawa: Statistics Canada.

Stewart, J. E., & Cannon, D. A. (1977). Effects of Perpetrator Status and Bystander Commitment on Response to a Simulated Crime. *Journal of Police Science and Administration, 5*, 308–323.

Stroud, C. (Ed.). (1993). *Contempt of Court: The Betrayal of Justice in Canada.* Toronto: Macmillan.

Sutherland, E. H. (1937). *The Professional Thief.* Chicago: University of Chicago Press.

———. (1949). *White Collar Crime.* New York: Holt, Rinehart and Winston.

Thomas, G., Reifman, A., Barnes, G., & Farrell, M. P. (2000). Delayed Onset of Drunkenness as a Protective Factor for Adolescent Alcohol Misuse and Sexual Risk Taking: A Longitudinal Study. *Deviant Behavior: An Interdisciplinary Journal, 21*(2), 181–210.

Thompson, C. Y. (1998). The Psycho-Femme: Identity Norm Violations and the Interactional Dynamics of Assignment. *Deviant Behavior: An Interdisciplinary Journal, 19*(3), 207–226.

Tittle, C. R., & Paternoster, R. (2000). *Social Deviance and Crime: An Organizational and Theoretical Approach.* Los Angeles: Roxbury.

Vail, D. A. (1999). Tattoos Are Like Potato Chips … You Can't Have Just One: The Process of Becoming and Being a Collector. *Deviant Behavior: An Interdisciplinary Journal, 20*(3), 253–273.

Van Dijk, J. J. M., Mayhew, P., & Killias, M. (1990). *Experiences of Crime across the World.* Boston: Kleuwer.

Williams, J. R., & Gold, M. (1972). From Delinquent Behavior to Official Delinquency. *Social Problems, 20*, 209–229.

Wolf, D. R. (1991). *The Rebels: A Brotherhood of Outlaw Bikers.* Toronto: University of Toronto Press.

Wright, R. T., & Decker, S. H. (1997). *Armed Robbers in Action: Stickups and Street Culture.* Boston: Northeastern University Press.

Zimbardo, P. G. (1972). Pathology of Imprisonment. *Society, 9*, 4–8.

———. (1973). A Pirandellian Prison. *The New York Times Magazine*, pp. 30–60.

Zwolinski, M. (1995). *The John Kordic Story: The Fight of His Life.* Toronto: Macmillan Canada.

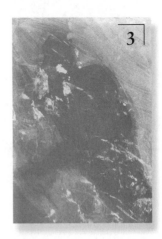

PRESCIENTIFIC APPROACHES TO DEVIANCE

In this chapter, we will look at the ways in which deviance was understood before the great transition to rationalism and science (the Enlightenment) in the late seventeenth century. The earliest sacred stories (myths) illustrated the character of deviance and warned people about the consequences of excessive control as well as excessive deviance. The spread and penetration of monotheistic religions—especially Christianity—led to a more causal, but still supernatural, explanation according to which the devil caused deviance and all other ills. Deviance no longer evoked feelings of ambivalence; it was evil, as were those who failed to oppose it. This chapter devotes considerable space to explaining the nature, origins, and consequences of the witchcraft craze that shook Europe from roughly C.E. 1400 to C.E. 1700.

Witchcraft is important to the study of deviance because it provides a paradigmatic example of the process (identified in our definition of deviance in Chapter 1) whereby authorities can create deviants. It is relatively easy, looking back through contemporary eyes, to see that "witches," as seen by the medieval authorities, did not really exist, even if there were (as now) some people who claimed to have supernatural powers. Once we make clear the way in which the deviantization of witches came about, we can look at other kinds of deviance closer to our own time and raise the same questions. For example, how much of both the glamour and the horror of the drug trafficker is real, and how much is a construct of some truths and many inaccuracies? What is the underlying reality, and why is distortion of that reality so common?

PAST AND PRESENT REPRESENTATIONS OF DEVIANCE

MYTHS, PARABLES, AND STORIES

Before the Enlightenment brought us science, rationality, and an empirically bound reality, people understood life in terms of myths, folklore, parables, and stories. These tales described their experiences and, in a nonscientific way, explained them. This tradition is carried on in modern art, drama, and literature that present us with examples of deviance and its consequences. Although they may or may not also provide moral instruction, these stories give us an understanding of how deviance fits in the scheme of things.

The ethical message of each major religion is supported by collections of historical or mythical tales in which various kinds of offences against the powers of creation, or against social regulation, happen. The offence is not always intended by—or even known to—the·offender. The response of heaven and earth, however, is usually punitive unless mitigated by ritual reconciliation. The prodigal son, for example, may be welcomed home. For the most part, deviants are expelled from the garden, turned into pillars of salt, or condemned to perform eternal tasks. Temptation and its consequences are central to many stories of this kind. Eve was tempted into tasting the forbidden fruit of knowledge. Pandora's curiosity led her to open the box containing all the evils of the world. Buddha, Christ, Mohammed, and other important religious figures all had experience, at least in figurative terms, of demons or temptations.

Secular or magical stories also reinforce cultural images of deviance and control. In Heinrich Hoffmann's *Der Struwwelpeter* (1861) (translated as *Slovenly Peter: Or Cheerful Stories and Funny Pictures for Good Little Folks*), a little girl plays with matches; her dress catches fire, and soon all that remains of her is a pile of ashes, two shoes, and two cats whose tears flow like a stream across the page. In another story, a boy insists on sucking his thumbs and a tailor (with legs like long scissors) leaps across the page to cut them off. Slovenly Peter's long fingernails inspired the film *Edward Scissorhands*, which is itself a moral parable (see Figure 3.1). This book has recently been reissued in a bilingual (German–English) version, *Struwwelpeter 2000*, which attempts to remain faithful to Hoffmann's original while rewriting parts unsuitable for small children (Hoffmann & Blyth, 2000).

Figure 3.1　Slovenly Peter

Source: Struwwelpeter: In English Translation, by Heinrich Hoffmann.

Many other children's stories have similar cautionary intentions. The boy who cried wolf when there was no wolf is denied help when he needs it. Little Red Riding Hood talks to a stranger in the woods and gets herself and her grandmother eaten. Cinderella's ugly stepsisters have their eyes plucked out and eaten by doves (Tatar, 1987, p. 182). The vain emperor is revealed as naked. These stories conform to the common cultural practice of warning and admonishing to induce polite language, table manners, caution, cooperation, modesty, and responsibility.

Trickster Legends

Despite the above examples, most of our secular tales are ambivalent about deviance in that they do not regard it as unconditionally bad. Indeed, the deviant character is frequently more likable and sympathetic than the characters who teach and correct. This ambivalence about deviance and control is reflected in the culturally universal trickster (Radin, 1972, p. iii). In trickster stories, the smart little guy outwits the stupid, greedy authorities. The trickster circumvents the usual rules in disrespectful ways.

> Unburdened by scruples, tricksters dupe friends, acquaintances, and adversaries alike in the pursuit of their selfish ends and blithely reward their benefactor's generosity with sometimes deadly betrayals. In addition, they have a pronounced weakness for food but are plagued by an inveterate aversion for work, a trait that forces them to rely on trickery to obtain food both in times of want and of plenty. (Owomoyela, 1990, p. 626)

Everything the trickster does is permeated with laughter, irony, wit—and deviance.

The trickster is also a god, a god that is not above us all but rather immanent in life itself and in the community. The audience reaction is laughter tempered with awe (Radin, 1972, p. xxiv). The trickster is often the "fire-bringer" who brings the sun or fire to mankind but is also the one blamed for earthquakes, chaos, war, and the end of all things.

The trickster takes many forms. He is usually masculine but also gender bending (Hyde, 1998). Even if he appears as a female, he may have a penis that wanders into unacceptable places. He does not take the realities of the human world seriously. In many tales, he shockingly violates many of the customary norms of honesty, mannerliness, and loyalty. When the trickster is present, complacency and comfort are at risk.

Brer Rabbit, Roger Rabbit, and Bugs Bunny have their origins in African trickster figures, Anansi and Legba. Their Disneyfication has almost eliminated the demigod features of the original, but they do convey the amusing, iconoclastic, and likable side of the trickster. One could say the same for Kokopelli, a sanitized and commercialized version of a more complex trickster figure. The trickster also encompasses darker, uncontrolled, less human forces. Batman's archenemy, the Joker, is funny, in a campy way; he can take on animal forms or the shape of inanimate objects; and he is violent, unpredictable, homicidal, and sadistic. The mean and mischievous imp Mr. Mxyztplk in *Superman* comic books combines both comedic and demonic features.

Box 3.1   The Trickster in Native Mythology

Nanabush (Weesagechack), the Canadian Cree Indian version of the trickster, is a force that, in modern Native literature, breaks through layers of cultural oppression. In Tomson Highway's celebrated plays *The Rez Sisters* and *Dry Lips Oughta Move to Kapuskasing,* Weesagechack is a tricky, shape-shifting, humorous, infinitely subversive, god-like figure, who often appears as a vulgarly seductive not-quite-female animal with human characteristics. In *Kiss of the Fur Queen*, the trickster is a "torch-singing fox" (fox is *maggeesees* in Cree) with "fur so white it hurts the eyes,... missile-like tits, ice-blond meringue hair.... She presents herself in the story as 'Miss Maggie-Weesageechak-Nanabush-Coyote-Raven-Glooscap-oh-you-should-hear-the-things-they-call-me-honey-pot-Sees, weaver of dreams, sparker of magic, showgirl from hell'" (pp. 231–234). According to Highway, she is "The clown who bridges humanity and God—a God who laughs, a God who's here, not for guilt, not for suffering, but for a good time." Highway continually contrasts the trickster's liberating discourse with the rigid dualisms and abusive forces of residential school religion. His trickster forces people to engage in making their own way, without relying on fixed rules and precepts (Johnson, 1990).

Many other writers of Aboriginal descent or identification make use of the trickster. Louis Owens gives us a wisecracking Indian drag queen at a college in California (Owens, 1994). Gerald Vizenor's Almost Browne wears four ordinary wrist watches whose "hands are set at arcane hours," and "outsize shoes ... tied with copper wire." Browne represents chance, which is "the unnameable creation of natives" (1989, pp. 1–2), who remain unnameable (free) within the dominant stories of North America. In *Green Grass, Running Water* (1993), Thomas King's Coyote guilelessly subverts the accepted truths of religion, economics, and John Wayne films but is ultimately the one element that holds the story, and its shifting levels of reality, together.

In another variation of the trickster, Christopher Moore "rescues" his central character—a Native who has "gone white" and has a very boring life—by having him encounter a trickster who magically destroys everything that supports his current choices. The hero is driven back to his roots, with much humour, and forward into a new and risky relationship (Moore, 1994). Although most modern Native literature celebrates the trickster's contribution to change, negative energy is also part of these stories. In *The Coyote Bead* (1999) Gerald Hausman deals with the Navaho perception of Coyote, who is seen as a violent destroyer of balance and peace. Coyote is blamed for the horrors visited on the Navaho by Whites and by the Utes. This negative side of the trickster is also seen in Tony Hillerman's *Coyote Waits.* Finally, as a note of caution, "old man Coyote is not a scholarly character. He has consistently evaded academic capture and definition and has tricked nearly every commentator into at least one outrageous and laughable generalization" (Lopez, 1977, p. xi).

Thus, the trickster embodies the paradox of deviance—its attractiveness and dangers and also its many faces.

Whether the figure is that of Blue Jay, Mink, Spider, or even Salmon, the American Aboriginal trickster is uniquely local in variations but universal in being a creative–chaotic force (Christie, 1997; Leeming & Page, 1999, p. 22). Among the Haida of the Queen Charlotte Islands, the trickster takes the form of Raven (Wilkins, 1994, p. 73) or, in other Native cultures, is very often Coyote (Bright, 1993). In European lands, the trickster is found in the Norse mythologies as Loki (Loki the creator, Loki the destroyer: a creative destroyer) and in the form of Hermes, messenger of the Greek gods of Mount Olympus (Combs & Holland, 1996). The trickster is also found in many European/Near Eastern picaresque tales—such as the German Til Eulenspiegel, "the merry prankster"—and in the Turkish "wise-fool" Nasreddin Hodja, who represents "revolt against the rigidity of tradition" or exposure of pretentious nonsense (Chirol, 1923; Radin, 1972, p. 185). Goethe's *Reynard the Fox* and Thomas Mann's *The Confessions of Felix Krull, Confidence Man,* also fit within this genre.

The trickster tradition is often called on in a postmodern way (Vizenor, 1989), which we discuss in Chapter 13, and as a moving force in novels. For example, in Charles de Lint's urban fantasy *Someplace to Be Flying* (1998) the trickster Raven is a central force. As in the original trickster tales, in these stories characters are inspired (often by having their lives turned upside-down) to free their lives from oppression or rut-like routine.

We find elements of the trickster in rock music (Michael Jackson); the bad heroes of film, sports, and art (Dennis Rodman, Jack Nicholson); and political protests (the antics of masked protestors at demonstrations, for example) (Santino, 1990).

Cross-dressers (people who wear clothes designed for the opposite sex) sometimes fall into the trickster category. They make fun of the established order and question one of its most fundamental dichotomies, the great gender divide. Thus, the role of the trickster is a contrary one that turns the accepted order of things on its head.

Contemporary Legends

Contemporary legends differ from legends of the past in that they claim to be factual rather than fantastic. These legends, although highly believable, are based on hearsay rather than fact (Goode, 1992, p. 306; Pearson, 1984). Some of them are horror stories reflecting urban fears, while some, like the trickster tales, are stories with a humorous, slightly ambiguous moral twist. An example of the first is the perennial legend of the Halloween candy poisoned (by strangers) that stirs up parental anxieties each October (Best, 1985; Brunvand, 1981). For an example of the second, see Box 3.2.

Most students have heard many legends spawned by essay anxieties, such as the one about the student who handed in a recycled essay and received a good mark on it, but with a note from the professor saying "I only got a C on this, but I always thought it was a lot better than that." Jan Harold Brunvand, University of Utah English professor and folklorist, has collected hundreds of these tales, which always

> ## Box 3.2   Naval Intelligence
>
> This is ostensibly a radio conversation between a U.S. naval ship's crew with Canadian authorities. It is purported to be based on an actual transcript, but it has appeared in a variety of different forms and has never been validated. The author's first record of this one was made 20 years ago, and the Web site where it currently resides claims that it is at least 35 years old (Ro, 2000).
>
> **Americans:** Please divert your course 15 degrees to the north to avoid a collision.
> **Canadians:** Recommend you divert *your* course 15 degrees to the south to avoid a collision.
> **Americans:** This is the captain of a U.S. Navy ship. I say again, *divert your course.*
> **Canadians:** No, I say again, you divert *your* course.
> **Americans:** This is the aircraft carrier *U.S.S. Lincoln,* the second-largest ship in the United States' Atlantic fleet. We are accompanied by three destroyers, three cruisers, and numerous support vessels. I *demand* that you divert your course 15 degrees north, that's one-five degrees north, or countermeasures will be undertaken to ensure the safety of this ship.
> **Canadians:** This is a lighthouse. It's your call.

betray their spuriousness by being told far too many times and with far too many embellishments and revisions, and always as told by a reliable source or a friend of a friend (FOAF) (Brunvand, 1981, 1986). Urban legends deal with understandings of deviance and control. They tell us that certain ways of living (deviance) are likely to lead to grief or humiliation, and in the process they express our fears (and sometimes our sense of humour).

EARLY EXPLANATIONS OF DEVIANCE:

THE DEMONIC PERSPECTIVE

The earliest recorded attempts to *explain* rather than describe the nature of deviance did not, as modern science does, seek causes in the empirical world. Deviance, like everything else, was deemed to be caused by forces in the supernatural realm (see Figure 3.2). In theoretical terms, the independent variables were supernatural forces, often demons or devils of some kind, who acted through particular human beings to cause harm in the world. Thus, when floods came, crops failed, farm animals sickened, or women miscarried, people did not look for the causes in nature, physiology, or medicine. Ordinary folks did not understand that mould on the crops could produce hallucinations, miscarriages, and other problems. They looked instead to the supernatural—to witches, sorcerers, demons, and the like—as an explanation for these events. In this world, there were no coincidences: if a man walked along a path

Figure 3.2   The Causal Model of Demonic Deviance

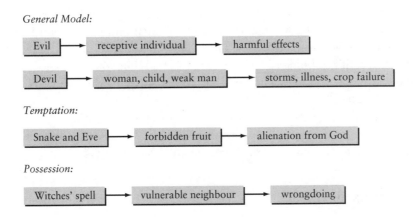

General Model:

Evil → receptive individual → harmful effects

Devil → woman, child, weak man → storms, illness, crop failure

Temptation:

Snake and Eve → forbidden fruit → alienation from God

Possession:

Witches' spell → vulnerable neighbour → wrongdoing

and something fell on him, someone else must have willed that event to happen by invoking the powers of the supernatural.

Over time, there have been many versions of the demonic perspective, each corresponding with the different ideas about the supernatural that were typical of the particular age and culture. Pantheistic religions each espoused a belief in gods and goddesses who had selfish, egotistical, or violent natures and a wide range of supernatural powers. Such gods, although capable of goodness, were also capable of malice in their treatment of human beings. They could tempt them or put them into situations in which evil would result. Madness or other forms of punishment might be visited upon humans who crossed the will of a powerful god, even if they did so inadvertently or while serving the interests of another god. Pantheism encompassed the notion of demons or other evil beings, none of which, however, achieved the status of Christianity's Satan. Hinduism and Buddhism recognize demons (although not in the form of a conspiracy theory whereby the demonic is part of an extensive, sinister plot against the forces of good). Many Aboriginal cultures include a belief in powerful evil sorcerers such as the Ojibwa *bearwalker* or the Navaho *skinwalker*. Fear of such a sorcerer has been successfully used in a Canadian courtroom as a defence against a murder charge (Laghi, 1997).

Monotheistic religions like Judaism, Christianity, and Islam have tended to see the goodness of an all-powerful creator as offset by a single, purely evil power (sometimes personified as a type of devil) bent on wresting power from the Almighty. In the Judeo-Christian view (which is partially also the view of Islam and which has precursors in Manichaeism and Neoplatonism), the supernatural primarily reflects a cosmic struggle between good and evil, personified by God and the devil (Satan). In the battle for human souls, the devil turns people into deviants. Such people are bad, not just because of what they do to others but also because of their treasonous role in the battle between good and evil. The demonic deviant commits physically harmful acts that weaken the system while at the same time challenging the order of things. In Shakespeare's *Macbeth*, for example, both Christian and pagan traditions are called on to describe the cosmic effects of Macbeth's capitulation to his wife's ambition and greed. Macbeth's stabbing of Duncan is not just a killing on earth—it is also an event that disturbs cosmic forces and as such is accompanied by thunder, screeching horses, and baying dogs.

This view of the world as dualistic, a matter of pure good and stark evil, had a profound impact on conceptions of deviance from the Middle Ages up until the 1970s. Only with the rise of postmodern alternatives has this duality been seriously challenged.

THE PAGAN AS DEVIANT

In their efforts to discredit and displace other religions, dominant religions have demonized the other religions' gods, made wizards and sorcerers of their sages, and treated their times of ritual ceremony as occasions of demonic celebration (Simpson, 1973). The idea of a Witches Sabbath, a time when witches supposedly gathered to engage in sex with the devil and his demons, was largely a Christian propaganda distortion of the rites of older religions seen as dangerous pagan cults. Similarly, Baal-Zeebub, the Lord of the Flies, was a fertility god worshipped by the Philistines and other Semitic groups. The Old Testament Israelites transformed him into Beelzebub, a powerful devil. Both the horned Celtic god Cerunnos and the Greco-Roman Pan were remade into Judeo-Christian images of devils with horns and cloven hooves (Russell, 1984, p. 63). Other demonized residuals of pagan times include the immoral or amoral humanlike creatures depicted as elves, fauns, trolls, satyrs, fairies, leprechauns, werewolves, dragons, ghosts, and jinn. Although now the tame stuff of children's storybooks, these creatures were once an accepted part of everyday life, both feared and respected. Anticipating retaliation if they failed to do so, people spoke kindly about fairies (Briggs, 1978) but also used them to explain such events as a husband going missing for a year. (The fairies had kidnapped him and made him dance.) Bad children are still sometimes seen as changelings—evil replacements for good children stolen by goblins or trolls; the deviance of such children is in no way the fault of their parents.

The pantheistic view of the world saw deviance and suffering as phenomena more or less beyond human control. The actions of both gods and hostile spirits were neither predictable nor always preventable. In the monotheistic cosmos, however, humans bear some responsibility for evoking, or giving in to, the forces of evil. The two main paths to deviance in this view are temptation and possession. The devil tempts or possesses weaker human beings such as children or morally weak (irreligious) adults. Sometimes the deviant contributes to the process by dabbling in the occult, indulging in heretical ideas, or living a lifestyle open to corruption.

EXAMPLES OF DEMONIC DEVIANCE: TEMPTATION AND POSSESSION

In the monotheistic tradition, Satan appears in multiple guises to promote our fall into the seven deadly sins of sloth, anger, lust, pride, envy, gluttony, and greed. In the Old Testament, the snake seduces Eve with promises of God-like knowledge. In the New Testament, the devil tempts Jesus to test God's love by jumping from the pinnacles of the temple, and Judas submits to evil when he accepts 30 pieces of silver in exchange for his betrayal of Jesus. In hundreds of folktales, the devil promises humans earthly pleasures in exchange for their eternal souls. This explanation gives humans a role in invoking the forces of evil but still explains the wrongdoing in terms of supernatural powers.

Sometimes the person is not tempted into evil but experiences a sense of being taken over by destructive forces. These forces may be conceived as demons lying in wait for the unsuspecting passerby or as evil spirits unleashed by witches or sorcerers by way of curses, spells, or enthrallments. Possession has been reported in every society (Levack, 1992b). Among North American Indians, the *windigo* was a spirit that could possess humans and entice them to their deaths or turn them into cannibalistic monsters (Largent, 1998). In many cultures, people who suddenly run amok and kill others are deemed to be possessed.

Thus, in the demonic perspective, mental illness, the birth of deformed children, repeated crop failures, and the like could be blamed either on violations of supernatural laws by humans or on the actions of supernatural beings engaged in possessing or tempting humans. Even mundane vices such as drinking or gambling could be blamed on the devil. In sixteenth-century Germany (a time in which few people could read), more than 100 000 copies of "devil books" were on the market. This popular literature singled out particular offences as proof of "how powerful and ubiquitous the devil and his followers were" (Coudert, 1992, p. 68).

The two solutions to the problem of demonic deviance were exorcism—cleansing the individual of demonic influence—or destroying the demonic influence by purifying the individual through extreme suffering or death.

THE SOCIAL CONTROL OF DEMONIC DEVIANCE

Exorcism is a religious ritual designed to bind or cast out—from either a place or a person—troublesome evil spirits, ghosts, demons, or other nonphysical, malign entities. Exorcisms persist to this day and are usually performed by teams (rather than individuals) led by a specially trained religious expert (e.g., a priest) or by a magical/occult adept, who acts as a kind of "ghostbuster." (Whether one believes in them or not, exorcisms are often extremely traumatic for the person being "cured" and may even result in death.) Some exorcisms are less formal and less demanding. In September 2000, it was reported that Latino gang members housed in the Santa Clara County jail in San Jose, California, had been allowed an exorcism to remove dangerous spirits that they had accidentally disturbed by playing with a makeshift Ouija board (Dotinga, 2000). The priest said a few prayers and sprinkled holy water on those afflicted and on their beds. This procedure seems to have solved the problem. Some exorcisms have even been performed by psychologists and psychiatrists as a means of relieving patients of obsessive-compulsive symptoms (Peck, 1983, p. 182) and, as reported in the journal of the Toronto-based Centre for Addiction and Mental Health, there is renewed acceptance of exorcism as an adjunct to the treatment of mental disorders, at least as a respectful response to patients who have strong religious beliefs (Centre for Addiction and Mental Health, 1999). Exorcism techniques range from the prayers, holy water, and confrontations of the newly revised Roman Catholic *Rituale Romanum,* to the laying on of hands practised in Pentecostal churches, to dances, trances, and the burning of animal dung of ritual paganism (Bonthrone, 2000; Guiley, 1991, p. 192).

Although exorcism is no longer a dominant method of social control, it is still practised. It appears to be enjoying a revival in response to the perceived failure of other forms of control. The remaking of films such as the *Exorcist* both reflects and feeds this trend.

Historically, however, the authorities often executed those who illegitimately acquired supernatural powers. It was believed that the death, if painful enough, would result in the salvation of the person's soul while at the same time driving the devil out. An added bonus was that such executions provided a highly educational (and sometimes profitable) form of entertainment for the people who came to watch.

THE WITCH CRAZE OF THE EUROPEAN RENAISSANCE, 1400–1700

HISTORICAL BACKGROUND

Virtually all societies have maintained some beliefs about witchcraft or sorcery. Before the witch craze, European beliefs were similar to those found on other continents. Witches and sorcerers were sometimes feared, sometimes persecuted, but often respected and recognized as people who served a useful role in the social order (e.g., by providing charms and amulets to protect people from harm or sickness, or by acting as oracles to decide the innocence or guilt of accused people). Magic directed against political leaders, however, was regarded as treason.

Belief in witches was "a continuing preoccupation of villagers, but not an obsession" (Garrett, 1977, p. 462). The penalties for unauthorized or malicious practice of witchcraft were commensurate with those enforced for other kinds of assault on individuals or their property.

Before C.E. 1000, church canon law (as reflected in the *Canon Episcopi* of about C.E. 906, a compendium of popular lore on demons) tended to hold that it was both un-Christian and illegal to believe in the reality of witches (Trevor-Roper, 1969, p. 13; Webster, 1996, p. 77). Witchcraft was not treated as part of the conspiracy theory of the demonic versus God, except for the *Canon*'s claim that women who believed themselves able to use love incantations or to fly at night with the pagan goddess Diana were suffering from delusions planted by the devil (Groh, 1987, p. 17). The *Canon* asserted that that the folkloric practice associated with such beliefs would disappear as all people became Christian (Ben-Yahuda, 1985, p. 34; Richards, 1990, p. 77). Catastrophes were sent by God to test humankind, and witches were deluded in believing that they could affect such things. In this period, attacks on presumed witches were regarded as superstitious pagan behaviour and sometimes resulted in protests to Rome.

Between C.E. 1000 and 1480, witches and sorcerers (along with other manifestations of supernatural beings) were redefined. Rather than harmless and misunderstood relics of pagan life, they became agents of the devil—a vast subversive conspiracy against everything that was right, orderly, and holy. In fact, many of the accusations made against heretics and witches in this period (incest, infanticide, sex orgies, and cannibalism) were the same as those that had been levelled against the early Christians by classical pagan writers (Cohen, 1987; Richards, 1990, p. 78). The process whereby folklore, witchcraft beliefs, ritual magic, and devil worship became one overall and world-shattering conspiracy was neither smooth nor gradual: it was contested in some areas and embraced in others.

The witch craze has been described as a collective psychosis or mania (Trevor-Roper, 1969). Although it has connections with modern fears of Satanism, its scale was much broader and its impact far more devastating. Episodes broke out repeatedly in towns, villages, and cities throughout Europe, the British Isles, and the American colonies, sometimes receding in one area only to break out in others. The exact number of victims is difficult to ascertain, given the widespread (but nonetheless local and episodic) nature of the witch-hunt and the fact that records were often not kept at all in the early period. Later records were often destroyed, deliberately or not.

> The chronicler of Trèves reported that in the year 1586, the entire female population of two villages was wiped out by the inquisitors, except for only two women left alive. Two other villages were destroyed completely and erased from the map. A hundred and thirty-three persons were burned in a single day at Quedlinburg in 1589, out of a town of 12,000.... In 1524, one thousand witches died at Como. Strasbourg burned five thousand in a period of 20 years.... A bishop of Bamburg claimed 600 witches in ten years; a bishop of Nancy, 800 in 16 years; a bishop of Wurzburg 1900 in 5 years. Five hundred were executed within three months in Geneva, and 400 in a single day at Toulouse.... The slaughter went on throughout Christian Europe for nearly five centuries. (Walker, 1996, p. 444)

Events such as plagues, wars, and famines were likely to be followed by outbreaks of witch-hunting. In all, somewhere between 100 000 and 200 000 executions probably took place (Barstow, 1995; Ben-Yahuda, 1985, p. 23), although figures as low as 40 000 to 60 000 (Levack, 1987, p. 21) and as high as 500 000 (Harris, 1978, p. 237), and even nine million (Murray, 1921; Pelka, 1992), have been cited. Although this means that the overall total number of executions amounted to no more than a small part of 1 percent of the total population of women, and an even smaller proportion of men, it is untrue to state (as Katz does), that "even at its peak, 99.9 plus percent of women in Europe were safe from the annihilatory impact of the panic"(Katz, 1994, p. 502). No one was safe, and when an outbreak occurred, it was lethal.

CONTRIBUTING FACTORS: THE INQUISITION AND THE *MALLEUS MALEFICARUM*

Although the witch craze can be seen as a symptom of the new dualist (monotheistic) way of looking at the world, its immediate sources were found within the dominant churches of the time, first among the Roman Catholic authorities, and then the Protestant ones. The witch craze, as a craze, began with the work of the Roman Catholic Inquisition.

The Inquisition caught in its net not only heretics who challenged what the authorities felt were the appropriate forms of belief and behaviour but also people who, like Galileo, put forward alternative interpretations of the empirical world (Christie-Murray, 1989; Redondi, 1987). The first Inquisition was set up in the eleventh century to combat heresy (false belief) by baptized Christians. It was followed in the fifteenth century by the Spanish Inquisition, which directed its energies against residual Muslim and Jewish elements in Spain, and, in 1542, by the Roman Catholic Inquisition, which was established primarily to combat Protestantism (see Figure 3.3). All three Inquisitions took the form of judicial bodies and operated under the assumption that witchcraft (which was seen to include the belief that the devil should be worshipped) was heresy of the worst kind and a special kind of crime (Larner, 1980).

Witch-hunting received a considerable boost from the work of the Franciscan and Dominican brotherhoods. These "begging friars" were missionaries, healers, and preachers. Part of their mandate, which came directly from Rome, was to fight heresy in those areas not well controlled by the Church (towns, mountains, and outlying areas where feudalism had failed to take hold). Heresy was often interpreted as any resistance to the control of feudal authorities and could also exist entirely in the minds of the people who were appointed, or appointed themselves, hunters of heretics. Conrad of Marburg, appointed first Inquisitor of Germany in 1231, conducted a reign of terror, discovering "nests of devil-worshippers" until his death in 1233. Like him, many of these witch-hunters, after killing hundreds, were themselves killed. Peter of Verona, founder of the Inquisition in northern Italy, was murdered in 1252. He was

Figure 3.3   Heretics about to Be Burned to Death by the Inquisition at Valladolid in 1559

Source: Mary Evans Picture Library. Reprinted by permission.

promptly canonized the following year as St. Peter Martyr (Richards, 1990, p. 57). *The Name of the Rose,* written by medievalist Umberto Eco and later made into a film of the same name, is a dramatization of the forces involved. In this story Bernard Gui (a historically real Dominican inquisitor) meets a dramatic and sticky end.

Two Dominicans in particular—Heinrich Kramer (also called Institor) and Jakob Sprenger—played a major role in systematizing and giving shape to the definition of witchcraft as a conspiracy. Together they wrote a treatise on witchcraft called the *Malleus Maleficarum* (The Hammer of the Witches) (1971). First published in 1486, this was not the first book to codify all that was then known or believed of witchcraft—or even the first to set standards for the prosecution of witches—but it was the most systematic, complete, and compelling. One of the first books to be printed on the newly invented printing press (Trevor-Roper, 1969, p. 101), it quickly became one of the first bestsellers in the history of books, outselling every book except the Bible (Groh, 1987, p. 17; Russell, 1988, p. 166). The "papal bull" that declared the jurisdiction of the authors to be the extirpation of witches in the Germanic countries was issued in 1484 and reprinted with the *Malleus Maleficarum* in 1486. By printing the "bull" as an introduction to the *Malleus Maleficarum,* the book itself seemed to carry

Rome's blessing, as it eventually did. Sprenger and Kramer were unable to obtain the endorsement of the theological school at Cologne, so they forged the endorsement they wanted and published this with the book as well (Ben-Yahuda, 1985, p. 52). This act did a great deal to provide apparent legitimacy to the prosecution of witches.

The *Malleus* compiled all the existing sources of belief about witches and witch-craft, most of which were taken from common superstitions, biblical references, Greek and Roman writings, and the confessions of "witches." From this material the authors fashioned an impressive work that put witches in the worst possible light. Hailed for centuries as a work of great knowledge and scholarship, this book is now regarded as a compilation of pseudo-knowledge fuelled by the fantasy projections of misogynistic and power-hungry men.

The book was divided into three parts. The first sought to convince readers that witches were dangerous heretics and that their gatherings (*sabbats*) were subversive. The ability of witches to raise hailstorms, cause crop failure, and emasculate men was only the tip of the iceberg. The real danger lay in the alliance with Satan. In contrast with previous church doctrine, the *Malleus* stated that those who rejected the reality of the witchcraft conspiracy were themselves part of it. The second section of the book was devoted to the identification of witches by devil's marks and other criteria, and the third section outlined the proper procedure for prosecuting a witch. This section included an extensive discussion of the kind of torture to be used at each point in the formal examination of accused witches.

TREATMENT OF THE ACCUSED

In Europe, torture was authorized in 1252 to elicit confessions from Albigensian heretics; in 1468, its use was extended to accused witches. Torture was needed to pro-duce convictions because the Roman canon law of proof (valid in most European courts) required, for a conviction, the evidence of two eyewitnesses or a confession. Eyewitnesses were often impossible to find for something as conspiratorial as witch-craft, and thus confessions became crucial (Inverarity, Lauderdale, & Field, 1983, pp. 251–254). As for the tortures, the six main methods (often combined with others, such as whipping) were the *ordeal of water*, which the victim was forced to ingest large quantities of water; the *ordeal of fire*, which might involve forcing the feet against burning coals, or literally roasting them before a fire; the *strappado,* in which the prisoner was hung from the wrists, behind the back, hoisted, and dropped by a pulley system; the *wheel*, in which the prisoner was tied to a large cart wheel and clubbed until all the bones were broken; the *rack*, in which the body was stretched on a frame with rollers at each end. Tightening the rollers stretched the body beyond endurance. Finally, there was the *stivaletto*. Boards, tied as tightly as possible, encased each leg and then wedges were driven between the boards and the leg, splintering or crushing the bones (Burman, 1984, pp. 63–65). These tortures were not punishments; they were merely adjuncts to interrogations. Torture was not supposed to be repeated, but it could be stopped and continued at a later time. Inquisitors were not supposed to participate in tortures, but a second inquisitor was allowed to absolve the first of any guilt for doing so (Burman, 1984, p. 63).

In Anglo-Saxon territories (England, North America), torture was not as regular or systematic as that practised on the continent of Europe (Inverarity et al., 1983; MacFarlane, 1970). Those who confessed to witchcraft in the Salem witch trials of 1692 were spared execution but were expected to name their co-conspirators—a bargain that provided a steady stream of new accusations. Whatever country we look at, however, we find that accused witches were regularly subjected to rough and humiliating treatment.

Under the pressure of torture (in Scotland and on the European continent) or rough treatment (in England and America), the accused were expected to answer leading questions: When had they attended meetings with the devil (*sabbats*)? What had they eaten at the meetings? How had they had sex with the devil? Whom had they seen there? The resulting confessions were similar, whether they were made in France, Germany, Italy, Spain, or England. This apparent uniformity across widely separated places seemed to confirm the objective reality of the events described, which spurred the inquisitors to ever-greater industry (Trevor-Roper, 1969, p. 44). Those who understood what was going on were often silenced. For example, Father Friedrich von Spee (also called Friedrich Spee von Langenfeld), a Jesuit, was confessor to those condemned to die at the stake in the German city of Würzburg (Sagan, 1995, p. 407). He attempted to console more than 260 victims, many of them girls under age 10. He wrote a vivid, sharply critical, and sarcastic exposé of the horrible abuses associated with the witch-hunt (especially the use of torture, the corruption of officials, and the absence of liability for damages on the part of the judges).

> Why do you search so diligently for sorcerers? I will show you at once where they are. Take the Capuchins, the Jesuits, all the religious orders, and torture them—they will confess. If some deny, repeat it a few times— they will confess. Should a few be obstinate, exorcise them, shave them, only keep on torturing—they will give in. If you want more, take the Canons, the Doctors, the Bishops of the Church—they will confess. (quoted in Walker, 1996, p. 443)

His *Cautio Criminalis seu de Processibus contra Sagas Liber* (Precautions for Prosecutors) (1631) was unsigned. Nevertheless, he was widely known to be its author, and was lucky to escape the fires himself. He spent the rest of his life (cut short by the plague) in exile, writing mournful nature poetry and working with plague victims (Cornwell, 1991, p. 359). Nevertheless, the *Cautio* helped to bring about the abolition of the witch-hunt in a number of places, such as Mainz, and can be credited with promoting its eventual abolition (Cardauns, 1999).

The examination process, although it assumed various forms, was generally self-reinforcing. Either a priest would ask for names of witches, or a witch-hunter (who

Figure 3.4   Trial by Water

The suspected witch was flung into a pond or stream with her hands and feet bound together. If she sank, she was innocent; if she floated, she was found guilty of witchcraft and then had to endure an even more horrible death.

Source: Reproduced from *Fireburn: Tales of Witchery,* by Ken Radford (London: Michael O'Mara Books Ltd., 1989).

was often paid on a per-witch basis) would name one. Almost any distinguishing behaviour or physical trait could be taken as an initial sign of a person's association with witchcraft. Being old and ugly, or even unusually beautiful or lucky, could necessitate further testing. If the woman was afraid, it meant her conscience was accusing her; if unafraid, then she was confident that Satan would rescue her. If she had led an exemplary life, that life was evidence of dissembling (only appearing to be virtuous); if she had not led an exemplary life, this was proof that she kept company with demons. Commonly, the accused would be thrown into water; sinking meant the person was innocent, while floating denoted guilt (see Figure 3.4). This form of judicial torture almost always produced the desired effect of more names and yet more confessions. The snowballing effect of each trial seemed to confirm the existence of an extensive, ever-growing, and terrifyingly conspiratorial underworld.

On the Continent, the court usually confiscated the witch's property. The whole process became "an expense account scam" (Sagan, 1995, p. 12). The witch's family was often forced to pay for the services of the torturers and executioners, the wood for burning, and the banquet held after the burning. In England, where those who were found guilty were hanged rather than burned and where any confiscated property went to the state, not the court, far fewer executions took place, and there were far fewer wealthy victims (Inverarity et al., 1983, pp. 251–254).

EXPLANATIONS FOR THE CRAZE

The demonic explanation for the witch craze was built on faith, and no amount of empirical evidence could refute it. More worldly interpretations of the causes of witch-hunting can be demonstrated by considering the kinds of people who were accused of witchcraft, the kinds of people who profited from their persecution, and when or under what conditions the accusations were made. All these aspects are considered in the following list, which summarizes the 16 characteristics of those selected for prosecution as witches in the initial stages of the witch-hunt. Once a hunt was under way, of course, no one was completely safe from accusation and conviction, and the only commonality among the victims was the fact that they had been accused.

Characteristics of the Accused

1. *Women.* By most accounts, at least 80 percent of those executed were women (Kieckhefer, 1976; Levack, 1992a). Thus, to understand the witch-hunts, it is necessary first to "confront the deeply imbedded feelings about women—and the intricate patterns of interest underlying those feelings—among our witch-ridden ancestors" (Karlsen, 1989, p. xiii). The selection of women as targets was hardly surprising given a patriarchal church that excluded women from all leadership roles and feared them as potential subversives (Worobec, 1995). Women who stepped out of their assigned roles as bearers of children and servants to men were especially vulnerable. Thus, women who were "old maids," widows, lesbians, or openly intelligent were likely to be targeted (Worobec, 1995, p. 176).

2. *Women in conflict with other women.* According to Willis, "village-level witch-hunting was women's work" (Willis, 1995). Briggs, for example, writes, "It

appears that women were active in building up reputations by gossip, deploying counter-magic and accusing suspects; crystallization into formal prosecution, however, needed the intervention of men, preferably of fairly high status in the community" (Briggs, 1996, p. 282). Before the craze, such conflicts would have been settled at the local level and would only very rarely have involved the courts.

3. *Women who gave birth to deformed babies.* These infants were regarded as "Satan's spawn," the product of sexual orgies involving the mother and the devil or his demons.

4. *People seen in the dreams of others* (especially if in the form of a sexual partner).

5. *Men or women who claimed to have occult powers.* In every society, there have been people with "second sight," who have forecast the future, dispensed spells or charms, or threatened others with supernatural vengeance. In the 1692 Salem witch trials, the first accused was Tituba, a West Indian servant who entertained the local girls with stories of voodoo and with fortune telling by palmistry. When the girls began falling into unexplained fits, Tituba's employer, the Reverend Parris, beat a confession of witchcraft out of her. People such as Tituba are tolerated in normal times, when there is no anxiety about demonic conspiracies, but are often among the first condemned when such fears are raised.

6. *People believed to be involved in treasonous conspiracies.* When the inheritance of a throne could depend on the birth of a living male baby and when poisoning was a major factor in royal succession, the practice of witchcraft for political purposes was often suspected. This form of accusation was particularly common in the early witchcraft trials (around C.E. 1400). For example, under James III of Scotland, several witches were executed on the grounds that they had been conspiring with the king's brother against the king (Larner 1980, p. 53). Also, the elimination of the Christian Order of Knights Templar (and the execution of its leaders, after confessions induced by torture) was treated as an issue of treason and witchcraft. Fifty-four Templars were publicly burned in Paris in May C.E. 1310, and many others followed (Burman, 1984, p. 98).

7. *People who got in the way.* The most famous witch trial in European history was that of a priest, Urbain Grandier. Grandier was handsome, charming, a brilliant speaker, and popular with his parishioners. His support for local power against the central government made him powerful enemies (a cardinal and the king). The accusation against him involved the "possession" of a group of Ursuline nuns. These women barked, screamed, blasphemed (swore), and contorted their bodies in erotic ways. Grandier was accused of sorcery. Despite torture, during which all of the bones in his legs and feet were mangled, he refused to confess. He was executed by fire, before a crowd of more than 6000 who had come for the spectacle (Huxley, 1996, pp. 211–218; Rapley, 1998).

8. *People who did not fully accept Church dogma and practice.* Besides free thinkers and early scientists, this group consisted of people who continued to follow the

customs of the earlier pagan religions. Evidence presented at the heresy trial of Joan of Arc included the fact that she had participated in ancient Celtic practices that were traditional in rural areas but forbidden by the Church.

9. *Healers, herbalists, and naturopaths.* People involved in issues such as fertility, midwifery, and abortion were particularly vulnerable. Known as "cunning men" and "wise women" in England and by equivalent names in Europe, they had "powers" that were not under the regulation of the authorities (Cassar, 1993, p. 319). Abortion, for example, was associated with beliefs that newborn babies were being used in obscene rituals with the devil. Curing people by "magical" means was also condemned. Midwives and herbalists were in competition with the rising all-male, university-based medical establishment (Eastlea, 1980; Watts, 1984, p. 28). People knowledgeable about drugs were also suspect because the effects of drugs such as atropine, henbane, and thornapple, which have narcotic and poisonous properties, seemed to reveal supernatural powers (Worobec, 1995, p. 171). Such drugs, whether they were given to people by women healers or whether they simply came to them as mould on bread (some fungi that attack grain have LSD-like properties), may lie at the root of beliefs about witches flying at night and being able to change shape (Harris, 1978, p. 190).

10. *People blamed for the misfortune of others.* Many accusations of witchcraft had their root in quarrels in which one party apparently threatened another, who later became sick or experienced some misfortune. Illnesses attributed to witchcraft or sorcery included "impotence, stomach pains, barrenness, hernias, abscesses, epileptic seizures, and convulsions" (Worobec, 1995, pp. 166–167). Many cases involved beggars who seemed to be retaliating against those who had denied them assistance (Groh, 1987, p. 19; Thomas, 1997, pp. 506, 564), or people who *ought* to have been seeking revenge for some previous insult or harm (Worobec, 1995, p. 181). The most frequent cases were those in which someone repudiated a neighbour—usually an old woman seeking a favour—and then attributed personal misfortunes to her (Garrett, 1977, pp. 462–463; Macfarlane, 1970, p. 196). Situations of this kind became increasingly common as the mutual-help systems typical of rural communities were disrupted by population growth and the arrival of early capitalist forms of economy; people who had some wealth began to feel threatened by the rising numbers of beggars and indigents.

11. *Exceptional people.* Sometimes personal characteristics like an unusual appearance, or perhaps extraordinary success or talent, were seen as the result of a Faustian bargain with Satan. The story of Faust, who sells his soul to the devil in exchange for knowledge and power, goes back at least to the ninth century. Niccolo Paganini, a composer and violin virtuoso of the nineteenth century, was treated as a Faustian figure, primarily because his playing was so extraordinary. Canadian fiddler Ashley MacIsaac has similarly been accused of having made a demonic pact. Unlike Paganini, MacIsaac will not have to worry about being harmed or refused burial rites.

12. *People named by accused witches under torture or persuasion.* Almost anyone could be named, but most confessing witches did not try to implicate court officials or other powerful people; such accusations, when they occurred, were often suppressed by the court.

13. *People named by those suffering from illness or hardship.* In Salem in 1692, the young girls who showed signs of "possession" (screaming unaccountably, falling into grotesque convulsions, mimicking the behaviour of dogs) named everyone they had a grudge against (Erikson, 1966, p. 142). In total, 142 persons were named, ultimately resulting in the death by hanging of 21 men and women (and one dog). A man who refused to plead either guilty or not guilty was crushed to death under heavy stones; his refusal to enter a plea was interpreted as a denial of the legitimacy of the proceedings. Only when the accusations began to include prominent people (e.g., Lady Phipps, wife of the Massachusetts colony's governor) was the process seriously questioned and, ultimately, rejected (Rosenthal, 1993).

14. *People with mental illnesses.* Allowed to wander freely in normal times, those suffering from mental illness were particularly vulnerable to being caught up in the witch-hunt. Also singled out were people with psychoneurotic symptoms (manifested, for example, in a failure to react when pricked with a pin) and "hysterics," who acted out because of physical or emotional stress. As Ben-Yahuda (1985) notes,

> While Freud himself virtually ignored the European witchcraze, it contains elements to warm any analyst's heart: cruel and destructive persecutions, women, sex, and violence. These could easily be integrated into psychoanalytic interpretations, emphasizing the projection of hostility, reaction-formation, incestuous wishes, and impulses of the id. (43)

15. *People with physical disabilities or neurological disorders.* Such individuals might be seen as victims of the witchcraft of others or as suitable partners for Satan. They were likely to be accused of giving others the evil eye. Also included in this group were the elderly and the physically unattractive.

16. *Scapegoats for the system.* As long as people believed that plagues, wars, famines, and personal troubles were caused by demons, they needed religious protection. The control of witchcraft became a very significant reason to pay tithes to the church and to obey its rules; only the church authorities knew how to diagnose and treat supernatural ills, and only they were powerful enough to oppose the devastating powers of Satan. Anyone could be named for the purpose. The witch craze divided people against each other in suspicion and fear and forced them to depend on the Church (Erikson, 1966).

The above list tells us a great deal about the conditions that informed the craze. Whether on the European continent, in England, or in the American colonies, witch-victims represented resistance to the sacred canopy erected over society by their respective churches. Some of these victims were actually deviant in some way. Others served as scapegoats for the threat posed to churches by the fundamental changes that were taking place around the world.

Disruptive Social Change

Plagues and famines were especially acute between 1400 and 1700, as was social change (Behringer, 1998; Watts, 1984, p. 7). Events such as Columbus's voyage to the Americas in 1492, the opening up of trade routes to the East, and the invention of the printing press all contributed to a growth in knowledge that had the potential to undermine Church rule.

Throughout the witch-craze period, most of the trials were held in the cultural borderlands, where social diversity and religious conflict were the greatest, or in places where war and plague had created disorder (Briggs, 1996; Thomas, 1997). Even in later outbreaks, such as in pre-Revolutionary Russia (in the late nineteenth century), the background of the craze was anxiety-provoking social change and economic upheaval.

Places that were sheltered from change did not develop the craze. For example, while the French in France were burning Huguenot heretics and witches, the stable French settlement in Canada was not affected; the belief in witches existed, but no panic was associated with it (Morison, 1955, p. 248). The same was true of Ireland, whose Catholic people were unshaken in their ways and unwilling to make use of the oppressive courts imposed on them by the English. In Ireland between 1534 and 1711, only nine proceedings against witches were recorded, most of them initiated by English or Scottish immigrants, and less than half of these resulted in an execution (Lapoint, 1992, pp. 77, 84). Similarly, in confidently Catholic Italy and Spain, few witches were burned.

During the eighteenth century the craze finally burned out. Courts gradually ceased to treat witchcraft as a reality other than in its associations with fraud and extortion. The Criminal Code of Canada, for example, makes it an offence to pretend to exercise or use any kind of witchcraft, sorcery, enchantment or conjuration (section 365). However, when an Ontario Supreme Court judge said to murderer Peter Demeter (sentenced to five life terms in 1988), "You certainly appear to ooze evil from every pore of your body," few people in the courtroom thought that Demeter was being told he was possessed or in the service of Satan (Claridge, 1988).

MODERN BELIEFS ABOUT DEMONIC DEVIANCE

Despite the predominance of secular definitions of deviance, the demonic remains a theme recognized and sometimes used in our society. The antichrist has been seen in everything from political opponents and enemy countries to supermarket bar codes (Fuller, 1995).

The belief that evil exists in the world does not necessarily result in panic over hidden conspiracies. When it does emerge in this form, however, the modern identifying label for those suspected of conspiring is likely to be Satanist, and the suspects are male as often as they are female. Indeed, the emphasis on female witches has receded, and the term witchcraft is rarely used in this sense. A huge divide has emerged between those who use the concepts of Satanism and those who speak of witchcraft. Contemporary witches consider themselves practitioners of faiths such as the Mother-Goddess religion. They neither believe in nor worship Satan, and they are usually (but not always) ignored rather than feared by people with different religious convictions (Guiley, 1991; Marron, 1989).

Belief in satanic deviance is, not surprisingly, found mainly (but not exclusively) in areas with a high degree of religious consciousness, such as the Bible Belt areas of Canada and the United States.

MODERN VERSIONS OF WITCH-HUNTING

Demonic evil remains a powerful metaphor for our fears of the unknown and for our awareness of the frightening and disgusting aspects of reality. Fundamental to this way of thinking is the theory that a conspiracy exists against public order and decency. What distinguishes the "moral panic" version of social menace conspiracy from *real* cases of conspiracy is that the former rests on almost no empirically verifiable evidence and the data that do exist are treated cavalierly. The story, spread through rumour, gossip, and innuendo, is accepted and passed on by credulous or ill-motivated people without being meaningfully tested. The same pattern is found in Hitler's campaign against Jews, McCarthy's persecution of communists, and accusations that childcare workers can fly through the air or would cannibalize babies.

THE HOLOCAUST

In Nazi Germany, the witch-hunt involved all those who seemed to oppose Hitler's new order. Like the witchcraft craze, it spread far beyond those who really were a threat and served purposes other than those admitted to by authorities. As with witches, systems were set up to identify a hidden enemy and destroy it, and the web of suspicion grew ever wider until no one could feel entirely safe. The Nazis widely disseminated a forgery called *The Protocols of the Elders of Zion*, which purported to be a record of a Jewish plot to take over the world. This work explicitly linked Jews with the antichrist:

> There is no room left for doubt. With all the might and terror of Satan,
> the reign of the triumphant King of Israel is approaching our unregen-
> erate world; the King born of the blood of Zion—the Antichrist—is near
> to the throne of universal power. (quoted in Cohn, 1976, p. 255)

The *Protocols* served to justify persecution of Jews and their allies in much the same way as the *Malleus* had done to witches several centuries earlier.

THE RED SCARE

In the 1950s, many people in both Canada and the United States believed in communism and sometimes even secretly belonged to communist organizations. Nonetheless, the "red menace" notion greatly exaggerated their numbers and influence and resulted in the harassment and blacklisting of thousands of citizens.

The belief that hidden conspirators were at work fuelled paranoia and turned people against one another. *McCarthyism* (named after Senator Joseph McCarthy, who made a career of communist-hunting) also spread into Canada. Most victims were deprived of their jobs, and many were also treated as social pariahs (Scher, 1992). Leopold Infeld, a Polish-born University of Toronto professor, was denounced in the House of Commons and harassed by the RCMP. Ultimately he returned to Poland. The reason for the harassment was that when some of his friends' names turned up on the list of spies in Canada that Igor Gouzenko (a Soviet who defected to Canada in 1945) gave to the Canadian government, Infeld joined a small organization formed to defend them. For this "crime," he was dubbed a "fellow traveller" and suspected of abusing his knowledge of atomic energy. The fact that he was not an atomic scientist carried little weight at the time (Zeidenberg, 1990). The main difference between the Canadian and U.S. persecution is that the Canadian authorities engaged in a hidden campaign. Canada's victims suffered job loss and ostracism without being told the reason for them (Sher, 1992).

SATANIC CHILD ABUSE: McMARTIN, MARTENSVILLE, AND INGRAM

McMartin

Other witch-hunting outbreaks concerned cases in which accusations of child molesting were made against daycare workers. Particularly notorious was the case of Peggy Buckey and her son Raymond, who in May of 1989 were together charged with 65 counts of child molestation. The Buckeys ran the McMartin Nursery School in Manhattan Beach, near Los Angeles. According to newspaper accounts, the first complaint came from a woman who later died from conditions often associated with alcoholism. This same accuser maintained that McMartin teachers had put staples in her child's ears, nipples, and tongue, and that her son (aged $2^{1}/_{2}$) had taken part in a human sacrifice ritual (Fukurai, Butler, & Krooth, 1994, p. 47). She claimed that Ray Buckey "flew through the air." Following her complaint, police sent a form letter to each of the families of the children who attended the nursery. Parents were asked to question their children about possible criminal acts such as oral sex and sodomy (Reed, 1989). They were also informed that

> photos may have been taken of children without their clothing. Any information from your child regarding ever having observed Ray Buckey leave a classroom alone with a child during any nap period, or if they have ever observed Ray Buckey tie up a child, is important. (Reed, 1989, p. 5)

As a result of this highly suggestive letter, about 360 children who had attended McMartin were sent to a Los Angeles child-abuse therapy group. Therapists there elicited stories of activities that included sodomy, oral copulation, nude photography, and exhibitionism. Films of the interviews show that the children were praised if they reported abuse; if they did not report abuse, the therapist rephrased the question or repeated it. The therapists used dolls with adult-sized genitalia, which could have shocked the children and induced fantasies. The McMartin Nursery School and seven others were closed. Peggy Buckey, her son Raymond, and five other childcare workers were charged. Raymond Buckey spent four years in custody before the trial. Costs for the prosecution's part of the trial alone amounted to $15 million (Fukurai et al., 1994, p. 44). After six years, a destroyed business, and ruined reputations, the defendants were acquitted on all 135 charges that came before the court.

In the 1980s, Satanism, ritual abuse, past lives, and recovered memories became popular fare on talk shows and in tabloids. Books such as *Michelle Remembers* (Smith & Pazder, 1980) popularized the practice of searching for repressed memories of incest and ritual abuse. This book was exposed as a fraud a few years later (Nathan & Snedeker, 1996). Experts' seminars on ritual abuse were funded by governments and attended by teachers, police officers, social workers, and parents, sometimes for educational credits (Hertenstein & Trott, 1993). From 1985 on, various allegations about satanic elements in the murder of unbaptized children, ritual abuse, mutilation, sexual trafficking of children, human sacrifice, and cannibalism were publicized on network television programs such as ABC's *20/20*, specifically its story "The Devil Worshippers" (1985); NBC's "1986"; and Geraldo Rivera's Halloween special "Devil Worship: Exposing Satan's Underground" (1986). Journalistic accounts appeared in newspapers and books, and an explosion of exposés, "recovered memory" auto-biographies, and anti-cult organizations followed. Satanists were accused of 60 000 Americans deaths each year, even though no evidence existed to support these repeated claims (Jenkins & Maier-Katkin, 1992, pp. 54, 60). Accusations against alleged perpetrators peaked in the late 1980s, and by 1992, interest was beginning to decline. For the most part, police and prosecutors no longer believe the more extreme claims, even though they still prosecute when the evidence supports it (Hicks, 1991).

Martensville

A Canadian daycare case took place in the town of Martensville, Saskatchewan (population about 3000), in 1992. Nine people, including five police officers, were charged with more than 100 sex-related charges. The triggering event occurred when a child's diaper rash came to the attention of a young police officer who had been trained to identify sexual abuse and who had apparently experienced abuse herself. Even though the resulting medical investigation of the rash concluded that no abuse had taken place, the initial fears had already led to the interrogation of other children, who were exposed to intense and repetitive interviews in which leading and suggestive questioning techniques were used. Children reported that they were "cut with knives," forced to take part in sex acts with dogs and flying bats, and held in cages in a church. They claimed that they had watched a baby being skinned, roasted, and eaten. No physical evidence supported these allegations, and a good deal of evidence suggested induced and malleable memories rather than recovered memories. The lengthy trial resulted in only one unrelated conviction, for the fondling of a 10-year-old in 1988. Although serious, such a charge is not at all on the same scale as the multiple-offender, multiple-abuse accusations that made this case infamous (Harris, 1998).

Many accusations of sexual abuse are true, and deserve to be heard. In 1995, Colin Ross estimated that about 10 percent of the recovered memories of dissociative identity disorder (multiple personality syndrome) are based in real events (Ross, 1995). The distinctive aspects of the McMarten and Martensville cases, however (the use of leading questions under pressure, the total absence of physical evidence, and the importance of untested assumptions based in beliefs), place them firmly in the realm of satanic panic (Victor, 1993).

Although the snowballing effect of a craze was averted in the Ingram case (Box 3.3), it nonetheless illustrates the closed circle of reasoning that defies contradiction: the victim or perpetrator's initial disbelief in sexual abuse is taken as evidence of a psychiatric state of denial. The more emphatic the feeling of disbelief, the more likely that the thing denied actually occurred (Frow, 1997).

Box 3.3 Ingram

Following his arrest on charges of child abuse in 1988, Paul Ingram, a "zealous member of a born-again church" (Wright 1993) in Olympia, Washington, confessed to abusing his daughters and to years of participation in a satanic child-abuse ring that practised pornography and ritual sacrifice. His confession implicated more than a dozen other people, two of whom were also charged.

But there was a problem. No physical evidence of any kind existed to back up Ingram's confession: no videotapes or photographs of satanic, pornographic activities; no visible scars on the daughters (other than those resulting from acne and an appendectomy), even though both of them claimed they had been cut and burned. The alleged activities had left no traces at all, other than the wildly improbable and inconsistent—and increasingly horrifying—stories recounted by Ingram's daughters and, later, his wife. Ingram maintained that he had no memory of the acts he was being accused of, but at the same time he did not deny doing them. His belief that the devil could make him do things of this kind and then remove the memory of them meant that he was motivated to retrieve memories of this kind. His confession was elicited after four hours of interrogation. Experts who heard the taped confession said Ingram sounded like someone in a hypnotic state and that he was influenced by suggestions put forward by the interrogators.

Box 3.3   Ingram (cont.)

The three accused men spent months in jail before their trials, were forced to pay for their defences ($90 000 in one case), and continue to be ostracized by others in the community (Ofshe & Watters, 1994; Watters & Ofshe, 1999; Wright, 1993). Although charges against Ingram's two co-conspirators were dropped, Ingram himself pled guilty and was sentenced to 20 years in prison. His later efforts to withdraw his guilty plea have, to date, been denied (Wright, 1993). He was denied a pardon in 1996 and is currently completing his 20-year sentence.

The parallels between this case and the witchcraft craze are clear:

> One could say that the miracle of the Ingram case is that it did not go any further than it did. If Ingram's memories had not finally become too absurd for even the investigators to believe, if Rabie or Risch [Ingram's alleged co-conspirators] had accepted the prosecution's deals, if the alleged crimes of other people implicated in the investigation [some 30 in all] had occurred within the statute of limitations—if any of these quite conceivable scenarios had taken place, then the witch-hunt in Olympia would have raged out of control, and one cannot guess how many other lives might have been destroyed. (Wright, 1993, p. 76)

MORAL PANIC AND ROLE-PLAYING AS ASPECTS OF SATANISM

There are two distinct aspects of Satanist and anti-Satanist thinking. The first, moral panic, expresses the ideological pattern of the witch-hunt. Fears are raised that are out of all proportion to the empirical evidence. In role-playing, the second aspect, individuals recognize the pattern of deviance being described by authorities and proceed to become what others fear. They act out the role provided to them, sometimes developing it still further. The cases of murderers Leonard Lake, David Berkowitz, and cult leader Charles Manson, for example, follow this pattern.

Thus, Satanism as a modern phenomenon involves (1) monsters in the mind (the innocent who are accused) and (2) monsters in reality (people who deliberately live up to the evil images of those who fear Satanism). Although some occult gang members engage in horrifying acts, far more of them are playing with the satanic image and not acting on it (Korem, 1994, pp. 171–197; Trostle, 1986). In the following sections, we will look at both aspects of Satanism—at the exaggerated claims of the anti-Satanists, which often entrap and destroy innocent people, and at the behaviour of people who call themselves Satanists.

SATANISM AS MORAL PANIC

The 1980s witnessed a sudden increase in reports of satanic cult activities—reports that originated from religious groups in both England and North America; however, little physical evidence of such activities existed (Hicks, 1991; Marty, 1990, p. 308; Marron, 1989). For example, although accusations of kidnappings and ritual murders rose, there were no corresponding increases either in missing person reports or in the discovery of places where such activities could have occurred.

Another example of anti-Satanism can be seen in the furor that erupted over the traditional logo of Procter and Gamble (see Box 3.4) and over a flyer circulated about the company. The flyer (disseminated by fundamentalist churches and posted on supermarket bulletin boards first throughout the southern United States then on into the northern states and Canada) claimed that the president of Procter & Gamble had appeared on *The Phil Donahue Show* to announce that he was "coming out of the closet" with respect to his (and P&G's) financial support for the Church of Satan (Blumenfeld, 1991; Victor, 1993, pp. 13–14).

Between 1986 and 1991, Procter & Gamble gradually phased out its traditional moon-and-stars symbol, largely because of the accusation that the beard on the man-in-the-moon logo has the evil number 666 in it and that the 13 stars are also a sign of evil, and it has fought back with lawsuits against individuals and some distributors for a rival company who have allegedly helped to spread the story. Despite evidence that the facts reported in the message are false, the rumour still finds sufficient believers to support its continued spread (Brunvand, 1986; Emery, 2000).

SATANISM AS ROLE-PLAYING

The second aspect of Satanism involves the way in which the socially constructed role of the Satanist is taken over by people who then attempt to enact it in real life. One of these was Aleister Crowley (1875–1947), who called himself "The Great Beast" and was pleased to be known as "the wickedest man in the world" (Wilson, 1987). Crowley deliberately cultivated his beast role and spent his life in devotion to the occult. He was described in the liner notes from Colin Wilson's *Aleister Crowley: The Nature of the Beast* (1987) as an "insatiable ambisexual athlete, a pimp who lived on the immoral earnings of his girlfriends, and a junkie who daily took enough heroin to kill a roomful of people." In 1934, Crowley attempted to sue a biographer who had accused him of involvement in black magic and human sacrifice; the testimony given at the trial was so repulsive to both judge and jury that Crowley lost his case (Guiley, 1991, p. 131). On another occasion, a friend of Crowley's lost a libel suit mainly because the jury accepted the argument "that anyone who was a friend of Crowley's had no reputation to lose" (Wilson, 1987, p. 25).

Satanist elements have, in varying degrees, entered the personal lives of many well-known writers and performers. Horror novelist Shirley Jackson played with ideas of witchcraft and the occult in her own life, as well as in her novels (Oppenheimer, 1988). Other writers have both sought out and felt "possessed" by occult forces. William Burroughs, for example, tried to explain how he came to shoot his wife, toward whom he felt no anger:

> I live with the constant threat of possession, and a constant need to escape from possession, from Control. So the death of Joan brought me into contact with the invader, the Ugly Spirit, and maneuvered me into a

Box 3.4   Satanism: Procter & Gamble's Problem

The following appeal to Christians to boycott P&G products arrived on a computer in Kamloops, British Columbia, from an unidentified source e-mail (computer spam), in July 1999. It is almost identical to flyers circulating since the early 1980s claiming that the president of P&G bragged about supporting Satanism in an appearance on The Phil Donahue Show, *and like those flyers is full of credible but untrue assertions of fact.*

Date: Tuesday, July 13, 1999

Subject: Let's stop supporting satan!

The president of Procter & Gamble appeared on the *Sally Jesse Raphael Show* on March 1, 1998. He announced that "due to the openness of our society" he was coming out of the closet about his association with the Church of satan. He stated that a large portion of his profits from Procter & Gamble products goes to support this satanic church.

When asked by Sally Jesse whether stating this on TV would hurt his business, he replied: *"There are not enough Christians in the United States to make a difference."*

[This is followed by a fairly accurate list of P&G products.] If you are not sure about the product, look for "Procter & Gamble" written on the products or for the symbol of a ram's horn, which will appear on each product beginning January 1, 2000. The ram's horn will form the number 666, which is known as satan's number. Christians should remember that if they purchase any of these products, they will be contributing to the Church of satan. Inform other Christians about this and *stop* buying Procter & Gamble products. Let's show Procter & Gamble that there are enough Christians to make a difference. [Original was in capital letters:] On the *Jenny Jones Show*, the owner of Procter & Gamble said that if satan would prosper him, he would give his heart and soul to him. Then he gave credit to satan for his riches.

Anyone interested in seeing this tape, should send $3.00 to Sally Transcripts, 515 West 57th Street, New York, NY, 10019. We urge you to make copies of this and pass it on to as many people as possible.

Liz Claiborne also professes to worship satan and recently openly admitted on the *Oprah Winfrey Show* that half of her profits go toward the Church of satan. This needs to stop!

The only reasonably accurate part of this message is the list of products. Other than the addition of Liz Claiborne at the end and the change from *The Phil Donahue Show* to the *Jenny Jones Show* and the *Sally Jesse Raphael Show,* this is the same story as told in the 1980s. March 1, 1998, was a Sunday, not a day when the *Sally Jesse* program airs, and profits from P&G go to shareholders, not to the Church of Satan. The new logo for P&G is not a ram's horn.

lifelong struggle, in which I have had no choice except to write my way out. (quoted in Morgan, 1988, p. 199)

The writer-artist Jack Pollock also expressed the feeling that his excesses in life were somehow demonically caused:

I do have a "mad motor" and the brakes are very difficult to locate most of the time. If I don't keep positively active, then the negative takes over.... I feel possessed. Your enquiry whether I feel that there is a foreign power within me strikes a familiar chord. (Pollock, 1989, p. 121)

Though few in number, some psychiatrists entertain the possibility that satanic possession may be real. M. Scott Peck, for example, has written about people he believes are demonically evil. In one such case, his patient (the brother of a suicide) received, as a birthday present from his parents, the weapon with which his brother had killed himself. Peck felt that parents who could do such a thing were evil, and he acted to rescue the boy from them. Another case involved a man who "made a pact with the devil" to rid himself of obsessive-compulsive thoughts. Peck feels that the devil may really have been involved. Finally, Peck describes two modern exorcisms at which not only demons but also the antichrist appeared (Peck, 1983, pp. 31–35, 51–59, 185–211).

Those who are committed to a "bad" identity may acquire pentagram tattoos and other symbols of the occult, or they may seek to participate in occult rituals (Lowney, 1995). People may acquire their knowledge of the satanic role from religious authorities (by reversing or reframing their teachings) or by perusing Church documents such as the *Malleus Maleficarum* or Guasso's *Compendium Maleficarum*. As noted by Stephen Kent, "readily accessible religious texts that often are central to our culture may provide inspiration to people who either want to sanctify their deviance or venerate the reputed god of this world (i.e., Satan)" (Kent, 1993a, p. 229). Some may acquire this knowledge through other "deviant" religious traditions, such as the Masonic Order (Kent, 1993b). Or they may discover it through popular culture (e.g., books and movies with satanic themes). Jenkins and Maier-Katkin have found that most youths arrested for satanic crimes are "dabblers ... whose notion of the occult is derived from horror films or role-playing games" (Jenkins & Maier-Katkin, 1992, p. 61). The controversial role-playing game *Dungeons and Dragons*, in the judgment of the Reverend John Torrell, as quoted on CBC's *Ideas,* provides teaching on

demonology, witchcraft, voodoo, murder, rape, blasphemy, suicide, insanity, sex perversion, homosexuality, Satan-worship, gambling, Jungian psychology, barbarism, cannibalism, sadism, demon-summoning, necromantics, divination, and many more teachings brought to you in living colour direct from the pit of Hell. (Canadian Broadcasting Corporation, 1991, p. 1)

The people involved in role-playing games reject this viewpoint and instead insist that these games have very positive effects on the players.

Heavy-metal music has assumed a Satanic character in the public eye. In 1990, the families of two young men sued CBS Records and the rock band Judas Priest. The families claimed that subliminal messages in the band's *Stained Glass* album had prompted the pair to shoot themselves. The suit failed, largely because there was ample evidence that the youths had been self-destructive long before the album was released (Dorn, Murji, & South, 1992).

Sometimes Satanism's primary aspects, moral panic and role-playing, overlap, as was evident in 1990, when the suicides of three Lethbridge, Alberta, teenagers were reported alongside accounts that they had been involved in devil worship. The story made front-page news across Canada. Some newspapers also interpreted completely unrelated suicides as being part of an overall satanic problem (Chruscinski & Gabor, 1990). The media used the suicides as a basis for discussing allegations (mostly from American sources) that devil worshippers were kidnapping children and animals and using them for ritual rapes, pornographic films, and human sacrifices. Despite these allegations, police investigation failed to uncover any organized cult ("Albertan Denies Suicide Link," 1990; Oake, 1990; Victor, 1993, p. 351).

EVIL AS METAPHOR

In modern times, the demonic has become more of a metaphor than an explanation when applied to deviance. Alcoholics speak of the "devil in the bottle," and many drug addicts see their addiction as a consequence of demonic-like trickery—the drug promises euphoria but delivers death. Some people even see evil behind the apparently secular surface of everyday life:

> The iniquitous roster of evil all around us is an unending list of dark powers that are proliferating: racism, genocide, monstrous crimes, drug gang wars, merciless and random slaughter of innocent civilians, gas bombing of cities, pestilence, famine and war, governmental policies of racial cruelty, death squads, violent or insidious suppression of human rights, forms of slavery, abuse of children, bestial military action against civilians, callousness to the homeless, the AIDS victims and the poor, abuse of the elderly, sexism, rape, wanton murder, cults, terrorism, torture, the unremitting aftermath of past holy and unholy wars, the Holocaust, heinous cruelty and hatred, and the seven deadly sins: wrath, pride, envy, sloth, gluttony, lust, and avarice.
>
> We go on polluting the air, the soil and the water. We think the unthinkable: atomic destruction of civilization and the earth itself. We trash outer and inner space. We literally are in danger of running amok.

All the while we feed an unbridled and insatiable appetite for horror; demonic projections are made on enemies as "Evil Empire" and "The Great Satan," governments conspire with organized crime, assassinate and massacre, destroy the souls of people for power and money, arm nations and individuals, and, as a consequence, human beings are now exploding in every corner of the globe. Such things as these are often nourished and cunningly abetted by the media: television, film, newspapers, and even art, literature and music. (Wilmer, 1988, pp. 2–3)

SUMMARY

Long before academics attempted to understand deviance, it was the subject of folklore and mythology, which gave it a place in the social order. Although many of the early formulations were moralistic and presented the deviant as a pitiful or evil creature, the dominant kind of story emphasized the multifaceted, frightening, and humorous aspects of deviance, and did not always side with the forces of control. These forms of understanding persist in their modern descendants: children's literature (and sometimes that for adults) and the oral tradition of the urban myth, which plays on our anxieties about danger and trouble.

The first attempt to provide a fully causal explanation of deviance was the demonic theory, which was rooted in the idea that powers of both good and evil cause all events in the world. The demonic explained not only deviance but also other kinds of troubling events, including storms, crop failure, and plagues, as well as religious doubt.

In the late Middle Ages, beginning slowly in the twelfth century and becoming a veritable holocaust by the seventeenth century, the idea that deviance resulted from supernatural causes was transformed into a terrifying conspiracy theory. Believers felt themselves surrounded by a swelling confederacy of witches who were in league with Satan to defeat the armies of Christ.

The dominant modern interpretation of the witchcraft craze is that the witch-as-part-of-demonic-conspiracy was a social construct, created and maintained by religious authorities in a manner that reflected the common beliefs of the people, reinforced dependency on the church, and served to suppress the enemies of patriarchal authority. The witchcraft mania had its start in the challenge to church hegemony posed by mountain regions and residual cultures that empowered women, and it reached its peak in the period in which religious wars and the rise of secular thought and science seriously threatened Church authority. It continues to emerge in places where a powerfully positioned religious world view is challenged by alternative ideas. Thus, witchcraft beliefs were both functional for the authorities and representative of the increasing conflict between a religiously validated patriarchy and alternative views of the world.

The witch-hunt provides a paradigm that can be applied to events such as the Nazi persecution of the Jews, the McCarthyite "red scare" in North America, and the panic over child molesters and Satanists. In modern times, demonology is used to explain deviance—generally in its most serious manifestations—only after all natural (as opposed to supernatural) explanations have failed. However, the paradigm can also be applied to more mundane forms of deviance such as drug trafficking when political authorities demonize those forms of deviance.

STUDY QUESTIONS

1. The trickster is a wonderful metaphor for a holistic conception of deviance in society—deviance is not just bad or evil, nor is it just fun and creativity. Think about some form of deviance in your life, on screen, or in literature: How does the trickster idea illuminate the phenomenon of deviance?

2. When was the last time you were caught in believing a story that turned out to be an urban legend? Why did you believe the story at the time?

3. How do movie directors and authors convince you to accept a demonic explanation for deviance?

4. Is evil real?

5. Find the *Malleus Maleficarum* using an Internet search. What does this book tell us about its authors?

6. Why did the witchcraft craze *not* occur in Canada, despite the presence of supernatural beliefs?

7. How does the "red scare" fit the paradigm of the witchcraft craze?

8. What purpose did the witch prosecutions in Salem have? (Refer to Erikson, cited in the text, for further information.)

9. Should police be taught about satanic cults? Why or why not?

10. What is the evidence that performers such as Judas Priest cause evil things to happen?

REFERENCES

Albertan Denies Suicide Link: Satanist Cult Cited in Trio of Teen Deaths. (1990, March 15). *The Toronto Star.*

Barstow, A. L. (1995). *Witchcraze: A New History of the European Witch-hunts.* San Francisco, CA: HarperCollins.

Behringer, W. (1998). *Witchcraft Persecutions in Bavaria: Popular Magic, Religious Zealotry and Reasons of State in Early Modern Europe* (J. C. Grayson & D. Lederer, Trans.). Cambridge, UK: Cambridge University Press.

Ben-Yahuda, N. (1985). *Deviance and Moral Boundaries: Witchcraft, the Occult, Science Fiction, Deviant Sciences and Scientists.* Chicago: University of Chicago Press.

Best, J. (1985). The Razor Blade in the Apple: The Social Construction of Urban Legends. *Social Problems, 32*(5), 488–499.

Blumenfeld, L. (1991, July 18). Procter and Gamble's Devil of a Problem. *The Toronto Star.*

Bonthrone, P. J. (2000). News: Loss of Faith "Has Led to Increase in Exorcisms." *Daily Telegraph.*

Briggs, K. M. (1978). *The Vanishing People.* London, UK: B. T. Batsford.

Briggs, R. (1996). *Witches and Neighbors: The Social and Cultural Context of European Witchcraft.* London, UK: HarperCollins.

Bright, W. (1993). *A Coyote Reader.* Berkeley, CA: University of California Press.

Brunvand, J. H. (1981). *The Vanishing Hitchhiker.* New York: W. W. Norton.

———. (1986). *The Choking Doberman and Other "New" Urban Legends.* New York: Norton.

Burman, E. (1984). *The Inquisition: Hammer of Heresy.* New York: Dorset Press.

Canadian Broadcasting Corporation. (1991). Dungeons and Dragons. *Ideas.* Toronto.

Cardauns, H. (1999). Friedrich Von Spee. *The Catholic Encyclopedia* (Vol. XIV). Kevin Knight. [On-Line]. <http://www.newadvent.org/cathen/14213b.htm>.

Cassar, C. (1993). Witchcraft Beliefs and Social Control in Seventeenth-Century Malta. *Mediterranean Studies, 3*(2), 316–334.

Centre for Addiction and Mental Health. (1999). Exorcism Therapy. *CAMH: The Journal 1*(Nov–Dec), 1–3.

Chirol, S. V. (1923). *Tales of Nasr-Ed-Din Khoja* (H. D. Barnham, Trans.). London, UK: C.M.G. Nisbet and Co.

Christie, S. (1997). Trickster Gone Golfing: Vizenor's Heirs of Columbus and the Chelh-ten-em Development Controversy. *American Indian Quarterly, 21*(3), 359–379.

Christie-Murray, D. P. (1989). *A History of Heresy.* New York: Oxford University.

Chruscinski, T., & Gabor, P. (1990, March 28). Meeting the Needs of Troubled Teens. *The Globe and Mail.*

Claridge, T. (1988, July 29). You Ooze Evil, Demeter Told, as Judge Adds Two Life Terms. *The Globe and Mail*, p. A1.

Cohen, S. (1987). *Folk Devils and Moral Panics: The Creation of the Mods and Rockers.* Cambridge, MA: Blackwell.

Cohn, N. (1976). *Warrant for Genocide: The Myth of the Jewish World Conspiracy and the Protocols of the Elders of Zion.* Toronto: Scholar's Press.

Combs, A., & Holland, M. (1996). Chapter 5: Hermes the Trickster. In *Synchronicity: Science, Myth and the Trickster* (pp. 79–102). New York: Marlowe and Company.

Cornwell, J. (1991). *Powers of Darkness, Powers of Light: Travels in Search of the Miraculous and the Demonic.* London, UK: Penguin.

Coudert, A. P. (1992). The Myth of the Improved Status of Protestant Women: The Case of the Witchcraze. In B. P. Levak (Ed.), *Witchcraft, Women and Society: Articles on Witchcraft, Magic and Demonology* (Vol. 10). New York: Garland.

de Lint, C. (1998). *Someplace to Be Flying.* New York: Tor Books.

Dorn, N., Murji, K., & South, S. N. (1992). *Traffickers: Drug Markets and Law Enforcement.* London, UK: Routledge.

Dotinga, R. (2000, September 1). Officials Commission Jailhouse Exorcism: Inmates Claim to Be Terrified by Ouija Board Spirits. [On-Line]. Available: <http://www.APBNews.com>.

Eastlea, B. (1980). *Witch-hunting, Magic and the New Philosophy.* Brighton, UK: Harvester.

Emery, D. (2000). *Urban Legends and Folklore.* [On-Line]. Available: <http://www.about.com>.

Erikson, K. T. (1966). *Wayward Puritans: A Study in the Sociology of Deviance.* New York: John Wiley.

Frow, J. (1996). Recovering Memory. *Australian Humanities Review, 4* (December). [On-Line]. Available: <http://www.lib.latrobe.edu.au/AHR/archive/Issue-Dec-1996/frow.html>.

Fukurai, H., Butler, E. W., & Krooth, R. (1994). Sociologists in Action: The McMartin Sexual Abuse Case, Litigation, Justice, and Mass Hysteria. *American Sociologist, 25*(4), 44–71.

Fuller, R. C. (1995). *Naming the Antichrist: The History of an American Obsession.* New York: Oxford University Press.

Garrett, C. (1977). Women and Witches: Patterns of Analysis. *Signs: Journal of Women in Culture and Society, 3*(2), 461–470.

Goode, E. (1992). *Collective Behavior.* Fort Worth, TX: Harcourt Brace Jovanovich.

Groh, D. (1987). The Temptation of Conspiracy Theory, Part II. In C. F. Grauman & S. Moscovici (Eds.), *Changing Conceptions of Conspiracy.* Berlin: Springer-Verlag.

Guiley, R. E. (1991). *Harper's Encyclopedia of Mystical and Paranormal Experience.* San Francisco, CA: HarperCollins.

Harris, F. (1998). *Martensville: Truth or Justice?* Toronto: Dundurn Press.

Harris, M. (1978). *Cows, Pigs, Wars and Witches: The Riddles of Culture.* New York: Random House.

Hausman, G. (1999). *The Coyote Bead.* Charlottesville, VA: Hampton Roads.

Hertenstein, M., & Trott, J. (1993). *Selling Satan.* Chicago: Cornerstone Press.

Hicks, R. D. (1991). *In Pursuit of Satan: The Police and the Occult.* Buffalo, NY: Prometheus.

Highway, T. (1998). *Kiss of the Fur Queen.* Toronto: Doubleday.

Hoffmann, H. (1861). *Slovenly Peter: Or Cheerful Stories and Funny Pictures for Good Little Folks* (M. Twain, Trans.). Philadelphia: John C. Winston. (Original work *Der Struwwelpeter: Oder Lustige Geschichten und Drollige Bilder für Kiner von 3–6 Jahren,* published in 1861)

Hoffmann, H., & Blyth, C. (2000). *Struwwelpeter 2000.* Kingston, ON: Iolair.

Huxley, A. (1996). *The Devils of Loudon.* New York: Barnes and Noble.

Hyde, L. (1998). *Trickster Makes This World: Mischief, Myth and Art.* New York: North Point Press (Farrar Straus and Giroux).

Inverarity, J. M., Lauderdale, P., & Field, B. C. (1983). *Law and Society: Sociological Perspectives on Criminal Law.* Boston: Little, Brown.

Jenkins, P., & Daniel Maier-Katkin. (1992). Satanism: Myth and Reality in a Contemporary Moral Panic. *Crime Law and Social Change, 17*(1), 53–75.

Johnson, D. W. (1990). Lines and Circles: The "Rez" Plays of Tomson Highway. In W. H. New (Ed.), *Native Writers and Canadian Writing* (pp. 254–264). Vancouver: University of British Columbia.

Karlsen, C. F. (1989). *The Devil in the Shape of a Woman: Witchcraft in Colonial New England.* New York: Random House.

Katz, S. (1994). *The Holocaust and Mass Death before the Modern Age* (Vol. 1). New York: Oxford University Press.

Kent, S. A. (1993a). Deviant Scripturalism and Ritual Satanic Abuse Part One: Possible Judeo-Christian Influences. *Religion, 23,* 229–241.

———. (1993b). Deviant Scripturalism and Ritual Satanic Abuse Part Two: Possible Masonic, Mormon, Magick and Pagan Influences. *Religion, 23,* 355–367.

Kieckhefer, R. (1976). *European Witch Trials, Their Foundations in Popular and Learned Culture 1300–1500.* Berkeley, CA: University of California Press.

King, T. (1993). *Green Grass, Running Water.* Boston: Houghton Mifflin.

Korem, D. (1994). *Suburban Gangs: The Affluent Rebels.* Richardson, TX: International Focus Press.

Kramer, H., & Sprenger, J. (1971). *The Malleus Maleficarum of Heinrich Kramer and James Sprenger.* New York: Dover.

Laghi, B. (1997, May 31). Bearwalker Still Haunts Some Ojibwa. *The Globe and Mail,* p. A5.

Lapoint, E. (1992). Irish Immunity to Witch-Hunting 1534–1711. *Eire-Ireland. A Journal of Irish Studies, 27*(Summer), 76–92.

Largent, F. (1998). Windigo: A Native American Archetype. *Parabola, 23*(3), 22–26.

Larner, C. (1980). "Criminum Exceptum"? The Crime of Witchcraft in Europe. In V. A. C. Gatrell, B. Lenman, & G. Parker (Eds.), *Crime and the Law: The Social History of Crime in Western Europe Since 1500* (pp. 49–75). London, UK: Europa.

Leeming, D., & Page, J. (1999). *Myths, Legends and Folktales of America.* New York: Oxford University Press.

Levack, B. P. (1987). *The Witch-Hunt in Early Modern Europe.* New York: Longman.

———. (1992a). Witchcraft, Women and Society. In *Articles on Witchcraft, Magic and Demonology* (Vol. 10). New York: Garland.

———. (Ed.). (1992b). *Possession and Exorcism: Articles on Witchcraft, Magic and Demonology* (Vol. 9). New York: Garland.

Lopez, B. (1977). *Giving Birth to Thunder, Sleeping with His Daughter: Coyote Builds North America.* New York: Avon.

Lowney, K. S. (1995). Teenage Satanism as Oppositional Youth Subculture. *Journal of Contemporary Ethnography, 23*(4), 453–484.

Macfarlane, A. (1970). *Witchcraft in Tudor and Stuart England.* London, UK: Routledge and Kegan Paul.

Marron, K. (1989). *Witches, Pagans, and Magic in the New Age.* Toronto: McClelland-Bantam Seal Books.

Marty, M. E. (1990). "Satan and the American Spiritual Underground." In D. Daume (Ed.), *Britannica Book of the Year* (pp. 308–309). Chicago: Encyclopaedia Britannica.

Moore, C. (1994). *Coyote Blue*. New York: Avon.

Morgan, T. (1988). *Literary Outlaw: The Life and Times of William S. Burroughs*. New York: Avon Books.

Morison, S. E. (1955). *The Parkman Reader: From the Works of Francis Parkman*. Boston: Little, Brown.

Murray, M. (1921). *The Witch Cult in Western Europe*. London, UK: Oxford.

Nathan, D., & Snedeker, M. (1996). *Satan's Silence: Ritual Abuse and the Making of a Modern American Witch Hunt*. New York: Basic Books.

Oake, G. (1990, November 12). Tales of Devilworship Chill Albertans. *The Toronto Star*.

Ofshe, R., & Watters, E. (1994). *Making Monsters: False Memories, Psychotherapy, and Sexual Hysteria*. New York: Charles Scribner's.

Oppenheimer, J. (1988). *Private Demons: The Life of Shirley Jackson*. New York: Putnam's Sons.

Owens, J. B. (1994). *Bone Game*. Norman, OK: University of Oklahoma.

Owomoyela, O. (1990). No Problem Can Fail to Crash on His Head: The Trickster in Contemporary African Folklore. *The World and I* (April), 625–632.

Pearson, I. (1984, November). The Cat in the Bag and Other Absolutely Untrue Tales from Our Urban Mythology. *Quest Magazine*.

Peck, M. S. (1983). *People of the Lie: The Hope for Healing Human Evil*. New York: Simon and Schuster.

Pelka, F. (1992). The "Women's Holocaust." *The Humanist 52*(5), 5–9.

Pollock, J. (1989). *Dear M.: Letters from a Gentleman of Excess*. Toronto: McClelland and Stewart.

Radin, P. (1972). *The Trickster*. New York: Schocken Books.

Rapley, R. (1998). *A Case of Witchcraft: The Trial of Urbain Grandier*. Montreal: McGill-Queen's University Press.

Redondi, P. (1987). *Galileo: Heretic*. Princeton, NJ: Princeton University Press.

Reed, C. (1989, May 20). Diabolical Debauchery or Mere Stories from the Mouths of Babes? *The Globe and Mail*, p. 5.

Richards, J. (1990). *Sex, Dissidence and Damnation: Minority Groups in the Middle Ages*. New York: Barnes and Noble.

Ro, A. (2000, August 9). Naval Intelligence. [On-Line]. Available: <http://users.uniserve.com/~abe/joke980510.html>.

Rosenthal, B. (1993). *Salem Story: Reading the Witch Trials of 1692*. Cambridge, UK, and New York: Cambridge University Press.

Ross, C. (1995). *Satanic Ritual Abuse: Principles of Treatment*. Toronto: University of Toronto Press.

Russell, J. B. (1984). *Lucifer: The Devil in the Middle Ages*. Ithaca, NY: Cornell University Press.

———. (1988). *The Prince of Darkness: Radical Evil and the Power of Good in History*. Ithaca, NY: Cornell University Press.

Sagan, C. (1995). *The Demon-Haunted World: Science as a Candle in the Dark*. New York: Random House.

Santino, J. (1990). Fitting the Bill: The Trickster in American Popular Culture. *The World and I* (April), 661–668.

Scher, L. (1992). *The Un-Canadians: True Stories of the Blacklist Era.* Toronto: Lester.

Simpson, J. (1973). Olaf Tryggvason versus the Powers of Darkness. In V. Newall (Ed.), *The Witch in History.* New York: Barnes and Noble.

Smith, M., & Pazder, L. (1980). *Michelle Remembers.* New York: Congdon and Lattes.

Tatar, M. (1987). *The Hard Facts of the Grimms' Fairy Tales.* Princeton, NJ: Princeton University Press.

Thomas, K. (1997). *Religion and the Decline of Magic: Studies of Popular Beliefs in Sixteenth and Seventeenth Century England.* New York: Oxford University Press.

Trevor-Roper, H. R. (1969). *The European Witchcraze of the Sixteenth and Seventeenth Centuries.* Harmondsworth, UK: Penguin.

Trostle, L. C. (1986). The Stoners: Drugs, Demons and Delinquency. A Descriptive and Empirical Analysis of Delinquent Behavior. Unpublished doctoral dissertation. Claremont Graduate University, Claremont, CA.

Victor, J. S. (1993). *Satanic Panic: The Creation of a Contemporary Legend.* Chicago: Open Court.

Vizenor, G. (1989). *Narrative Chance: Postmodern Discourse on Native American Literatures.* Albuquerque, NM: University of New Mexico Press.

Walker, B. G. (1996). *The Women's Encyclopedia of Myths and Secrets.* Edison, NJ: Castle Books.

Watters, E., & Ofshe, R. (1999). *Therapy's Delusions: The Myth of the Unconscious and the Exploitation of Today's Walking Worried.* New York: Simon & Schuster.

Watts, S. (1984). *A Social History of Western Europe, 1450–1720.* London, UK: Hutchinson University Library.

Webster, C. (1996). *From Paracelsus to Newton: Magic and the Making of Modern Science.* New York: Barnes and Noble.

Wilkins, C. (1994). The Bird the Haida Call the Trickster. *Canadian Geographic* (March/April), 71–79.

Willis, D. (1995). *Malevolent Nurture: Witchhunting and Maternal Power in Early Modern England.* Ithaca, NY: Cornell University Press.

Wilmer, H. A. (1988). Introduction. In P. Woodruff & H. A. Wilmer (Eds.), *Facing Evil: Light at the Core of Darkness.* LaSalle, IL: Open Court.

Wilson, C. (1987). *Aleister Crowley: The Nature of the Beast.* Northamptonshire, UK: Aquarian Press.

Worobec, C. (1995). Witchcraft Beliefs and Practices in Pre-Revolutionary Russian and Ukrainian Villages. *Russian Review, 54,* 165–187.

Wright, L. (1993, May 17, May 24). A Reporter at Large: Remembering Satan (Parts 1 and 2). *The New Yorker.*

Zeidenberg, J. (1990, March 16). Persecuted Professor: Celebrated Scientist Was Driven into Exile by Cold War Witch-Hunt in Canada. *The Globe and Mail.*

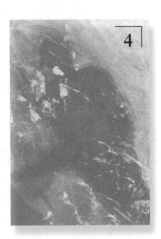

CLASSICAL THEORIES OF DEVIANCE AND THEIR INFLUENCE ON MODERN JURISPRUDENCE

This chapter examines the long, slow process whereby demonic-supernatural theories of deviance were pushed aside by powerful new ideas about the nature of man and of reality. By the late seventeenth and early eighteenth centuries, the sacred canopies of Catholicism and Protestantism were no longer sufficient to explain everything that happened in the world. Travel, science, and newer philosophies challenged these religious perspectives with knowledge that simply would not fit religiously bounded cosmologies.

The new "enlightened" classical view of deviance saw it as behaviour that detracted from the overall happiness or well-being of members of society. No longer was the deviant seen as a person in league with the forces of evil or as a purveyor of heretical thoughts. Heretics might still be deviant in the courts of the churches, but not in the civil courts. The deviant was one whose self-interest was not sufficiently constrained by his or her expectation of cost, so that he or she was willing to commit acts detrimental to the community as a whole. The infliction of excruciating pain and violent death was no longer viewed as a means to salvation but rather as a futile expression of the impotence and erratic rage of the system being displaced. Since deviance was a rational calculation, the way to reduce it was to increase the swiftness, certainty, and severity of punishment precisely to the point at which the potential deviant would be deterred; that is, to the point at which the individual would decide that the risk of deviance was not worth it and that conformity was the better choice.

The new thinkers devoted much of their attention to devising controlled systems of punishment that would warn would-be deviants that the cost of their offences would be higher than the pleasure they might gain. These thinkers argued that punishments beyond this were criminal in themselves, since they reduced happiness without contributing to the overall good. Classical theorists worked toward making the system of social control more reliable and accountable. Judges were no longer permitted to devise their own laws and sentences and were restrained by legislation. As well, accused individuals no longer stood alone against the system. Measures of due process were instituted to ensure they had the right to a fair trial and, if convicted, to punishment that would not be cruel and unusual.

RATIONAL CALCULATION IN AN IMPERFECT WORLD:
THE ENLIGHTENMENT, 1680–1800

The Enlightenment was characterized by a new, strictly empirical view of the world. Hell was no longer a physical place into which an unlucky sailor might accidentally fall (Jenkins, 1984, p. 126), and it was no longer "common to feed a consecrated Host to a sick cow in order to drive out a demon" (Raulston Saul, 1992, p. 38). In this disenchanted world, the deviant was no longer seen as a creature possessed by devils, tormented by sorcerer's spells, or tempted by Satan. The deviant was a rational person who made self-serving choices. Interest in deviance turned from the outrages of heresy and witchcraft to the disruptions of crime. The five central tenets of the classical view were as follows:

1. People are *hedonistic.* They seek pleasure (gain) and avoid pain (harm).

2. People have *free will.* They choose whether to commit offences or conform to rules when solving their problems and meeting their needs.

3. Society represents a form of *social contract* whereby each individual gives up some of his or her right to hedonistic pleasure to partake of the greater good provided by social order.

4. *Punishment* is justified as a means of transforming the hedonistic calculation so that the performance of duty is more rewarding than following the criminal path. In classical utilitarian terms, the solution for all kinds of crime is to make the punishments sufficiently severe and predictable that the calculation is changed and conformity is preferred over crime.

5. Reform of the secular world is worthwhile and appropriate since the chief goal in life is not to achieve salvation but rather to reach the utilitarian goal, which is *the greatest good for the greatest number.* Armageddon is not imminent: abuses, injustice, and oppression are the chief evils to be fought against, not the armies of the antichrist.

With crime as the focus, other forms of deviance tended to be neglected, but the paradigm of the classical school can readily be extended to include the explanation of noncriminal forms of deviance. Just as we may weigh the likelihood of a fine or jail, we may also weigh the likelihood that our actions will cause our families to disown us, our best friends to shun us, or some nasty disease to shorten our lives. Although the classical view is sometimes described as "noncausal" because of its emphasis on free choice (Henry & Milovanovic, 1996, p. 127), it does implicitly invoke pain and pleasure as causal factors (Beirne, 1991, p. 807) and so overlaps considerably with modern psychological theories.

The classical view became dominant only after several centuries of transition, during which the ideas of religion, rationality, and science overlapped and competed with one another in a violent, disruptive way. Those who first espoused these new

Figure 4.1   The Classical Paradigm

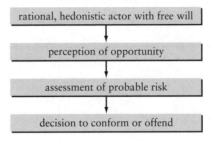

ideas needed powerful friends if they were to avoid the fires of the Inquisition. Giordano Bruno (executed in 1600) and Galileo (sentenced to penance, first imprisoned in a dungeon and then released into house arrest in 1633) argued that the earth moved around the sun, a position that was inconsistent with Church dogma at the time. To accept these scholars' heretical ideas would have forced a rapid and unsettling change at every level of the medieval Church. Galileo's *Dialogue Concerning the Two Chief World Systems* (1632) uses three characters to argue the issue of the nature of the universe. Salviati, the mathematically and empirically correct expert, Sagredo, the intelligent layman, and Simplicius, "a pompous Aristotelian philosopher who loved to drop Latin phrases, would often wax prolix on a topic before being played for a fool" (Sobel, 1999, p. 144). As the Church's position at the time was Aristotelian, Galileo's belief that he was being careful may have been delusional. He survived only because he recanted on the position that he firmly believed to be true (Lerner & Gosselin, 1986; Peters, 1989; Redondi, 1987).

The Enlightenment was rooted in the rediscovery of early Greek and Roman prescientific writing (which had been preserved in monastic libraries) and in the work of the emerging geological, astronomical, and medical sciences, which were being aided by new technology—the telescope and microscope—and by improvements in transportation and communication. Many of the discoveries were incompatible with established medieval cosmology. If the world was older than 6000 years and was not the centre of the universe, many other aspects of dogma might be questioned as well (Russell, 1988, pp. 212–213).

The strongest champions of the changing world view, the *philosophes,* often used material provided by scientists. These thinkers were advocates of a new faith in reason, toleration, materialism, and empiricism (Russell, 1988, p. 208). They were activists, not just philosophers. Nor were scientists the empiricists they have since become. In this period, the natural and supernatural worlds were not so clearly divorced. Paracelsus, a founder of clinical medical science, was, for example, a firm believer in some aspects of sorcery and demonology. His credulous description of the witch has been described as a "folklore classic" (Webster, 1996, p. 77). Newton's

Table 4.1	Demonic and Classical Perspectives Compared	
	Demonic	**Classical**
Time of dominance	1400–1700	1700–1800
Conception of deviance	Evil	Violation of social contract
Explanation	Moral weakness, temptation	Free will and hedonism
Remedies	Exorcism, execution	Imprisonment

science was profoundly theological and mystical (Dobbs, 1975; Figala, 1977). The work of astronomists and astrologists overlapped, as did chemistry and alchemy, medicine and curative incantations, and mathematics and number mysticism. As the philosopher Immanual Kant observed of the late eighteenth century, this was an age that aspired to enlightenment but was not actually an enlightened age (Kant, 1784/1977). "It was an age whose literary spokesmen preached the virtues of reason and good sense and humane regard for one's fellow man. But it was not an age that had achieved these virtues" (Gay, 1966, p. 53).

Only gradually did Hume's idea that the universe was governed by immutable natural laws become the dominant assumption in science and philosophy. In the meantime, the classical thinkers discussed in this chapter occupied a middle ground. They rejected what they regarded as the superstitious, misguided oppression of the Church, but at the same time were disturbed by what they saw as the displacement of humanism by the forces of science. The scientific attempt to study humanity as one would any other phenomenon (rocks, trees, insects) seemed to downgrade humanity in that it left no room for people's essential qualities of morality, dignity, and faith (E. Becker, 1968, p. 7). The anguished, heartfelt writings of Jean-Jacques Rousseau, which are often interpreted as "anti-science," reflect the clashing and incompatible world views that characterized the period (E. Becker, 1968, p. 16; Dent, 1988).

SOCIAL JUSTICE IN THE EIGHTEENTH CENTURY

The ideas of the Enlightenment arrived on a scene that was anything but enlightened. The practice of the courts was demonstrably irrational, corrupt, unjust, cruel, harsh, and arbitrary. Holy terror was the law of the times. Most forms of misbehaviour went totally unpunished, so that life for most people was unpredictable and hard. Although few became entangled in the justice systems of government or Church, those who did were treated as terrible examples for everyone else. The process of accusation was capricious at best and biased against the powerless at worst. Court officials were often unpaid and all too willing to be bought. Throughout Europe, courts accepted anonymous denunciations. In France, for example, a *lettre de cachet* (an anonymous letter to the king) was sufficient to send a person to prison. Those accused were imprisoned until tried, and investigation of the case often required that they be put to judicial (investigative, not punitive) torture. These painful investigations produced surprisingly few confessions, although it was not uncommon for a person's health to be irreparably damaged. In typical cases, judges answered to no higher authority, apart from the rich and powerful whom they feared to antagonize. They made up the law as they went along and decided punishments according to their own interpretations of appropriate standards. Particularly when the accused was of low status, punishments were deliberately made as horrifying as possible and often took the form of public rituals of pain, which attracted large crowds, as a circus might do. The safeguards of due process, which we now take for granted, were completely absent.

Despite the terror, social control was not well maintained. The system was so unpredictable that the guilty might well escape punishment, while the innocent were tortured into confessions and executed. In this period, there was growing fear of the "dangerous classes," a category that included all those who were not under the control of a master and who were thus free to commit crimes and engage in the actions of the urban mob.

Several factors contributed to the growing crime and disorder. Disastrous wars meant increases in taxation and the periodic return of disaffected soldiers hardened by war and unsuited to peacetime employment. Typhus and cholera epidemics brought on by urban conditions affected the social balance. In England, gin became a staple "food" for the poor because it was cheaper and more filling than nonalcoholic alternatives. *Gin Lane,* a painting by Hogarth, dramatically presents the depravity of people who were undernourished, drunken, and living in squalor. The response to all this social chaos was greater punishment. In England, law reforms in 1722 and 1758 added more than 350 crimes to the list of those punishable by death. Most of these crimes were crimes against property, such as putting graffiti on London Bridge, or stealing food. Executions came to be scenes of drunken revelry or rioting. Ignatieff (1978) explains:

> In theory, the processional to the gallows and the execution itself were supposed to be a carefully stage-managed theater of guilt in which the offender and the parson acted out a drama of exhortation, confession and repentance before an awed and approving crowd. The parson's sermons were set pieces on social obligation, delivered at the gallows and subsequently hawked in the streets with an account of the offender's life and descent into crime.
>
> The trouble was that if the spectators did not approve of the execution, the parson would find his worthy sentiments drowned in the abuse welling up from the crowd. Moreover, the crowd had a highly developed sense of the rights due the condemned, and if any of these rights were abridged, they were quick to vent their wrath on the authorities, especially if the condemned also happened to contest the justice of the execution itself. (pp. 21–22)

The crowd sometimes rescued prisoners, and the executioner (especially one who bungled the job) was sometimes killed. A legal system as disorderly as this one could not last long.

THE *PHILOSOPHES* AND THE CLASSICAL SCHOOL

The *philosophes* expressed anger and scorn over the inconsistencies, stupidities, and abuses of the social order; at the same time, they developed a new vision of how society could be if it were based on rational principles that would ensure the greatest happiness for the greatest number.

One of these courageous crusaders against the tyranny, bigotry, and cruelty of his time was François-Marie Arouet (1694–1778), who is usually known by his pen name, Voltaire. As a youth, he had experienced some of the inequities of the French justice system firsthand when an anonymous accusation landed him in the Bastille, an infamous prison later to figure as a symbol of tyranny. In his first book, *The Philosophical Letters* (1734), Voltaire took issue with the religious philosopher and mathematician Pascal, arguing that the purpose of life was not to reach heaven through suffering, but rather to assure the greatest amount of happiness through material progress in the sciences and the arts. In *Candide* (1759), he satirized almost every aspect of eighteenth-century life. At one point in his travels, Candide is ship-wrecked off Lisbon on the eve of the great earthquake of 1755. Voltaire goes on to describe the event and, in the following passage, its aftermath:

> After the earthquake had wiped out three-quarters of Lisbon, the learned men of the land could find no more effective way of averting total destruction than to give the people a fine auto-da-fé [burning of heretics]. The University of Coimbra had established that the spectacle of several persons being roasted over a slow fire with full ceremonial rites is an infallible remedy against earthquakes. (quoted in Peters, 1989, p. 179)

Here Voltaire attacks the blind stupidity of those who regard natural disasters like earthquakes as religious phenomena and then proceed to punish and torture innocent people for them. In 1762, Voltaire led the successful lobby for "rehabilitation" (a postmortem declaration of innocence) on behalf of Jean Calas, a Protestant (Huguenot) merchant of Toulouse. Calas's son had been mentally unstable and had committed suicide. The prosecutor maintained that the son had been about to convert to Catholicism. Although he continued to deny the charges, Calas was convicted for the murder of his son and executed by being broken on the wheel on March 10, 1762. His family was arrested and his property was confiscated by the state (Brown, Esbensen, & Geis, 1991, pp. 215–216; Pfohl, 1985, pp. 59–60).

Some of the *philosophes* maintained that the greatest good is served when each of us give up some of our freedom to do as we please in order to preserve the safety and well-being of all—a kind of social contract that each member of society enters into as a condition of membership. Further, any law that goes beyond what is necessary to uphold the social order is oppressive and wrong. One of these social-contract writers, Thomas Hobbes (1588–1679), argued in his best-known work, *Leviathan*, that moral rules should have a purely secular basis. Hobbes (1881) describes human beings in their natural state as being engaged in a "war of all against all," a war fuelled by their desires for gain, safety, and reputation. In such a society, there could be no industry or agriculture, no importation or building, no arts or letters because "the fruit thereof is uncertain." To escape this unpleasant condition, men make a social contract with one another to give up their freedom to the sovereign, whose sole obligation is to protect the people. Without this contract, neither justice nor injustice exists.

> To this warre of everyman against every man, this also is consequent; that nothing can be Unjust. The notions of Right and Wrong, Justice and Injustice have there no place. Where there is no common Power, there is no Law: where no Law, no Injustice. (Hobbes, 1881, p. 96)

The Leviathan (state), a huge, artificial monster made for our protection, establishes what is right and wrong and punishes to protect the common good (Hobbes, 1881, p. 91).

The two main representatives of the classical school—Cesare Beccaria (1738–94) and Jeremy Bentham (1748–1832)—drew on the work of many writers, particularly the *philosophes* and the social-contract writers.

CESARE BECCARIA

Born of a noble Italian family, Cesare Beccaria was an indifferent student who often objected to the accepted notions taught in his day. He graduated with a degree in law from the University of Padua at the age of 20, was a professor of political economy for a brief period, and later enjoyed a reputation as a brilliant mathematician who found new applications for quantitative methods in social and political affairs. His famous essay "*Dei delitti e delle pene*" ("On Crimes and Punishments") was first published in 1765 (Beccaria, 1765/1995). It was written as his contribution to the Society of Fists, a socially conscious literary club started by his friend Pietro Verri. Verri's brother, Alessandro, held the position of "protector of prisoners" in Milan, and gave Beccaria firsthand access to local penal institutions.

Beccaria was deeply disturbed by what he saw and heard in these prisons. Although his essay did not express new ideas but rather those whose time had come, it did so with such eloquent logic that it was widely read and became a focal point for action against barbaric practices in criminal law and procedure in Europe, England, and the colonial settlements. Indeed, it may have had more practical effect than any other treatise ever written on the subject. It was highly praised by intellectuals of the time, including Voltaire, Diderot, Rousseau, and Hume. Its main six points are summarized in the following list:

1. All people are motivated by pain and pleasure. They are rational pain/pleasure machines. Crime is reasonable behaviour and represents neither the devil nor illness. To reduce crime, it is necessary to make it less rational by changing social conditions.

2. The basis of all social action must be the utilitarian concept of the greatest happiness for the greatest number, not the salvation of the soul or preparation for Armageddon (the end of the world).

3. The greatest happiness is ensured by the social contract whereby each individual gives up some of his or her right to hedonistic pleasure for the benefit of the whole. This is represented in the ruler (sovereign), who is thereby entitled, through the legislature, to make laws for the society.

4. The social contract is supported when the laws are openly made by the legislature, clearly written, widely known, and uniformly enforced.

5. Crime must be considered an injury to society, and the only rational measure of crime is the extent of this injury. Any act of authority of one person over another that is not justified by absolute necessity is tyrannical. The act, not the intent, is the measure of the crime. The most serious crimes are those that "immediately tend to the dissolution of society" (e.g., treason). Just below this are crimes that injure people and property. Least serious are crimes that disrupt public peace, such as being drunk in public. Punishment should be in proportion to the seriousness of the crime (hence banishment for treason, fines for property damage, and humane imprisonment for other crimes). Execution is not justifiable, especially since it cannot be reversed should an error later be found.

6. Punishment is justified only on the grounds that it helps prevent further criminal conduct. It does this by increasing the costs of unlawful conduct through such mechanisms as the law and a system of punishment that results in the minimum occurrence of crime. Imprisonment is one way of meting out just enough punishment to prevent further crime.

Beccaria did not put his name on the work at first, fearing repression by the Inquisition (Paolucci, 1963, pp. ix–xi). The inquisitors did commission an investigation of the book, and Beccaria was charged with sedition, sacrilege, and impiety. The provincial governor, however, interceded on his behalf (Brown et al., 1991; Maestro, 1972, p. 64). The Vatican denounced the book, and it remained on the index of proscribed books until that list was abolished in 1962 (Maestro, 1973). As is often the case with censorship, however, while it was banned, the book only became more popular.

JEREMY BENTHAM

Like Beccaria, the English gentleman-of-means Jeremy Bentham found the law of his time an appalling mass of incongruities, absurdities, and barbarities. Justice went to those who could pay for it. Men were given the death penalty for stealing food to feed their starving children, and the majority of executions were for crimes against property.

Bentham spent most of his life obsessed with a vision of social reform based on utilitarianism, the principle that all things should be organized in such a way as to ensure the maximum happiness for the greatest number. Bentham emphasized hedonism, and his works discuss the issue of effective punishment more than they do Beccaria's ideas about social contract and an accountable, predictable judicial system. Bentham began with the premise that "Nature has placed mankind under the governance of two sovereign masters, pain and pleasure." From there he developed the idea of a *felicific calculus* whereby actions are evaluated based on their tendency to produce either pain or pleasure. The calculus would include the pains and pleasures of wealth, benevolence, desire, hunger, and even piety (Rennie, 1978, p. 22).

According to Bentham's *Principles of Morals and Legislation* (1789), the law in particular needed to be totally reformed to meet utilitarian standards. The utility of any law could be measured by the extent to which it promoted the pleasure, good, and happiness of the people. The actions of individuals could be judged according to whether, on balance, they contributed to or detracted from the happiness and benefit of all. Criminal acts detracted from the collective happiness and, therefore, should be prevented. Acts that did not detract from the collective happiness should not be the subject of criminal law, even if many people thought they should be regulated.

This opened up, for Bentham, the opportunity to write in great detail on whether certain practices that he called "offences against one's self," or "offences of impurity" should be treated as crimes. In an unpublished 60-page essay, he considers whether homosexual activities are harmful beyond harm to the consenting participants. He considers, for example, that such practices might disturb a marriage or cheat women (Bentham, 1978/1785). In Bentham's time, such ideas were unusual. Sodomy was punished by hanging.

For utilitarians, such as Bentham, laws and punishments that were unnecessary were themselves evil. "All punishment is mischief: all punishment is in itself evil … it ought only to be admitted in as far as it promises to exclude some greater evil" (Bentham, 1830/1988, p. 170). Thus, in Bentham's system, people could do as they pleased, as long as it was not harming the overall happiness of the people around them.

Since humans were hedonistic, crime (harm to happiness) could be prevented if all citizens were made to understand that the punishment would be swift, certain, and slightly greater than the pleasure of the crime. Like Beccaria, Bentham argued that deviance could be controlled not by changing deviants but by changing the rules, not by terrorizing people but by showing them that conformity was the best way to find happiness. His *felicific calculus* would assign definite values to pleasure and pain. If a thief gained X units of pleasure from a crime, it would be up to the court to assign X + 1 units of pain (Jenkins, 1984, p. 128). For each offence, it was appropriate to adjust the punishment (adapted from Rennie, 1978, p. 22).

- The value of the punishment should not be less than what is sufficient to outweigh that of the profit gained by the offence.

- The more serious the offence, the more time and money should be invested to make sure that it is punished enough.

- The punishment for the various offences should be set in such a way that, if a person decided to commit an offence, he or she would be induced to choose the less serious one.

- If an offence has several aspects, the punishment should be set to discourage all parts of it, not just the most serious part.

- The punishment should never be more than what is necessary to outweigh the value of the offence to the offender. Since punishment involves pain and is, therefore, intrinsically evil, it should be used only to exclude some greater evil.

- The punishment should be generally consistent across similar offences but should take into account the differences between offenders that influence their sensitivity.

These ideas led to the invention of various kinds of punishment that could be meted out in measured doses. Typical of these were the tread wheel on which offenders would be forced to keep walking uphill, as if going up a down escalator, and various gadgets that would count how many turns of a crank had been made (the prison governor could determine how many turns had to be made before earning a meal). The point of these boring, repetitive, and useless tasks was to make sure that the convict got no intrinsic pleasure out of the work. Bentham also attempted to develop a beating machine, which he felt would be preferable to the inconsistencies of the usual practice of flogging. A revival of this kind of thought can be found in Graeme Newman's *Just and Painful: A Case for the Corporal Punishment of Criminals* (1983), in which Newman argues for the use of electric shock as an alternative to imprisonment or fine. Newman's 1983 argument is the same as Bentham's: the use of punishment can be scientifically controlled and precisely calibrated to fit the offence. In a later publication, however, written after reading Michel Foucault's 1979 *Discipline and Punish*, Newman retreats from this position. Having questioned why we persist in punishment when research leaves us in uncertainty and doubt about its efficacy, Newman says, "I have given historical and cultural answers to this question. Perhaps the more obvious answer is that we are simply all sadists" (Newman, 1985, p. 249).

NEOCLASSICAL THEORY

Classical ideas were quickly tested in the aftermath of the French Revolution. Beccaria's recommendations were used—almost word for word—in the drafting of the French Declaration of the Rights of Man in 1791 (Bellamy, 1997, p. 24). They also became an important part of the Constitution of the United States (1787) and were enshrined in the English Reform Act of 1832. Jeremy Bentham was honoured with citizenship in the French Republic in 1792. The classical approach, when tested by prac-

Box 4.1   The Panopticon Prison

In Bentham's time, prison was rarely a punishment in itself. People were held in prisons until trial, and then subjected to execution, a fine, the pillory, transportation (banishment), or short-term confinement in old ships moored just off the coast called prison hulks (Geis, 1973, p. 63; Radzinowicz, 1948). Bentham felt that imprisonment was an ideal form of punishment since it would give the felon the opportunity to adjust his *felicific calculus* toward a belief in the value of conformity. Punishments could be meted out in measured days and years exactly proportionate to the need for reform. The panopticon (all-seeing place) was to be a different sort of prison, one aimed at returning the offender to the society as a productive, disciplined person.

Source: B. F. Barton & M. S. Barton (1993), Modes of Power in Technical and Professional Visuals, *Journal of Business and Technical Communication, 7(1),* 139. Reprinted with the permission of University College London, Bentham 115/44.

Bentham envisioned the panopticon as a circular or polygonal building with a tower in the centre. The tower would be designed for observation, with wide windows opening onto the inner side of the building, which would contain the cells. Each cell would have two windows, one permitting light from outside the prison to backlight the cell (thus revealing any activity on the part of its occupant), and the other permitting constant surveillance from the tower. In this arrangement, an omniscient prison inspector, protected from view, could observe any particular prisoner or prison employee. Visible to the supervisor and guards, the prisoner would be isolated by thick walls from his fellow inmates. "He is seen, but he does not see; he is the object of information; never the subject of communication" (Foucault, 1979, p. 200).

The panopticon manager would derive income from the money earned by convict contract labour (which would enable convicts to develop useful work skills) but at the same time would be held financially liable to the government for failing to reform the convict or for an unusually high number of deaths among inmates over a given period. The panopticon was also to be placed close to a dense population centre, where it would be a visible reminder to those tempted to go astray (Geis, 1973, p. 64).

Box 4.1   The Panopticon Prison (cont.)

Bentham campaigned vigorously for such a prison and even imagined himself as its omniscient manager (Bentham, 1830/1988). Other than the small-scale version that still exists as Cellhouse F at Stateville Correctional Center (in Joliet, Illinois), the panopticon has remained an idea on paper. Its principles, however, have had widespread influence.

An example of panoptical principles is seen in the Special Handling Unit (SHU) at the Regional Reception Centre for the Correctional Service of Canada (Quebec Region), in operation since 1997:

> Inside the SHU, the greyness of the day beyond the walls blends with the artificial light of the Unit, leaving the central area clearly lit but with few shadows.

> The SHU has five cellblocks, each including a small, triangular exercise yard. These cellblocks fan out around a central control post equipped with tinted windows. Inside this control post, correctional officers monitor all inmate activity and control all cell doors and the barriers that mark the range. (Chartier, 2000, p. 4)

As we shall discuss in Chapter 12, Foucault (1979) turned Bentham's panopticon idea into a kind of symbolic representation of the omnipresent and omniscient forces of control in modern society, extending beyond the prison and into everyday life.

tical experience, however, proved too rigid and was gradually modified by neoclassical thinkers.

The classical school of thought had maintained that all crimes were to be judged only in terms of their harm to the social fabric and punished only according to the pain necessary to deter further offences. As formulated in codes of law, such as the French Code of 1791, classical thought meant that each offence had the same penalty regardless of the circumstances under which it occurred. The theft of a loaf of bread would be treated in the same way whether the thief was a starving adult, a mischievous child, or a vandal. The person who killed in anger would receive the same penalty as the person who killed in a state of insanity. Dissatisfaction with this arrangement led to the French Declaration of Rights being modified in 1810 and 1819 to provide more discretionary power to the judge, although this discretion was still nothing like the unbridled power held by judges in the seventeenth century (Brown et al., 1991, p. 229).

The neoclassicists introduced three new concepts:

1. *Mitigating factors.* In the classical system, all assaults of a particular degree of seriousness were treated in the same way; under the neoclassical system, the judge could take into account, for example, whether the attack was perpetrated by a vicious bully, by someone engaged in self-defence, or by a person suffering delusions of persecution.

2. *Past record.* In the classical system, every offence was treated in the same way, whether it was a first-time, repeat, or a multiple-repeat offence. The neoclassical system would punish the repeat offender more severely.

3. *Differences in free will.* It was increasingly recognized that the classical assumptions of free will and rational capability were not always corroborated by reality. Some classes of offenders—minors, people with mental disabilities, and the insane—were clearly not as capable as the average person of choosing between right and wrong. Neoclassical systems put into effect procedures for measuring the degree of responsibility possessed by the offender, as seen in the separation of adult and juvenile courts, the provision of legal defences such as insanity, and distinctions in the degree of premeditation required for conviction, such as the distinction between accidental and premeditated homicide.

To put neoclassical theory into perspective, it is useful to compare its approach to a specific offence with the way in which the demonic and classical systems would respond. In the demonic system, the treatment an offender receives depends on social status and degree of influence over the judge. If a rich, powerful man murders a

---

Box 4.2   Classical Thought without Social Contract: The Unbridled Pursuit of Pleasure

A contemporary of Bentham's was the infamous Donatien Alphonse Francois, Comte de Sade (1740–1814). De Sade's life and his writings illustrate what happens to classical thought when the social-contract element is rejected. De Sade regarded most laws as wrong—laws against theft, for example, are unjust because they force the man who has nothing to respect another who has everything (Hood & Crowley, 1995, p. 129). De Sade went further than other thinkers in rejecting the moral force of God or the laws of nature. For him, no absolute standards of right and wrong existed, nothing except the pursuit of the maximum self-gratification, even if this caused great pain to others or ultimately ruined one's own body. In de Sade's view, the maximum pleasure was the maximum good, while virtue, kindness, and love were perversions because they restricted indulgence in pleasure (Russell, 1988, pp. 211–212). Although many others (called *libertines* at the time) shared de Sade's personal excesses, de Sade's writings attracted official attention. Approximately one-fourth of de Sade's writings were destroyed by authorities, and his last effort, a 10-volume work (called *The Days of Florabelle*), which he wrote secretly while in prison and banned from writing, was burned by his son (Hood & Crowley, 1995, p. 156). De Sade's challenge to the forces of law and order, and the repression it engendered (represented by the sinister Dr. Royer-Collard) are dramatized Hollywood-style in the Fox Searchlight film *Quills* (2000, directed by Philip Kaufman; see <http://www.foreverkate.com/quills/presskit.htm>).

peasant, there will likely be no arrest, much less confinement and trial. Should the roles be reversed, however, the murderer will in all probability be arrested, treated very roughly before trial, subjected to judicial torture, and condemned to an extremely painful and public execution.

In the classical system, the offender's treatment depends solely on the nature of the murder and the harm done as a result of it. It makes no difference whether the person who committed the murder was sane or whether the killing was an unintended result of some other action. The execution itself will be swift (if not painless), "a medical operation performed in an antiseptic environment by dispassionate experts" (Bowers, 1974, p. 29).

In the neoclassical system, the rich and powerful offender will receive greater punishment than the poor one if it can be determined that the offender had more choices in the situation or was motivated more by greed than by fear or rage. The accused is permitted to argue that he had no free will because of mental illness, duress, "mistake of fact," or any of the other mitigating circumstances specified in the law books.

TESTING CLASSICAL THOUGHT: THE MODERN LEGACY

Classical theory has continued into the present in several different ways. The principal theoretical forms of this continuation are deterrence theory, routine activities/rational choice theory (both discussed below), and social control theory (discussed in Chapter 11).

DETERRENCE THEORY

Cesare Beccaria enumerated the three principles of punishment that became the hallmark of classical deterrence doctrine. He argued that crime control is a function of *certainty*, *celerity* (speed), and *severity* of punishment. Taken together, these amount to a fourth criterion, *exemplarity*—that is, the example set for would-be offenders. Research has been directed toward finer analysis of what deterrence is and of the circumstances under which deterrence succeeds or fails (Schneider & Laurie, 1990). The following sections introduce several types of deterrence: absolute, relative, general, specific, and restrictive.

Absolute Deterrence

Penalties are so sure, so soon in coming, and so terrible that no crime is committed. We might create near-absolute deterrence for parking offences by raising the penalty to some amount greater than the value of the car—and enforcing it. This action would violate other principles of classical thought.

Relative Deterrence

Penalties are frequent enough, and serious enough, to encourage other choices. Raising the price of alcohol and reducing liquor store hours may have a general effect of reducing (though not eliminating) alcohol-related problems. Increasing the visibility of police (e.g., by using more marked cars or by making public announcements through the media) may reduce the number of drivers willing to risk speeding. Increasing penalties without increasing surveillance is not successful in reducing the offence rate, despite the commonsense belief that it should (Broadhurst & Loh, 1993, p. 251; Campbell & Ross, 1988).

General Deterrence

The demonstration effect: we see others caught and decide that we will not do what they have done. For instance, the number of airplane skyjackings dropped noticeably following several highly publicized disastrous attempts (Chauncey, 1975, pp. 447–473). The criminal court demonstrates how particular kinds of crime are treated, and parallels can be found in the "courts" of everyday life. Consider, for instance, your own reaction when someone is caught saying something stupid in class or on a date.

General deterrence is a controversial concept. Not only does it sometimes seem unjust to punish an offender so that others will not offend but it is also not clear that general deterrence works well enough to be justifiable. Fattah (1976) reports on some historical cases in which general deterrence apparently failed. Charlie Justice, who devised the clamps used to hold condemned persons in the electric chair, was himself convicted of murder and electrocuted. Alfred Wills, a convict who helped install a prison gas chamber, later killed three people and was gassed.

Specific Deterrence

The direct personal effect: The actual personal experience of punishment encourages different choices. This effect is not as clear-cut as we think. While rewards generally make repetition of the rewarded behaviour more likely, punishments are not

---

Box 4.3 Justice or Deterrence?

Judges find themselves faced with a dilemma when the crime is serious but severe punishment would be unjust, as in a murder trial that took place on Canada's East Coast. In what at first appeared to be a clear-cut case of murder, Jane Stafford admitted to killing her husband while he slept. The evidence showed, however, that Billy Stafford had been an appallingly abusive father and husband—a violent man who made serious death threats against his wife and her children and who blocked all avenues of escape. He was so violent that police were afraid to intervene, even on occasions when Jane Stafford begged for help. Although convicted (of manslaughter, not murder), she served only two months in jail before being paroled. The case attracted a great deal of attention, including one documentary, one feature film, one trial drama (Jonas, 1986), and at least two books (Vallée, 1986, 1995). Although some observers feared that Stafford's light sentence would create an open season on imperfect spouses, no such effect has been observed.

predictably effective. Some punishments actually increase the likelihood of further offences. Punishment gives an offender attention, (negative) recognition, and often a reason for resentment; it can confirm a negative identity and cut off access to legitimate places, people, and jobs.

Restrictive Deterrence

The individual avoids punishable acts selectively (a selective reduction of offending). The concept of restrictive deterrence is a relatively recent entry in the deterrence arena (Gibbs, 1975, p. 33). Jacobs (1996, pp. 409–410) provides the example of drug dealers who stay in business but who will not sell to people they perceive to be possible "narcs" (narcotics officers), or who sell drugs that are not targeted by police (Katyal, 1995). Fear causes them to redirect their activities but does not make them stop.

WHEN DOES DETERRENCE WORK?

Between actual penalties and offence rates is an actor who (1) perceives, or fails to perceive, the penalties; (2) calculates, or does not calculate, the risks and benefits that are involved; and (3) acts or does not act. The main findings from the studies that test deterrence ideas are treated in the following sections.

Certainty

Beccaria argued that the certainty of punishment is much more important than its severity, and later research seems to confirm this. Certainty can be measured in three main ways: (1) by actual rate of detection and punishment, (2) by the beliefs about the rate of punishment held by the population, and (3) by the beliefs of individuals about their own vulnerability to detection and punishment (Green, 1989, pp. 799–800). When proactive policing (increased patrols and targeting of particular groups of offenders) increases the likelihood of apprehension and punishment, the offences will probably decline or become less observable, at least temporarily. A displacement effect may well be observed: offenders move to new locations or engage in less visible deviance.

People who believe they are not vulnerable to the penalties associated with a particular offence are less likely to take them seriously. For example, Claster's (1967) study of juvenile delinquents found that, although the delinquents in the sample assessed the likelihood of *anyone* getting caught in a hypothetical criminal act in about the same way as the nondelinquents did, they assessed their *personal chances* of getting caught as much less. Claster attributed this to a "magical immunity belief" (pp. 80–86). People who feel they are lucky or invulnerable are more likely to offend. In the highly publicized case involving the murder of JoAnn Wilson by (or on behalf of) her husband Colin Thatcher, Thatcher was frequently depicted in the media as a

---

Box 4.4   Faculty Parking and Deterrence

Chambliss (1966) describes a "natural experiment" he observed at a Midwestern American university where parking regulations underwent a sudden and dramatic change. Before the changes were introduced, professors were among the most flagrant offenders. If caught, they seldom paid the one dollar, which was the penalty for violation. The new policy involved stiffer fines, towing, and rigid enforcement—in other words, a dramatic increase in certainty and severity. Thirteen professors in the sample were "frequent violators" before the new policy was introduced. After it went into effect, six of the professors stopped offending altogether, another six reduced their violations, and one began parking in an alley beside his office where he was less likely to be tagged (Chambliss, 1966). In this case, increasing severity and certainty was effective. It is debatable, however, whether such a policy would work as well with offences motivated more by passion than by reason or those strongly supported by a subculture.

---

man who believed—and based on previous experiences had some reason to believe—that he was above the law and invulnerable to its penalties (Bird, 1985).

Severity

Fear of pregnancy or incurable disease probably deters a great deal of sexual deviance but not all. Increasing the severity of punishment may reduce the offence rate, as long as belief in certainty is maintained. For example, a road traffic act introduced in Germany in 1962 provided very stiff penalties for drunk driving. The new regulations were widely publicized, and the number of reported offences immediately declined. However, as drivers became aware that police were not rigorously enforcing the law, violation numbers crept back up to former levels (Middendorf, 1968).

Similar down-then-up findings have been reported in other settings (Green, 1989, pp. 785, 799; Potter, 2000). A study by Phillips (1980) on the effects of well-publicized executions over the 63 years from 1858 to 1921 showed the same pattern: a decline in homicides for about two weeks, followed by an increase in the homicide rate over the next three weeks.

In the early 1970s, a delinquency prevention program called Scared Straight! was introduced by the Juvenile Awareness Project at Rahway State Prison in New Jersey. Fuelling the treatment program was the classical notion of deterrence. Youths were to visit prisons and be shown by convicts just how bad the consequences of delinquency would be, with the expectation that at least some of them would be shocked into abandoning their criminal lifestyles to avoid such a fate. The program, and those modelled after it, provided youths with a no-nonsense view of the humiliations and abuses typical of prison life. The programs were popular because they seemed to provide an inexpensive form of education. However, evaluation has failed to confirm their deterrent effects. In fact, Finkenauer (1982) found that youths who were exposed to the Scared Straight! program had higher rates of offending in the six months that followed than did control group members who were not exposed to it. Clearly, the deterrence effects of severity are overrated.

Celerity (Speed)

A punishment or penalty that is immediate is expected to be more effective than one received long after the offence. In many European countries, traffic fines are levied on the spot. Classical theory would predict this to be a more effective deterrent than receiving notification of an offence in the mail. If, as in most cases, bank robbers are caught only after they have had time to enjoy some of the fruits of their offence, this pattern would tend to reinforce the offence rather than correct it. The clearest support for the importance of celerity has come from laboratory research on animals. Studies of human beings have been quite inconclusive. Human behaviour is most predictably influenced by rewards.

UNANTICIPATED CONSEQUENCES: WHEN DOES DETERRENCE *INCREASE* OFFENDING?

Making an offence such as kidnapping punishable by death may actually contribute to more serious crime, since the kidnapper has even more to lose should the kidnap victim be allowed to live and end up providing useful evidence to the police.

When newer cars were produced with antitheft devices, such as locking steering wheels, the rate of cars being forcefully taken away from their owners increased. Similarly, the number of nighttime safe-cracking raids on banks decreased as security systems evolved and less money was kept overnight, but the number of hold-ups increased.

If the penalty is just as heavy for a small offence as for a larger one, the offender may decide that it is "as good be hanged for a sheep as a lamb" and commit the greater offence (Friedmann & Sjostrom, 1993). In addition, heavy penalties may make juries reluctant to convict, thus reducing the certainty of punishment (Foucault, 1979, p. 14). Heavy penalties can also lead to a brutalization effect, increasing overall levels of violence in the society (Bowers & Pierce, 1980). Parents who try to teach their children not to hit other children but do so by spanking or hitting provide a role model of violence as a means of solving problems. Finally, the process of punishment may have unintended effects on the offender's future ability to find legitimate work and avoid deviant companions. Thus, whenever policymakers offer increased deterrence, as with "tough on crime" policies, it is important to examine the possibility of unanticipated consequences.

On the whole, deviant behaviours that are engaged in for rational (instrumental) reasons (e.g., cheating, stealing, lying, and deceiving for economic gain) are more likely to be affected by changes in the likelihood of detection and punishment than are behaviours with less rationally controlled components (e.g., compulsions and addictions) (Brown et al., 1991, p. 443). Deterrent sanctions also work best on individuals who have low commitment to crime as a way of life (they may have a job and family and be unwilling to risk losing them) and who are older, future-oriented, nonimpulsive, and pessimistic about their chances of criminal success (Brown et al., 1991, p. 451).

THE CLASSICAL INHERITANCE:
MODERN RATIONAL THEORIES

Many modern theories incorporate the utilitarian ideas of Bentham and Beccaria. Here we will look at just two: the utilitarian economic theory of deviance and rational choice theory. Like classical theory, these theories focus more on crime than on other forms of deviance.

ECONOMIC THEORY

In the late 1960s, a paper on the "economy of deviance" by Gary S. Becker (1968) inspired a flood of articles that depicted criminals as being just like everyone else with respect to rationally maximizing "their own self-interest (utility) subject to constraints (prices, incomes) that they face in the marketplace and elsewhere" (Rubin, 1980, p. 13). This version of utilitarianism points to the fact that a "market" for offence opportunities exists, just as a market for legitimate ones does (Ehrlich, 1996). The cost–benefit ratios of various crimes and infractions show that deviants often act *as if* they were the rational actors of the classical model, affected not just by penalties but also by other kinds of costs and rewards.

> The notion of the criminal as a rational calculator will strike many readers as highly unrealistic, especially when applied to criminals having little education or to crimes not committed for pecuniary gain. But ... the test of a theory is not the realism of its assumptions but its predictive power. A growing empirical literature on crime shows that criminals respond to changes in opportunity costs, in the probability of apprehension, in the severity of punishment, and in other relevant variables, as if they were indeed the rational calculators of the economic model—and this regardless of whether the crime is committed for pecuniary gain or out of passion, or by well or by poorly educated people. (Posner, 1977, pp. 164–165)

In this view, it is possible to work out the cost–benefit ratios for particular acts (Lo, 1994). On one side of the ledger, we can put the potential costs: risks (whether from other deviants, from victims, from the act itself, or from legal authorities);

difficulty (distance, skills needed); lost opportunities (the deviant lifestyle may preclude certain legitimate activities); expenses (supporting a particular lifestyle or obtaining weapons, a getaway car, a stash of drugs); and time (planning and executing a plan, recruiting others for group activities). On the other side of the ledger are the benefits, which may be material (property or money) or emotional (revenge, power, respect, excitement, acceptance). Any increase in the likelihood of detection (arrest and exposure) and punishment (imprisonment, societal rejection, job loss) changes the balance of the ledger. One economist has seriously argued that we should raise the costs for possession of pornography. Recognizing that the demand for pornography is relatively inelastic (people still try to get it, even when it is harder to get) Katyal argues that the pornography users will commit fewer crimes (such as rape) if getting the pornography causes them to have less free time. This would, of course, be true if they were in prison for pornography offences (Kahan, 1997, pp. 9–11; Katyal, 1995).

RATIONAL CHOICE THEORY

Rational choice theory (Cornish & Clarke, 1986) was developed mainly by Ronald V. Clarke in the 1980s, partly in response to criticisms of Becker's fairly narrow economic model (Clarke, 1997b, p. 9). Rather than modelling the crime decision in complex mathematical formulas, rational choice models tend to take the form of decision diagrams, tracing the path of the offender's reasoning in each situation or context. Deviance (whether theft or suicide or something else) occurs when, after considering such situational factors as how easy the task will be and how rewarding it will be, the individual decides that the expected cost of violating the rules is outweighed by the expected gain (Clarke & Lester, 1988). Clarke sees crime, for example, as "purposive behavior designed to meet the offender's commonplace needs for such things as money, status, sex, excitement," and argues that "meeting these needs involves the making of (sometimes quite rudimentary) decisions and choices, constrained as they are by the limits of time and ability and the availability of relevant information" (Clarke, 1997b, pp. 9–10).

Rational choice theory includes, however, the possibility that the offender will weigh other elements. Parents, deciding whether to abide by the rules for safe car-seat use, may weigh not only the likelihood of a fine but also the likelihood of a humiliating lecture by the police officer, their personal commitment to good parenting, the possibility of an accident, and the amount of time and energy it will take to install the seats in the approved manner (Carlin & Sandy, 1990). Factors such as group spirit and loyalty, situational ethics, fear, and subcultural norms may compromise the effectiveness of many deterrence programs. People who are furious with one another may not weigh the consequences of their actions (Brown et al., 1991, p. 443), although even in cases apparently characterized by blind rage, deterrence is not completely irrelevant (Katz, 1988).

Rational choice theory is often associated with the policies of situational crime prevention, whereby architecture, social structure, and social meanings are manipulated to reduce the presence of deviance opportunities. Situational crime prevention has been credited with the reduction of shoplifting, cigarette sales to minors (O'Grady, Asbridge, & Abernathy, 2000), and obscene phone calls (Clarke, 1997a), as well as making a dent in hard-core crimes such as bank robbery. An example of situational crime control is Disney World (see Box 4.5).

Women and Rational Choice Theory

Classical theorists and their rational followers have normally spoken of the deviant as male. They have rarely discussed, much less studied, the question of whether these general theories can account for both men's and women's deviance (Daly & Chesney-Lind, 1988; Gelsthorpe & Morris, 1994). On the whole, theorists have tended to accept the folk prejudice that men are instrumental (rational) and women are expressive (emotional), or dominated by their gender in irrational ways, such as committing deviant acts because of sexual frustration or menopausal disorder (Klein, 1996). And yet, it seems clear that, when we eliminate women's deviance that is identified simply because it varies from a male standard, then most women's deviance seems to be economic—that is, women tend to write bad cheques, shoplift, and engage in welfare fraud or prostitution more than they tend to involve themselves in irrational assaults, vandalism, or extreme risk taking. If women have been less active in enterprise crime (such as organized crime cartels), this may be "less a result of single-mindedness in the rational pursuit of crime than because they lack access to organizations and social contacts that would enable them to pursue criminal enterprise more safely and profitably" (Steffensmeier, 1983, p. 1025). Even with respect to sex-trade work, it is only in the past few decades that a substantial literature has emerged suggesting that the choice to engage in this occupation may be a rational rather than a pathological one (Scrambler & Scrambler, 1997, p. xv).

The solutions proposed by rational choice theorists and economic theorists reflect classical thinking in their call for increased speed and certainty of penalties (but not brutalizing penalties) to deter crime. They focus on the ways in which rational choice is bounded: the decisions of deviants are not made in a vacuum. In recent work, an emphasis is placed on the reduction of deviant opportunities, largely through "target-hardening," which makes the unwanted behaviour harder to accomplish (Cohen, Felson, & Land, 1980; Posner, 1977, p. 164), and incapacitation (by imprisonment or banishment), which removes the offender from the target area. Parents, for example, may accomplish both target-hardening and incapacitation by keeping their children in supervised settings and banishing troublesome playmates. Workplaces increasingly use surveillance to deter poor work habits and eliminate employees who are found wanting. Airports use security screening to identify potential terrorists and

Box 4.5   Social Control in the Theme Park

Social control in theme parks is often hidden behind other functions so that it takes the form of help and elicits grateful cooperation rather than resistance. Shearing and Stenning (1985) have written a perceptive account of how the use of special vehicles and strategically placed photographic opportunities at Disney World not only keeps visitors in their designated places but also controls the kinds of images they take away from their experience.

> It will be apparent ... that Disney Productions is able to handle large crowds of visitors in a most orderly fashion. Potential trouble is anticipated and prevented. Opportunities for disorder are minimized by constant instruction, by physical barriers which severely limit the choice of action available, and by the surveillance of omnipresent employees who detect and rectify the slightest deviation.... The coercive edge of Disney's control system is seldom far from the surface, however, and becomes visible the moment the Disney–visitor consensus breaks down, that is, when the visitor attempts to exercise a choice that is incompatible with the Disney order. This can be illustrated by an incident that occurred during a visit to Disney World by Shearing and his daughter, during the course of which she developed a blister on her heel. To avoid further irritation she removed her shoes and began to walk barefooted. They had not progressed ten yards before they were approached by a very personable security guard dressed as a Bahamian police officer with white pith helmet and white gloves that perfectly suited the theme of the area they were moving through (so that he, at first, appeared more like a scenic prop than a security person), who informed them that walking barefoot was, "for the safety of the visitors," not permitted. When informed that, given the blister, the safety of this visitor was likely to be better served by remaining barefooted, at least on the walkways, they were informed that their safety and how best to protect it was a matter for Disney Productions to determine while they were on Disney property, and that unless they complied he would be compelled to escort them out of Disney World. [She put her shoes back on.]
>
>   ... It is thus, paradoxically, not to Orwell's socialist inspired Utopia that we must look for a picture of contemporary control, but to the capitalist-inspired disciplinary model conceived of by Huxley, who, in his *Brave New World*, painted a picture of consensually based control that bears a striking resemblance to the disciplinary control of Disney World and other corporate control systems. Within Huxley's imaginary world people are seduced into conformity by the pleasures offered by the drug "soma" rather than coerced into compliance by threat of Big Brother, just as people today are seduced to conform by the pleasures of consuming the goods that corporate power has to offer. (pp. 301–304)

Source: C. D. Shearing and P. C. Stenning,   "From the Panopticon to Disney World: The Development of Discipline," in *Perspectives in Criminal Law,* edited by A. Doob and E. L. Greenspan (Aurora, ON: Canada Law Book, 1985), pp. 336–347.

resort to the courts to produce incapacitation of offenders. Target-hardening may be physical (the use of electronic merchandise tagging, hidden cameras, and architectural improvements) or educational (warning elderly people about the bank inspector scam and similar rip-offs directed at them by con artists). As the proponents of these rational approaches expand their attention to include issues of opportunity and the analysis of situational elements, their work overlaps with that of control theorists, which we will discuss in Chapter 11.

SUMMARY

Classical theory introduced a radically new view of the deviant as a person who rationally chooses to increase pleasure by acting in a way that violates the rules of society. Classical theorists criticized the existing justice system for providing a social milieu that encouraged crime. Although punishments were severe to the point of being crimes in themselves, their erratic application precluded any deterrent effect.

The classical theorists devoted themselves to elaborate schemes to make punishment more predictable and consistent and to calibrate it at a level severe enough—no more, no less—to counterbalance the rewards of crime. They argued for greater swiftness and certainty of punishment. As a consequence of their work, horrifying public executions began to give way to punishments that could be administered in precisely measured doses.

Classical theorists focused more on crime than on other forms of deviance, more on the criminal justice system than on informal social controls. Modern economic criminologists and rational choice theorists have revitalized the classical view of crime as a rational choice, but they have expanded the rational view to include consideration of the ways in which society structures the opportunities for rule violation. Although classical theory (especially as adjusted by the neoclassical thinkers) has enjoyed considerable support when applied to the actions of apparently rational predators and cheaters, it seems much less able to deal with deviance in which rationality seems absent or diminished. The theory's fundamental assumption of human rationality and free choice came under increasing attack as biological science and the emerging fields of psychology and sociology began to provide alternative assumptions and explanations.

STUDY QUESTIONS

1. How does the image of the deviant change when viewed from classical theory instead of religiously based theory?

2. Was it safe to be a rational thinker in the eighteenth century? What were the dangers?

3. Why did rational thought become more accepted in the eighteenth century than it had been since the fall of Rome?

4. Who were the *philosophes*? Were they scientists?

5. Why were demonic punishments so dramatic, when compared with those favoured by the classical theorists?

6. Who was Jeremy Bentham? What were his inventions like?

7. Why is the panopticon idea often treated as a dangerous one?

8. What is a social contract? How does it justify the use of punishment in society?

9. Canada's criminal justice system still reflects classical and neoclassical thought more than any other influence. Examine a particular case, such as that of Robert Latimer, convicted for the murder of his daughter, who had severe physical disabilities, highlighting how we try to hold individual citizens responsible for their choices (free will) and how we use the courts to send a message (deterrence) to the public.

10. Who were the leaders responsible for bringing in the classical system? Why were these people able to take on the might of the Church when previous critics had been silenced?

11. Is the idea of free will better grounded in empirical reality than the idea of demonic possession? How does one set of beliefs win out over another?

12. It is ironic that much of the strength behind the *philosophes* came from writings that had been preserved by monasteries and that many of the leaders of the classical school were initially educated in religious institutions. To what extent did the Church, while trying to serve its own interests, actually contribute to its own loss of dominance?

13. As we move through this textbook, you will notice that, although all the theories claim to explain deviance, each focuses mainly on a particular kind of deviance. Why was *crime* central to classical thought, while *heresy* was central to demonic thought?

14. Why were executions moved indoors, away from public scrutiny? Why did sanitized, isolated death fit the classical theory better than the demonic theory?

15. No convincing evidence exists that the death penalty is an effective deterrent (compared with long prison sentences) for committing murder. How does classical theory evaluate the death penalty?

16. What kind of injustice was corrected by neoclassical theory? Is there a danger that mitigating and aggravating circumstances can become an excuse for inequality in the court?

17. When does deterrence work? Does our system reflect the classical emphasis on certainty and speed?

18. How is it possible that programs meant to deter crime and deviance can actually increase these problems?

REFERENCES

Beccaria, C. (1995). On Crimes and Punishments. In R. Bellamy (Ed.), *On Crimes and Punishments and Other Essays*. Cambridge, UK: Cambridge University Press. (Original work published in 1765)

Becker, E. (1968). *The Structure of Evil: An Essay on the Unification of the Science of Man.* New York: Free Press.

Becker, G. S. (1968). Crime and Punishment: An Economic Approach. *Journal of Political Economy, 76,* 169–217.

Beirne, P. (1991). Inventing Criminology: The "Science of Man." In Cesare Beccaria's Dei delitte della Pene (1764). *Criminology, 29*(4), 777–820.

Bellamy, R. (1997). Crime and Punishment. *History Review, 28,* 24–26.

Bentham, J. (1978). Offences against One's Self. *Journal of Homosexuality, 3/4*(4/1), 389–405. (Original work published in 1785)

———. (1988). Panopticon (Chapter 3). In J. Bentham (Ed.), *The Rationale of Punishment: Book 5 of Complex Punishments.* (Original work published in 1830)

Bird, H. (1985). *Not Above the Law: The Tragic Story of JoAnn Wilson and Colin Thatcher.* Toronto: Key Porter.

Bowers, W. J. (1974). *Executions in America.* Lexington, MA: Heath.

Bowers, W. J., & Pierce, G. L. (1980). Deterrence or Brutalization: What Is the Effect of Executions? *Crime and Delinquency, 26*(October), 453–484.

Broadhurst, R., & Loh, N. (1993). The Phantom of Deterrence: The Crime (Serious and Repeat Offenders) Sentencing Act. *Australia and New Zealand Journal of Criminology, 26*(3), 251–271.

Brown, S. E., Esbensen, F.-A., & Geis, G. (1991). *Criminology: Explaining Crime and Its Context.* Cincinnati, OH: Anderson.

Campbell, D. T., & Ross, H. L. (1988). The Connecticut Crackdown on Speeding. In E. S. Overman (Ed.), *Methodology and Epistemology of Social Science: Selected Papers.* Chicago: University of Chicago Press.

Carlin, P., & Sandy, R. (1990). The Value of Time and the Effect of Fines on Child Car Safety Seat Usage. *Applied Economics, 22,* 463–476.

Chambliss, W. J. (1966). The Deterrent Effect of Punishment. *Crime and Delinquency, 12,* 70–75.

Chartier, G. (2000). Inside the SHU. *Let's Talk (Correctional Service of Canada), 25*(3), 2–5.

Chauncey, R. (1975). Deterrence, Certainty, Severity and Skyjacking. *Criminology, 12*(February), 447–473.

Clarke, R. V. (1997a). Deterring Obscene Phone Callers: The New Jersey Experience. In R. V. Clarke (Ed.), *Situational Crime Prevention: Successful Case Studies* (2nd ed.). Guilderland, NY: Harrow and Heston.

———. (1997b). Introduction. In R. V. Clarke (Ed.), *Situational Crime Prevention: Successful Case Studies* (2nd ed.). Guilderland, NY: Harrow and Heston.

Clarke, R. V., & Lester, D. (1988). *Suicide: Closing the Exits.* New York: Springer Verlag.

Claster, D. S. (1967). Comparison of Risk Perception between Delinquents and Nondelinquents. *Journal of Criminal Law, Criminology and Political Science, 58*(March), 80–86.

Cohen, L. E., Felson, M., & Land, K. C. (1980). Property Crime Rates in the United States: A Macrodynamic Analysis, 1947–1977, with Ex-Ante Forecasts for the Mid-1980s. *American Journal of Sociology, 86*(July), 90–118.

Cornish, D. B., & Clarke, R. V. (1986). *The Reasoning Criminal.* New York: Springer.

Daly, K., & Chesney-Lind, M. (1988). Feminism and Criminology. *Justice Quarterly, 5*(4), 497–538.

Dent, N. J. H. (1988). *Rousseau: An Introduction to His Psychological, Social and Political Theory.* Oxford, UK: Basil Blackwell.

Dobbs, B. J. T. (1975). *The Foundations of Newton's Alchemy.* Cambridge, NY: Cambridge University Press.

Ehrlich, I. (1996). Crime, Punishment and the Market for Offenses. *Journal of Economic Perspectives, 10,* 43–67.

Fattah, E. A. (1976). *Deterrence: A Review of the Literature, Fear of Punishment.* Ottawa: Law Reform Commission of Canada.

Figala, K. (1977). Newton as Alchemist. *History of Science, 15,* 102–137.

Finkenauer, J. (1982). *Scared Straight! and the Panacea Phenomenon.* Englewood Cliffs, NJ: Prentice-Hall.

Foucault, M. (1979). *Discipline and Punish.* New York: Vintage.

Friedmann, D., & Sjostrom, W. (1993). Hanged for a Sheep: The Economics of Marginal Deterrence. *Journal of Legal Studies, 12*(June), 345–366.

Gay, P. (1966). *Age of Enlightenment.* New York: Time Inc.

Geis, G. (1973). Jeremy Bentham. In H. Mannheim (Ed.), *Pioneers in Criminology* (2nd ed.). Montclair, NJ: Patterson Smith.

Gelsthorpe, L., & Morris, A. (Eds.). (1994). *Feminist Perspectives in Criminology.* Milton Keynes, UK: Open University Press.

Gibbs, J. P. (1975). *Crime, Punishment and Deterrence.* New York: Elsevier.

Green, D. E. (1989). Past Behavior as a Measure of Actual Future Behavior: An Unresolved Issue in Perceptual Deterrence Research. *Journal of Criminal Law and Criminology, 80*(3), 781–804.

Henry, S., & Milovanovic, D. (1996). *Constitutive Criminology: Beyond Postmodernism.* Thousand Oaks, CA: Sage.

Hobbes, T. (1881). *Leviathan.* Oxford, UK: James Thornton.

Hood, S., & Crowley, G. (1995). *Marquis de Sade for Beginners.* Cambridge, UK: Icon Books (Penguin).

Ignatieff, M. (1978). *A Just Measure of Pain: The Penitentiary in the Industrial Revolution, 1750–1850.* New York: Columbia University Press.

Jacobs, B. A. (1996). Crack Dealers and Restrictive Deterrence: Identifying Narcs. *Criminology, 4*(3), 409–431.

Jenkins, P. (1984). *Crime and Justice: Issues and Ideas.* Monterey, CA: Brooks/Cole.

Jonas, G. (Ed.). (1986). *The Scales of Justice: Ten Famous Criminal Cases Recreated* (Vol. 2). Toronto: Lester and Orpen Dennys/CBC Enterprises.

Kahan, D. M. (1997). Response: Between Economics and Sociology: The New Path of Deterrence. *Michigan Law Review, 95*(8), 2477–2497.

Kant, I. (1977). What Is Enlightenment? In H. Reiss (Ed.), *Kant's Political Writings.* Cambridge, UK: Cambridge University Press. (Original work published in 1784)

Katyal, N. (1995). Deterrence's Difficulty. *Michigan Law Review, 95*(8), 2385.

Katz, J. (1988). *Seductions of Crime: Moral and Sensual Attractions in Doing Evil.* New York: Basic Books.

Klein, D. (1996). The Etiology of Female Crime. In J. Muncie, E. McLaughlin, & M. Langan (Eds.), *Criminological Perspectives: A Reader.* London, UK: Sage.

Lerner, L. S., & Gosselin, E. A. (1986). Galileo and the Specter of Bruno. *Scientific American, 255*(5), 126–133.

Lo, L. (1994). Exploring Teenage Shoplifting Behavior: A Choice and Constraint Approach. *Environment and Behavior, 26*(5), 613–639.

Maestro, M. (1972). *Voltaire and Beccaria.* New York: Octagon.

———. (1973). *Cesare Beccaria and the Origins of Penal Reform.* Philadelphia, PA: Temple University Press.

Middendorf, W. (1968). *The Effectiveness of Punishment Especially in Relation to Traffic Offences.* South Hackensack, NJ: Fred E. Rothman.

Newman, G. (1983). *Just and Painful: A Case for the Corporal Punishment of Criminals.* New York: Free Press.

———. (1985). *The Punishment Response* (2nd ed.). Albany, NY: Harrow and Heston.

O'Grady, W., Asbridge, M., & Abernathy, T. (2000). Illegal Tobacco Sales to Youth: A View from Rational Choice Theory. *Canadian Journal of Criminology, 42*(1), 1–20.

Paolucci, H. (1963). Translator's Introduction to *Cesare Beccaria: On Crimes and Punishments.* New York: Bobbs Merrill.

Peters, E. (1989). *Inquisition.* Berkeley, CA: University of California.

Pfohl, S. (1985). *Images of Deviance and Social Control: A Sociological History.* New York: McGraw-Hill.

Phillips, D. P. (1980). The Deterrent Effect of Capital Punishment: New Evidence on an Old Controversy. *American Journal of Sociology, 86,* 139–148.

Posner, R. (1977). *Economic Analysis of Law* (2nd ed.). Boston: Little, Brown.

Potter, G. W. (2000). Cost, Deterrence, Incapacitation, Brutalization and the Death Penalty: The Scientific Evidence: Statement Before the Joint Interim Health and Welfare Committee. *The Advocate, 22*(1), 24–29.

Radzinowicz, L. (1948). *The Movement for Reform* (Vol. 1). London, UK: Stevens.

Raulston Saul, J. (1992). *Voltaire's Bastards: The Dictatorship of Reason in the West.* New York: Vintage Books.

Redondi, P. (1987). *Galileo: Heretic.* Princeton, NJ: Princeton University Press.

Rennie, Y. (1978). *The Search for Criminal Man.* Lexington, MA: Lexington Books.

Rubin, P. H. (1980). The Economics of Crime. In R. Andreano & J. J. Siegfried (Eds.), *The Economics of Crime*. New York: John Wiley.

Russell, J. B. (1988). *The Prince of Darkness: Radical Evil and the Power of Good in History*. Ithaca, NY: Cornell University Press.

Schneider, A. L., & Laurie, E. (1990). Specific Deterrence, Rational Choice, and Decision Heuristics: Applications in Juvenile Justice. *Social Science Quarterly, 71*(3), 585–601.

Scrambler, G., & Scrambler, A. (Eds.). (1997). *Rethinking Prostitution: Purchasing Sex in the 1990s*. London, UK: Routledge.

Shearing, C. D., & Stenning, P. C. (1985). From the Panopticon to Disney World: The Development of Discipline. In A. Doob & E. L. Greenspan (Eds.), *Perspectives in Criminal Law: Essays in Honor of John L. L. J. Edwards* (pp. 336–347). Aurora, ON: Canada Law Book.

Sobel, D. (1999). *Galileo's Daughter: A Historical Memoir of Science, Faith and Love*. Toronto: Penguin, Viking.

Steffensmeier, D. (1983). Organization Properties and Sex-Segregation in the Underworld: Building a Sociological Theory of Sex Differences in Crime. *Social Forces, 61*(4), 1010–1032.

Vallée, B. (1986). *Life with Billy*. Toronto: McClelland Bantam-Seal Books.

———. (1995). *Life after Billy*. Toronto: McClelland Bantam-Seal Books.

Webster, C. (1996). *From Paracelsus to Newton: Magic and the Making of Modern Science*. New York: Barnes and Noble.

CHAPTER 5

BIOLOGICAL AND PHYSIOLOGICAL EXPLANATIONS OF DEVIANCE

It is difficult to explain some kinds of deviance, such as gender-bending or delusional thinking, in classical terms. Consider the following excerpts:

> She was beautiful, seductively beautiful in a streetwise way. Her big eyes sparkled. Her skin glowed. A broken incisor tooth punctuated her smile and gave her a naughty look.
>
> "I dance, I do lip sync, and I emcee," she said. "Shit like that. My mama got the name Chablis off a wine bottle.... 'Ooooo, *Chablis*. That's nice. I like that name.' And mama said, 'Then take it, baby. Just call yourself Chablis from now on.' So ever since then I've been Chablis."
>
> "A cool white wine for a cool black girl," I said.
>
> "Y-e-e-e-s, child!"
>
> "What was your name before that?" I asked.
>
> "Frank," she said. (Berendt, 1994, p. 97)

> Jack Freedman, a "very structured, very business-orientated ... nonstop go, go, go" and basically "unaffectionate" man (according to his daughter), suddenly started to change. He ditched his business suits in exchange for brightly colored clothes, took art classes, and became warm and accessible. He began to have "open periods" of intense awareness of color and nature. At the same time, he had "closed periods" of depression, anger and antisocial behavior, including purposely bumping into strangers on the street and stealing tips from restaurant tables. Mr. Freedman has been diagnosed as having a degenerative brain disorder. (Based on an ABC *20/20* program, April 25, 1999, which included interviews with Mr. Freedman, his daughter, and his psychiatrist.)

Positivism (sometimes also called scientism) is based on the belief that the methods of natural science should be adapted to the study of human beings. Positivist theory assumes that knowledge can be discovered only through sensory experience, observation, and experiment. Its early proponents claimed, sometimes only half-truthfully, that they employed the scientific method of sampling, controls, and analysis. When the assumptions and techniques used in the scientific study of rocks, plants, and insects were applied to human affairs, the result was an entirely new view of our species, one that seemed to address kinds of deviance not well explained by classical theory, such as craziness, self-injurious compulsions, or extreme impulsiveness.

Although classical thinkers frequently invoked the spirit of science, most of their work was not scientific, either because it was untested by empirical data or because no effort was made to collect empirical data in a disciplined, systematic manner. Thus, positivism—and the "positive school of criminology" it gave rise to—represents what Kuhn (1970) terms a paradigm shift. It constituted a new kind of lens through which human nature and human behaviour could be understood (see Table 5.1).

This paradigm achieved dominant status as an explanation of deviance in the late nineteenth and early twentieth centuries, when sociological versions of positivism challenged it with yet another paradigm. Sociology still competes vigorously, and sometimes quite acrimoniously, with the biologically oriented paradigms. Students should be aware that this competition causes many biologically oriented theorists to deny the importance of sociological insights and many sociologists to deny the relevance of biology to social action (Udry, 1995).

Some of the early attempts to discover the biological level of social action were crude and fraudulent examples of deviance in science, and some terrible uses have been made of this fraudulent material by racist, sexist, and homophobic policymakers. As we will show (see Box 5.5), the perspective itself has sometimes been "deviantized." Nonetheless, it is likely that a final theory of social action will have to incorporate biological variables.

Understanding the contribution of biological theories, and their limits, is particularly important given the fact that the average citizen is bombarded with psychobiological interpretations in newspapers, television documentaries, soap operas, films, and other media. Whether we agree with these theories or not, it is important to

Table 5.1　Comparison of Classical and Positivist Schools

	Classical	Positivist
Time of dominance	1700–1800	1800–1900
Conception of deviance	Violation of social contract, crime	Pathology, constitutional inferiority, sickness
Explanation	Free will, balance of punishment	Determinism, symptoms of constitutional faults
Remedies	Swift, certain, graduated punishment	Treatment, separation, elimination

understand and evaluate them. As we will show, none of the biological or psychological theories explains so much that no room remains for other contributions.

Positivists assume that, underlying all empirical reality, there are discoverable laws that can be used to explain everything in nature, including human behaviour. A person whose every action was a symptom of dark, biological impulses, evolutionary position, and environmental forces replaced the hedonistic self-directed actor depicted in classical thought. This view of human beings argued that all behaviour is determined by forces no individual ever fully controls. Free will, in this view, is nothing but an illusion through which human beings try to establish their superiority over other animals.

> The illusion of a free human will (the only miraculous factor in the eternal ocean of cause and effect) leads to the assumption that one can choose freely between virtue and vice. How can you still believe in the existence of a free will when modern psychology, armed with all the instruments of positive modern research, denies that there is any free will and demonstrates that every act of a human being is the result of an interaction between the personality and environment of man?... The positive school of criminology maintains, on the contrary, that it is not the criminal who wills; in order to be a criminal it is rather necessary that the individual should find himself permanently or transitorily in such personal, physical and moral conditions, and live in such an environment, which become for

Box 5.1   Crime and Punishment in *Erewhon*

The illogic of punishing sickness was parodied by the English humorist Samuel Butler in his 1923 novel *Erewhon Revisited Twenty Years Later* (*Erewhom* is an anagram for nowhere). In Erewhon, criminals receive treatment while sick people are punished.

> Prisoner at the bar, you have been accused of the great crime of labouring under pulmonary consumption [lung cancer or tuberculosis], and after an impartial trial before a jury of your countrymen, you have been found guilty.... I find that though you are now only twenty-three years old, you have been imprisoned on no less than fourteen occasions for illnesses of a more or less hateful character; in fact, it is not too much to say that you have spent the great part of your life in jail. It is all very well for you to say that you came of unhealthy parents, and had a severe accident in childhood which permanently undermined your constitution; excuses such as these are the ordinary refuge of the criminal.... You are a bad and dangerous person, and stand branded in the eyes of your fellow-countrymen with one of the most heinous known offenses ... had not the capital punishment for consumption been abolished, I would certainly inflict it now. (1923/1967, pp. 77–78)

Butler simultaneously attacks and pokes fun at the practice of sentencing criminals, who were seen as being no more responsible for their actions than were sick people for their symptoms.

him a chain of cause and effect, externally and internally, that disposes
him toward crime. (Enrico Ferri, 1897, quoted in Grupp, 1968)

Just as the classical theorists satirized the practice of curing earthquakes by
burning heretics, so the positivists ridiculed the classical notion that deviance was
willed and thus could be deterred by punishment.

SOCIAL DARWINISM

The English philosopher Herbert Spencer (1820–1903) coined the phrase "survival of
the fittest" to describe the implications of evolutionary theory for human society.
Spencer argued that every field—industry, art, science, or human biology—reflected a
pattern of development from lower to higher, from less complex to more complex, from
inferior to superior. He took from Darwin's *Origin of the Species* (1859) and *Descent
of Man* (1871) the notion that the development in human societies followed the principles of natural selection through competition. The more fit competitors win, survive,
and procreate, while the less fit die out—unless, of course, the fit commit race suicide
by not breeding or the unfit (the poor, the criminal, and those with mental illnesses) are
artificially supported by well-meaning but misguided people. Social Darwinists believed
that those living organisms—whether human, plant, or animal—best able to adapt to a
particular set of living conditions were the ones with the greatest chances of survival.
Darwin's concept of evolution was used by Social Darwinists, including sociologist
William Graham Sumner, to justify policies that reduced the chances of survival among
those designated as "unfit" (Dennett, 1995; Eldredge, 1995).

Social Darwinists reason that the powerful and rich are that way because they are
more "fit," not in Darwin's original meaning of reproductive capacity but in a social
meaning of having health, intelligence, and good moral qualities. If England dominated the world with its imperialist system, it was because the English were a superior race who had to carry the burden of responsibility for those less fit to govern
themselves. Fitness became a synonym not only for healthy but also for deserving.
Darwinian ideas, more extreme than Darwin's own, still play a notable role in
modern social thought.

MENDEL AND THE DISCOVERY OF GENETIC INHERITANCE

Gregor Mendel (1822–84) studied plant seeds and discovered the genetic principles
whereby variations of colour and size are transmitted by heredity through predictable
mutations and combinations of genes. This finding was often misinterpreted as
meaning that environment played no role in determining individual traits.
Consequently, there were those who attributed "feeblemindedness," deviance, and
criminal behaviour entirely to heredity (Jeffrey, 1990, p. 181); for them, heritable was
synonymous with inevitable and immutable (Gould, 1981, p. 156).

The popularity of Social Darwinist and Mendelian genetic explanations grew throughout the nineteenth century and reached its apex by the early twentieth century. In the 1930s, Hitler used these theories to establish breeding programs for the Aryan race, including the infamous *Lebensborn* program, and to justify the mass execution and abuse of millions of Jews, Gypsies, homosexuals, Jehovah's Witnesses, and others whose politics or physical traits were interpreted as signs of degeneracy and unfitness (Lilienthal, 1985; Toland, 1977, p. 1046n).

BORN CRIMINAL THEORY

The idea that criminality was not only inborn but also marked a person's appearance was common in antiquity. The newly emerging criminal anthropology promised the possibility of using physical features to identify actual and potential criminals.

The earliest researchers sought to find statistical connections between external characteristics such as facial features, skull size, and body shape. Later, science would move into the less visible realms of genes, blood-sugar counts, and neurochemical markers. In roughly chronological order, the early efforts took the form of physiognomy, phrenology, craniometry, atavism, and degeneracy.

PHYSIOGNOMY

As far back as Aristotle, facial features were used to draw analogies between humans and animals. If a person looked like a bull, she would be stubborn and tenacious; if he looked like a lion, he would be brave.

Physiognomy, the science of judging character based on facial features, had widespread support and appeal in the late-eighteenth and early-nineteenth centuries. John Caspar Lavater (1741–1801) produced a detailed four-volume map of the human face, which associated various shapes and structures with specific personality traits. In this work, entitled *Physiognomical Fragments* (1775), criminals were characterized as tending to have shifty eyes, weak chins, and large, arrogant noses. A physiognomist's report on Lizzie Borden, said to have murdered her parents with an axe in 1892 (but acquitted in court), was typical of reports done at the time. The physiognomist diagnosed from Borden's face that she was "high tempered, secretive, and fond of property" and that strongly suggested she had committed the crime (Lane, 1992, p. 467, from *Phrenological Journal*, 1892). Although physiognomy may be used as a quick indicator of conditions like Down syndrome, its value today is negligible.

PHRENOLOGY

Phrenology (*phrenos* = mind, *logos* = study) was most popular in the mid-nineteenth century. It was based on the theory that functions such as cautiousness, firmness, benevolence, mirthfulness, and intellect were located in distinct parts of the brain (see

Figure 5.1), and that the stronger the functions, the larger their physical manifestations. The enlarged parts, it was held, would push the skull out so that a trained technician could feel the bumps and thus "read" the person's character (Brown, Esbensen, & Geis, 1991, p. 231). In the early nineteenth century, Franz Joseph Gall (1758–1828) and his student and colleague, Johann Caspar Spurzheim (1776–1832), published a two-volume work on phrenology, presenting it as a new science (Leek, 1970). If a person was cruel or benevolent, the dominant quality would appear as a bump in the contour of the skull in the appropriately mapped area. In the normal person, the higher faculties of friendship, religion, and intellect were dominant. Deviant tendencies might reveal themselves through bumps in the "combativeness" area or the "amativeness" area (Fink, 1938, pp. 1–19). In the mid-nineteenth century, it was customary to make a cast of the head of executed criminals so that degenerate features of the skull could be recorded (Lane, 1992, pp. 157, 463). Authors as diverse as Balzac, Hawthorne, and Conan Doyle made use of phrenology for characterization, in much the same way that a modern novelist would incorporate insights from modern psychology. For example, on meeting Sherlock Holmes (the cerebral hero of deductive detection) for the first time, arch-villain Moriarty comments that Holmes has "less frontal development than I should have expected" (Wohl, 2000, p. 1).

Figure 5.1   The Brain as Seen by Phrenologists

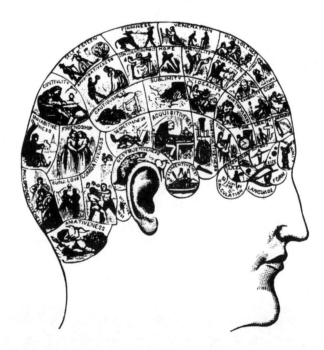

Source: Reproduced by permission of the Bettmann Archive.

A phrenological analysis of Adolf Hitler by Alfred Richter, which was published in the late 1930s with the approval of Hitler's National Socialist Party, claimed that Hitler's facial expression was that of "a genius, a creative, spiritual leader, powerful, tenacious, filled with great love, unspeakable pain, and renunciation," while the upper part of his head showed "universal love, lofty religion, beauty and nobility of nature" (Richter, 1938, cited in Fest, 1970).

Long since discredited as a science, phrenology booths can be found today at psychic fairs, along with those offering palmistry, astrology, tarot cards, and other forms of fortune telling.

CRANIOMETRY

Craniometry was a system of classifying human types based on skull measurement, particularly measurement of the size of the skull. Leading practitioners like Swedish anthropologist Anders Rolf Retzius thought of themselves as objective observers who merely recorded and honestly interpreted the weights and volumes of the brains and skulls they studied. At first, larger brains were believed to indicate greater brain activity (and thus the superiority of the individual), but when it was found, for example, that the largest female brain ever recorded belonged to a woman who had killed her husband, the theory had to be revised (Gould, 1981, p. 94). Eventually, most craniologists held that the brain that was too large or too small could be the sign of deviance in the individual.

Craniometric data usually corroborated prevailing social, ethnic, national, and gender biases. Gustave Le Bon, a popular French psychologist and follower of craniologist Broca, put forth these ideas:

> [T]here are a large number of women whose brains are closer in size to those of gorillas than to the most developed men's brains.... All psychologists who have studied the intelligence of women, as well as poets and novelists, recognize today that they represent the most inferior forms of human evolution and that they are closer to children and savages than to an adult civilized man. They excel in fickleness, inconstancy, absence of thought and logic, and incapacity to reason. (quoted in Gould 1981, pp. 60–61)

The limits of craniometry were soon reached, as most investigators turned to more defensible and reliable indicators of human characteristics. Some researchers still refer to this kind of data (see Box 5.5), but they face serious criticism for it.

LOMBROSO'S THEORY OF ATAVISM

The controversial theories of Cesare Lombroso (1835–1909) have inspired more commentary, praise, and condemnation than those of any other criminologist (Wolfgang, 1972, p. 232). Though often credited with being the father of criminology, his biological approach to crime causation, sometimes called forensic anthropology, proved full of unlikely assumptions and questionable statistical tests. Central to Lombroso's conception of crime was his theory of biological atavism. According to this theory, the criminal (or troublemaker) was an evolutionary throwback, a reversion to a more primitive stage in human evolution. Physical characteristics (*stigmata*) such as sloping foreheads, bushy eyebrows, and protruding jaws and cheekbones were evidence of atavism and its attendant deviant propensity. Different kinds of criminality were indicated by head and body size, hair colour, and abnormalities of the ears, nose, arms, and body. For example, "ravishers have short hands, medium-sized brains, and narrow foreheads; there is a predominance of light hair with abnormalities of the genital organs and of the nose" (Lane, 1992, p. 161; Lombroso, 1885). Lombroso's follower Enrico Ferri coined the term "born criminal" to describe the biologically determined criminal type (Brown et al., 1991, p. 233).

Just as Beccaria had turned against the theological and supernatural theories that were part of his education, Lombroso found himself increasingly at odds with the classical ideology of free will dominant in Italian academic circles of his period. He was influenced by evolutionary theory through the work of Auguste Comte (1798–1853), who argued that society goes through evolutionary stages just as the human species does; by the biological work of Gall; and by the French alienist (psychiatrist) B. A. Morel, who argued that degeneracy was expressed in epilepsy, insanity, mental deficiency, and crime (Wolfgang, 1972, pp. 234, 242).

While working as a physician in the Italian army, Lombroso systematically studied some 3000 soldiers. He observed, "From the beginning I was struck by a characteristic that distinguished the honest soldier from his vicious comrade: the extent to which the latter was tattooed and the indecency of the designs that covered his body" (quoted in Lombroso-Ferrero, 1911/1972, p. xii). In Lombroso's terms, tattooing reflected primitive people's love of adornment and insensitivity to pain (Wolfgang, 1972, p. 245).

This early work inspired Lombroso to test the theory that physical and psychological traits were correlated. Soon he was conducting anthropometric studies of inmates and inmate cadavers in Italian prisons. In one of these prisons, he uncovered the skull of a notorious brigand, which he used in his public lectures to illustrate the idea of the atavistic criminal.

> This was a revelation. At the sight of that skull I seemed to see all of a sudden, lighted up as a vast plain under a flaming sky, the problem of the nature of the criminal—an atavistic being who reproduces in his person the ferocious instincts of primitive humanity and inferior animals. Thus were explained anatomically the enormous jaws, high cheek bones, prominent supercilliary arches, solitary lines in the palms, extreme size of the orbits, handle shaped or sessile ears found in criminals, savages and apes, insensitivity to pain, extremely acute sight, tattooing, excessive idle-

ness, love of orgies, and the irresistible craving for evil for its own sake, the desire not only to extinguish life in the victim but to mutilate the corpse, tear its flesh, and drink its blood. (Lombroso-Ferrero, 1911/1972, pp. xiv–xvi)

In addition, he used the case of Misdea, a young Italian soldier, as an illustration of the epileptiform nature of criminality. Misdea had suddenly attacked and killed eight officers and men. He then fell into a deep sleep for 12 hours and awoke with no memory of his deed (Wolfgang, 1972, p. 248). Lombroso classified all criminals as "epileptoids" on a scale in which epileptic was at the top, followed by criminal moral imbecile, born criminal, criminaloid (occasional criminal), and criminal by passion (Lombroso, 1885, cited by Wolfgang, 1972, p. 254).

Lombroso did not claim that all criminals were born criminals. He adjusted his argument repeatedly to meet the criticisms of other researchers. He finally proposed that about 30 to 40 percent of criminals took this form, while the rest (i.e., those without epilepsy, mental illness, or atavistic stigmata) were brought to crime by force of circumstance (Gould, 1981, p. 132). Lombroso believed, however, that born criminals were the most serious and chronic offenders. Lombroso's ideas entered into the public awareness and literature of his time. Leo Tolstoy's novel *Resurrection*, written after Tolstoy had an argument with Lombroso, uses its story to denounce Lobrosian theories (Mazzarello, 2001). Lombroso stimulated the interest of contemporary sociologist Émile Durkheim in the study of deviance and crime (Bosc, 1999).

Lombrosian Theory and Social Control

Lombrosian theory became a factor in determining guilt or innocence in the courtroom and in deciding how a convicted criminal should be treated. Called as an expert witness in a case in which the court was trying to determine which of two stepsons had killed a woman, Lombroso testified that one of them was the perfect type of born criminal. In *Criminal Man* (1911/1972), he described this man (who was convicted) as having "enormous jaws, frontal sinuses and zygomata, thin upper lip, huge incisors, unusually large head, tactile obtuseness with censorial manicinism" (p. 436). The precise meanings of these terms are lost to us, but it is clear that the signs of atavism had replaced warts, black cats, and unusual abilities as indicators of criminality.

When it came to social control of the born criminal, relatively few options existed. Neither suffering for salvation (the demonic approach) nor the manipulation of free will (classical theory) was appropriate for the born criminal; this left as possible solutions execution, isolation, or treatment. At the time, few treatments were available, especially if the problem was seen as congenital. Lombrosians tended to favour the death penalty or isolation in institutions for the insane. Mussolini supporters Raffaele Garofalo (1852–1934) and Enrico Ferri, both followers of Lombroso, argued for the elimination of the unfit in terms similar to those invoked by the Nazis (Brown et al., 1991, p. 236).

Box 5.2   Lombroso and the Female Offender

In every country that keeps records of such things, women have much lower rates of criminality than do men. To be logically consistent, Lombroso should have concluded from this that women were more evolutionarily advanced than men (Hagan, 1985, pp. 76–78). Instead he argued that women were nearer to their atavistic origins than were men but that criminal propensities in women were neutralized by their natural passivity, which he attributed to the "immobility of the ovule [egg] compared with the zoosperm [sperm]" (Lombroso & Ferrero, 1895, p. 109). The typical woman, Lombroso claimed, was characterized by piety, maternal feelings, sexual coldness, and an underdeveloped intelligence. Criminal women, on the other hand, were either born with masculine qualities (intelligence and activeness) conducive to criminal activity or encouraged to develop these qualities through such things as education and exercise. Furthermore, Lombroso wrote, "[Women's] evil tendencies are more numerous and more varied than men's, but generally remain latent. When they are awakened and excited they produce results proportionately greater" (quoted in Wolfgang, 1972, p. 255).

Lombroso argued that when not restrained by religious sentiments, maternal feelings, and stupidity, the "innocuous semi-criminal present in the normal woman" emerges as a born criminal "worse than any man" (Lombroso-Ferrero, 1911/1972, quoted in Wolfgang, 1972, p. 255).

For the most part, Lombroso found that women escaped the "atavistic laws of degeneration." He felt that prostitutes were the one exception and that they were the closest to the typical representative of criminality, even to a greater extent than the male homicidal robber (Wolfgang, 1972, p. 254). Autopsies of women from Italian prisons showed criminal women of Lombroso's day were more masculine, with darker skin, a more "virile cranium," and excess body hair. Today, these results would be interpreted as evidence of the hard lives lived by women who ran afoul of the law and of prejudice against poor migrant Sicilians, who were, overall, darker than northern Italians.

The Displacement of Lombrosian Theory

Paul Topinard, a contemporary of Lombroso, observed that Lombroso's atavistic criminals looked much like Topinard's own collection of friends (Brown et al., 1991, p. 237), concluding that those symptoms of degeneracy were not valid indicators of behaviour. No matter how accurate Lombroso's measurements of ears, noses, and brains were, this evidence did not support the conclusion that particular sizes, weights, and shapes of anatomical parts were associated with particular criminal proclivities. In addition, Lombroso was severely criticized for using ill-defined measurements, unwarranted deductions, and inadequately chosen control groups, as well as for relying too frequently both on reasoning by analogy and on anecdotal illustration.

Charles Buckman Goring (1870–1919), a doctor and medical officer in the British prison system, accepted Lombroso's challenge to do a real test of the theory of atavism. With the help of the well-known statistician Karl Pearson, he collected, beginning in 1902, biometric data on more than 3000 English chronic offenders. In comparing these convicts with control groups made up of hospital patients, Cambridge and Oxford students, and British Royal engineers (military), Goring found that the physical and mental constitutions of both criminal and law-abiding persons of the same age, stature, class, and intelligence were virtually identical with respect to Lombroso's atavistic stigmata. Goring showed that Lombroso's version of the "anthropological monster" did not exist (Goring, 1913). Goring continued to believe, however, that offenders, who had narrower heads than the controls and appeared to be "feeble-minded," were genetically inferior to normal people. Aspects of the "criminal man," from his "bulbous fingertips" to his "malformed ears," continue to surface in modern works on criminal profiling (Lane, 1992, p. 165).

Lombroso's chief long-term contribution to criminology and the study of deviance was not his atavism theory or his methods, but rather the fact that he inspired others to observe firsthand and systematically what criminals looked and sounded like, what they had in common, and how they differed from others.

EUGENICS AND THEORIES OF DEGENERACY

Eugenics

The term *eugenics* (good birth) was coined in 1883 by Sir Francis Galton (1822–1911) (see Figure 5.2), who saw selective breeding as the antidote to the social problems produced by those who were genetically unfit. Positive eugenic policies were proposed to encourage those with the best genes to reproduce. Negative eugenics involved programs to exclude inferior populations (immigration controls), compulsory sterilization programs for those identified as unfit, and, in Germany, extermination programs for the ethnically, mentally, and politically unfit.

Although eugenics spread to include people in many countries, most of the work was done in the United States and Germany, and it was in these countries that it came to dominate policy.

U.S. eugenicists primarily used family pedigree charts provided by family members. Based on a study of such charts, Charles E. Davenport claimed that "thalassophilia" (love of the sea) was a sex-linked gene (since only males became naval officers). Davenport also concluded that alcoholism, pauperism, prostitution, and "train wrecking" were determined by genes. In the 1920s the American Eugenics Society (co-founded by Davenport) sponsored "Fitter Families Contests" at state fairs across the United States. Just as cows and sheep were appraised by judges at the fairs, so were human entrants (Horgan, 1993).

Eugenics also played a role in Canada, where it was used to justify policies of sterilization practised on people defined as "morons," who were often simply people from deprived backgrounds or those suffering from conditions such as deafness or the after-effects of polio. Eugenic ideas were also adopted by some early Canadian feminists,

Figure 5.2   Francis Galton in 1864

Source: Mary Evans Picture Library. Reprinted with permission.

who wanted to improve women's status by ensuring that women had fewer but better babies. Nellie McClung, for example, who was a prominent figure in the battle to give women the vote, was also a strong supporter of Alberta's Sexual Sterilization Act. An example of the impact of this legislation is the case of Leilani Muir, a woman who was sterilized in 1959 and who in 1996 become the first victim to successfully sue the government of Alberta for taking away her right to have a child.

Eugenicists have tended to form close attachments with those developing new techniques of psychometrics—IQ tests, MRI brain scanning techniques, and similar measures. This empiricism lends a spurious scientific veneer to work that typically involves huge leaps between empirical evidence and conclusions (Allen, 1996).

Robert Dugdale and the Jukes

In 1875, a year before the publication of Lombroso's *Delinquent Man,* an American investigator for the Prison Association of New York named Robert Dugdale (1841–83) published a study of a so-called degenerate family entitled *The Jukes: A Study in Crime, Pauperism, Disease, and Heredity.* In 1873, Dugdale had been present in a Kingston, New York, court when a youth was being tried for receiving stolen goods. Five of the youth's relatives were present, and the group struck Dugdale as a particularly depraved-looking clan. The family, it turned out, lived in caves in a nearby lake region and had a reputation for all sorts of criminal and moral wrong-doing (Adams, 1955, p. 411). Although the accused youth was acquitted, Dugdale's opinion was already formed. He made inquiries about relatives of the youth who were in court and concluded that one was a burglar, two had been involved in pushing a youth over a cliff, and two were "harlots" (defined by Dugdale as any woman who had ever experienced a "lapse"). Dugdale investigated other relatives and came up with the mathematically unsound finding that 17 of the 29 adult males were criminals, while 15 others had been convicted of some degree of offence.

Dugdale traced the family back to its beginnings 150 years earlier in the person of Max Jukes, who became "exhibit A in the Dugdale rogues' gallery, although nothing criminal appears in his record" (Adams, 1955, p. 42). Dugdale spent a year hunting through prisons, almshouses, asylums, and public records in search of Jukes. He uncovered approximately 1200 of Max Jukes's descendant progeny, of whom only 709 could be fully traced. More than 25 percent of these (180) were paupers, while about 20 percent (140) were "criminals" (including 7 murderers, 60 thieves, and 50 prostitutes) and about 30 others had been charged with the crime of "bastardy."

Despite the appallingly inept methodology of Dugdale's study, it was widely influential, and the name Jukes became a synonym for depravity. In Canada, A. P. Knight, a professor at Queen's University, spread the word about how the Jukes had cost New York more than a million dollars in public expenses (McLaren, 1990, p. 41). All of this fostered the idea that criminality, poverty, and degeneracy were inherited, feeding into the public demand for policies that would reduce the size of this burden on society. Dugdale favoured environmental changes to help the defectives, but his work was used to support policies of negative eugenics.

Henry Goddard and the Kallikaks

Henry Herbert Goddard (1866–1957) psychologist and director of research at the Vineland Training School for Feeble-Minded Boys and Girls in New Jersey, was influenced both by Mendel's research in genetic heritability and by the newly developing science of IQ testing. In his view, intelligence was inborn and inherited and was a measure of many other aspects of human worthiness, especially human morality.

Goddard published the "pedigrees" of hundreds of defective people who would not have existed had their feeble-minded ancestors been prevented from breeding (Gould, 1981, p. 168). One such study was the history of Martin Kallikak, a respectable young soldier in the colonial army at the time of the American Revolution. Goddard coined the name from the Greek words *kallos* meaning beautiful and *kakos* meaning bad (Gould, 1981, p. 168).

Kallikak, a normal soldier, had a sexual liaison with a feeble-minded barmaid, which resulted in a family tree full of hopeless ne'er-do-wells (as Goddard characterized them) who were living in great poverty in the pine barrens of New Jersey. Later, Kallikak returned home, married a respectable Quaker woman, and started another family line. In contrast to the previous union, all but three of the 496 descendants from this match were "normal." Goddard's presentation of his findings appears to have been somewhat dishonest. Photographs of the degenerate Kallikaks in Goddard's book were amateurishly doctored to make the family members appear unintelligent and vaguely diabolic (Gould, 1981, p. 171).

Goddard believed that delinquency and immorality were caused by degeneracy and that this degeneracy showed itself in low IQ scores. He administered IQ tests to Vineland training school residents and compared their scores with those of inmates in several New Jersey jails and prisons. Since none of the inmates at Vineland scored higher than a mental age of 13 on the Binet scale, he set the cutoff point for feeblemindedness at the mental age of 12. When he found that a median of 20 percent of the prisoners scored below this point, he interpreted the result as support for his theory. As intelligence tests became more widely used, however, this interpretation was challenged. Carl Murchinson's 1926 study *Criminal Intelligence* found that the rate of feeble-mindedness was higher in the army than it was in the prisons (Pfohl, 1985, p. 93).

BORN CRIMINAL THEORY REVISITED

Body-type theory was developed in a new form in the work of two Americans: anthropologist Earnest Albert Hooton and psychologist William Sheldon. Both men were professors at Harvard University, and both believed that their work proved that crime and immorality were aspects of physical inheritance.

EARNEST ALBERT HOOTON AND THE HIERARCHY OF DEGENERATION

Earnest A. Hooton (1887–1954) described the biological component of criminal behaviour as degeneracy. Hooton argued that crime was the result of normal environmental stress on low-grade organisms (humans). He conducted a massive study of more than 17 000 people (including about 14 000 prisoners), collecting 197 distinct bodily measurements for each of them. This study was published as the three-volume *The American Criminal* in 1939; a shorter version, *Crime and the Man*, appeared the same year.

Despite the fact that his evidence, reinterpreted by other scholars, shows there were more differences among prisoners than between prisoners and the noncriminal controls, Hooton concluded that prisoners were distinctive and inferior. Like Lombroso, Hooton pointed to features such as tattooing and sloping foreheads as signs of degeneracy, although his finding that there was an excess of blue-grey and mixed eye colours among criminals might have surprised other degeneracy specialists. Hooton claimed to have discovered a natural "hierarchy of degeneration."

> If one considers in order, sane civilians, sane criminals, insane civilians
> and insane criminals he finds that each succeeding group tends to mani-

fest greater ignorance, lowlier occupational status, and more depressing evidence of all-round worthlessness. The same hierarchy of degeneration is evidenced in physical characteristics. The lower class civilian population is anthropologically fair to middling, the sane criminals are vastly inferior, the insane civilians considerably worse than sane criminals, and insane criminals worst of all.... The specific criminal proclivities found in certain races and nationalities among the sane prisoners are carried over, to a great extent, into the offenses committed by insane criminals of the same ethnic or religious origin. (Hooton, 1939, p. 382)

Hooton presented his data by racial and national-origin groups, illustrated by drawings of Germans in lederhosen, Spanish with sombreros, and other "friendly" icons. He argued that although race did not affect whether a person would be a criminal or not, it *did* affect what kind of crime would be committed. Thus, he divided Caucasians into nine different groups, including the "pure Nordic" type, which he characterized as "an easy leader in forgery and fraud; a strong second in burglary and larceny and last or next to last in all crimes against the persons." "Negroids," he maintained, "commit a great deal of homicide, are parsimonious in sex offenses, and perpetuate [*sic*; perpetrate] a modest amount of robbery" (Hooton, 1939, pp. 249, 382).

It should come as no surprise that Hooton was an enthusiastic supporter of eugenics. He argued that, in all racial groups, it is the inferior organisms that succumb to the adversities of natural temptations in their environment, and that it is impossible to correct the environment to the point "at which these flawed and degenerate human beings will be able to succeed in honest social competition" (Hooton, 1939, p. 388). Hooton believed that both crime and war could be ended for all time by a stringent policy that would either extirpate the physically, mentally, and morally unfit or else segregate them into a "socially aseptic" environment (Hooton, 1939, p. 309).

Hooton was criticized by other academics for improperly selecting (and using) his control samples, for suppressing data that did not fit his hypotheses, and for making the very basic research error of defining as "inferior" all characteristics found most often among prisoners and then proceeding to show that the data demonstrated how inferior prisoners were—an example of "circular reasoning" (Reuter, 1939; Sutherland, 1939). Nonetheless, the work enjoyed instant and widespread success among the public, confirming as it did popular prejudices of the day against Blacks, immigrants, various ethnic groups, and the lower socioeconomic classes in general (Moran, 1980, p. 220).

WILLIAM H. SHELDON AND SOMATOTYPING

William H. Sheldon (1898–1977) took the ideas of the German psychiatrist Ernst Kretschmer, who had identified three distinct body types—asthenic (frail, weak), athletic (muscular), and pyknic (short, rotund)—and associated them with different behavioural predispositions.

In *Varieties of the Human Physique* (1940), Sheldon mapped out the relationships among human physique, personality, and criminal propensity. His method of making objective bodily measurements is called somatotyping (see Figure 5.3). The basic divisions or somatotypes are *endomorph* (soft, round, easygoing, sociable, self-indulgent), *mesomorph* (hard, rectangular, restless, energetic, insensitive), and *ectomorph* (lean, fragile, introspective, sensitive, nervous). Sheldon argued that the human embryo comes with three forms of skin tissue—the endoderm, the ectoderm, and the mesoderm. The endomorph was a person in whom the organs associated with the endoderm (e.g., the digestive system) were most highly developed relative to the other two tissue types. Mesomorphs had a preponderance of the muscle- and bone-related mesoderm tissue, while ectomorphs had relatively little body mass and relatively great surface area.

Each individual in Sheldon's sample would be assigned a score from 1 to 7 for endomorphy, mesomorphy, and ectomorphy. Anyone who scored an average of four for the three measures would be classified as average. If, however, the score was close to 7–1–1 (or 1–1–7), the person was mainly an endomorph (or an ectomorph) (Brown et al., 1991, p. 263). In *Varieties of Delinquent Youth* (1949), Sheldon reported on an eight-year test in which he had compared 200 boys from the Hayden Goodwill Inn (a reform school for delinquent boys) with a control group of 200 college students. He developed a "D" scale and tried to show how it was related to somatotype. His D scale brought together measures such as IQ insufficiency, medical problems, psychotic problems, psychoneurotic traits, cerebrophobic delinquency (alcoholism, drug use), gynandrophrenic delinquency (homosexuality), and primary criminality (legal delinquency). Sheldon found that his delinquents not only had a much worse rating on the D scale but also had an average mesomorphically dominated somatotype of 3.5–4.6–2.7. The college students scored much lower on mesomorphy, which led Sheldon and his associates to conclude that physical inadequacy was the basic cause of crime, and that eugenics should be practised as the best long-term solution to crime (Sheldon, Hartl, & McDermott, 1949, p. 19).

Sheldon's work, like Hooton's, entered into the popular imagination without being particularly well received by the academic community. Sutherland (1951) re-analyzed Sheldon's data using what he thought was a more meaningful criterion of delinquency (conviction in a court of law, instead of measures of homosexuality and intelligence). He found no significant body-type differences between Sheldon's seriously delinquent boys and the college boys. Although later research has confirmed that incarcerated offenders tend to be more mesomorphic than control groups (Corte & Gatti, 1972; Glueck & Glueck, 1950), biological explanations for this finding have given way to sociological ones. Thus, the relationship between mesomorphy and delinquency may be a reflection not of biological determinism, but rather of opportunity (the mesomorph is better able to carry out delinquent acts), labelling (the mesomorph is more likely to be suspected of delinquent acts), and incarceration (in a prison environment of controlled food intake and incentives for muscular develop-

Figure 5.3   Sheldon's Somatotypes

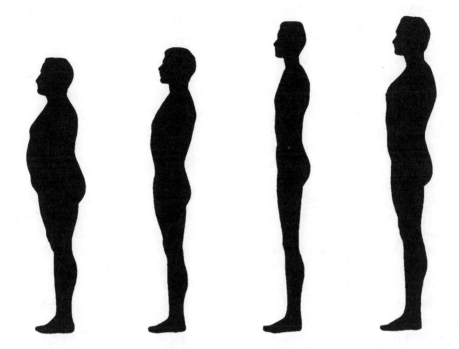

From left to right: endomorph, mesomorph, ectomorph, normal

Source: Reproduced by permission of *The Encyclopedia of Sociology: New & Updated,* 2nd ed., by Dushkin Publishing Group. Copyright © 1981, The Dushkin Publishing Group/Brown & Benchmark Publishers, a division of McGraw-Hill Higher Education Group, Guilford, CT. All rights reserved.

ment, the ectomorph and endomorph take on mesomorphic features). Despite the dubious utility of such measures, somatotype information is still collected in many institutional settings.

BIOLOGICAL POSITIVISM REVISITED

As studies of degenerate families and body types ran their course, new approaches were being developed, the most important of which involved the use of twin and adoption studies.

TWINS STUDIES

If I had any desire to live a life of indolent ease, I would wish to be an identical twin, separated at birth from my brother and raised in a different social class. We could hire ourselves out to a host of social scientists and practically name our fee. For we would be exceedingly rare representatives of the only really adequate natural experiment for separating genetic from environmental effects in humans—genetically identical individuals raised in disparate environments. (Gould, 1981, p. 235)

The nature versus nurture debate has dogged the efforts of those who want to prove that behaviour, whether criminal or conforming, is determined by inborn characteristics. For example, the finding that one of the best at-birth indicators of antisocial behaviour in a young boy is his father's criminal record can be interpreted as supporting either a genetic-inheritance argument or a social-learning argument. Twin studies have been looked on as a means of sorting out these conflicting interpretations.

In nature, monozygotic (identical) twins are formed from one egg and have virtually identical chromosomes; in contrast dizygotic (fraternal) twins share about half the same chromosomes, as do brothers and sisters born apart. The differences among the three groups (ordinary brothers and sisters, fraternal twins, and identical twins) provide opportunities to test the importance of inheritance and environment. If behavioural traits are largely inherited, then identical twins, whose genetic makeup is the same, are more likely to have similar traits than are fraternal twins, who have on average half of the same genes. In most studies we find that the *concordance* (the chance of both having the same trait) is greater for identical twins, even when these individuals were raised in different families. *Discordance* is defined as contrasting outcomes, for example, when one twin is a heterosexual Casanova and the other is monogamously homosexual.

No study shows a 100 percent concordance, even for identical twins; however, evidence exists that some traits show higher concordance for identical twins than for nonidentical twins. These include alcoholism, schizophrenia, Alzheimer's disease, autism, and affective disorders (depression, for example) (Plomin, Owen, & McGuffin, 1994).

Twin study research was initially proposed by Sir Francis Galton, the inventor of eugenics, as a means of distinguishing "the type of humanity that is exceedingly ill-suited to play a respectable part in our civilization (Galton, 1907, p. 868, cited in McInerney, 1999). One of the earliest twin studies was German geneticist Johannes Lange's *Crime as Destiny.* Lange located 30 pairs of twins in which at least one of each pair was in prison. He found a very high concordance for apparently identical twins. Fraternal twins were only slightly more likely than ordinary siblings to both be criminals (Lange, 1931). The title of Lange's book reflects the conclusions that he drew.

One of the most authoritative twin studies was conducted in Denmark by Christiansen (1977a, 1977b). Christiansen was able to use the Danish twin register (a full listing of all twins born in Denmark between 1870 and 1920) and the Danish national register of criminal behaviour to establish the criminal or noncriminal paths

Box 5.3   Fame, Fortune, and Fake Data

Studies by English psychologist Sir Cyril Burt (1883–1971) on genetically identical twins raised apart initially seemed to constitute strong support for the argument that heredity was much more important than environment with respect to both measured intelligence and behaviour. Burt's findings were used as recently as 1969 by Arthur Jensen to support his belief that IQ differences between Blacks and Whites were inherited and ineradicable. Burt's work is an interesting (and extreme) example of wishful, prejudiced thinking and fraudulent data. Despite the recent publication of two books intended to vindicate him (Fletcher, 1991; Joynson, 1989), it seems quite clear that Burt not only fabricated his twins but also invented research associates and research papers authored by these phantom assistants (Butler & Petrulis, 1999; Gould, 1981, chap. 6).

Thomas Bouchard claims that twins tend to exhibit similar physical and mental traits, including habits and fears, brain waves, and heart patterns (Bouchard, 1984; Bouchard et al., 1990; Langinvainio et al., 1984). Bouchard's research is represented in the film *Twins*, in which the raised-apart twins (Schwarzenegger and DeVito) both double-flush the toilet. Bouchard has had much more public acceptance of his ideas than academic acceptance, however, and considerable skepticism remains concerning his more dramatic, televised claims (Dusek, 2000). Like Philippe Rushton (see Box 5.5), much of Bouchard's research is funded by the Pioneer Fund. The Pioneer Fund was originally established to support activities that would enable the spread of the genes of the original White settlers in the United States. Over time, the fund has been associated with people whose work has favoured segregation, restriction of immigration, and White supremacy (Dusek, 2000; Rosenthal, 1995).

Overall, identical twins (most of whom are raised together) are approximately two to three times as likely as fraternals to be similar with regard to their criminal record, or lack thereof, but the record for other traits is quite varied. George Ebers (University Hospital, London, Ontario), for example, reported a concordance rate for homosexuality in a series of identical twin studies that was no higher than might be due to chance (cited in Wertz, 1996, n. 871; Wickelgren, 1999). Even among identical twins who are raised together (i.e., those with both genetic and environmental commonalities), if one twin is psychopathic it is still reasonably possible that the co-twin will not be (Bohman, 1996; Plomin et al., 1994). As Lykken (1982, p. 26) observes, "among persons as close as twins, individual unshared experiences often play a decisive role." Thus, although the findings of twin studies provide some support for the inherited-predisposition (genetic) argument, they do not support the idea that most or all "bad seeds" are born that way.

of 14 344 twins (7172 pairs). He found prison, police, or court records on 926 people, involving 799 of the twin pairs (Wilson & Herrnstein, 1985, p. 94). Concordance was found for 35 percent of the identical twins, compared with 13 percent of the fraternal twins.

ADOPTION STUDIES

Adoption studies are used to assess the likelihood that a child whose parents have a particular trait will also have that trait through genetic inheritance rather than upbringing. Adoption studies are problematic, mainly because adoption is an unusual event. It may be associated, in itself, with disruption, mental disorder, or antisocial behaviour. Also, the placement of adopted children is not random, so environmental factors cannot really be excluded from the studies.

In an early adoption study, Crowe (1972) compared 52 adopted children whose biological mothers had criminal convictions with a sample of adopted children whose biological mothers had no convictions. The groups were matched in terms of age, sex, ethnicity, age of separation from the mother, and type of adopting family. As expected, the rate of arrests and convictions was higher in the first group than in the control group.

Most large-scale adoption studies have been done in Scandinavian countries, which have relatively small, immobile, and homogeneous populations and which are noted for their excellent records on births and adoptions, arrests and convictions, treatment for alcoholism, and other social data (Brennan, Mednick, & Jacobsen, 1996; Crowe, 1972). One Swedish study (Goodwin et al., 1974) showed that adopted men whose biological parents had a history of alcohol abuse were more likely to become alcohol abusers than those whose parents had no such problem, even though they had been adopted before the age of six weeks. Similarly, men whose biological parents were criminals were four times more likely to have criminal records than were men whose biological parents had no record.

Another Swedish study (Cloninger et al., 1982) had similar results. This study distinguished between "milieu-limited alcoholism" and "male-limited alcoholism." The first type was found among both men and women, was usually not severe, and seemed strongly influenced by environmental conditions. The other type of alcoholism was less common but more serious. It was found among men whose biological relatives displayed the same characteristic heavy-drinking pattern, and it was not influenced by the drinking habits of the adoptive parents.

Although both of the above studies maintain that a connection exists between the behaviour of biological relatives and the behaviour of children who are adopted, the relationship is far from deterministic. In fact, most of these youths do not follow their biological parents' example. For example, Mednick, Gabrielli, & Hutchings (1984) conducted a series of studies of parents and children involved in all nonfamilial adoptions in Denmark between 1927 and 1947. If either biological parent (mother or father) had a criminal record, the parents were counted as criminal. Findings for the sample of 4065 male adoptees showed that in the worst case, when both the adoptive and the birth parents had criminal records, less than 30 percent of the adoptees had criminal records themselves (Mednick et al., 1984). The least criminal group were those whose parents, biological and adoptive, had no criminal record. Even so, 13.5 percent of these adoptees had a record. This result supports the view that inheritance has a slight effect, but it is far from determining one's destiny.

MODERN BIOLOGICAL EXPLANATIONS OF DEVIANCE

As research continues and knowledge of organic processes accumulates, more sophisticated biological paradigms have emerged, mainly focusing on the operation of the human brain. The resulting explanatory maps often combine the study of inherited genetic conditions with consideration of how noninherited genetic abnormalities, brain damage, and the ingestion of chemicals (food or drugs) combine to increase the likelihood that specific kinds of behaviour may be programmed to occur. Modern psychological research often builds on the findings of the biological sciences, particularly with respect to the origins of persistent differences in individual temperament and behaviour.

Box 5.4   The State of Behavioural Genetics

Crime: Family, twin, and adoption studies have suggested a heritability of 0 to more than 50 percent for predisposition to crime. (Heritability represents the degree to which a trait stems from genetic factors.) In the 1960s researchers reported an association between an extra Y chromosome and violent crime in males. Follow-up studies found that association to be spurious.

Bipolar disorder: Twin and family studies indicate heritability of 60 to 80 percent for susceptibility to bipolar disorder (also known as manic depression). In 1987 two groups reported finding different genes linked to bipolar disorder, one in Amish families and the other in Israeli families. Both reports have been retracted.

Schizophrenia: Twin studies show heritability of 40 to 90 percent. In 1988 a group reported finding a gene linked to schizophrenia in British and Icelandic families. Other studies documented no linkage, and the initial claim has now been retracted.

Alcoholism: Twin and adoption studies suggest heritability ranging from 0 to 60 percent. In 1990 a group claimed to link a gene—one that produces a receptor for the neurotransmitter dopamine—with alcoholism. A recent review of the evidence concluded that it does not support a link.

Intelligence: Twin and adoption studies show a heritability of performance on intelligence tests of 20 to 80 percent. One group recently unveiled preliminary evidence for genetic markers for high intelligence (an IQ of 130 or higher). The study is unsubstantiated.

Homosexuality: In 1991 a researcher cited anatomic differences between the brains of heterosexual and homosexual males. Two recent twin studies have found a heritability of roughly 50 percent for predisposition to male or female homosexuality. These reports have been disputed. Another group claims to have preliminary evidence of genes linked to male homosexuality. The data have not been published.

Source: Adapted from *Scientific American*, "Behavioral Genetics: A Lack of Progress Report," June 1993, p. 125. Copyright © 1993 by Scientific American Inc. All rights reserved.

THE XYY MALE

Chromosomes are thin threads of genetic material (DNA) that contain hereditary instructions (genes) for the growth of every living cell in an organism. They have been implicated in a number of syndromes, both physiological and behavioural. One of the earliest attempts to link genetic anomalies to criminal deviance is contained in the swift rise and fall of the "XYY monster myth" between 1969 and 1977. Normal cells have 46 chromosomes, two of which determine the gender of the individual. In the normal female, the two chromosomes are both Xs (hence XX equals female), while in the normal male, the two chromosomes are XY. Different combinations are possible, however. Ever since it became possible to test for these anomalies (the XYY anomaly was first reported in 1961), researchers have attempted to establish syndromes of behaviour and their accompanying physical traits. One such anomaly is the 47-XYY aneuploidy.

In 1965, Patricia Jacobs and her colleagues at a maximum-security prison hospital in Edinburgh published their findings concerning 197 male patients with mental disabilities who had been institutionalized because of "dangerous, violent, or criminal propensities." Seven of these inmates (3.5 percent) were XYY genotypes (Jacobs et al., 1965). Given that the estimated frequency of XYY in the general population was assumed to be about 1.3 percent (or 1 case per 1000), this finding led researchers to speculate that XYY might predispose a person toward the kind of behaviour that results in imprisonment. Underlying this research was the assumption that, since the Y chromosome is the male hormone, the XYY genotype must be some kind of supermale.

> The Y chromosome is the male-determining chromosome; therefore, it should come as no surprise that an extra Y chromosome can produce an individual with heightened masculinity, evinced by characteristics such as unusual tallness, increased fertility … and powerful aggressive tendencies. (Jarvik, Klodin, & Matsuyama, 1973, pp. 679–680)

Stories and reports about "XYY men" began to appear in the scientific literature (often based on one or two cases), which linked the syndrome to slightly heightened chances for behavioural problems and aggression, psychosis and schizophrenia, paraphilias and criminal offending (Ike, 2000). XYY was prominently featured in newspaper accounts of criminal cases, such as that of Richard Speck, convicted for the murder of eight student nurses. Speck entered a not-guilty plea based on the XYY chromosomal "disorder." Speck did not actually have the disorder. As could be expected the idea also entered popular entertainment. In the film *Alien 3*, the heroine crash-lands on a remote planet that serves as an off-world penal colony for hardened, violent XYYs.

In 1970, Dr. Arnold Hutschnecker, a medical adviser to President Nixon, suggested a program whereby every six-year-old in the United States would be screened for chromosomal or psychological abnormalities; those testing positive—"hard-core six-year-

Box 5.5   Rushton: Scientific Racism as a Deviant Perspective

Although the XYY myth seems to have run its course, attempts to find genetic roots for various kinds of behaviour continue. Genetic explanations often merge into race-based ideologies of the society. For example, Philippe Rushton (a full professor in the Department of Psychology, University of Western Ontario) has produced many scientific findings concerning alleged differences among Asians, Whites, and Blacks. His main theme is that skull size, brain size, and IQ are correlated with the present and potential achievements of people in these racial categories.

In "The New Enemies of Evolutionary Science" (1998), Rushton describes a paper that he delivered January 1989 in which he concluded that "East Asians, on average, were slower to mature, less fertile, less sexually active, with larger brains and higher IQ scores than Africans, who tended to the opposite in each of these areas." Whites, he found, fell between these groups. He argued at that time that these differences had evolved as man had migrated out of Africa into regions that selected for more cognitive development. The Europeans and Asians were forced to evolve toward larger brains, lower sexual potency and aggression, and greater family stability. Rushton regarded these traits as continuing to influence a variety of present and future possibilities for people of different racial inheritance.

Rushton's (1995) *Race, Evolution and Behavior* expresses the same ideas but in more detail. This small book was distributed (unsolicited and free) among academics, many of whom protested receiving what they regarded as hate literature in scholarly dress. This monograph presents data on brain size, intelligence, crime, personality, sex hormones, twinning rate, family stability, and social organization and basically extends Rushton's original assumptions about the genetic, inherited causes of aggression, crime, and other traits, which can be interpreted to mean that Blacks commit more offences than Whites because they are, incurably, a lower form of animal, not because of the many forms of disadvantage and oppression they have faced or the differential policing applied to them, or any other variable; Rushton does not control for such differences.

Rushton, recently described as "the bad boy of academe" (Grace, 2000), seems to have been surprised that his assertions produced an immediate reaction from scholars (on scholarly grounds) and from various activist groups (on grounds of racism). In Rushton's view, he is treated as a deviant simply because his views are not shared by those who prioritize political correctness over facing of the facts. He feels he is justified in standing up (as Galileo tried to do) to what he sees as persecution. It is certainly true that Rushton has been attacked, not only in works such as Stefan Kuhl's *The Nazi Connection: Eugenics, American Racism and German National Socialism* (1994) but also in many forums of academic opinion. The chief support he has found has been that he has the right to be wrong and the right to say what he believes to be true.

Rushton's research (and also that of other scientific racists) has at least two problems. First, much of this work is seriously flawed, both in its assumptions and in its execution, so that the facts are highly suspect. Second, the research carries with it an

---

Box 5.5   Rushton: Scientific Racism as a Deviant Perspective (cont.)

ethical claim that, if something is part of nature (red in tooth and claw) we should go along with it, even help it to unfold more rapidly. This claim needs to be brought out into the open and discussed. Do you want to live in a society that is run on Darwinian principles? Do you believe that strengthening the strong people will reduce crime, poverty, and other social ills?

The taint of scientific racism extends—sometimes inappropriately—to other researchers who want to understand the biological component of human behaviour. In 1992, a conference on genetic factors and crime was given support by the Human Genome Project and the National Institutes of Health (NIH). Due to protest, the NIH withdrew its funding. The conference was eventually held in 1995 after being renamed and moved to a rural location in Maryland. Even so, it was briefly invaded by protesters chanting "Maryland conference, you can't hide. We know you're pushing genocide" (Coombs, 1999, p. 227). For these protesters, the very topic of the conference indicated a deviant form of science.

---

olds"—would be sent to "therapeutic camps" (Conrad & Schneider, 1992). The policy was, however, abandoned because it was not feasible at the time (Hunt, 1973). The image of the XYY violent supermale has subsequently proved to have been a great exaggeration (Borgaonkar & Shah, 1974; Fox, 1971; Owen, 1972; Pyeritz et al., 1977; Sarbin & Miller, 1970). Most XYY males have nonviolent and noncriminal life histories.

GENETICS AND THE BELL CURVE ARGUMENT

One of the most widely discussed books on biologically based differences, including differences in criminality, is *The Bell Curve*. A central argument in this work is that IQ is heritable, Blacks have a lower IQ range than Whites, and IQ and criminality are linked traits. Co-author Charles Murray has been quoted as saying that his book sells because it makes well-meaning Whites "who fear that they are closet racists feel better" about acknowledging what they "already think but don't know how to say" (de Parle, 1994, p. 48 quoted in Coombs, 1999, p. 229). This book has earned the criticisms directed against its implicit racism and its neglect of environmental variables, but it has also strongly influenced policymakers in the United States.

GENETIC LOADING

Certain types of predatory aggression and seemingly senseless, explosive violence may be related to physical damage or malfunction in specific parts of the brain. Recent biologically based explanations are more open to the role of such things in combination with environmental factors. In the hypothetical case of a man who commits sudden, unpredictable acts of violence against women, this perspective would seek some inherited genetic condition or biological malfunction that is loading him toward aggression. Environmental factors such as his use of drugs, alcohol, or pornographic material, and stress at work or in his home would be seen as triggers that precipitate his violent episodes. This pattern can be diagrammed as in Figure 5.4.

Thus, the person with an inherited predisposition is like a loaded gun, with the environment serving as a trigger. (This conceptualization differs from the typical social science viewpoint, which sees the environment as a factor *shaping* the behaviour rather than merely releasing it.) Men with high (genetically based) levels of the hormone testosterone are more likely than other men to commit aggressive acts, although only when they are in a situation with an appropriate target (i.e., they usually don't attack their employers or people twice as big as they are). Similarly, women who suffer hormone imbalances after childbirth are more likely to kill their babies if they are simultaneously experiencing severe stress in the home. Many researchers regard mental illnesses like schizophrenia as pathological conditions that result from an interplay between genetic loading and an environmental trigger such as complications at birth, viral infection, head trauma, or severe stress. In the same way, anorexia nervosa, an increasingly recognized eating disorder, may have a genetic basis but emerges only in stressful social environments that strongly favour a cultural norm of thinness. Also supporting this idea is the finding that persons who become addicted to heroin while under conditions of stress free themselves from it quite readily when the stress is removed (Robins, 1993).

A wide variety of sexually deviant behaviours called paraphilias, in which individuals are turned on by exposure to unusual or forbidden stimuli, have been blamed on the functioning of the limbic system of the brain. According to Money (1983), the particular need is programmed and the program is released when the opportunity is found, sometimes following ideas found in the reading of pornography but often invented in response to the situation. Paraphilias range from the need for a sexual partner who is an amputee (acrotomophilia), or dead (necrophilia), or unwilling (rapism or raptophilia) to involvement in dirty talk (scatophilia or narratophilia), or actual dirt (mysophilia), or human waste (coprophilia or urophilia) (Money, 1983, pp. 169–170). Paraphilias can lead to serial homicide, as in the case of Jeffrey

Figure 5.4   A Biological Model of Deviance

Heredity *(genetic loading)*	+	*Biological* *process*	+	*Environmental* *stress*	=	*Deviance* *as symptom*
defective genes		nutrition needs		available diet		
high sensory threshold		allergies		pollutants (air, noise)		
hormones (testosterone)		exercise		work demands		
somatotype				family demands		

Dahmer, a cannibalistic necrophiliac who killed several young men, or to activities such as armed bank robbery. Robber Ronald Keyes, for example, claims that his masochistic paraphilia made him act in ways that were dangerously illegal and wrong and that this was part of his girlfriend's sexual domination over his life (Keyes & Money, 1993).

Seeing drug use or other addictions as inborn characteristics is less easy. Although some evidence supports the view that some people have an inborn predisposition to explore and take risks, it is difficult to deduce from this that some of them have a specific, inborn need for cocaine, heroin, or alcohol. It has been argued, however, that although the initial use of a drug like crack cocaine is mainly voluntary and very much influenced by the environment, once ingested the chemical properties of the drug trigger a continuing physiological disorder characterized by craving for the drug. In this view, the brain is either temporarily or permanently altered by the continuing use of the drug such that withdrawal symptoms persist for hours or days when the drug is withheld, while craving for the drug may continue long after its use is terminated—sometimes permanently. It follows from this that the best cure would be some new drug intervention to reverse the brain pattern established by the original drug. Mounting evidence shows, however, that the physiological aspect of addiction is not the only—or even the most important—factor in the continuing use of recreational drugs (Blackwell & Erickson, 1988). Studies of addictive behaviour have shown that, for many people in treatment, breaking away from the drug-using culture is at least as, if not more, difficult than breaking free of the physical need for drugs (Blackwell & Erickson, 1988).

Whether we look at evidence from genetic inheritance studies or focus on other sources of chemical or structural differences in brain functioning, such differences do seem, under certain conditions, to be related to offending behaviour. "If you have low levels of a certain neurotransmitter in your brain *and* an alcoholic father, your chances of being able to live a normal life are worse than if you simply had a drunken father *or* a chemical deficit" (Moir & Jessel, 1995, p. 2; italics in original). The causal pattern between such factors and actual behaviour is not direct and deterministic. You can inherit a predisposition toward particular kinds of behaviour based on one abnormality, or an even stronger predisposition based on several, but you will not necessarily act on it.

SOCIOBIOLOGY AND THE SELFISH GENE

In the early 1970s, a rather different angle on the question of genetic influence on behaviour was put forward in the controversial book *Sociobiology* (1975) by entomologist E. O. Wilson. Most sociobiological work has involved nonhuman subjects, and in this guise it has been relatively uncontroversial. The leap from what is found in other species to humanity has not been so easy to make, even though sociobiology has avoided the taint of racism better than its eugenic counterparts. Human socio-biology is, in principle, indistinguishable from evolutionary psychology (Lynn, 1995; Pinker, 1997). As such, its focus is on individual personality characteristics such as selfishness and altruism. It has also pronounced on inborn causes of specific behav-iours like rape, infanticide, suicide, marital infidelity, and homosexuality (along with religion, war and peace, slavery, and genocide).

Sociobiologists argue that all living bodies are driven by an innate need to ensure that their genetic material survives, and, furthermore, that their behaviour is often unconsciously "programmed" toward this end (Crippen, 1994, pp. 318–319). Organisms (individuals) are always seeking "inclusive fitness," defined as the sum of the individual's own reproductive success plus the reproductive success of others who carry that person's genes (his or her children, for example). Humans, like insects and animals, strive to enhance the number of genes they leave behind, "whether directly through their own offspring, indirectly through the offspring of their relatives, or through a reciprocal exchange of services with nonrelatives" (Maryanski, 1994, p. 381).

The theory is used to explain or justify many characteristics imputed to be immutable in humans, including gender roles (mainly male promiscuity, rape, aggres-sion, warfare), status hierarchies, racial bigotry, cheating, and lying (Freese, 1994, p. 347; Maryanski, 1994, p. 380). According to Dawkins, each of us is primarily a walking container for the genes that use us. In other words, we are "survival machines"—robot vehicles blindly programmed to preserve these selfish molecules (Dawkins, 1976, p. 19). This does not mean that every detail of cultural life is genet-ically programmed. Most sociobiologists allow for considerable variation in the expression of biological imperatives, and "for a dynamic coevolution of genetic, behavioral and cultural traits" (Freese, 1994, p. 347). An example of this is Sarah Hrdy's work on parenting, based mainly on nonhuman research. Hrdy argues that mothers who have careers are actually performing a role that is shared with other species, one that fosters their children's chances for successful competition (Hrdy, 1981). Other sociobiologists use Darwinian thought to justify restrictions on women's nonparenting roles. Sociobiologists such as E. O. Wilson take a conservative stand against phenomena such as egalitarianism and women's liberation. Wilson, for example, felt that women did not belong in politics, law, or science (Wilson, 1978).

Preservation of the gene pool does not always mean the survival of the individual. When a person altruistically undertakes a suicide mission and in doing so saves others, the gene is preserved more effectively than if all members of the group exposed themselves to extreme danger. As the central sociobiological concept of inclu-sive fitness predicts, we are most likely to sacrifice ourselves if the people we are saving are kinfolk or people so like ourselves that they may be carriers of the same genes (Dawkins, 1976, p. 97). Similarly, sociobiologists feel that marriage laws restricting people to one partner violate the innate demand that the genes be passed on through a maximum number of partners. Adultery is a natural consequence of this form of sexual restriction. Similar arguments have been used to explain why step-children are more likely than biological children to be abused or killed (Daly, 1996; Dawkins, 1976, chap. 9; Zimmer, 1996).

How might sociobiologists explain lifestyles that are *not* driven by reproductive needs, in particular homosexuality? It has been pointed out in response to this question that homosexuals have often filled the altruistic roles of shaman, diplomat, artist, and artisan and are frequently found in human-service occupations where their social roles serve to improve the fitness of the group (Wilson, 1975, p. 555).

The idea that a gene exists that programs those who possess it to be homosexual (or possess any other social characteristic) remains speculative and controversial. Some observers, hostile to homosexuality, think that it takes away the moral blame that homosexuals somehow deserve; others, who see homosexuality as a valid choice, argue that it pathologizes them and could result in massive screening or genetic engineering to eliminate them (Bullough, 1994, p. 231).

Most researchers today feel that we should be looking for combinations of genes rather than single genes and that the influence of genes on behaviour is more like "open programming" than determinism. Mapping of the three to six billion chemical components that make up the human genetic code has been completed (Sherrid, 2001), but it will be a long time before genetic researchers are able to isolate particular genes or genetic combinations that control specific behavioural events in the body. Nor should it be forgotten that the leap from these inner events to behaviour is wide; one can feel rage without necessarily acting on it, just as one can feel a craving without having to engage in consummatory behaviour.

Most sociobiologists have explicitly disavowed the idea that "biology is destiny." In arguing that a particular genetic inheritance makes certain kinds of behaviour more likely, they do not deny that environmental factors may play a deciding

---

Box 5.6   How Is the Gene for Homosexuality Passed On? An Answer from Sociobiology

McNight (1997) suggests that ... the "gay gene" is not only to be found in gay men, but also in straight men (genetic closeting, if you like). So there are three kinds of genetic sexual orientation to be found in men: homozygotic gay men, homozygotic straight men (who have no homosexual genetic loading), and heterozygotic straight men (who carry homosexual genetic material, but who are not themselves gay)....

It is these "homosexually enabled straight men" that are at the centre of McNight's explanation. Homosexuality survives, not because gay men, *per se*, are adaptive, but because the gay gene makes straight men more successfully heterosexual. McNight hypothesises that this homosexual genetic loading endows some straight men with two crucial characteristics—enhanced sexual drive and charm. Such sexually enhanced and charming straight men become highly successful heterosexuals, i.e. they produce more offspring than their un-enhanced straight brothers. (Wilson, 1997)

Source: Elizabeth Wilson, "Fossilized Homosexuals," *Australian Humanities Review*, November, 1997. Reprinted with permission.

role in whether the behaviour manifests itself. Nonetheless, some observers are concerned that sociobiological views lend support to unacceptable controls such as involuntary sterilization, abortion, and genetic screening for criminological or insurance purposes.

SUMMARY

The rise of natural science, particularly the biological sciences, provided a new model of explanation for deviance theorists that seemed better able than the classical model to account for all kinds of behaviour, including behaviour that did not seem to be rational or chosen. The biological positivist approach denied free will and saw human beings as puppets whose strings were pulled by the bodies they inhabited.

Early biological positivism drew together the Darwinian evolutionary model and the Mendelian genetic model to create the science and the social movement of eugenics, which was grounded in the assumption that Caucasian males were the fittest of the species, and which led to the search for the "hereditary degenerate" and policies designed to eliminate crime, poverty, and war by eliminating "inferior" specimens of humanity. The search for the born criminal began with consideration of external characteristics such as facial features and body shape and gradually progressed to the less visible features of the mind, such as brain chemistry. Family studies of hereditary degeneracy gave way to more scientifically appropriate twin and adoption studies. These were soon supplemented by the discovery of chromosomes, which led to premature and exaggerated claims about the relationship between single genes and specific behaviours, as exemplified by the characterization of XYY males as supermales. Sociobiology gained popularity and influence in the 1970s, but is still strongly opposed, on both methodological and ideological grounds, by mainstream evolutionary researchers.

The search for connections between the genetic level of human existence and behaviour continues. Much of this research, and certainly the most readable and public part of it, is consciously or unconsciously tainted by racist and sexist biases and comes close to being a deviant version of science. Nonetheless, it is possible that both the shape of our institutions and the pattern of typical deviations from institutional expectations will be influenced by (but probably not determined by) genetic codes that underlie both the genetic and the cultural evolution of humankind. We should proceed with caution.

STUDY QUESTIONS

1. Is it possible to be too scientific? Are there some things that a purely scientific approach to gender-bending or drug use is going to miss? Does it matter?

2. Although classical theorists observed the world around them, often without using the lens of religion, their work was not scientific. What is the difference between

the objective observations of the classical theorists and the objective observations of social scientists?

3. What things were criminal in Samuel Butler's *Erewhon?* What was Butler trying to say about criminal justice in England?

4. What is the difference between evolutionary theory (Darwinism) and Social Darwinism? (Consider in particular the concept of race.)

5. What is the connection between physical appearance and deviance? How might this be proven?

6. What did Lombroso have in common with Beccaria? (Hint: Both rebelled against the dominant theories of their time and did rather poorly in school, possibly because of this.)

7. What features of research methodology supported the claims of eugenicists that White European males were the fittest humans on earth?

8. In what way is the work of Philippe Rushton similar to the work of Sir Cyril Burt, even though there is no evidence that Rushton falsifies data?

9. What do adoption studies show about the heritability of criminal and deviant tendencies? If you have a twin, raised separately from you, what are the chances that you will both be criminal?

10. Why was there a major outcry from Blacks and criminologists against the claims of *The Bell Curve?*

REFERENCES

Adams, S. H. (1955). The Jukes Myth. In E. A. Schuler, T. F. Hoult, D. L. Gibson, & W. B. Brookover (Eds.), *Readings in Sociology* (5th ed.). New York: Thomas Y. Crowell.

Allen, G. E. (1996). Science Misapplied: The Eugenics Age Revisited. *Technology Review, 99,* 22–32.

Berendt, J. (1994). *Midnight in the Garden of Good and Evil.* New York: Random House (Vintage).

Blackwell, J. C., & Erickson, P. G. (1988). *Illicit Drugs in Canada: A Risky Business.* Toronto: Nelson Canada.

Bohman, M. (1996, March). Predisposition to Criminality: Swedish Adoption Studies in Retrospect. In CIBA Foundation Symposium (Ed.), *Genetics of Criminal and Antisocial Behavior—Symposium No. 194* (pp. 99–108). New York: John Wiley and Sons.

Borgaonkar, D., & Shah, S. (1974). The XYY Chromosome, Male—or Syndrome. *Progress in Medical Genetic, 10,* 135–222.

Bosc, D. (1999). L'Invitation à l'Exposition (The Invitation to the Exposition: Unedited Correspondence from Émile Durkheim to Cesare Lombroso in 1895). *Durkheim Studies, 5,* 13–20.

Bouchard, T. J. (1984). Twins Reared Together and Apart: What They Tell Us about Human Diversity. In S. W. Fox (Ed.), *Individualism and Determinism: Chemical and Biological Bases.* New York: Plenum.

Bouchard, T. J., Lykken, D. T., McGue, M., Segal, N. L., & Tellegen, A. (1990). Sources of Human Psychological Differences: The Minnesota Study of Twins Reared Apart. *Science, 250,* 223–228.

Brennan, P. A., Mednick, S. A., & Jacobsen, B. (1996, March). Assessing the Role of Genetics in Crime Using Adoption Cohorts, In CIBA Foundation Symposium (Ed.), *Genetics of Criminal and Antisocial Behavior—Symposium No. 194* (pp. 115–122). New York: John Wiley and Sons.

Brown, S. E., Esbensen, F.-A., & Geis, G. (1991). *Criminology: Explaining Crime and Its Context.* Cincinnati, OH: Anderson.

Bullough, V. L. (1994). *Science in the Bedroom: A History of Sex Research.* New York: Basic/Harper Collins.

Butler, B., & Petrulis, J. (1999). Some Further Observations Concerning Sir Cyril Burt. *British Journal of Psychology, 90*(1), 155–160.

Butler, S. (1967). *Erewhon Revisited Twenty Years Later.* New York: New American Library. (Original work published in 1923)

Christiansen, K. O. (1977a). A Preliminary Study of Criminality among Twins. In S. A. Mednick & K. O. Christiansen (Eds.), *Biosocial Bases of Criminal Behavior.* New York: John Wiley.

————. (1977b). A Review of Studies of Criminality among Twins. In S. A. Mednick & K. O. Christiansen (Eds.), *Biosocial Bases of Criminal Behavior.* New York: John Wiley.

Cloninger, C. R., Sigvardsson, S., Bohman, M., & von Knorring, A.-L. (1982). Predisposition to Petty Criminality in Swedish Adoptees: II. Cross-Fostering Analysis of Gene-Environment Interaction. *Archives of General Psychiatry, 39,* 1242–1247.

Conrad, J., & Schneider, J. W. (1992). *Deviance and Medicalization: From Badness to Sickness.* Philadelphia, PA: Temple University Press.

Coombs, M. (1999). A Brave New Crime-Free World? In J. R. Botkin, W. M. McMahon, & L. P. Francis (Eds.), *Genetics and Criminality: The Potential Misuse of Scientific Information in Court.* Washington, DC: American Psychological Association.

Corte, J. B., & Gatti, F. (1972). *Delinquency and Crime: A Bio-Psychological Approach.* New York: Seminar Press.

Crippen, T. (1994). Toward a Neo-Darwinian Sociology. *Sociological Perspectives, 37*(3), 309–335.

Crowe, R. R. (1972). The Adopted Offspring of Women Criminal Offenders. *Archives of General Psychiatry, 27*(November), 600–603.

Daly, M. (1996, March). Evolutionary Adaptationism: Another Biological Approach to Criminal and Anti-Social Behavior. In CIBA Foundation Symposium (Ed.), *Genetics of Criminal and Antisocial Behavior—Symposium No. 194* (pp. 183–247). New York: John Wiley and Sons.

Dawkins, R. (1976). *The Selfish Gene*. New York: Oxford University Press.

Dennett, D. (1995). *Darwin's Dangerous Idea: Evolution and the Meanings of Life*. New York: Simon and Schuster.

Dusek, V. (2000). *Sociobiology Sanitized: The Evolutionary Psychology and Genetic Selection Debates*. [On-Line]. Available: <http://www.shef.ac.uk/~psysc/rmy/dusek.html>.

Eldredge, N. (1995). *Reinventing Darwin: The Great Debate at the High Table of Evolutionary Theory*. New York: John Wiley.

Fest, J. (1970). *The Face of the Third Reich*. New York: Pantheon.

Fink, A. E. (1938). *The Causes of Crime: Biological Theories in the United States, 1800–1915*. Philadelphia, PA: University of Philadelphia Press.

Fletcher, R. (1991). *Science, Ideology and the Media: The Cyril Burt Scandal*. New Brunswick, NJ: Transaction.

Fox, R. G. (1971). The XYY Offender: A Modern Myth. *The Journal of Criminal Law, Criminology and Police Science, 62*(March), 71–72.

Freese, L. (1994). The Song of Sociobiology. *Sociological Perspectives, 37*(3), 337–373.

Glueck, S., & Glueck, E. (1950). *Unravelling Juvenile Delinquency*. Cambridge, MA: Harvard University Press.

Goodwin, D. W., Schlusinger, F., Moller, N., Hermansen, L., Winokur, G., & Guze, S. B. (1974). Drinking Problems in Adopted and Nonadopted Sons of Alcoholics. *Archives of General Psychiatry, 31*, 164–169.

Goring, C. (1913). *The English Convict: A Statistical Study*. Montclair, NJ: Patterson Smith.

Gould, S. J. (1981). *The Mismeasure of Man*. New York: W. W. Norton & Co.

Grace, K. M. (2000). The Bad Boy of Academe. *Alberta Report, 26*(48), 50–52.

Grupp, S. E. E. (1968). *The Positive School of Criminology: Three Lectures by Enrico Ferri*. Pittsburgh, PA: University of Pittsburgh Press.

Hagan, J. (1985). The Assumption of Natural Science Methods: Criminological Positivism. In R. Meier (Ed.), *Theoretical Methods in Criminology*. Beverly Hills, CA: Sage.

Herrnstein, R. J., and Murray, C. (1994). *The Bell Curve: Intelligence and Class Structure in American Life*. New York: Free Press.

Hooton, E. A. (1939). *Crime and the Man*. Cambridge, MA: Harvard University Press.

Horgan, J. (1993). Trends in Behavioral Genetics: Eugenics. *Scientific American, 268*, 122–131.

Hrdy, S. B. (1981). *The Woman That Never Evolved*. Cambridge, MA: Harvard University Press.

Hunt, J. (1973). Rapists Have Big Ears: Genetic Screening in Massachusetts. *The Real Paper,* 4.

Ike, N. (2000). Current Thinking of XYY Syndrome. *Psychiatric Annals, 30*(2), 91–97.

Jacobs, P. A., Brunton, M., Melville, M., Brittain, R. P., & McClermont, W. F. A. (1965). Aggressive Behavior, Mental Subnormality, and the XYY Male. *Nature, 208*(December), 1351–1352.

Jarvik, L. F., Klodin, V., & Matsuyama, S. S. (1973). Human Aggression and the Extra Y Chromosome: Fact or Fantasy? *American Psychologist, 28*, 674–682.

Jeffrey, C. R. (1990). *Criminology: An Interdisciplinary Approach*. Englewood Cliffs, NJ: Prentice-Hall.

Joynson, R. B. (1989). *The Burt Affair*. London, UK: Routledge.

Keyes, R. W., & Money, J. (1993). *The Armed Robbery Orgasm*. Buffalo, NY: Prometheus Books.

Kuhl, S. (1994). *The Nazi Connection: Eugenics, American Racism and German National Socialism*. New York: Oxford University Press.

Kuhn, T. (1970). *The Structure of Scientific Revolutions* (2nd ed.). Chicago: University of Chicago Press.

Lane, B. (1992). *The Encyclopedia of Forensic Science*. London, UK: Headline.

Lange, J. (1931). *Crime as Destiny*. London, UK: Allen and Unwin.

Langinvainio, H., Kaprio, J., Koskenvuo, M., & Loanqvist, J. (1984). Finnish Twins Reared Apart: III. Personality Factors. *Acta Geneticae Medicae et Cemellologlae: Twin Research, 33, 259–264.*

Leek, S. (1970). *Phrenology*. New York: Macmillan.

Lilienthal, G. (1985). *Der "Lebensborn e.V.": Ein Instrument nationalsozialistischer Rassenpolitik (The Lebensborn Society: An Instrument of National Socialist Race Policy)*. Munich, Germany: Urban and Fischer.

Lombroso, C. (1885). Criminal Anthropology Applied to Pedagogy. *Monist, 6, 50–59.*

Lombroso, C., & Ferrero, W. (1895). *The Female Offender*. London, UK: Fisher Unwin.

Lombroso-Ferrero, G. (1911/1972). *Criminal Man: According to the Classification of Cesare Lombroso*. New York: Putnam and Sons.

Lynn, R. (1995). The Moral Animal: Why We Are the Way We Are. *National Review, 47,* 70–72.

Lykken, D. T. (1982). Fearlessness: Its Carefree Charm and Deadly Risks. *Psychology Today* (September), 20–28.

Maryanski, A. (1994). The Pursuit of Human Nature in Sociobiology and Evolutionary Sociology. *Sociological Perspectives, 37*(3), 375–389.

Mazzarello, P. (2001). Lombroso and Tolstoy. *Nature, 409*(6823), 983–984.

McInerney, J. D. (1999). Genes and Behavior: A Complex Relationship. *Judicature, 83*(November–December), 1–4.

McLaren, A. (1990). *Our Own Master Race: Eugenics in Canada, 1885–1945*. Toronto: McClelland and Stewart.

McNight, J. (1997). *Straight Science? Homosexuality, Evolution and Adaption*. London, UK: Routledge.

Mednick, S. A., Gabrielli, W. F., & Hutchings, B. (1984). Genetic Influences in Criminal Convictions: Evidence from an Adoption Court. *Science* (May 25), 891–989.

Moir, A., & Jessel, D. (1995). *A Mind to Crime: The Controversial Link between the Mind and Criminal Behaviour*. London, UK: Michael Joseph.

Money, J. (1983). Paraphilias: Phyletic Origins of Erotosexual Dysfunction. In S. G. Shohan (Ed.), *Israel Studies in Criminology*. New York: Sheridan House.

Moran, R. (1980). The Search for the Born Criminal and the Medical Control of Criminality. In P. Conrad & J. W. Schneider (Eds.), *Deviance and Medicalization: From Badness to Sickness*. St. Louis, MO: Mosby.

Owen, D. R. (1972). The 47, XYY Male: A Review. *Psychological Bulletin, 78, 209–233.*

Pfohl, S. (1985). *Images of Deviance and Social Control: A Sociological History*. New York: McGraw-Hill.

Pinker, S. (1997). *How the Mind Works*. New York: W. W. Norton.

Plomin, R., Owen, M., & McGuffin, P. (1994). The Genetic Basis of Complex Human Behaviors. *Science, 264*, 1734–1739.

Pyeritz, R., Schreier, H., Madansky, C., Miller, P., & Beckwith, J. (1977). The XYY Male: The Making of a Myth. In Ann Arbor Science for the People Editorial Collective (Ed.), *Biology as a Social Weapon*. Minneapolis, MN: Burgess.

Reuter, E. B. (1939). Review of *Crime and the Man*, by E.A. Hooton. *American Journal of Sociology, 45*, 123–126.

Robins, L. (1993). Vietnam Veterans, Rapid Recovery from Heroin Addition: A Fluke or a Normal Expectation? *Addiction, 88*, 1041–1054.

Rosenthal, S. J. (1995). The Pioneer Fund. *American Behavioral Scientist, 39*(1), 44–62.

Rushton, J. P. (1995). *Race, Evolution and Behavior*. New Brunswick, NJ: Transaction.

———. (1998, March). The New Enemies of Evolutionary Science. *Liberty, 4*(March), 31–35. [On-Line]. Available: <http://www.lrainc.com/swtaboo/stalkers/jpr_liberty.html>.

Sarbin, T. R., & Miller, J. E. (1970). Demonism Revisited: The XYY Chromosomal Anomaly. *Issues in Criminology, 5*(Summer), 197–207.

Sheldon, W., Hartl, E., & McDermott, E. (1949). *Varieties of Delinquent Youth*. New York: Harper and Row.

Sheldon, W. H. (1940). *Varieties of the Human Physique: An Introduction to Constitutional Psychology*. New York: Harper.

Sherrid, P. (2001). After the Breakthrough. *U.S. News and World Report, 130*(8), 48–50.

Sutherland, E. H. (1939). Reviews of *Crime and the Man* and *The American Criminal*: An *Anthropological Study*, Vol. 1, by Earnest Hooton. *Journal of Criminal Law and Criminology, 29*, 911–914.

———. (1951). A Critique of Sheldon's *Varieties of Delinquent Youth*. *American Sociological Review, 16*, 10–13.

Toland, J. (1977). *Adolf Hitler*. New York: Byzantine Books.

Udry, J. R. (1995). Sociology and Biology: What Biology Do Sociologists Need to Know? *Social Forces, 73*, 1267–1279.

Wertz, D. C. (1996). Crime Genes: The Danish Adoption Studies. *GeneLetter* (November). [On-line]. Available: http://www.geneletter.com/archives/danishcrime.html>.

Wickelgren, I. (1999). Discovery of Gay Gene Questioned. *Science, 284*(5414), 571–575.

Wilson, E. (1997). "Fossilised Homosexuals": Elizabeth Wilson Reviews Jim McNight's *Straight Science? Homosexuality, Evolution and Adaptation. Australian Humanities Review*. [On-Line]. Available: <http://www.lib.latrobe.edu.au/AHR/archive/Issue-November-1997/wilson.html>.

Wilson, E. O. (1975). *Sociobiology: The New Synthesis*. Cambridge, MA: Belknap Press.

———. (1978). *On Human Nature*. Cambridge, MA: Harvard University Press.

Wilson, J. Q., & Herrnstein, R. J. (1985). *Crime and Human Nature*. New York: Simon and Schuster.

NTL

Wohl, A. S. (2000). *Phrenology and Race in Nineteenth-Century England*. [On-Line]. Available: <http://landow.stg.brown.edu/victorian/race/rc3.html>.

Wolfgang, M. E. (1972). Cesare Lombroso. In H. Mannheim (Ed.), *Pioneers in Criminology*. (2nd ed.). Montclair, NJ: Patterson Smith.

Zimmer, C. (1996). First, Kill the Babies: Evolutionary Explanations of Infanticide. *Discover, 17*, 72–78.

C H A P T E R

THEORIES OF THE MIND: PSYCHOANALYTIC AND PSYCHOLOGICAL EXPLANATIONS OF DEVIANCE

In this chapter we review some of the most popular theories of deviance, explanations that focus on the mind. Many cases seem to call for a mental explanation of deviance. An example is murderer David Snow. Snow was regarded as a small-town (Orangeville, Ontario) eccentric with body odour—a man given to long silences, compulsive TV watching, and frequent tirades against others. He was also obsessed with pornography and military weaponry. Suspected of being the "House Hermit" (breaking into cottages), he eluded capture by heading to the West Coast of Canada, only to surface as a kidnapper and rapist of women there. Finally, Snow was convicted of the murders of Ian and Nancy Blackburn, found in the trunk of their car in Toronto in 1992 (Shaw, 1998).

Another example is William Lyon Mackenzie King (1874–95), a former Prime Minister of Canada. Regarded as a bland organization man by the public, it was only after his death that Canadians became aware that he participated in séances to communicate with his dead mother and that these and similar psychic activities helped him to make important governmental decisions. At least once King experienced an episode of psychiatric hospitalization during which he believed that others were influencing him with electric currents (Roazen, 1999). We are unlikely to find a satisfactory explanation for either of these examples in the rational calculations of classical theory or in the degeneracy theories discussed in Chapter 5. Theories of the mind are usually rooted in biology, but they also take into account the effects of society on mental processes, such as developing a conscience and learning. They differ from sociological theories in that they focus mainly on the individual, while sociology deals with broader "group" phenomena. Ideas drawn from psychiatry and psychology have merged with popular culture in the Western world. These ideas play a dominant role in our everyday accounts of deviance and in our art and literature, particularly the part that deals with unconscious and hidden motives behind human choices.

PSYCHOANALYTIC EXPLANATIONS OF DEVIANCE

FREUDIAN AND POST-FREUDIAN THEORIES

The psychoanalytic theories of Sigmund Freud (1856–1939) and his followers have had—and continue to have—a substantial impact on explanations of deviance. These theories emphasize motives for deviance that are nonrational and largely unconscious. Freud's conception of the human personality as a three-part structure of *id, superego,* and *ego* is a useful conceptualization of how biological and social factors come together in the individual mind. The *id*, the only part of the personality present at birth, is the completely selfish, biologically rooted drive for the gratification of instinctual needs such as food and sex (Freud's *pleasure principle).*

The *superego*, in contrast, is developed through the process of socialization and incorporates within itself the expectations of society, as taught by significant others (parents and role models). It is the cornerstone of what most of us call the "conscience" and controls whether we feel proud or guilty about our actions. It demands that the primitive urges of the id be channelled, curbed, or repressed.

The *ego* stands between the id and the superego, balancing their conflicting demands and keeping the individual in touch with both inner reality and the reality of the environment (Freud's *reality principle).* Freud also postulated the existence of the life instinct *(Eros),* which consists of impulses and drives toward self-preservation and reproduction, and the death instinct *(Thanatos),* which consists of an individual's impulses toward self-destruction and which may be expressed as aggression and hostility toward others. Needless to say, these principles conflict with each other. Attempts to resolve the conflicts may result in the development of anxiety and deviant adaptations, such as psychosomatic illness or drug dependence. Joan and William McCord (1960), for example, explain male forms of alcoholism as reflecting the conflict between men's dependency needs and the social requirements of independence imposed by our society. Women are less susceptible, in this view, because society allows them to retain their dependency into adulthood.

Deviant behaviour of almost any kind may be blamed on the id, the superego, the ego, or some combination of all three. Aggressive behaviour like murder or rape may express the transformed death wishes of the uncontrolled id. Neurotic behaviour like self-mutilation or nervous habits might be the consequence of an overly repressive superego. Aichen (1935) argued that some delinquents are love-deprived and fail to develop a strong superego. Others are overindulged and their id impulses are not restrained. Still others develop a criminal superego by identifying with criminal parents (in organized crime families, for example) or by identifying with other youths in crime-ridden neighbourhoods. Redl and Wineman (1951) similarly explain delinquent aggression as the product of inadequate ego and superego development caused by the lack of close relationships with adults.

In the Freudian system, the deviance that emerges is related to the stage of psychosocial development at which the individual experienced some difficulty, such as a traumatic event or sustained abuse. Freud outlined the stages of development as a sequence, moving from the oral stage through anal, genital, and eventually phallic stages. A person who did not receive enough nurturing or experienced trauma during the oral stage of development might be more likely to engage in smoking, gum-chewing, drinking, or compulsive shopping; a more socially acceptable resolution might involve learning to play a wind instrument or becoming a wine taster. Trouble in later stages of psychosocial development might result in disturbances of gender identity, such as homosexuality, transsexualism, transvestism, or prostitution. For Freud, we are all, and are always, sexual beings, but that sexuality is not always erotic. The ego forces us to sublimate many of these sexual urges, diverting them into athletics, economic competition, and other civilized pursuits—or into deviant outlets. For Freud, much of women's deviance was based on jealousy of men's anatomy. Girls who cannot resolve their "penis envy" overidentify with maleness and become unfeminine in a variety of unacceptable ways, including aggression and crime (Freud, 1933).

Not all psychologists or psychiatrists accept Freud's concept of biologically based reasons for human behaviour. Eric Erikson, Alfred Adler, Harry Stack Sullivan, Karen Horney, Eric Fromm, Thomas Szasz, and R. D. Laing place far more emphasis on environmental factors than did Freud, but all of these thinkers have been marginalized as deviant from the mainstream of psychiatric orthodoxy.

Many variants of psychoanalytic interpretation exist. In courtrooms, lawyers often try to explain that their clients' behaviour was not willfully chosen but rather caused by forces they neither understood nor were able to control. Freud (1948, p. 52) suggested that some criminals are driven by an unconscious desire to bring punishment down on themselves, either as a way of retaliating against their unacknowledged, forbidden desires (e.g., sexual feelings toward a parent), or as a means of justifying the sense of guilt produced by those desires. Similarly, people who engage in destructive, but noncriminal, behaviour such as compulsive spending may be trying to fill an inner emptiness, which may be the consequence of parental failure to provide unconditional love during infancy, or the result of childhood sexual abuse. Compulsive spending may also reflect conflict within a marriage as one partner makes the other "pay" for mistreatment of some kind (Lieberman, 1991). Psychiatrists have been criticized as "whores of the court" (the title of Hagen's 1997 book) because of their dual role in shoring up or undermining the guilt of accused persons, depending on which side is paying the bill.

FRUSTRATION–AGGRESSION THEORY: SCAPEGOATS AND ROAD RAGE

Freud (1948) argued that civilization engenders frustration by restricting the primal urges of the id. Frustration can be channelled in many directions, but it often results in anger and aggression. This idea was developed and dubbed "frustration–aggression theory" by psychologists in the late 1930s. Dollard et al. (1939) and Dollard et al. (1987) proposed that frustration and aggression always follow when goal attainment

Box 6.1   Mind Control

All theories of deviance have implications for social control of those they identify as abnormal. Psychiatry has sometimes been accused of being an extension of the Inquisition in that it ferrets out "heretical" ideas and makes scapegoats of any who dissent (Szasz, 1970). People who have been hospitalized for mental illnesses and given shock treatments or drug therapy sometimes refer to themselves as "the psychiatrized" and have formed self-help and advocacy groups such as Toronto's On Our Own and the Vancouver Mental Patients Association. Patients whose recovered memories of childhood abuse turned out to be figments of the therapists' heated imagination have sued for high damages.

One particularly egregious example of deviant psychiatric control occurred at the Allen Memorial Institute at McGill University in Montreal during the late 1950s and into the 1960s. Ewen Cameron, the man in charge of this experiment, was a very well connected and prestigious psychiatrist who enjoyed status as Head of the Quebec Psychiatric Association, the Canadian Psychiatric Association, and the American Psychiatric Association. He was founder of the Canadian Mental Health Association and the World Psychiatric Association. In the 1940s, Cameron had participated in the drafting of the Nuremberg Code on medical research (a code that his own work violated), which later became the basis for successful court action—unfortunately after Cameron's death.

Cameron's work was funded by the Canadian military and the United States' CIA as part of a broader CIA program called MK-Ultra. Patients came to Cameron for help with depression, alcoholism, and many conditions for which electroshock was not the normal treatment. They were used in drastic experiments—intensive repeated electroshock, psychosurgery, massive doses of dangerous drugs (curare, LSD), hypnosis, and experimental "psychic driving"—designed to further military knowledge related to brainwashing. The first step was to deprogram the mind, virtually obliterating the existing personality. After being kept in a state of sensory deprivation for as long as 65 days, the "patient" was put into a coma-like immobile state and subjected to recorded messages designed to reprogram the mind in the desired form. Patients who survived lost large chunks of their memories and often suffered incontinence and similar difficulties. A majority remain in mental hospitals, with little likelihood of recovery. Cameron gave up on this technique in 1964 and simply walked away from it, having finally realized that, despite the depth of its invasiveness, it simply didn't work.

Most of what we know about this horrifying case is found in the work of investigative journalists (Collins, 1998; Marks, 1977), United States congressional and senate investigations, and trial documents of a civil suit brought by Canadian Member of Parliament David Orlikow and his wife, Val, for damages done to Val when she went to Dr. Cameron for the treatment of postpartum depression (*Orlikow et al. v. United States*), and biographical materials (Weinstein, 1988). These events were first reported in Canada by CBC's *Fifth Estate* in 1984 and have been the subject of the CBC TV miniseries *The Sleep Room* (Zuckerman & Wheeler, 1998).

is blocked. The aggression is not necessarily or even usually against the original cause of the frustration (see Figure 6.1). The early theorists focused most on displaced aggression, for example, the aggression of White southerners against Blacks when the Whites were frustrated by the economy (Berkowitz, 1962; Hepworth & West, 1988) or intergroup violence among children when they were denied an expected treat (Miller & Bugelski, 1948). More recently, incidents of road rage (Fumento, 1998) and air rage (Luckey, 2000), brawls over disputed decisions at sports events, and ("going postal") harassment and mass murders on work sites (Fox & Spector, 1999) have attracted theoretical attention. It is notable that frustrated individuals tend to displace their anger onto targets who are less likely to fight back, such as visible minorities, less powerful employees, wives, and children.

Displaced aggression may also explain attacks on particular kinds of people (Hughes & Dagher, 1993, p. 302). Gay bashers, for example, may be unsure of their own sexual identity and express this by attacking those who, in some way, represent the part of themselves they have disowned (Dollard et al., 1987, n. 956). People who feel insecure in other ways may develop an inferiority complex that reveals itself in arrogance and aggression against others.

Frustration may be linked with relative deprivation, the belief that one is not getting as much as one should have, relative to others. This kind of frustration has been linked to civil violence (riots) and other forms of protest and rebellion (Gurr, 1970). During the 1992 riots in Los Angeles, most of the targets were businesses run by new immigrants, who seemed to be getting more opportunities for success than were experienced by Black Americans (Ong & Hee, 1993).

Figure 6.1 The Classic Frustration–Aggression Chart

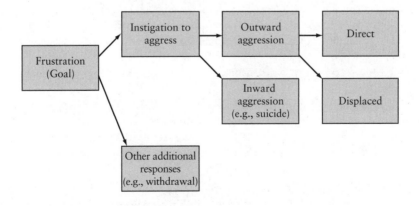

Source: Dollard et al., *Frustration and Aggression* (Yale University Press, 1939). Reprinted with permission.

Finally, we can note that most of the research on frustration–aggression has involved men or boys. Some evidence exists, mainly anecdotal, to support the view that women and girls may use relational aggression more often than physical aggression; that is, women are more likely to harm others' relationships (through gossip, innuendo, and social exclusion) than they are to engage in physical violence. Recent reported rises in female violence have been exaggerated in the news media and seem to be restricted to episodic gang-type violence and bullying perpetrated by adolescents.

Psychoanalytic explanations can help deviants understand how their behaviour is related to unmet needs, and thus provide them with the opportunity to find more acceptable ways of meeting those needs. And yet, some observers feel that what psychoanalytic explanations really provide deviants with are excuses for their behaviour—excuses that free them from feelings of guilt, place the guilt on parents or society, and thus enable them to commit more offences. Criminals who use psychiatry in this fashion look on punishment as further persecution and become bitter instead of reformed. Psychiatry has also been used as a means of political control. In the

Box 6.2   Gender and Psychiatric Explanations: Are Women Morally Better Than Men—or Just Sneakier?

Freud, echoing the dominant patriarchal notions of his time, maintained that normal women exhibit feminine traits of passivity, masochism, and narcissism that leads them into self-destructive forms of deviance or compulsive nonrational actions such as kleptomania. In his view, deviant women were a biological perversion or were expressing a psychiatric rebellion against their biologically natural female role. They were people who had developed a masculinity complex out of their jealousy of males' anatomical advantages, or who were neurotic because they had been, or wished to have been, seduced by their fathers (Masson, 1985; Schimek, 1987).

Otto Pollack (1950) has argued that women are more deviant than men are, even though statistics on most forms of misbehaviour, apart from prostitution and neonatal infanticide, seem to indicate that the reverse is true. According to Pollack, girls are not more moral than boys, just more cunning and conniving. Many girls learn to resolve their problems in passive–dependent ways, while males resolve theirs in aggressive–competitive ways. Women learn trickery and manipulation; men learn fighting and pushing. Pollack linked the female's ability to hide her feelings about the sex act from her husband and her sexuality from her children to her greater ability to get away with deceit. He argued that women are more devious when they commit offences (using poisoning instead of a gun, for example) or they use feminine wiles to induce men into committing offences for them. In Pollack's view, the authorities also treat them leniently because they evoke male chivalry. Taking note of the disadvantaged economic position of most women, Pollack argued that women experience sentiments of frustration and resentment that motivate them to make false accusations against men.

former Soviet Union, political dissidents were treated for their political views in psychiatric hospitals (Podrabinek, 1980). Conventional psychiatry has also been accused of pushing women back into dependent roles, sometimes aided by pharmaceuticals and hospitalization.

COGNITIVE THEORY: THE DEVELOPMENT OF MORAL JUDGMENT

Cognitive theories of moral judgment are based on child-development studies that show how a person's understanding of the meaning of rules develops, in a fixed sequence, at various stages of life. Jean Piaget (1896–1980) theorized that two main stages of moral development exist, the first characterized by an acceptance of rules as absolute, unchangeable, and valid in all circumstances, and a second, more mature stage in which the spirit of the law takes precedence over the letter of the law, and in which factors such as the motivation and intention of the rule breaker are considered (Piaget, 1932).

LAWRENCE KOHLBERG'S STAGES OF MORAL DEVELOPMENT

In a more complex version of Piaget's formulation, Kohlberg (1969, 1981, 1986) presented his core sample of 72 boys with "story problems" (moral dilemmas) and recorded their solutions over a period of years. One of these problems was "Heinz's Dilemma": a woman has a rare cancer and will die without a specific drug. The pharmacist charges $2000 for a small dose of the drug (even though it does not cost much to make) and, by borrowing, Heinz can come up with only half the amount. The pharmacist wants a steep return on his discovery of the drug and will not sell the drug for less. Heinz steals the drug. Should Heinz have done that? Kohlberg was interested mainly in the way in which his subjects justified the choices that they made, rather than the choices themselves.

Kohlberg classified his subjects' responses into three major stages of moral development: *preconventional, conventional,* and *postconventional.* Each major level has an early and late phase. The preconventional level (ages 4 to 10) is one of obedience–punishment thinking. At stage 1 Heinz should not steal because he will be punished, or Heinz should steal because he probably will not be punished. At stage 2, Heinz should get what he wants, if he can (utilitarian thinking).

The conventional level involves stereotypical "good person" thinking. At stage 3, Heinz should try to win social approval and acceptance, probably by abiding by the rules that others think are important. At stage 4, Heinz should not steal because the rules against stealing serve society as a whole.

The postconventional level is rarely attained. In the early phase (stage 5), rules are judged in relation to the individual's own personal standards and values. At the highest stage (6), rules are judged according to universal principles of justice, and this might mean that Heinz should rebel against the capitalist order.

People at the postconventional level may go so far as to break rules they see as wrong or unjust (Rest et al., 1999). They may find the present social system so intolerably corrupt that they actively attempt to destroy it. This thinking may be found in people regarded as heroes because they stand up to oppressive regimes but also in the thinking of people like Theodore (Ted) Kaczynski, who, despite diagnosed mental illness, was frighteningly rational. As the Unabomber, Kaczynski's mailed bombs killed 3 and injured 26, as he attempted to publicize his rage against modern technology and the impact of civilization on nature (Dube, 2000). Political offenders may commit exactly the same offences as their nonpolitical counterparts, but they do it for a cause—their reward is not personal gain but the cause itself.

Kohlberg found that most American adults reached stages 3 or 4 (conventional) but that very few moved beyond this. Common criminals were found to be significantly lower in their moral-judgment development (mainly stages 1 and 2) than were noncriminals from the same social background (Henggeler, 1984).

Carole Gilligan (1982), who worked as one of Kohlberg's research assistants in the 1970s and has proposed extensive revisions to his theory, noted that Kohlberg's system placed justice-based decision making highest on his scale. That is, when subjects decided what to do based on equality, justice, and respect for individual rights, they scored a 5 or 6 on Kohlberg's scale. Gilligan argues that this privileges men's morality over a different mode favoured by women. Women, when given the choice, tend to frame their responses in terms of concepts such as caring, restoring relationships, being kind, and balancing the needs of others with the needs of the self. On Kohlberg's scale, women cluster at level 3 (below, or the same as, the men), even though the high proportion of males who are criminal or close to it seems to belie the idea that men are more highly moral than women.

Gilligan proposed an adjusted scale for females, which, like Kohlberg's, has three levels: a *selfish level*, a *conventional level (conformity)*, and a *postconventional level*. At the conventional level, women reflect the common social norm that putting their own interests first is selfish and wrong. They make decisions in terms of looking after others. At the postconventional level, women recognize that looking after themselves is part of maintaining strong connectedness and responsible relationships. Just as legality is a higher level of awareness, so is the broader view of maintaining overall harmony. Gilligan also finds that women's refusal to make judgments ("I'm not really sure, it depends on the situation") is a sign of higher moral development, rather than (as in Kohlberg's schema) a lower one.

Although Gilligan points to the omission of female subjects and the caring dimension from Kohlberg's work, it is probably wrong to assume that the problem is simply a gender one. The theory is better if it includes both, and it needs to be tested in ways that allow the full participation of male and female subjects. An example of this testing is a study by Sarah Gordon that showed differences in males and females who write computer viruses. She finds Gilligan's work useful in explaining the rarity of female virus writers (Gordon, 1994). Other studies, however, have found that, at least with respect to mundane deviance such as classroom cheating, women may espouse higher moral values, but their actual behaviour does not differ much from men's (Whitely, Bichlmeier Nelson, & Jones, 1999).

THE CRIMINAL-MIND PERSPECTIVE

Another approach has been put forward by psychologist Stanton Samenow, who argues that the criminal is distinctive in his or her "thought patterns" (Samenow, 1984; Yochelson & Samenow, 1976). Like Lombroso, Samenow maintains that the criminal is "a different breed of person" (p. 31), only in this case the criminal traits are not physical but cognitive; the criminal exhibits different thinking patterns or precisely 52 "errors in thinking" that characterize the white-collar offender as much as the street criminal and that are found in criminally minded people who do not (yet) have a criminal record (Harris, 1984). Samenow (1984) maintains that when ordinary people enter a drugstore, they assess how easy it will be to find what they want and then pay for it. In contrast, the criminally minded assess how the cash register is protected and where the store's exits are; they do this automatically, even if they are not currently planning to rob the store. According to Samenow, this kind of thinking can be traced to the criminal's earliest consciousness. As a child, the criminal-to-be is deceitful and rebellious and constantly lies as a means of disarming other people. As an adolescent, he uses school as a training ground for "fighting, lying, stealing and engaging in power plays against teachers and other pupils" (Samenow, 1984, p. 14).

According to the criminal-mind perspective, the criminal is an abuser of family, school, and employer, not a victim of these institutions. Bad neighbourhoods, inadequate parents, television, schools, drugs, and unemployment do not cause crime. If they did, Samenow argues, we would have far more criminals than we do (Samenow, 1984, pp. 6–13). People with criminal minds can be trained to behave normally, he suggests, but just as the recovering alcoholic will always be an alcoholic, so the criminal will always be a criminal (Samenow, 1984, p. 229). Samenow's version of the psychopath (see Box 6.3) is potentially controllable, and yet it conforms to the popular stereotype that the criminal is fundamentally different from the rest of us. Samenow's work has been well received by the public (his 1984 book is in its tenth printing), has been implemented in some programs for delinquent youth (Goodman, 1983), and (according to Samenow's Web site, 2000) has attracted attention in the media (*60 Minutes, Good Morning America, The Phil Donahue Show, The Larry King Show,* and *The CBS Morning News*).

THEORIES OF LEARNING

Psychological studies of the learning process provide an important underpinning for sociological theories of learning, which we discuss in Chapter 9. Most psychologists would agree with Hebb (1980) that learning is "a changed pattern of conduction in the brain that results from experience and makes a change of response potential" (p. 81). Based on our biological capacities and our experiences, we develop a stable repertoire of potential responses to events in our lives.

TEACHING, TRAINING, AND MODELLING

Human beings learn in several ways. The most significant of these are teaching, training (operant and classical conditioning), and modelling. The most obvious way we learn is through *teaching,* which is the conscious transmission of information and techniques that may be used to solve problems (Nettler, 1978, p. 315; 1982, p. 114). Teaching tends to be intellectual and cognitive, and the learner is virtually always aware of the process. *Training* need not always be obvious, aware, or even intended. One mode of training is *classical conditioning* or associative learning. An experiment conducted by Ivan Pavlov (1849–1936) is the best-known example of this. In it, dogs were placed in an experimental situation in which food was paired with the ringing of a bell. Eventually, the sound of the bell triggered a salivation response in the dogs, even in the absence of food. The dogs had learned to associate the bell with food and responded accordingly (Goldstein, 1986, p. 32). Humans also can learn in a comparable fashion by associating something new with something that is strongly liked or disliked. This kind of learning is the root of our preference for the familiar.

Classical conditioning can also be used to reverse an acquired behaviour in a process known as *desensitization.* In simple terms, this technique involves removing the negative feelings associated with an object or event and replacing them with positive ones. People who have a phobia (extreme fear reaction) can be desensitized by repeatedly pairing the feared thing (whether it be snakes, flying, or open or enclosed spaces) with something that they like or that has a calming effect on them. The technique has also been used to deal with feelings closely associated with such behaviours as problem drinking, sexual exhibitionism, chronic kleptomania (due to anxiety), reckless driving, racial hostility, and aggression in general. It is sometimes argued that the constant deluge of images of deviance we receive from the media and other sources has desensitized people—not to mention the deviants themselves—to the real meaning of acts like murder, rape, and child abuse.

The second important mode of training is called *operant* or *instrumental conditioning,* so named because the learner operates on the environment to produce the effect. Although classical conditioning involves pairing a new stimulus with an existing response, in operant conditioning the individual learns to associate a particular behaviour with a particular consequence. If the individual finds the consequence of an action rewarding (positive reinforcement), the behaviour will continue and may increase.

The only limits on this type of learning are the biological capability of the organism to perform the behaviour and the cognitive ability of the organism to link the consequence with the act. If a pleasurable consequence is not forthcoming, the behaviour will probably be extinguished and replaced by other actions. When an action has been repeatedly associated with unwanted consequences, the autonomic nervous system (which is not under conscious control) responds by increasing heart rate, blood pressure, and the production of hormones in a way that creates feelings of anxiety. Thus, most of us would feel acutely uncomfortable with the idea of picking a pocket or assaulting someone to rob them (Fishbein, 1990; Moffitt, 1983).

Psychological research has shown that the timing, intensity, and consistency of rewards and punishments have strong effects on how well a particular kind of behaviour is learned—just as the classical deterrence theorists would have predicted. Bank robbers, for example, are usually not caught immediately, and they reap the rewards for their behaviour (excitement and the chance to spend money) long before their eventual punishment (which is then associated with getting caught, not with committing the crime). In terms of reinforcement, the prison term comes much too late to be very effective, and the offenders may very well resolve to not get caught the next time, rather than resolving not to commit the crime again.

Many things affect operant conditioning. For example, in prison, different rewards and styles of reinforcement may be managed by the institution, ranging from threats to actual punishments, and from money, food, tokens, and praise to more complex forms such as the negotiation of an earlier parole date. This reinforcement regime may be undermined by an informal system controlled largely by the strongest inmates. The effects of rewards and punishments on individuals can differ as well. Although rewards of money or pleasurable experiences are usually positive reinforcers, punishments are more difficult to evaluate in this respect. Standing up to pain and deprivation may bring feelings of pride, which are positive rewards. Nonetheless, "contingency management" or "reality therapy" programs use operant conditioning to influence behaviour in a wide variety of contexts: psychiatric institutions, homes for people with mental disabilities, classrooms, reform schools, prisons, and many other settings (Glasser, 1965; McKain & Anthony, 1990; Schaefer & Martin, 1966).

The third major way of learning is through *modelling* (imitating the behaviour of others). In many languages, the verb "to teach" is the same as the verb "to show," and our awareness of this lies behind such things as the media's policy not to publicize suicides that occur in places like subway systems or at Niagara Falls. In modern life, each of us is exposed to a wide range of alternative models of behaviour, and we select from them those that attract us or suit our interests and capabilities. Seeing other people rewarded, apparently for behaving in particular ways, is part of this, as is admiring people who are higher than ourselves in one or all of life's hierarchies and identifying with their behaviour. It is this aspect of learning that makes the misbehaviour of popular entertainment figures distressing to parents. The intentional shock tactics of performers like Madonna or Blink-182 disturb many observers, who see these people as role models for the young (Edwards, 2000).

TEMPERAMENT AND LEARNING

Temperament refers to an individual's mental, physical, and emotional characteristics. Many psychologists argue that temperament is formed through a combination of genetic predisposition and perinatal environment (e.g., drug use on the part of the mother), and that its basic components are in place at birth. From earliest infancy, children display differences in terms of activity level, rhythmicity (regularity), distractibility, and responsiveness (Cattell, 1979; Eysenck, 1960). The baby who is very slow to establish routines of sleep and bowel movements is likely to become the child who has difficulty adjusting to the routines of school and the adult who struggles with the routines of work.

Research psychologist Hans Jürgen Eysenck (1916–1997), student of Cyril Burt, developed a theory of temperament that fits within the category of behaviour genetics (sometimes called "differential psychology") and shares a common base with the work of Galton, Rushton, Bouchard, and others discussed in connection with eugenics and scientific racism in Chapter 5.

Eysenck used factor analysis (a statistical technique) to produce scales that differentiate individuals from one another along a dimension of *neuroticism* (degree of stability or instability of behaviour) and *extroversion or introversion* (impulsive, outgoing behaviour versus controlled, withdrawn behaviour) (Eysenck, 1960). In a psychiatric hospital, virtually all patients scored high on neuroticism (instability of behaviour) but differed in the kind of disturbance they showed. Those who scored high on introversion as well as neuroticism tended to suffer from depression, phobias, and compulsions; those who scored high on extroversion and neuroticism were more likely to have been hospitalized because of personality disorders, manias, and hysteria. Various studies using the Eysenck scales have found deviant behaviour (car accidents, unwed motherhood, repeated criminal conviction, psychopathy) to be concentrated in the high-neuroticism/high-extroversion (NE) quadrant formed by the two scales (Eysenck, 1960, 1964).

In the original studies, violent criminals tended to be non-neurotic extroverts—people who enjoyed the excitement of robbing or raping, for example, and did not dwell on the possibility that things could go wrong. (It is hard to imagine a painfully shy bank robber, especially one who agonizes over what can go wrong.) A rather late addition to Eysenck's theory was the trait of *psychoticism* (1977; Eysenck & Eysenck, 1976). This trait reflects many of the same characteristics as are attributed to the psychopath. The person who is high on Eysenck's psychoticism scale shows inappropriate emotional responses, a disregard for common sense or social conventions, and heightened recklessness. Psychotics (persons with schizophrenia, for example), geniuses, and sexual perverts also score highly on this trait, as measured by the Eysenck scale. Although Eysenck's two original scales (extroversion and neuroticism) have been widely adopted for diagnostic purposes, his underlying genetic explanation for them has been controversial (de Jong, 2000). The idea that psychopathy, genius, and psychotic and sexual disorders have a common genetic root has not been well received by scholars outside the behavioural genetics group and Eysenck's ideas about racial inheritance of IQ and other eugenic ideas—he was a Fellow of the British Eugenics Society—even less.

Like Philippe Rushton, Eysenck accepted funding from the Pioneer Fund, and like Rushton, he faced an international campaign to deny him the chance to speak on university campuses. On several occasions, violent disruptions of his lectures took place (Eysenck, 1990).

Temperament theories, whether biological or not, are based on the observation that temperament does not change a great deal during an individual's life unless brain damage occurs (or is reversed) or the immediate environment changes drastically and for a long time (Nettler, 1982). For example, people can change dramatically when they are cut off from their roots, brainwashed, and kept in an environment that sustains the change. Even so, the person who compulsively sought drugs may become a person who compulsively does good deeds. The A+ student who drops out of school to join a cult may become the cult's best fundraiser or most devout member. An example of this kind of consistency of temperament despite an apparent transformation of behaviour can be found in the case of Patty Hearst. Before her kidnapping in 1974 by an ultra-leftist urban guerrilla group, Hearst—a California college student and granddaughter of publishing magnate William Randolph Hearst—was a compliant individual who lived very much according to the ideas of her boyfriend and family. Although the public was shocked by a photograph of Hearst (as group member "Tanya") holding a machine gun during a bank robbery undertaken in the name of the "revolution," her change of behaviour was consistent with her compliant temperament (Watkins, 1976). What had changed—traumatically—was the nature of the people who had authority over her (the kidnappers). Following her release, Hearst returned to a conventional lifestyle.

The Psychopathic Personality

The term *psychopath* combines the Greek word for soul (*psyche*) with the word for illness or suffering (*pathos*). This name is somewhat misleading, since the essence of psychopathy is the absence of real feelings—the psychopath may recognize empathy, compassion, or feelings of guilt in others but does not experience these emotions as others do (Cleckley, 1976). The term psychopath was invented long after the reality that it refers to was recognized. In the nineteenth century, the main corresponding term was "moral insanity," in which "the emotional and ethical capacities are impaired while the intellect remains intact" (Pritchard, 1835; Rafter, 1997, pp. 236,

241). The intact intellect distinguishes the sane psychopath from the psychotic, who is not fully in touch with the world.

The early use of the concepts of moral degeneracy, moral insanity, psychic degeneration, and constitutional psychopathy included a range of deviant types, from simple troublemakers, to chronic liars, to serious violent offenders. The definitions were also extended to include gender rebels, women who were defiantly promiscuous, and men who were effeminate or homosexual. Not all researchers included sexual deviation as part of the psychopathic personality, but many did, and originally the greatest concern was for women's sexual deviance. German psychiatrists such as Emil Kraepelin (1917, p. 284) said that sadism, masochism, and fetishism are to be expected in degenerates as part of their "primeval tendencies" (cited in Rafter, 1997, p. 242), and these ideas were further developed by Bernard Glueck, who studied a sample of prisoners at Sing Sing and concluded that 20 percent of them—drinkers, gamblers, drug addicts, and sex perverts—were psychopaths. The rest were labelled as mental defectives or insane (Glueck, 1918, cited in Rafter, 1997, p. 243).

Box 6.3   The Psychopath

For seven months in 1989, a notorious convicted killer who had escaped custody terrorized the Miramichi region of New Brunswick. Allan Legere was an accomplished liar, a manipulator of other people, and a cold-blooded killer. Concerned only with his own well-being, he appears to have been completely unresponsive to normal feelings of love, caring, and responsibility. While on the run, he robbed and sexually assaulted several people. His victims included two elderly sisters (sexually assaulted and beaten to death), an elderly priest (robbed and beaten to death), and another pair of elderly sisters, one of whom was beaten to death and one of whom survived to testify against him (MacLean, Veniot, & Waters, 1992).

Not all psychopaths are criminals. It is likely that the famous "love them and leave them" cad Don Juan was a psychopath. He manipulated women into loving him and enjoyed their suffering when he abandoned them. Not all psychopaths have abnormal needs and desires, but they are likely to cross the line into illegality if they do. The psychopath may be the conniving salesperson who charms people into buying things they don't need and can't afford, or the heartless Scrooge who would deny Tiny Tim a bit of Christmas cheer. The psychopath can be a woman, as shown by the pitiless and apparently guilt-free behaviour of Karla Homolka, who participated in the kidnapping, sexual abuse, and eventual deaths of two teenage girls and who apparently brought about the death of her sister, Tammy (Jenish & Driedger, 1995). The disparity between social image and inner pathology (paraphilias, serial sexual offending, and murder) was especially jarring in the case of Homolka and her equally attractive partner, Paul Bernardo (Jenish, 1995).

In *The Individual Delinquent* (1915) William Healy included a whole chapter on offenders characterized by "psychic constitutional inferiority" (PCI). Healy's offenders with PCI were typically unable to exercise self-restraint and showed evidence of physical abnormalities that could be interpreted as degeneracy or even "atavism" (Rafter, 1997, p. 45). Healy describes the female with PCI as quite rare and explains this in terms similar to Lomboso's sperm and ovule analogy. Women are passive and immobile while men are active (p. 245). The female with PCI is often a prostitute, is "hypersexual," and violates norms by bearing numerous illegitimate children, despite her unattractiveness. The male with PCI is described as effeminate and unemployed (p. 247). The first specialized institution for psychopaths (established in 1916) was designed for female prostitutes (Freedman, 1987). Edith Spaulding, its director, described the psychopathic woman as antisocial, uncooperative, and disruptive—an impulsive rebel (Spaulding, 1969, p. 915, cited in Rafter, 1997, p. 248). Over time, the public view of the psychopath came to be typified by the (male) serial killer celebrated in films such as *The Silence of the Lambs*.

Gradually though, through a process sometimes called "concept drift," the expert opinion has swung back toward the original image of a person without internalized social controls, and many practitioners now refer to it as *sociopathy*, even though most practitioners feel that the condition has physiological, as well as social, roots. Sociopathy is recognized in persistent violations of social norms of nonviolence, responsibility, honesty, accountability, and truthfulness (Huss & Langhinrichsen-Rohling, 2000). Psychopathy is now considered a subcategory of antisocial personality disorder (ASPD), according to the DSM, *The Diagnostic and Statistical Manual of Mental Disorders* (American Psychiatric Association [APA], 1994, pp. 645–650; Hare, 1996b).

In his book *Without Conscience* (1993), Robert Hare of the University of British Columbia argues that we live in a "camouflage society," one in which many of the traits characteristic of the psychopath are tolerated or even valued (Hare, 1996b). These include "egocentricity, lack of concern for others, superficiality, style over substance, being 'cool,' and manipulativeness" (Hare, 1996b). In these conditions, many psychopaths can avoid being "unmasked" as defective personalities (Hare, 1986; Reid, Walker, & Dorr, 1986).

AROUSAL THEORY

Although work on temperament and learning is diverse, considerable convergence is found in the area of differences in the responses of individuals to environmental stimuli. According to arousal theory, some people are *augmenters*. They see colours as brighter than other people see them, noises as louder, pain as more painful, and excitement as more exciting. Others are, physiologically, *reducers*, who perceive stimuli but do not react to them as much as average people do. These differences have been found to be associated with typical modes of behaviour, including risk-taking types of deviance.

Augmenters quickly find a given level of stimulation "too much" and attempt to retreat from it. As infants, they show a greater "startle response" to noise and light, and as adults, they tend to seek reduced stimulation. They are more likely to be seen as introverts, who seek quiet pastimes. If born into a crime family, they are likely to seek the role of bookkeeper rather than enforcer. If they become criminals, it will be in the less exciting, less risky forms of crime. Reducers, on the other hand, perceive the same stimulus as less stimulating than the average person, and are easily bored. They are likely to become "sensation-seekers" (Schrader & Wann, 1999; Zuckerman, 1984).

Reducers take longer to "get the message" from pain or pleasure (they are harder to train) and are more likely to enjoy the physical sensations that accompany risk-taking actions. Reducers who drink, for example, may drink hard, experiencing the drunkenness as an escape from boredom, and are less likely to be deterred by a colossal hangover than are augmenters. Reducers are more likely to drive fast, engage in unsafe sex, skydive, gamble, have criminal records, and acquire serious injuries (Mawson et al., 1996; Roberts, 1994). The majority of reducers are men (Schrader & Wann, 1999). Reducers are also more likely to be diagnosed as psychopaths (Day & Wong, 1996; Hare, 1996a). Controversy rages over the causes of these differences. Some regard the difference as related to humankind's history, in which the (male) hunter who was a reducer would have a survival advantage. Others see it as an inborn trait that can be controlled but not changed. Still others feel that sociopathy can be brought about through training, induced by growing up in a violent, abusive, or neglectful family, living in displaced persons' camps under wartime conditions, or even by participation in certain types of military or sports training. Many theorists combine the two ideas:

> The conventional psychological wisdom—that bullies are motivated by an underlying lack of self-esteem—is simply not the case. A boy with typically low levels of cortical arousal suffers from a stimulus hunger, a sort of craving for sensation. He becomes easily habituated, and therefore easily bored with his environment. Strong stimuli are not experienced as unpleasant and to be avoided—rather they can be exciting and engaging. The cycle becomes self-reinforcing; a child in a deprived community with nothing to do, and no hope of a creative stimulus, satisfies his hunger for sensation and novelty by an ever-increasing spiral of danger and impulsiveness. As he grows older, he associates this satisfaction with acting out of antisocial behavior. He has, indeed, become dependent on it in stronger and stronger doses. It's no use offering this boy a jigsaw or a bicycle—he'll get bored; it's no use offering him a dinghy or a skiing holiday to "let off steam"—the novelty soon wears off. He can be satisfied only with wrecking the regatta or crashing down the off-piste suicide runs. (Moir & Jessel, 1995, p. 76)

The hero and the psychopath, as Lykken (1982) says, "are twigs from the same branch" (22).

THE SOCIAL CONSTRUCTION OF MEDICALIZED CONDITIONS

What do the following accounts have in common?

Scott Falater, 43, killed his wife Yarmila by stabbing her 44 times and holding her head underwater. Defense specialists testified that his history of job stress and sleep deprivation could explain that this behavior was an episode of sleepwalking. The jury convicted him anyway. (Kelley, 1999) [medical excuse making]

Three weeks before this event, Falater had spoken with others about a Canadian case in which a man took a knife from his own kitchen, drove 14 miles to his in-laws' home, and killed his mother-in-law. He was judged not guilty, on the basis that his sleepwalking amounted to "non-insane automatism." (Callwood, 1990; *R. v. Parks,* 1992)

When the verdict came down, Lorena Bobbitt asked, "Is that good?" She had been acquitted by reason of temporary insanity in the infamous "penis-snipping" event that deprived her husband John Wayne Bobbitt, of an important part of his anatomy. Lorena was sent to a Virginia mental hospital for a 45-day period of evaluation, and then released. (Sachs, 1994, p. 99) [psychiatric excuse making]

On the evening of Sunday, August 20, 1989, Lyle and Erik Menendez (aged 21 and 18) killed their parents—they ran out of bullets on the first try, ran back to their car, and got some more. In the next few months, both boys spent huge amounts of their inheritance, indulging their childhood dreams (Davis, 1994). Although they eventually confessed, and there was ample evidence beyond this, their first jury could not decide to convict them. The reason? The boys claimed to have been sexually and emotionally abused by their father, and their mother had to die if he did. [abuse excuse]

A farmer from Blumenhof, Saskatchewan, became obsessed with singer Anne Murray and began a systematic campaign of harassment. He spent more than 4 years in custody and almost 20 years under various probation orders to stay away from Murray. After violating probation again, he was brought to court, declared unfit to stand trial, and committed to psychiatric care. He suffers from a rare mental disorder called erotic paranoia, which leads him to believe that he and the singer are involved in a secret affair. [psychiatric excuse]

Dan White resigned his position as a member of the San Francisco Board of Supervisors but then tried to retract his resignation. Backed by Harvey Milk—widely known as the man who brought homosexual politics to City Hall—Mayor Moscone refused to reinstate him. White sought out and killed both Moscone and Milk. At the trial, White's lawyer argued that his client was suffering from depression exacerbated by his intake of snack food, in what came to be known as the "Twinkie defense." The jury apparently agreed that White had been temporarily insane (depression) and convicted him of manslaughter, not murder. Shortly after he was released on parole, White committed suicide. (Miller, 1987) [medical–psychiatric excuse]

In England, a 37-year-old woman suffering from PMS killed her ex-lover by driving her car directly at him, pinning him to a telephone pole. She was found not guilty of murder, due to diminished responsibility. Although convicted of manslaughter, she was conditionally discharged, which meant that she was set free. (Rose, 2000, p. 11)

In each example, a serious attempt has been made to explain the behaviour in question in terms of a *medical model*. In these versions of the medical model, however, the behaviour itself can be the main evidence of the disease, the only evidence of the disease, or even just an accusation. Similarly, insulting words can be seen as a symptom of "stress," "Bobbettizing" as a symptom of spousal abuse, and a commuter-train mass murder can be blamed on "black rage syndrome" (Gregory, 1984). The mother with a child who is frequently ill or injured may be accused of Munchausen by Proxy Syndrome (a condition in which people with a pathological need for attention cause harm to those in their care). If the sick or injured child is a foster child, or is part of a custody battle, the child may be removed from the home (Siegel & Fischer, 2000).

The medicalized interpretation of the behaviour becomes a substitute for moral interpretations, lifting the burden of responsibility from the perpetrator—who is considered not responsible for his or her actions—but it also means that the person is no longer considered a responsible, respectable person. Note that, historically, women are disproportionately medicalized, while men are disproportionately criminalized (Conrad & Schneider, 1980, p. 272; Maticka-Tyndale & Bicher, 1996).

Most of the time, we are not aware that we have a choice: that we can choose to treat the drug addict as a criminal, as a sick person, or just someone with some problems. We can choose to identify a sick soldier's behaviour as malingering, paranoid schizophrenia, or a respectable syndrome such as posttraumatic stress disorder. We can choose to treat the wealthy customer's shoplifting as kleptomania and to treat the poor person's shoplifting as theft. The behaviour is the same, but its meaning is not.

Medicalization is a term that refers to the application of "disease" explanations (the medical model) to certain types of deviant behaviour. These behaviours include excessive drinking (alcoholism), overeating (obesity or greed) or undereating (bulimia and anorexia), addictions (drugs, sex, cleaning, shopping, exercise, work), and compulsions (hyperactivity, hair pulling, nail biting, child and spousal abuse). They also include deviant characteristics, such as being too short, too fat, or too unhappy, shopping too much, being too angry about sexual abuse, feeling too much, or feeling too little. Although we may sneer at the use of a sleepwalking defence to the attempted rape of a seven-year-old, we may not be quite so certain about postpartum depression as a reason for infanticide (Grossman, 1990).

Revisionist psychiatrists like Thomas Szasz and R. D. Laing believe that our modern tendency to medicalize life is just as misguided as the efforts of the Inquisition.

> [T]he concept of mental illness has the same logical and empirical status as the concept of witchcraft; in short … witchcraft and mental illness are imprecise and all-encompassing concepts, freely adaptable to whatever uses the priest or physician (or lay "diagnostician") wishes to put on them.… [T]he concept of mental illness serves the same social function in the modern world as did the concept of witchcraft in the late Middle Ages; in short … the belief in mental illness and the social actions to which it leads have the same moral implications and political consequences as had the belief in witchcraft and the social actions to which it led. (Szasz, 1970, p. xix)

Most observers, however, do not completely reject the claims of the medical model, even if they remain skeptical about some of its applications.

Conrad and Schneider (1980, 1992) have traced the path of social construction by which particular kinds of deviance have come to be treated as medical problems. They describe and analyze how madness became mental illness, drunkenness became alcoholism, opiate users became addicts, delinquency became hyperactivity, over-enthusiastic discipline became child abuse, and homosexuality became a psychiatric illness. In each case, although the behaviour changed little, if at all, over time, the explanation for it changed from "moral badness" to "pathological illness." Conrad and Schneider use a sociohistorical sequential mode to describe the process common to all these cases. The model has five broad stages (Conrad & Schneider, 1980, pp. 266–267):

1. definition of behaviour as deviant
2. prospecting (medical discovery)
3. claims making (medical and nonmedical interests)
4. legitimacy (securing medical turf)
5. institutionalization of a medical deviance designation

In the first stage (*definition*), a particular type of behaviour is defined as highly undesirable. This definition may have been part of the commonsense understanding embedded in the culture for a long time. For example, although masturbation had been negatively viewed since at least biblical times, it was not medicalized until the nineteenth century, when it was treated with all sorts of unpleasant restraining devices and even surgery. Similarly, restless inattentiveness in schoolchildren was regarded as "bad" long before it was diagnosed as hyperkinesis or attention deficit disorder and treated with drugs. In other cases, the definition of behaviour as deviant may have developed after a long period of not being noticed very much. For example, anorexia nervosa has a long history, and at one time, it was even associated with holiness (Bell, 1985). Only recently has it been recognized as a medical problem.

In the second stage (*prospecting*), a medical perception of a problem is first proposed to a professional audience, usually in a medical journal or at a conference. This stage is called prospecting because it is tentative; the proposal may or may not be picked up by others. Prospecting can include a new diagnosis, new physical cause, or new treatment. The most common of these, the proposal of a new diagnosis, is spelled out as a series of symptoms that add up to a physically based "syndrome." The second most frequent form of prospecting is the proposal of a new physical cause for the behaviour. Third, a new treatment—or new application of an old treatment—may be proposed.

An example of the prospecting of a *new diagnosis* or recently "discovered" syndrome is fetal alcohol syndrome (FAS). The physical and cognitive abnormalities that characterize victims are attributed to drinking on the part of the mother during the pregnancy (Astley & Clarren, 2001). Although the condition must have occurred often in the gin-soaked slums of nineteenth-century England, and in other places characterized by cheap, available, or culturally mandated use of alcohol, it has become a medically recognized syndrome only recently.

Sometimes a proposed diagnosis is unambiguous and specific. Other times it is quite vague. Ysseldyke and Algozzine (1982) found that official definitions of learning disabilities were so diverse and nonspecific that more than 90 percent of the students in public schools could be classified as having a learning disability.

Of the *new causes and new treatments* constantly being prospected, only a few catch on, and the treatment often precedes any full understanding of the cause. The use of estrogen to combat problems associated with menopause preceded the definition of menopause as a kind of deficiency disease, and the use of drugs for hyperactivity still precedes an understanding of why some children cannot sit still. Pharmaceutical companies have strong motivation to expand the number of conditions that can be treated with their products.

The third stage (*claims making*) is the key stage in the process of medicalization (Conrad & Schneider, 1980, p. 267). Medical definitions are sometimes not accepted if they compete with strongly held beliefs and interests. An interesting example of this is Daniels's (1979) study of combat psychiatry, which shows that the definition of mental illness changes according to the circumstances and context in which it occurs. It is a lot easier for a student to be diagnosed as mentally incapacitated than it is for a frontline soldier to be diagnosed as mentally unable to fight.

Those who take up the cause of the new deviance designation are often beneficiaries of the programs that result: the so-called experts gain both prestige and funding for their research; the administrators increase their resources for treatment services; the drug companies sell their pills and tonics; and the support groups gain interest, sympathy, and services for their area of interest (Horowitz, 1981, p. 750).

At the fourth stage (*legitimacy*), the claim makers exert pressure on medical associations and relevant government agencies (legislators, investigatory committees, and

Box 6.4 Gender and Medicalization: A Case of Inequality?

In 1985, when version four of the *Diagnostic and Statistical Manual* of the American Psychiatric Association was being prepared (it was published in 1994), two new diagnostic categories were proposed: Self-Defeating Personality Disorder and Late Luteal Phase Dysphoric Disorder. Both of these disorders were perceived as pathologizing characteristics associated with many women—women who put others' needs ahead of their own, and women who experience stress as an aspect of menstruation. Sociologist Margrit Eichler and psychiatrist Paula Caplan responded by describing a "macho man" disorder, tentatively named "Delusional Dominating Personality Disorder (DDPD)." Caplan and another colleague entered this into the process to be evaluated for the new DSM edition. Among the behavioural traits that would distinguish DDPD were "an inability to establish and maintain meaningful interpersonal relationships," "an inability to derive pleasure from doing things for others," and "a tendency to feel inordinately threatened by women who fail to disguise their intelligence" (Caplan, 1995, p. 171). DDPD was not accepted in the final version of the DSM-IV but, as pointed out by Kingwell and Donaldson (1993), it is a reminder that a great deal of socially accepted behaviour is essentially destructive, that more social violence is perpetrated by males than by the "(mostly imaginary) crazed witches of PMS," and that efforts such as Caplan's should remind us "that the line between normal and pathological is far from firm."

In fact, the 300 or so categories of the DSM-IV make it possible to pathologize almost everything we (males and females) do—from playing video games (under malingering) to losing our cool (Intermittent Explosive Disorder).

The heavy impact of dominant social norms can be read in the history of the DSM, arguably one of the most influential books of our time. In 1973, a vote forced the removal of "homosexuality" from the DSM-III, but ego-dystonic homosexuality remained. This meant doctors could still bill for the treatment of homosexuals who were unhappy about being homosexual. In the DSM-IV (1994), this vestige was removed, but the category of "Gender-Identity Disorder" (GID) remained. It is reasonably clear that the DSM reflects social control as much as it represents physical realities (Livesley, 1995).

the courts) to gain official recognition of and support for the new view. Success in the fourth stage is exemplified when a judge refuses to send a convicted person to prison because no appropriate treatment facilities are in place there for his or her particular disorder.

The fifth stage (*institutionalization*) is a direct outcome of successful work in the previous stages. It includes both acceptance of the diagnosis by medical authorities and the establishment of treatment programs based on the medical model. Thus, the establishment of programs for sex offenders has followed the demand of the courts that such people be "treated," even though most treatments are highly experimental at this point.

Almost anything can be pathologized. A good many of you may recognize the "Coffee Drinkers' Syndrome." According to the DSM-IV (APA, 1994, p. 708), coffee drinkers who abruptly stop or sharply reduce their intake of caffeine after "prolonged daily use" may experience headache and one or more other of a list of symptoms, including fatigue, anxiety, and nausea. More consequential, perhaps, is the medicalization of exceptions to the dominant male gender role.

THE SICK ROLE: MEDICALIZATION AND SOCIAL CONTROL

In the early 1950s, the way in which designations of sickness were related to social control in society were increasingly recognized. As the sociologist Talcott Parsons (1951) observed in that period, illness involves violation of the norms that structure role performance. Parsons argued that the "sick role" is a culturally available mechanism that minimizes the disruptiveness of deviance to the system as a whole. The sick role has four components: two exemptions from normal responsibilities and two new obligations (Parsons, 1951, pp. 428–479). (The exemptions are conditional on the performance of the obligations.)

1. The sick person is *exempt* from role obligations. The certifiably sick person does not have to write exams, show up for work, or even have a job if the illness is sufficiently serious.
2. The sick person is *exempt* from negative judgment *as well as the penalties* that normally attend failure to perform customary duties. (There may be some negative judgment if the illness is deemed self-induced.)
3. The sick person is *obligated* to recognize that illness is undesirable and to want to get well. It is not acceptable to embrace the illness or to abandon oneself to it.
4. The sick person is *obligated* to seek and cooperate with a qualified treatment agent. This may mean taking medication with unpleasant side effects, participating in behavioural modification programs, or submitting to psychosurgery.

Medicalized explanations of deviance that establish a sick role can have positive, negative, or mixed effects for the individuals involved. On the positive side, the person who is assigned a "sick" as opposed to a "bad" label is spared guilt and punishment and is sometimes helped by being able to hope that a cure or effective control will be found. In the case of a sleepwalking killer, the sick role can mean freedom instead of a lengthy prison sentence.

However, the sick role has its dark side. First, calling someone's behaviour sick means that the behaviour is seen neither as rationally willed nor as worthy of serious attention beyond its status as a symptom of illness. Often, the behaviour of rebels and nonconformists is labelled mental illness and thus demeaned. In 1885, when Louis Riel was charged with treason for leading the Northwest Rebellion, he rejected his lawyers' advice that he plead "not guilty by reason of insanity" on the grounds that, although it could spare his life, it would cost him his dignity; that is, his claim to "the moral existence of an intellectual being" (Bliss, 1974, p. 212). In other cases, pharmaceuticals may be used as chemical straitjackets.

Second, the fact that a diagnosis or label for a particular behaviour exists implies that an effective treatment for that behaviour also exists. Often this is not the case or is only partly the case. The individual may be forced to endure appalling treatment in the name of therapy. Psychosurgery has helped some marginal deviants (e.g., epileptics) but turned others into functional zombies. Similarly, electroshock therapy has helped some depressives but left others damaged and bitter. It may seem that any treatment is better than none with respect to violent, habitual criminals, but even here, some treatments, particularly those aimed at sex offenders, would appear to violate one of the major principles of Western democracy, which is the dignity and worth of each individual (Pellegrino, 1985).

Third, although some medical diagnoses, such as hyperactivity, include a prediction that the individual will outgrow the problem, many others come with the assumption that the condition is permanent. When this expectation is coupled with the assumption that the individual lacks control over the behaviour in question, the medicalized diagnosis may very well constitute a self-fulfilling prophecy in which the person who might otherwise have outgrown a problem, or taken charge of it, or gathered with others to make the behaviour legitimate, instead suffers repeated and lifelong "relapses," or is never given a chance to participate in society in a normal way.

Fourth, the use of medicalization to control behaviour has, according to some observers, brought about the tyranny of the "therapeutic state," in which the state bypasses the due process rights of the accused (i.e., those established under the classical model of the responsible criminal), substitutes diagnoses based on evidence that would not be acceptable in a courtroom, and sentences individuals to enforced treatment, for the good of the accused person (Kittrie, 1971). At its most extreme, the substitution of treatment for punishment can result in "selective incapacitation" whereby those who are most likely to offend are identified *before* they commit any offence and are either subjected to treatment or contained in an institution of some kind.

Finally, by focusing on the individual, illness models cause us to look inside the body rather than at the environment surrounding it. The medicalization of menopause, for example, results in emphasis on hormone therapy that tends to exclude any serious analysis of the social position of middle-aged women. Similarly, the medicalization of homosexuality, hyperactivity, radicalism, drug abuse, and domestic violence may preclude awareness of the wider, social aspects of these phenomena. The next chapter follows an alternative thread of explanation, one that emphasizes the social environment as the source of deviance.

SUMMARY

Many psychiatric and psychological theories are based on the Freudian idea that biological urges reside in the id portion of the mind and that these are subject to control or mismanagement by the ego and superego, both of which are influenced by environmental factors. Freudian theory has been used to explain violence against outgroups, self-destructive forms of deviance, and just plain "different" deviance.

Psychologists have also developed theories of cognitive and moral development that help to distinguish people who commit common offences from those who engage in political and morally motivated criminal activity. Psychological theories of temperament and learning also throw light on how deviants may learn deviant behaviour and deviant motives because of conditioning or social modelling in their environment.

Biological, psychological, and sociological research all converge in arousal theory. This theory predicts that people who are overstimulated in the normal environment will retreat, while those who are bored and insensitive to pain will take both legal and illegal risks. Arousal theory has particular relevance for sensation-seeking forms of deviance, especially with respect to those who fit the label "psychopath."

According to the medical model, deviant behaviour is a symptom of disease or, in some cases, is the disease itself in the sense that there are no other symptoms or obvious physical manifestations of illness. This model has been controversial when applied to mental illness, hyperactivity, and addictive-compulsive behaviours such as alcoholism, drug abuse, gambling, compulsive spending, and kleptomania. The medical model has been criticized on several fronts, most generally for addressing nonconformity as a symptom and treating it with drugs and psychosurgery, and for failing to consider the social conditions that may have contributed to the deviance.

STUDY QUESTIONS

1. Psychiatric and psychological theories (which are often reduced to "pop-psych") are the dominant theories featured in popular entertainment programming, the news media, and all the main communications media of our time. Partly because they are very familiar to us, they seem very convincing. Some of these theories are potentially powerful explanations of individual behaviour, but others are tainted. Try making a list of those with promise and those that are probably wrong.

2. Is postconventional thinking deviant?

3. What is the main point in the argument between Gilligan and Kohlberg?

4. Why do we not always realize when we have "learned" something new? (Hint: conditioning, reinforcement.)

5. How useful is the concept of the "psychopath"? Is it just a judgment of worthiness or is it meaningful?

6. Neoclassical thought allowed for the consideration of aggravating and mitigating circumstances, and this has led to the evolution of many defences against criminal conviction, including "diminished capacity" and " not guilty by reason of insanity." When taken into the courtroom, these positivist diagnoses become a battleground of defence expert witness versus prosecution expert witness. How useful are psychiatric and psychological theories in the pursuit of criminal justice?

7. To what extent is a craving for a drug similar to and different from a craving for pickles or a love of salt? How is it different?

8. How does the medical model differ from a merely scientific model? What else is involved?

9. In what way is the use of medicalization a double-edged sword? How can medicalization improve the lives of "rule breakers" while simultaneously making things worse?

10. Why are feminists unlikely to accept the medicalization of conditions such as menstruation and menopause? What is gained by this medicalization, and what is lost?

REFERENCES

Aichen, A. (1935). *Wayward Youth*. New York: Viking.

American Psychiatric Association [APA]. (1994). *The Diagnostic and Statistical Manual of Mental Disorders DSM-IV* (4th ed.). Washington, DC: American Psychiatric Association.

Astley, S. J., & Clarren, S. K. (2001). Measuring the Facial Phenotype of Individuals with Prenatal Alcohol Exposure: Correlative with Brain Dysfunction. *Alcohol and Alcoholism, 36*(2), 147–159.

Bell, R. M. (1985). *Holy Anorexia*. Chicago: University of Chicago.

Berkowitz, L. (1962). *Aggression: A Social Psychological Analysis*. New York: McGraw Hill.

Bliss, M. (Ed.). (1974). *The Queen v. Louis Riel*. Toronto: University of Toronto Press.

Callwood, J. (1990). *The Sleepwalker*. Toronto: Lester and Orpen Dennys.

Caplan, P. (1995). *They Say You're Crazy: How the World's Most Powerful Psychiatrists Decide Who's Normal*. Reading, MA: Addison Wesley.

Cattell, R. B. (1979). *Personality and Learning Theory* (Vol. 1). New York: Springer.

Cleckley, H. (1976). *The Mask of Sanity*. St. Louis, MO: Mosby.

Collins, A. (1998). *In the Sleep Room: The Story of the CIA Brainwashing Experiments in Canada*. Toronto: Lester and Orpen Dennys.

Conrad, P., & Schneider, J. W. (1980). *Deviance and Medicalization: From Badness to Sickness*. St. Louis, MO: Mosby.

———. (1992). *Deviance and Medicalization: From Badness to Sickness* (2nd ed.). Philadelphia, PA: Temple University Press.

Daniels, A. K. (1979). Normal Mental Illness and Understandable Excuses: The Philosophy of Combat Psychiatry. *American Behavioral Scientist, 14*(2), 167–184.

Davis, D. (1994). *Bad Blood: The Shocking True Story Behind the Menendez Killings*. New York: St. Martin's Press.

Day, R., & Wong, S. (1996). Anomalous Perceptual Asymmetries for Negative Emotional Stimuli in the Psychopath. *Journal of Abnormal Psychology, 105*(4), 648–652.

de Jong, H. L. (2000). Genetic Determinism: How Not to Interpret Behavioral Genetics. *Theory and Psychology, 10,* 615–637.

Dollard, J., Doob, L. W., Miller, N. E., Mowrer, O. H., & Sears, R. R. (1939). *Frustration and Aggression*. New Haven, CT: Yale University Press.

Dollard, J., Doob, L. W., Miller, N. E., Mowrer, O. H., Sears, R. R., & Ellis, C. S. (1987). Criminality, Psychopathy, and Eight Other Behavioral Manifestations of Sub-Optimal Arousal. *Personality and Individual Differences, 8,* 905–927.

Dube, J. (2000). *How Sane Is Ted Kaczynski? The Unabomber Argues on His Own Behalf.* [On-Line]. Available: <http://abcnews.go.com/sections/living/InYourHead/allinyourhead_ 64.html>.

Edwards, G. (2000). Blink-182: The Half-Naked Truth. *Rolling Stone 846*(36), 36–41

Eysenck, H. (1960). *The Structure of Human Personality*. London, UK: Methuen.

———. (1964). *Crime and Personality*. London, UK: Routledge and Keegan Paul.

———. (1977). *Crime and Personality*. London, UK: Routledge and Kegan Paul.

———. (1990). *Rebel with a Cause*. London, UK: W. H. Allen.

Eysenck, H., & Eysenck, S. B. G. (1976). *Psychoticism as a Dimension of Personality*. London, UK: Hodder and Stoughton.

Fishbein, D. H. (1990). Biological Perspectives in Criminology. *Criminology, 28*(1), 27–72.

Fox, S., & Spector, P. E. (1999). A Model of Work Frustration–Aggression. *Journal of Organizational Behavior, 20,* 915–931.

Freedman, E. (1987). Uncontrolled Desires: The Response to the Sexual Psychopath, 1920–1960. *Journal of American History, 74*(1 June), 83–106.

Freud, S. (1933). *New Introductory Lectures*. New York: W. W. Norton.

———. (1948). The Ego and the Id. In J. Strackey (Ed.), *The Complete Psychological Works of Sigmund Freud* (Vol. 19). London, UK: Hogarth.

Fumento, M. (1998, August). Notes and Comment: "Road Rage" versus Reality. *Atlantic Monthly*. [On-Line]. Available: <http://www.theatlantic.com/issues/98aug/roadrage.htm>.

Gilligan, C. (1982). *In a Different Voice*. Cambridge, MA: Harvard University Press.

Glasser, W. (1965). *Reality Therapy: A New Approach to Psychiatry*. New York: Harper and Row.

Goldstein, J. (1986). *Aggression and Crimes of Violence* (2nd ed.). New York: Oxford University Press.

Goodman, D. (1983). Do Juvenile Offenders Have "Criminal Personalities"? *Corrections Magazine, 9*(1), 30–35.

Gordon, S. (1994). The Generic Virus Writer. *Proceedings of the Fourth International Virus Bulletin Conference,* Jersey, UK.

Gregory, S. S. (1994). Black Rage: In Defense of a Mass Murder. *Time* (Domestic) *143*(23). [On-line]. Available: <http://www.time.com>.

Grossman, J. L. (1990). Postpartum Psychosis: A Defense of Criminal Responsibility or Just Another Gimmick? *University of Detroit Law Review, 67*(2 Winter), 311–344.

Gurr, T. R. (1970). *Why Men Rebel*. Princeton, NJ: Princeton University Press.

Hagen, M. (1997). *Whores of the Court: The Fraud of Psychiatric Testimony and the Rape of American Justice*. New York: HarperCollins.

Hare, R. D. (1986). Twenty Years' Experience with the Cleckley Psychopath. In Reid (Ed.), *Unmasking the Psychopath*. New York: W. W. Norton.

———. (1993). *Without Conscience: The Disturbing World of the Psychopaths among Us*. New York: Pocket Books.

———. (1996a). Psychopathy: A Clinical Construct Whose Time Has Come. *Criminal Justice and Behavior, 23*(1 March), 25–54.

———. (1996b). Psychopathy and Antisocial Personality Disorder. *Psychiatric Times, 13*(February). [On-Line]. Available: <http://www.mhsource.com/pt/p960239.html>.

Harris, H. (1984). The Criminal Personality: A Dialogue with Stanton Samenow. *Journal of Counselling and Development, 63,* 227–229.

Healy, W. (1915). *The Individual Delinquent*. Boston: Little, Brown.

Hebb, D. O. (1980). *Essay on Mind*. Hillsdale, NJ: Erlbaum.

Henggeler, S. (1984). *Delinquency in Adolescence*. Beverley Hills, CA: Sage.

Hepworth, J. T., & West, S. G. (1988). Lynchings and the Economy: A Time Series Reanalysis of Hovland and Sears (1940). *Journal of Personality and Social Psychology, 55,* 239–247.

Horowitz, A. (1981). Review of Medicalization of Deviance by Conrad and Schneider. *Current Sociology, 10*(6), 750.

Hughes, G., & Dagher, D. (1993). Coping with a Deviant Identity. *Deviant Behavior: An Interdisciplinary Journal, 14,* 297–315.

Huss, M. T., & Langhinrichsen-Rohling, J. (2000). Identification of the Psychopathic Batterer: The Clinical, Legal, and Policy Implications. *Aggression and Violent Behaviour, 5*(4), 403–422.

Jenish, D. A. (1995). Heart of Darkness. *Maclean's, 11,* 18–23.

Jenish, D. A., & Driedger, S. D. (1995). Ending the Secrecy. *Maclean's, 108*(28), 12–14.

Kelley, M. (1999, June 26). Jury Convicts Husband in Sleepwalking Murder Trial. *Detroit News*. [On-Line]. Available: <http://detnews.com/1999/nation/9906/25/06260012.htm>.

Kingwell, M., & Donaldson, G. (1993). Who Gets to Decide Who's Normal. *The Globe and Mail*.

Kittrie, N. (1971). *The Right to Be Different: Deviance and Enforced Therapy.* Baltimore, MD: Johns Hopkins University Press.

Kohlberg, L. (1969). *Stages in the Development of Moral Thought and Action.* New York: Holt, Rinehart and Winston.

———. (1981). *The Philosophy of Moral Development: Essays on Moral Development* (Vol. 1). San Francisco, CA: Harper and Row.

———. (1986). The Just Community Approach to Corrections. *Journal of Correctional Education, 37*(2), 54–58.

Kraepelin, E. (1917). *Lectures on Clinical Psychiatry* (3rd rev. ed.). New York: William Wood.

Lieberman, C. M. D. (1991). Shopping Out of Control. *Britannica Medical and Health Annual* (pp. 342–346.). Chicago: Encyclopaedia Britannica.

Livesley, W. J. (Ed.). (1995). *The DSM-IV Personality Disorders.* New York: Guilford Press.

Luckey, S. C. (2000, September). Air Rage. *Air Line Pilot,* p. 18.

Lykken, D. T. (1982, September). Fearlessness: Its Carefree Charm and Deadly Risks. *Psychology Today,* pp. 20–28.

MacLean, R., Veniot, A., & Waters, S. (1992). *Terror's End.* Toronto: McClelland and Stewart.

Marks, J. (1977). *The Search for the "Manchurian Candidate": The CIA and Mind Control.* New York: W. W. Norton.

Masson, J. M. (Ed.). (1985). *The Complete Letters of Sigmund Freud to Wilhelm Fleiss 1887–1904.* Cambridge, MA: Harvard University Press.

Maticka-Tyndale, E., & Bicher, M. (1996). The Impact of Medicalization on Women. In B. Schissel & L. Mahood (Eds.), *Social Control in Canada: Issues in the Study of Deviance.* Toronto: Oxford University Press.

Mawson, A. R., Biundo, J. J. J., Clemmer, D. I., Jacobs, K. W., Ktsanes, V. K., & Rice, J. C. (1996). Sensation-Seeking, Criminality, and Spinal-Cord Injury: A Case Control Study. *American Journal of Epidemiology, 144*(5), 463–472.

McCord, J., & McCord, W. (1960). *Origins of Alcoholism.* Stanford, CA: Stanford University Press.

McKain, S. J., & Anthony, S. (1990). Social and Independent Living Skills in a Prison Setting: Innovations and Challenges in Behavior Modification. *Behavior Modification, 14*(4), 490–518.

Miller, J. (1987, January 16). Is There Really a "Twinkie" Defense? *Lawyers Weekly.*

Miller, N. E., & Bugelski, R. (1948). Minor Studies of Aggression II. The Influence of Frustrations Imposed by the In-Group on Attitudes Expressed toward Out-Group. *Journal of Psychology, 25,* 437–442.

Moffitt, T. E. (1983). The Learning Theory Model of Punishment: Implications for Delinquency Deterrence. *Criminal Justice and Behavior, 10,* 131–158.

Moir, A., & Jessel, D. (1995). *A Mind to Crime: The Controversial Link between the Mind and Criminal Behavior.* London, UK: Michael Joseph.

Nettler, G. (1978). *Explanations.* New York: McGraw-Hill.

———. (1982). *Explaining Criminals* (Vol. 1). Cincinnati, OH: Anderson.

Ong, P., & Hee, S. (1993). *Losses in the Los Angeles Civil Unrest.* Los Angeles: Center for Pacific Rim Studies (UCLA).

Orlikow et al. v. United States, 682 F. Supp. 77 (D.D.C. 1988).

Parsons, T. (1951). Deviant Behavior and Mechanisms of Social Control. In T. Parsons (Ed.), *The Social System* (chap. 7). New York: Free Press.

Pellegrino, E. (1985). Oedipus, Original Sin and Genetic Determinism. In F. H. Marsh & J. Katz (Eds.), *Biology, Crime and Ethics*. Cincinnati, OH: Anderson.

Piaget, J. (1932). *The Moral Judgement of the Child*. London, UK: Kegan Paul.

Podrabinek, A. (1980). *Punitive Medicine*. Ann Arbor, MI: Karoma Publishers.

Pollack, O. (1950). *The Criminality of Women*. Westport, CT: Greenwood.

Pritchard, J. C. (1835). *A Treatise on Insanity and Other Disorders Affecting the Mind*. London, UK: Sherwood, Gilpert and Piper.

R. v. Parks, [1992], 2 S.C.R. 871.

Rafter, N. H. (1997). Psychopathy and the Evolution of Criminological Knowledge. *Theoretical Criminology, 1*(2), 235–259.

Redl, F., & Wineman, D. (1951). *Children Who Hate*. Glencoe, IL: Free Press.

Reid, W. H., Walker, J. I., & Dorr, D. (Eds.). (1986). *Unmasking the Psychopath: Antisocial Personality and Related Syndromes*. New York: W. W. Norton.

Rest, J., Narvaez, D., Bebeau, M., & Thoma, S. (1999). *Postconventional Moral Thinking: A Neo-Kohlbergian Approach*. Mahwah, NJ: Erlbaum.

Roazen, P. (1999). *Canada's King: An Essay in Political Psychology*. Oakville, ON: Mosaic Press.

Roberts, P. (1994). Risk. *Psychology Today, 27*, 50–56.

Rose, N. (2000). The Biology of Culpability. *Theoretical Criminology, 4*(1), 5–34.

Sachs, A. (1994). Justice: Now for the Movie: Lorena Bobbitt Is Not Guilty Owing to Temporary Insanity. *Time (Domestic), 143*(5), p. 99.

Samenow, S. E. (1984). *Inside the Criminal Mind*. New York: Times Books/Random House.

———. (2000). *Biographical Sketch of Dr. Stanton E. Samenow*. [On-Line]. Available: <http://www.kreative.net/samenowbio.html>.

Schaefer, H. H., & Martin, P. L. (1966). Behavioral Therapy for "Apathy" of Hospitalized Schizophrenics. *Psychological Reports, 19*.

Schimek, J. G. (1987). Fact and Fantasy in the Seduction Theory: A Historical Review. *Journal of the American Psychoanalytic Association, 35*, 937–965.

Schrader, M. P., & Wann, D. L. (1999). High-Risk Recreation: The Relationship between Participant Characteristics and Degree of Involvement. *Journal of Sport Behavior, 22*, 426–441.

Shaw, A. (1998). *A Friend of the Family: The True Story of David Snow*. Toronto: Macfarlane Walter and Ross.

Siegel, P. T., & Fischer, H. (2001). Munchausen by Proxy Syndrome: Barriers to Detection, Confirmation, and Intervention. *Children's Services: Social Policy Research and Practice, 4*(1), 31–50.

Szasz, T. S. (1970). *The Manufacture of Madness: A Comparative Study of the Inquisition and the Mental Health Movement*. New York: Harper and Row.

Watkins, J. G. (1976). Ego States and the Problem of Responsibility: A Psychological Analysis of the Patty Hearst Case. *Journal of Psychiatry and Law, 4*(4), 471–489.

Weinstein, H. M. (1988). *Father, Son and the CIA*. Halifax: Goodread Biographies-Formac.

Whitely, B. E. J., Bichlmeier Nelson, A., & Jones, C. J. (1999). Gender Differences in Cheating Attitudes and Classroom Cheating Behavior: A Meta-Analysis. *Sex Roles: A Journal of Research, 41*(9/10), 657–680.

Yochelson, S., & Samenow, S. E. (1976). *The Criminal Personality. Vol. 1, Profile for Change.* New York: Jason Aronson.

Ysseldyke, J., & Algozzine, B. (1982). *Critical Issues in Special and Remedial Education.* Dallas, TX: Houghton Mifflin.

Zuckerman, B. (Producer), & Wheeler, A. (Director). (1998). *The Sleep Room* [Miniseries]. Toronto: CBC.

Zuckerman, M. (1984). Sensation Seeking: A Comparative Approach to a Human Trait. *Behavioral and Brain Sciences, 7,* 413–471.

THE SOCIAL DISORGANIZATION PERSPECTIVE

In the summer of 1963, the federal government's Indian Affairs office in Kenora, Ontario, administered the relocation of the Ojibwa of Grassy Narrows from their old reserve to a new one, 5 km away, where they would be more easily served with the benefits of modern life (an on-reserve school, medical care, electricity, and the like). The move to the new reserve was not the first intrusion of government and outside industry into this community: it was preceded by a long history in which the Native way of life and religion had been undermined by White-run residential schools, governmental regulations, and the impact of industry. For example, Ontario Hydro's manipulation of water levels for the production of electricity destroyed wild rice beds, killed beaver and muskrat during the winter, and damaged sacred sites, including burial grounds. This move, however, dealt a particularly severe blow to the old community ways. The new reserve was laid out according to standards appropriate to a suburban non-Native population. It cut across the social boundaries of the Native community and placed homes too close together and too far from the natural environment. It took 20 years for the promised utilities to arrive.

In 1970, it was discovered that the Wabigoon River, which provided commercial fishing for the community, had been irreversibly poisoned by methyl mercury. As a result, the fishery shut down and, despite the provision of welfare support, the community began to self-destruct.

In the four years before the move, 91 percent of deaths in Grassy Narrows were due to natural causes. Between 1974 and 1978, 26 persons, or almost one-fifth of the population in the 11-to-19 age group, attempted suicide. Public disorder and criminal offences, such as assault, break and enter and theft, vandalism, and gang rape had reached crisis levels. Many of these offences were attributed to preteen boys and girls. Young people were particularly affected by community and family breakdown. Many experienced severe neglect and physical abuse as their parents' alcoholism deprived them of food, clothing, and family support. The Children's Aid Society took many into custody. Anastasia Shkilnyk, who studied the community from 1977 to 1978, reported that within the community, no blame is attached to acts of violence committed by children. One sixty-eight-year-old band member was beaten so viciously by a gang of children that he required lengthy hospitalization. Yet he did not press charges. When asked why, he said that he was very ashamed that the old way of life had gone, "because this would never have happened on the old reserve ... the kids, they had been drinking, and when a person is drinking, he is not himself." Most people forgive the youngsters, even for atrocious offenses, because they know that their violence is both a symptom of the general disorder in the community and an effect of the breakdown of the Indian family. (Shkilnyk, 1985, p. 34)

The situation at Grassy Narrows, as in many other Aboriginal communities in Canada, remains problematic. Although compensation from Ontario Hydro, the pulp mill, and the federal and provincial governments (Grassy Narrows and Islington Indian Bands Mercury Pollution Claims Settlement Act, 1986) has brought money to the community, money cannot solve its problems. Assaults on the traditional ways of life continue: in 1999, Abitibi-Consolidated Inc. reportedly used clear-cutting techniques within the area traditionally used by the community, resulting in damage to trap lines and hunting territories (Hare, Hull, & Pritchard, 1999). High rates of alcoholism, violence, family breakdown, corruption, and other kinds of deviance are typically found in communities that, like Grassy Narrows, experience severe and continuing disruption.

The production of deviance at Grassy Narrows introduces the first of several distinctly *sociological* approaches to the understanding of deviance. Deviance at Grassy Narrows cannot reasonably be blamed on genetic inheritance, since earlier generations of these families (before 1950) did not display exceptional levels of violent or self-destructive behaviour. It is also very unlikely that the problems were directly caused by mercury poisoning, since other cases of mercury poisoning (in Japan, for example) have not been associated with this kind of response. Most observers see the outbreak of alcoholism, murder, vandalism, and suicide at Grassy Narrows as symptomatic of a failure of the social order. The cultural beliefs and structural organization characteristic of the older Ojibwa community were disrupted and were no longer effective guides to personal behaviour.

SOCIOLOGICAL POSITIVISM: THE PATHOLOGY OF SOCIETY

The idea that "pathology" can exist at the social level is characteristic of the social disorganization perspective. This view dominated the sociology of deviance from the 1890s to the mid-1930s and later formed the basis for interactionist, social learning, and control theories, all of which will be discussed in later chapters.

ORIGINS OF THE SOCIAL DISORGANIZATION PERSPECTIVE

The idea that social conditions influence people's behaviour was not new or unique to the nineteenth century; philosophers had long engaged in debates about which forms of government, and which social institutions, were most conducive to higher public morality. What was new was the attempt to combine the idea of social causation with the investigative methods of science. Sociological positivism emerged when thinkers from various backgrounds (philosophy, theology, political science, and natural science) began to look for regularities in social life, just as natural science had sought regularities in plant and animal life.

Beyond a desire to follow the example set by the natural sciences, these early sociologists were motivated by the historical changes that had led to increasingly obvious concentrations of deviance among people in particular social classes and groups. The Industrial Revolution created entirely new social classes of people, including the urban middle class and the so-called dangerous and perishing classes of the poor, unemployed, and criminal, who lived in the unsanitary and overcrowded urban slums of rapidly growing cities. It seemed evident to many thinkers that the unhealthy physical conditions (such as those given graphic literary treatment by Charles Dickens in *Oliver Twist*) were matched by the unhealthy moral condition of the slums' inhabitants (Adler, 1994; Pearson, 1975, p. 161; Tobias, 1972).

Religion, which had been largely irrelevant (if not antagonistic) to classical theory, now served as a motivating factor in the scientific study of society. Those who were relatively well off were encouraged by their religious leaders to concern themselves with the quality of the physical, spiritual, and moral life around them. In part, this took the form of Social Gospel, a movement that became particularly strong along the eastern seaboard of the United States and in Canada's Maritime settlements.

In England and North America, many of the early sociologists had training in theology, and shared a commitment to religious views of social responsibility. Wesley College in Winnipeg (Methodist) was the first college to offer sociology courses (in 1906), followed by Acadia and McMaster (Baptist) in 1907. McGill University in Montreal shares this Baptist background; its sociology department (established in 1922) was headed by Carl Dawson, who had trained for the Baptist ministry.

Other precursors of sociological study took the form of cartographers' maps and public welfare surveys (Bulmer, Bales, & Sklar, 1991). The cartographical school, which emerged in the 1820s, used statistics about social issues to create social maps that showed that crime, dependency, and other social problems regularly occurred in some areas at a higher rate than in other areas and that these rates changed when social conditions changed. The cartographers established that the statistics for suicide, crime, and public health were stable over time from society to society and from area to area. Through their work, it became possible to demonstrate the predictability of overall rates of rule breaking, in a way that underlined the fact that crime was not just an individual, psychological fact.

Box 7.1   Description of Field-Lane 1850

Let the inspector of the London prisons—after emptying all his outer pockets, and buttoning-up his coat to secure his watch, pocket-book and handkerchief—penetrate this celebrated receptical [*sic*] for stolen goods. The lane is narrow enough for him to reach across from house to house, and the buildings so lofty that a very bright sun is required to send light to the surface. The dwellings on either side are dark.... The stench is awful. Along the narrow lane runs a gutter, into which every sort of poisonous liquid is poured. This thoroughfare is occupied entirely by receivers of stolen goods, which goods are spread out for sale. Here you may re-purchase your own hat, boots, or umbrella; and unless you take special precaution, you may have one of the importunate saleswomen ... attempting to seduce you into the purchase of the very handkerchief which you had in your pocket at the entrance.... Let him pause for a moment to contemplate this *hot-bed of crime and demoralization* [italics in original]. Here is one of the great dunghills on which society rears criminals for the gallows, as on other dunghills it rears melons for the table.... The flavour of the fruit depends upon the quality of the soil; and here we have some of the richest rankness in the world.

Source: W. H. Dixon, *The London Prisons*, edited by J. J. Tobias, David & Charles Publishers (Newton Abbot, Devon: 1972 [1850]), 31–33. Reprinted by permission.

The earliest studies made use of government statistics when these were available, but a tradition of independently sponsored social surveys soon developed as various agencies for public welfare and reform went into the slums to document conditions and to propose solutions. The predominant view was that the urban masses were ignorant, undisciplined, irreligious, and, especially if touched by radical economic beliefs, a danger to the society in which they lived. A variety of people took up the challenge to understand the sources of urban squalor and to do something about them. These included

- Religious (frequently evangelical) "do-gooders" who saw the moral uplift of the lower classes as a spiritual duty. They considered overcrowding, epidemics, infant mortality, crime, and other social problems as evidence of inadequate moral training.

- Humanitarian philanthropists from the industrial middle class who felt that impulsive and unsystematic charity was ineffective, even counterproductive, in that it maintained rather than relieved poverty and dependency. Their social engineering was intended to produce a more useful working class.

- Journalists who produced descriptive accounts for newspaper articles or books and muckraking investigative reporters who exposed the sources of corruption at the political and economic level. A ready market existed for stories of the depravity of the poor and the corruption of officials, whether they were real-life versions in such books as W. H. Dixon's *The London Prisons* (1850), Charles Booth's *Life and Labour of the People in London* (1891), and Charles Loring

Brace's widely read *The Dangerous Classes of New York* (1872), or fictionalized accounts as in the novels of Charles Dickens (Tobias, 1972, pp. 30–33).

- Public health and welfare officials who conducted surveys and investigations.
- Social reformers, like John Howard, Charles Booth, and Beatrice Webb, who studied society to improve it; and radicals, like Karl Marx, who hoped to end urban poverty (and its attendant problems) by overthrowing the entire system.

The combined efforts of these groups resulted in an outpouring of studies that used the social survey form in one way or another.

ÉMILE DURKHEIM AND SOCIOLOGICAL POSITIVISM

The founders of sociology—Auguste Comte, Herbert Spencer, Vilfredo Pareto, Émile Durkheim, Karl Marx, and Max Weber—were all influenced by Darwinist evolutionary theory in varying degrees. They saw societies as organisms that could adapt to their environments and evolve over time, and they felt that understanding the laws of social evolution might enable them to influence its course.

Although Émile Durkheim (1858–1917) wrote in the same period as Cesare Lombroso, Durkheim argued that "social facts are explained by social facts" and firmly rejected any explanation that invoked psychological or biological variables. In Durkheim's view, deviance is either natural to the social organism or it is a pathology of that organism. He felt that most deviance is natural and actually helps society to function effectively (Durkheim, 1897/1951, 1961).

Durkheim believed that societies, like other organisms, evolve from simple to more complex forms. The nature of deviance—and the way in which it is contained—differs according to the stage of development that is characteristic of the society. In the earliest societies (exemplified by small, tribal groups), most members of the

---

Box 7.2 The City below the Hill

One of the earliest sociological studies in Canada was *The City below the Hill* (1897/1972) by Sir Herbert Brown Ames, a successful industrialist and reformer. Like many of his contemporaries, Ames believed in the message of Social Gospel. He sought to use objective and scientific methods of study to identify problems and provide for effective social reform.

Ames organized a house-to-house canvass of a lower-class district of Montreal. Residents were systematically questioned about employment, family composition, housing, rent, ethnic background, and so on. The results were organized and transferred to a series of maps. Of particular concern to Ames was his discovery that drunkenness, crime, disease, death, and poverty were concentrated in the "rear tenements" of this area of Montreal, and he made numerous proposals for improving the area (Campbell, 1983, p. 20).

community did the same kind of work and shared similar daily experiences. The congruence of their lives fostered common ideas and beliefs, which constituted a *common conscience* shared by all. When a rule was broken, it offended virtually all members of the society equally, and the offender's punishment was likely to be severe, repressive, and approved by all. In Durkheim's terms, the members of a society share a common conscience that holds them together in a state of *mechanical solidarity*. Little individualism or real freedom exists in such a society, but the people do not feel repressed because they are in agreement with the rules.

Mechanical solidarity is transformed into *organic solidarity* when population pressure leads to an increasingly complex division of labour (see Figure 7.1). The new specialization and diversity that characterize members of a society are accompanied by a considerable diminishment of the common conscience. Police officers, bartenders, carpenters, priests, bankers, and others develop a slightly differing consciousness of moral issues such that few deeds—among them not even violent murder—offend all groups equally or compel them to respond in identical fashion. There are even places in society where deviants can live without fear of repression. Moral outrage now applies only to extreme offences (e.g., the torture of children) and rarely takes the form of commonly approved violent repression. Durkheim thus equated organic solidarity with greater variety in human expression, more freedom, and less moral outrage. But accompanying this was a danger of too much freedom and, therefore, too little control.

Figure 7.1 Durkheim's Forms of Solidarity

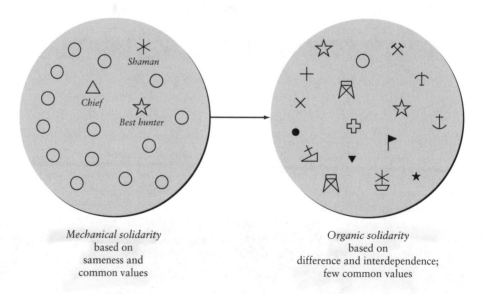

Mechanical solidarity
based on
sameness and
common values

Organic solidarity
based on
difference and interdependence;
few common values

Although Durkheim accepted the normalcy and desirability of social change from mechanical to organic solidarity, he argued that excessively rapid social change (e.g., urbanization and industrialization), or inconsistencies produced by crises of war, famine, or illness, could disrupt the natural adaptive processes of society, weaken its levels of integration and regulation, and thereby allow the development of socially harmful (pathological) forms of deviance.

As discussed in Chapter 2, Durkheim felt that social change in his time had created a society characterized by *anomie* (lack of integration in the group) and *egoism* (lack of regulation by the group), both of which led to high rates of suicide, mental illness, and crime. In anomic situations, people lack the firm moral values and commitments required to hold them in society, while lives that are not regulated or supervised allow the excessive development of egoism (Durkheim, 1897/1951). This analysis can be used today to interpret the evidence that crime rates are lower in countries such as Bahrain, which is characterized by a high degree of integration based on adherence to Islamic values and which is more highly regulated than any North American country (Helal & Coston, 1991), and to explain the rise of hate crimes and social disorder in those successor states of the former Soviet Union as they adjust to capitalist social norms (Glatzer & Bos, 1998).

SOCIOLOGY IN AMERICA: THE EMERGENCE OF THE CHICAGO SCHOOL

When sociological ideas crossed the Atlantic to the United States, they found a mixed reception. In the established educational centres of the eastern seaboard, sociology was regarded as an upstart discipline with a "bastard name and a barbarian terminology" (Matthews, 1977, p. 88). The discipline was seen as tainted by radicalism (i.e., socialism and feminism) and was often treated as subordinate to the more established disciplines of economics, political science, and theology. Sociologists in these departments had little independence and little access to departmental budgets for research. Many of these early sociologists considered themselves ministers, journalists, or natural scientists first, and no clear line existed between their professional sociology and their other activities. Thus, sociological work tended to be an uneasy combination of social ethics, social problems, and social science, and was sometimes funded by philanthropic or political reform groups, churches, or government.

The University of Chicago, which opened in 1892, was different in almost every way. The city of Chicago was particularly well suited to be a centre for ideas about the influence of rapid change on the social order. The site that in the 1830s had held only Fort Dearborn, a small log fort on the prairie–urban frontier, had evolved into a boomtown that gathered into its core a growing stream of migrants from both urban and rural areas and waves of immigrants from Ireland, Sweden, Germany, Poland, and Italy. Chicago's population expanded from 4470 people in 1840 to 1 099 850 by

Box 7.3   Hull House

At the University of Chicago, the study of society was bifurcated between the Department of Sociology (site of scientific sociological growth) and Hull House (site of practical, sociologically informed activism). This division was also largely one between men (at the University) and women (at Hull House). Both groups regarded Chicago as a social laboratory for research and the development of policy, but Hull House was more involved in day-to-day social assistance than was true of the Department of Sociology, and it was much more connected with reform ideologies (Sibley, 1995). Hull House was a "settlement house" that provided social services in the Chicago slums. Founded by Jane Addams, along with some of her friends (Ellen Gates Starr, Florence Kelley, Dr. Alice Hamilton, and others), Hull House concentrated its efforts on helping both immigrants and the rootless poor surmount the barriers created by social disorganization so that they could become successful participants in the American Dream.

Hull House provided childcare; an employment service; an art gallery; language, music, and art classes; a library; a theatre; and other supports for the men, women, and children of the surrounding community. A Russian immigrant later wrote about how he had been casually welcomed to "come often.... Such was my introduction to Hull House, the university of good will, good English, good citizenship" (Elshtain, 1998, p. 363).

The efforts were mainly reformist, rather than revolutionary, but much of the work was highly engaged with social issues, not scientifically detached from its subject matter. Jane Addams (1860–1935) often wrote in a satirical, polemical style (Addams, 1913). For example, she argued that wealthy men should be held responsible for the problem of prostitutes: "The men whose money sustains their houses, supplies their tawdry clothing, and provides them with intoxicating drinks and drugs, are never arrested, nor indeed are they even considered law-breakers" (Addams, 1913, p. 112). Hull House supporters created the Immigrants Protective League, the Juvenile Protective Association, and what was later known as the Institute for Juvenile Research. They started the first Juvenile Court and pushed the Illinois legislature to enact protective labour legislation for women and children and to provide compulsory education. Jane Addams was a leader in endeavours as widely diverse as Campfire Girls, the Consumers' League, and the American Civil Liberties Union. In 1931, she was awarded the Nobel Peace Prize for her pacifist activism.

The women of Hull House initiated and carried out much of the collection of statistical data and community mapping that is best remembered of the work of Chicago School academics (Becker, 1999; Platt, 1994). A groundbreaking and influential book by Jane Addams was *The Spirit of Youth and the City Streets* (1909). One of the first academic books to examine youth gangs, it dealt with how the urban environment distorted "the spirit of youth," by which Addams meant the need for play, adventure, and idealism. Another important contribution was *Hull-House Maps and Papers*, produced by a women's collective within Hull House. This book used detailed maps of community social life to analyze the effects of social disorganization, immigration,

Box 7.3   Hull House (cont.)

and the economy on Chicago's south side. And, as Deegan (1990, p. 24) notes, "this book established the major substantive interests and methodological technique of Chicago Sociology that would define the School for the next forty years." Much of this history, and with it, the history of the contribution of women to the Chicago School, however, was suppressed either purposefully, or simply as a by-product of Robert Park and Ernest Burgess's drive for a sociology that would be "scientific" and not contaminated with social reform and social work viewpoints (Deegan, 1990; Harvey, 1999; Hughes, 1973; Orcutt, 1996). It has also been suggested that the men of the Chicago School were not respectful of women and that they were "old fogies," afraid to risk their respectable positions (Delamont, 1992).

1890 and 3 375 329 by 1930 (Bulmer, 1984, p. 13; Burgess & Newcomb, 1931, p. 5). Bulmer (1984, p. 14) describes the Chicago of 1890 as a "boiling, turbulent, industrial metropolis that knew what it meant to be great, but hardly had time to absorb the knowledge."

Two years later, the University of Chicago began its work under the threat of serious urban disorder. In 1886, someone had thrown a bomb that killed seven police officers in Chicago's Haymarket Square, and the police had responded by firing on the crowd. This event, called the Haymarket Riot of 1886, was followed by similar outbreaks in other American cities. The apparent threat of class warfare, alien radicalism, and urban mass violence sent shock waves through the social classes that supported the university and lent urgency to their desire for effective urban research. Exacerbating the social unease was the 1893–97 depression, during which unemployment ran as high as 20 percent. Downtown streets in these years were flooded with both the jobless (who survived through various, often illegal, ways) and opportunists eager to take advantage of the relative lawlessness that characterized the urban centre.

The university itself was not a tradition-bound outgrowth of long development and social-establishment support but was created almost overnight with the assistance of $35 million in grant money from John D. Rockefeller and substantial gifts from the community, particularly from local Baptists and industrialists (Christakes, 1978, p. 15; Pfohl, 1985, p. 144). Right from the beginning, this gave the University of Chicago a reformist, liberal, and practical slant, providing a sharp contrast to both the elitist and pedantic style that characterized the eastern universities and the radical economic and political complexion of European schools.

The University of Chicago's first president, William Rainey Harper, instructed staff "not to stock the student's mind with knowledge of what has already been accomplished in a given field," but instead to "train him that he himself may be able to push out along new lines of investigation" (Bulmer, 1984, p. 15; Goodspeed, 1928, p. 145). The university recruited professors such as Robert Park, a former newspaper man who had studied and taught until he was "like Faust ... sick and tired of books" and wanted to see the world (Coser, 1977, p. 368). After a period of muckraking journalism, Park joined the University of Chicago in 1914, having had only one formal sociology course, and became the Chicago School's preeminent spokesperson.

Particularly important was the fact that Chicago had an independent sociology department, which meant the weight of traditional thought would not impede newer ideas. In addition, the university's enviable economic position enabled the first sociology head, Albion Small, to lure the best young minds away from other universities at salaries close to double those offered elsewhere, and then to encourage their research (Downes & Rock, 1981, p. 53). Though officially independent, the sociology department was, in the early years, closely associated with the social service–oriented (Baptist) divinity school and the departments of political science and philosophy. All of these departments were linked by the common objective of improving the social conditions of industrial America (Matthews, 1977, p. 89).

The Chicago Department of Sociology was associated with organizations such as the Institute for Juvenile Research. Among the Chicago School studies published by the Institute was Shaw and McKay's *Social Factors in Juvenile Delinquency* (1931). Clifford R. Shaw was a major force in founding and supervising the Chicago Area Project (CAP) in the mid-1930s. This program was an attempt to bring organization to disorganized areas. CAP employed local youths (often gang members) to work in recreation programs, community-improvement campaigns, and projects devoted to reaching and assisting delinquent youngsters and ex-convicts. The Chicago Area Project also spearheaded local improvements in education, sanitation, safety, and law enforcement and provided recreational outlets and summer camping for youth, and data for Chicago School research projects. Although CAP was maintained for almost 40 years, it was never rigorously evaluated. The program itself cannot be claimed to have had a clear success, but it provided plentiful research opportunities (Keys, 1987, pp. 27–28; Kobrin, 1955).

Because of these particularly favourable conditions, a "Chicago School" of sociology emerged. Although it involved collaborative and mutually supportive work that came to be characterized by a distinctive paradigm of interpretation (Bulmer, 1984, p. 2), the Chicago School was never a doctrine or an ideology. On the contrary, it was quite diverse in its expression. What its distinctive parts had in common was a tendency toward focused, grounded studies of observable social scenes.

Since graduate studies were only in their infancy in America, most of the original staff of the Chicago School had done at least some of their training in Germany, and the stamp of the German "research seminar" (as opposed to the mass lecture hall or the individual tutor style of education) became part of the Chicago tradition. This meant that students were challenged to become part of their own learning and find their own raw materials, rather than being passive recipients of traditional knowledge.

Students were assigned class exercises that took them outside the university and into the community. Dissertations, research projects, and (eventually) books documented almost every aspect of Chicago life. Studies were made of gangs, organized crime, prostitution, real-estate offices, local newspapers, the rooming-house district, the community known as Hobohemia, the central business district, and taxi-dance halls (where men came by taxi and paid women to dance with them). There were also studies of the ethnic groups that made Chicago a vibrant (albeit sometimes conflict-ridden) mosaic. Many of these studies reported on deviants and deviant lifestyles, largely because of their proximity and accessibility to the university. Wealthier, more organized neighbourhoods tended to be "defended communities" that were largely inaccessible to researchers (Suttles, 1972, p. 35). Chicago School sociologists did not concern themselves with the deviance of the stable middle and upper classes, concentrating instead on deviance as it was expressed among immigrants, bohemians, and the rootless poor.

Many staff members also shared a very strong rural or small-town Baptist background, which fit well with the idea of social science as a way of fulfilling one's responsibility toward disadvantaged groups by improving their quality of life, both materially and morally. Their origins also inclined them toward viewing the seeming chaos of the city as something that contributed to vice, crime, and personal demoralization, especially when contrasted with the apparent stability, order, and harmony of rural life. They often wrote as though the city itself was a deviant form. The Chicago School was reformist and positivist rather than radical or revolutionary. The kinds of deviance it described and explained were street crimes and deviant lifestyles, not white-collar crimes or the exploitation of the masses.

Chicago sociology became the sociology of Chicago, and then, in the 1920s, as its reputation spread, the sociology of urban forms of social life, the frontier, and the relations between metropolitan centres and hinterland regions. Under Robert Park's charismatic leadership, Chicago became the "hegemonic centre" (the dominant force) of sociology from 1915 to the mid-1930s, and, particularly in Canada, had a substantial influence on political science and history (Bulmer, 1984, p. xiii; Cortese, 1995). Many Canadian academics were drawn to the university. Roderick McKenzie, a Manitoban, entered the Ph.D. program in 1913. Having studied in Winnipeg, McKenzie brought with him an awareness of ethnic heterogeneity, the dominance of some groups over others, and the exploitation of the hinterland by the city, all of which entered into his work on natural areas and patterns of dominance. McKenzie became a leader of the Chicago School, and other Canadians like Carl Dawson brought these ideas back to Canada, particularly to McGill, where they fit well with the Baptist traditions and the utilitarian emphasis of that university. For these sociologists, the city was a laboratory for the study of social order and social process.

THE CHICAGO SCHOOL AND SOCIAL DISORGANIZATION THEORY

Although variations existed within the mainstream of Chicago theorizing, certain common threads can be identified. The main argument holds that rapid social change leads to a breakdown of common values and regulation in certain parts of society, thereby allowing anomic forms of deviance like suicide and mental illness to emerge. The Chicago School theorists regarded the following kinds of change as particularly germane to social disorganization:

- *Urbanization:* the transition from a relatively simple rural social order to a complex, crowded urban arrangement
- *Migration:* the movement of people from a close-knit, homogeneous rural society into an anonymous, heterogeneous urban setting
- *Immigration:* the movement of people with a wide variety of social backgrounds and customs, often European, into the American melting pot
- *Industrialization:* the transformation of employment patterns and the development of the industrial working classes and underclasses
- *Technological change:* runaway change that outstrips adaptation, thereby producing a gap in which social disorganization occurs

"Disorganization" tended to include anything that, when compared with the ideal of stable, small-town life, was negative or "pathological." Chicago theorists in the early period often overlooked the possibility that "disorganization" might really be another form of organization. They were aware, however, that the break-up of one form of order provided the basis for the growth of new forms.

PRIMARY AND SECONDARY RELATIONS

Chicago School work provided a base for the symbolic interactionist work we discuss in Chapter 10. Chicago theorists such as Charles Horton Cooley emphasized the importance of "primary relations" (informal, face-to-face, personal interactions) over "secondary relations," which are formal, direct, and less personally involving. According to the Chicago School perspective, the less someone is integrated and regulated by involvement in personally meaningful interdependent relationships, the more likely it is that he or she will engage in unregulated or deviant behaviour. In small towns, the individual is enmeshed in primary relations that impose limits on behaviour; surveillance and gossip provide strong controls. In the urban setting, anonymity weakens these ties. In small towns, people might engage in deviant sexual behaviour at their peril; in the urban setting, niches exist where such behaviour is accommodated (Laumann et al., 1994).

HUMAN ECOLOGY

Ecology can be loosely defined as a science that deals with the relationships of organisms to one another and to other factors that make up their environment. Human ecology is the study of spatial and temporal relations among people and how they are affected by social and economic competition for space and other resources; human ecology views ethnic groups, occupational cultures, and various other users of "social space" as "species" seeking individual and group survival in a competitive environment.

From ecology, Chicago sociologists borrowed and adapted many concepts to form what was sometimes called a "human ecology theory of urban dynamics." The nine most important concepts are outlined below.

1. *Invasion* is the introduction of a new group or culture ("species") into the territory, not necessarily involving any force. An ethnic group may "invade" a district formerly dominated by another group, or a new use for land may push out incompatible elements, as may occur when a central business district expands into the residential areas that surround it. A modern example of invasion called gentrification takes place when people in upper-middle socioeconomic classes buy properties in inner-city residential areas and transform them into areas in which the poor cannot afford to live.

2. *Segregation* is the separation of "species" (ethnic, racial, or business categories) from one another, so that each tends to be concentrated in some areas and absent in others. Various groups and institutions tend to settle in separate and distinct parts of the city, or even in distinct parts of a neighbourhood. Ethnic and racial groups often tend to be segregated, either voluntarily or (due to economic or political circumstances) involuntarily. Some land uses mutually profit from being close to each other, whereas others (factories and upscale residential communities, for example) have a detrimental effect on each other; for the latter group, segregation may be the result.

3. *Natural areas* are often the product of unplanned processes; these natural boundaries are rarely entirely consistent with official administrative territorial units such as census tracts. As Park (1916/1967, p. 10) observed, "Every large city has its occupational suburbs, like the stockyards in Chicago, and its residential enclaves, like Brookline in Boston, the so-called Gold Coast in Chicago, Greenwich Village in New York, each of which has the size and character of a completely separate town, village or city, except that its population is a select one."

4. *Conflict* is intense competition between groups over the use of territory. Conflict often occurs when a new group or new land use first invades an area. An example of conflict is gang warfare over street territory or racially motivated rioting.

5. *Dominance* is the strength of one group relative to others. The dominant group may lack the authority or right to command but manages to exercise control

Box 7.4   The Ecological Fallacy

The ecological analogy sometimes led to confusion between the characteristics of an area and those of its individual residents. The "ecological fallacy" is exemplified by the assumption that, if a high-crime area has a large number of immigrants, transients, or students, then these people are the criminals (Robinson, 1950). An alternative explanation is that the area is "undefended," which is to say it lacks the kind of social organization that can restrain violent or highly objectionable forms of deviance and, therefore, attracts opportunists. People in public housing projects are often victims of the ecological fallacy. They lack the power to prevent criminals (who may not live in the area) from using their stairwells and lobbies for illegal purposes. They may be denied jobs or treated unfairly because others assume that area residents are the main perpetrators of crime.

Slum areas may be similarly stigmatized as places where only undesirable people live. Seeley (1959, pp. 7–14) classifies slum dwellers into four types:

1. permanent necessitarians (social outcasts and long-term poor)
2. temporary necessitarians who are poor for the short term (e.g., students and recent immigrants)
3. permanent opportunists (e.g., prostitutes who work there, fugitives, and criminals)
4. temporary opportunists (e.g., short-term sellers and purveyors of illegal goods or services)

Most likely to be criminal or seriously deviant are the opportunists (both permanent and temporary) who use the disorganized area but do not always live in it. Stokes (1962, 187–197) makes a similar distinction between "slums of hope," which are inhabited by newcomers and recent immigrants looking for a better life, and "slums of despair," which show different kinds, and higher levels, of deviance.

---

through its ability to influence the conditions of life (Bogue, 1949, pp. 10–11). Dominance may be expressed between ethnic or racial groups, between land uses, or between urban centres and their dependent hinterlands.

6. *Accommodation* is the process whereby different "species" (groups or land uses) achieve a nonconflictual adjustment. This often means that the weaker groups have adjusted to the dominance of others.

7. *Assimilation* is the complete absorption of one group into the way of life of another, as exemplified by the incorporation of new immigrants into the American melting pot. Chicago School theorists generally approved of assimilation (i.e., as a sign of adjustment to the emerging urban order).

8. *Succession* is the takeover by a new group. Invasion may be followed by succession in a repeated pattern as group after group moves through an area. Succession may occur, for example, as wealthier residents move to better districts and the

housing they leave behind is divided into rooming-house accommodation for a different social class or new immigrant group.

9. *Symbiosis* is interdependence among groups, as when one ethnic group provides restaurants, another specializes in carpet cleaning, and another does auto repair—each serving the needs of the other communities.

In the eyes of the Chicago School theorists and their followers, the well-organized community is a kind of symbiotically integrated superorganism. When invaded by new groups or new land use, it responds by attempting to regain "biotic balance." Conflict and competition occur, possibly on a level sufficient to disrupt the super-organic controls of the community. Eventually, the community either goes into a final decline, or accommodation and assimilation occur around a new dominant form and order is restored.

LOCATION

The reliance of the Chicago sociologists on the ecological model made them more sensitive than later theorists to the locations of social activity. Location as a *geographical concept* refers to position on a land surface. Location as an *ecological concept* refers to the distribution of people in social as well as geographical space.

RESEARCH METHODS OF THE CHICAGO SCHOOL

ECOLOGICAL MAPPING

The research method most closely associated with the Chicago School is ecological mapping. In this procedure, detailed maps of a particular city or district are used to show where deviant activities and social problems are concentrated. An ecological map might be constructed by plotting on a census tract map the home addresses of people charged with criminal offences, receiving psychiatric care, or being treated for sexually transmitted diseases. Alternatively, the map might record which parts of the city experience the most break-ins, murders, or brawls, or have the highest concentration of brothels or drug dens. It is possible to create maps that show how people visualize their social space within the city.

The foremost exponent of the ecological approach was Canadian-born Roderick McKenzie. In the 1920s McKenzie developed the *zonal approach* to the study of cities and contributed to the extension of ecological ideas into the study of the Canadian and U.S. frontier. This approach has provided a unique perspective on the path and pattern of vice and disorder in the newly formed communities (Shore, 1987, p. xvi).

The best known of the ecological maps derived from McKenzie's work was published by Robert Park and Ernest Burgess and was developed still further by Frederic M. Thrasher. Thrasher's version of this map is presented in Figure 7.2. The map presents the city as a series of five concentric circles or zones (Burgess, 1925; Harris & Ullman, 1945, pp. 12–13). Large businesses, stores, banks, commercial offices, places of amusement, light industry, and transportation characterize zone 1, the central business district. Busy in the daylight hours, this area is deserted at night. It has few residents of any kind apart from those living in large hotels. Few criminals or deviants live here, but they may find within it crime targets or places conducive to deviant activities. Zone 1 tends to expand into the residential zone next to it.

Zone 2 is variously called the transitional area, zone in transition, or interstitial area. Rooming houses, flats, and hotels that are home to unskilled day workers, recent immigrants, and students characterize zone 2. As the central business district expands, land values in Zone 2 rise, encouraging speculators to buy residential properties and convert them into rental housing. Speculators have no incentive to maintain the buildings, which quickly degenerate into slum housing. In Zone 2, marginals like hobos, alcoholics, and prostitutes find their own space; transvestites, gays, and others can find places to meet without censure; and various kinds of criminals are able to operate without much concern about interference from the law or their neighbours.

Figure 7.2   The Place of Chicago's Gangland in Urban Ecology

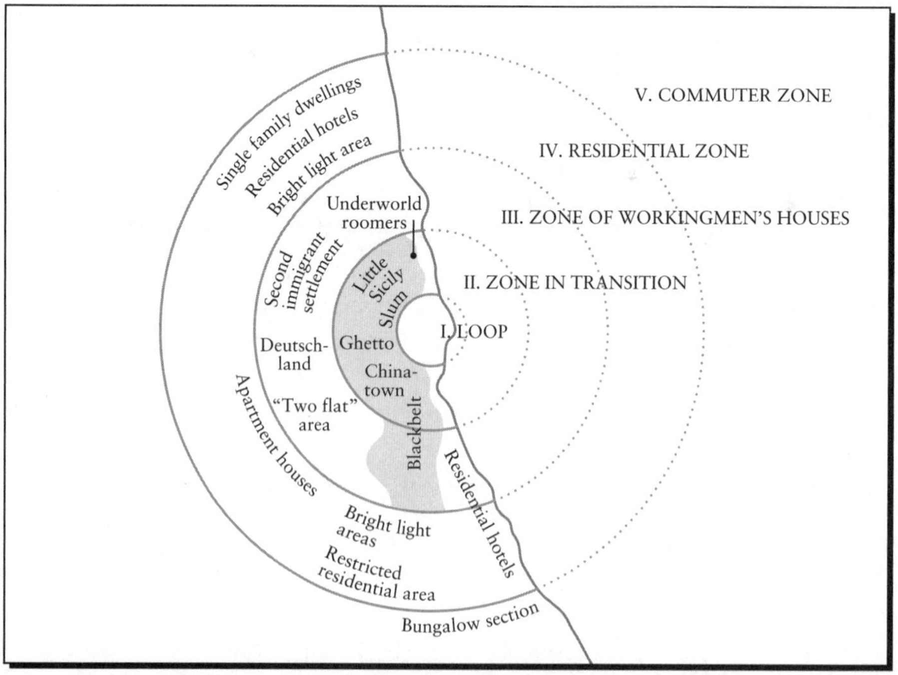

Source: Reprinted from *The Gang*, by Frederick Thrasher, by permission of the University of Chicago Press. Copyright © 1927.

Zone 2 is overwhelmingly the part of the city characterized by social problems, including school truancy, mental illnesses, suicide, infant mortality, venereal disease, and poverty. The problems of Zone 2 are compounded by the fact that it is the area of first settlement or immigrant reception area. With the arrival of each new group, the social order is freshly disrupted as the older, more established groups leave for better housing in other parts of the city.

Zone 3 is the area settled by the stable working class and the second generation of immigrants. Its carefully tended homes are small, similar in design, crowded together, and frequently accommodate more than one family. Zone 3 is much more stable than Zone 2 but not as stable as Zone 4.

Zone 4 is the suburban middle-class area, settled mainly by white-collar workers and executives. Homes are larger, less similar, and less densely situated than those in Zone 3, and apartments are likely to be upscale. People tend to own their own homes, to move infrequently, and to share a sense of community values and norms.

Zone 5 is "exurbia," a commuter zone characterized by large residential properties belonging to the relatively affluent. The area may also contain pockets of other kinds of use such as heavy industry or old rural slum.

Within the concentric zones are further subdivisions called natural areas. Harvey Warren Zorbaugh's *The Gold Coast and the Slum,* first published in 1929, focused on the natural areas of the near north side of Chicago. This small territory just north of the central business district included a wide range of lifestyles. Lake Shore Drive was one of the most desirable living areas in Chicago (it was also known as the Gold Coast), where most of the people listed in the social register made their homes. Next to it was a less favoured but still upper-class neighbourhood (although on its edge some houses had been converted into rooming houses).

Beyond this neighbourhood were the distinct communities of Hobohemia, Towertown, the rooming-house district, the North Clark Street strip, and the many small communities (like "Little Sicily") that were home base for at least 26 ethnic and immigrant groups. Hobohemia was "the last resort of the criminal and the defeated" (Madge, 1963, p. 95), an area in which individuals lived without any kind of meaningful attachments. Towertown was a run-down artist's colony and an immigrant reception neighbourhood that attracted the latest arrivals. Here Zorbaugh (1929, p. 92) found a population of "egocentric poseurs, neurotics, rebels against the conventions of Mainstreet or the gossip of the foreign community, seekers of atmosphere, dabblers in the occult, dilettantes in the arts, or parties to drab lapses from a moral code which the city has not yet destroyed." Towertown was a place where people who were not married to each other might live together without fear of censorship, and where homosexuality was said to be widespread.

In studying the rooming-house area, Zorbaugh documented how the lifestyles of the roomers were almost totally unregulated by any conception of communal life. The rooming-house keeper did not question the morality of the roomers, and the roomers had no control over one another. Zorbaugh contrasted this with the boarding house, in which people met over meals and established connections with one another. He also fleshed out his statistical and observational material with personal documents, including the story of a "charity girl" (prostitute) who had come to Chicago intending to become a pianist, only to end up a part of the lonely, unsettled, rootless population of the rooming-house world.

North Clark Street supplied the needs of the rootless population, "the hobos, the radicals, the squawkers [street vendors], the stick-up men, panhandlers, prostitutes, dopeys, jazz hounds, [and] gold diggers" (Madge, 1963, p. 100). In the slum area behind North Clark Street were many ethnic communities. Zorbaugh describes a community of young single Persian [Iranian] men who worked mainly as hotel help or janitors, a small Greek colony that focused on restaurant work and exuded a strong ethnic solidarity, and a small but growing community of Blacks from rural Georgia, Mississippi, and Arkansas who were displacing the Sicilian population. Altogether, he found within the slum 28 distinct nationalities living side by side, with comparatively little friction. The only regular external contacts these communities had were with social service agencies and the law. Residents treated the agencies as a resource to exploit, while they regarded the law as a source of constant interference and oppression (Madge, 1963, p. 103).

Comparative studies of Philadelphia, Boston, Cincinnati, Greater Cleveland, Richmond (Virginia), Montreal, and even cities in England found the same zonal patterns. In the 1940s, Hoyt's (1939) sector model of residential differentiation and Harris and Ullman's (1945) multiple-nuclei model joined the concentric zone model as major variations from the concentric circle pattern of development (Brantingham & Brantingham, 1984, p. 312). Each city developed natural areas that favoured the presence of deviant ways of life. In Canada, Toronto follows the Chicago concentric-zone pattern, while Winnipeg is characterized by the multiple-nuclei pattern.

More recent work in Canada and the United States has documented the massive changes in city organization brought about by the shift of business and commercial activities from the central business district to the suburbs. In many cities, suburban malls have become hangouts for those with time on their hands. These studies have generally confirmed the idea of "natural crime areas" in the sense that certain parts of the city, particularly its "undefended" neighbourhoods, tend to become places where crime and deviance concentrate.

Neighbourhoods rarely change from high-crime to low-crime areas (or vice versa) unless there has been change in the stability of the neighbourhood and its ability to organize for social control. When change does occur it may take the classic Chicago form of central business district expansion and immigrant pressure (Schuerman & Kobrin, 1986), but in modern times it is more likely to be caused by public policy decisions such as slum clearance, subsidized housing, or urban redevelopment projects. Owen Gill (1977) describes how Luke Street, a stable, working-class neighbourhood in an English city, was transformed into an area characterized by aggressive,

Box 7.5   Deviant Service Centres and Planned Communities

Canada's wilderness frontier has been characterized by the rise and fall of small communities that are created to exploit a single economic resource. Such communities grow up around a mine or a mill, for example, or the building of a railway, pipeline, or dam. They rise suddenly as the resource is discovered or the project is begun, and they last until either the project loses its economic viability or the resource is exhausted. These temporary communities are small centres of suburban life dropped into the bush or other isolated areas. Only air routes or summer roads may connect them to the urban centre, thousands of miles away. Some look like regular suburbs, while others are little more than trailer camps. There are three main periods in the lives of these communities.

In the initial phase, large numbers of mostly single young men come together to build the town and prepare the area for economic exploitation. During this phase some regulation and integration exists—revolving around a demanding work routine—and deviant opportunities are limited. The absence of women increases the likelihood of opportunistic forms of homosexuality (i.e., homosexual behaviour among men who would prefer to associate with women were they available). There are few controls such as family, church, or the mixing of generations to restrain behaviour. Social unrest at this stage is likely to take the form of alcohol abuse, brawls, and individual forms of violence. Organized strikes are unlikely, although wildcat strikes may occur in response to specific incidents.

The second phase has its "boomtown" and its "model town" versions. The gold rush encampment is an example of boomtown conditions. In the boomtown, people attracted to the town by job or prospecting opportunities flood in. Historically, most have been relatively young males able to do the physical labour involved and to hold their own against others' claims. They may be followed by women and older people who hope to provide services (bars, brothels, hotels) to those who are earning a great deal of money but have little time to look after their own needs. Confusion, disorder, and severe strains on the availability of provisions and accommodation initially characterize the boomtown. Services such as policing, medical care, sanitation, and fire control are only gradually achieved. The number of shared problems, however, tends to lead to community organization, and eventually these towns develop social controls that stabilize the community.

The model town emerges when the company (or the government) sets out formal plans for the community and controls who lives there and how they live. Issues such as housing for workers, middle management, and executives are settled in advance. Model town plans rarely if ever include vice areas. As a result, the model town usually develops a parasite community that provides prostitution, alcohol, drugs, gambling, and other vice activities. The parasite town may grow up "across the river" from the planned community, or it may take the form of ribbon growth along the highway leading into the community (e.g., Elliot Lake, Ontario). In cases where the company is able to prevent either of these developments, the vice centres of the most

> ## Box 7.5   Deviant Service Centres and Planned Communities (cont.)
>
> accessible free town or city will expand to meet the demand created by residents of the model town.
>
> Phase three occurs if a town lasts long enough to achieve stability. It then takes on the characteristics of an urban centre and may seem indistinguishable from other places, as long as the company or industry that is its primary support does not fail. Resource exhaustion or changes in the prices of resource products on the world market may turn such places into expensive ghost towns.

unemployed youth on the streets, heavy police attention, and high crime rates. Primarily responsible for the change was a housing policy that directed large, low-income families into the area, thereby overloading facilities like schools and playgrounds, undermining local community organizations, and creating stigmatization of the area.

ETHNOGRAPHY

A frequently used tool of the Chicago School was urban ethnography, a field inquiry technique first developed by anthropologists in their study of tribal societies (Lindner, 1996). Ethnography involved continual monitoring of events as they unfolded in their natural setting. Chicago School ethnographies documented social worlds and ways of life within city neighbourhoods through a combination of field work (participant observation), techniques such as door-to-door surveys, and the collection of publicly available data on sex ratios, age structures, and racial/ethnic residential segregation and interaction. Even such data as the sale of streetcar tickets could be used to enrich the picture of how people lived, communicated, and interacted within the city.

Ethnography looked at each group (prostitutes, hobos, delinquents, drug users) as if it were an urban tribe with unique characteristics reflecting its place in the urban order. Studies of vocational types—the shopgirl, the police officer, the vaudeville performer—laid the basis for understanding the interactive network in which these people lived, as well as the typical pattern that their careers followed. The Chicago School produced many studies showing how the city provided niches in which deviant lifestyles were able to flourish.

Nels Anderson's *The Hobo: The Sociology of the Homeless Man* (1923/1962) was an early ethnographic study that pioneered the use of participant observation, as its author collected the "life stories" of some 60 men who lived in Chicago's Hobohemia area (see Figure 7.3). In a work that exemplifies the classic perspective of social disorganization theory, Anderson—himself a mule driver ("skinner") and hobo before he entered the University of Chicago—depicted the "hobo" as a migratory worker who moves from place to place seeking temporary, often seasonal, work, the "tramp" as a migratory nonworker, and the "bum" as a nonmigratory nonworker.

LIFE DOCUMENTS

Other members of the Chicago School used "life documents," such as diaries and letters, to reveal how people experienced the transition to city life and how their ideas and behaviour changed in response to the urban environment. The principal example of this approach is *The Polish Peasant in Europe and America* (1920) by W. I. Thomas and Florian Znaniecki.*

Thomas and Znaniecki (1920) gathered data for their study by advertising for letters, diaries, and other personal documents of rural Polish peasants who had migrated to large U.S. cities in the early 1920s. Although they were particularly interested in what they called "undesigned records," such as letters that had not been written for publication (Bulmer, 1984, p. 51), Thomas and Znaniecki also made use of newspapers, records of court trials, sermons, and pamphlets issued by churches and political parties. Their analysis of these materials revealed a clear pattern whereby the second generation found Old World customs to be incompatible with participation in America. Although the first generation could choose to insulate itself in a community of fellow immigrants, members of the second generation were obliged to participate in school and work that took them away from this closed community. Their experience of conflicting values and norms often led to an "anything goes" attitude and the emergence of a stage in which the immigrant family was unable to prevent drift into forms of anomic deviance such as prostitution, delinquency, divorce, and mental illness.

Another life document approach was the "life history," a story of one person or several individuals that could assume the form of an autobiography or a series of interviews. Exemplifying the genre is Shaw's (1930) account of a delinquent named Stanley. Here the autobiography is framed by Shaw's chronological record of his subject's brushes with authorities, behavioural problems, and criminal convictions. Shaw felt that such stories should be supported by the use of outside data sources, including "the usual family history, the medical, psychiatric and psychological findings, the official record of arrests, offences, and commitments, the description of play-group relationships, and any other verifiable material which may throw light upon the personality and actual experiences of the delinquent in question" (Shaw, 1930, p. 2). Although each life story was unique, Shaw and others believed that an overall picture similar studies.

---

* This name is pronounced zuh-nan-*yet*-ski.

SOCIAL DISORGANIZATION THEORY IN CANADA

McGILL UNIVERSITY

The centre of social disorganization theory and research in Canada was Montreal's McGill University. Like the University of Chicago, McGill was shaped by its affiliation with the theological and industrial concerns of its benefactors, as well as by the personal and scientific aspirations of its faculty. McGill's strong utilitarian and social service ethos was in part a natural expression of the university's roots and in part a response to the conditions produced by World War I. Montreal experienced severe strains both during and after the war, including widespread work stoppages in 1919 and a panic over Bolshevism fuelled by the Russian Revolution of 1918. Concern was widespread about the quality, health, discipline, and loyalty of the working classes. This, and preoccupation with the process of "human efficiency," motivated the city's business and social welfare leaders to support the university in finding better ways than "charity" to deal with social problems (Shore, 1987, p. xiv).

McGill's sociology department fought much harder than its American counterparts—but with less success—for recognition and funding. The service-oriented Department of Social Services was created in 1918, but only in 1924 did sociology emerge from this social work domination to form an academic department of its own. By that time, McGill had developed an international reputation for scientific and medical achievements, and sociologists there found themselves under considerable pressure to imitate the methods of science and dissociate themselves from the more practically oriented, unscientific aspects of social work. Nonetheless, sociology at McGill was neither subordinated to political economy nor rejected as a shallow "American" discipline. (The same could not be said of other Canadian universities at the time; the University of Toronto, for example, offered courses in sociology, but did not have an independent sociology department until the 1960s.)

Under the leadership of Carl Dawson, who had come to McGill in 1922 with a background in divinity studies and Chicago School sociology, the McGill sociologists produced studies of Montreal that detailed patterns of physical growth, the impact of industries, residential and occupational patterns, and sequences of race relations. When mapped in Montreal, Burgess's concentric circles became concentric "kidneys," with many natural areas within them and a clear divide between French-speaking and English-speaking areas. McGill sociology went beyond the city—and beyond the Chicago School—into the study of frontier settlement and the processes whereby the interdependence of metropolis (major cities) and hinterland (resource-based communities) create new patterns of urban growth.

Box 7.6   Social Disorganization in the Zone of Transition

Montreal: The Dufferin District

In the early twentieth century, the part of Montreal that corresponded most closely with the Chicago School idea of the zone in transition was the Dufferin District, an area studied by Robert Percy, a master's student at McGill University (Shore, 1987, pp. 139–143). The Dufferin District had originally been settled by English, Irish, Scottish, and French members of the stable working class: skilled workers, artisans, teachers, and merchants, but with the expansion of the commercial district, it was invaded by machine shops, warehouses, and manufacturing establishments and by successive waves of immigrants, including Chinese, Russian Jews, Russians, Greeks, Italians, Germans, Poles, and Blacks. The original families departed, and their homes were remodelled into rental units and commercial places.

Percy found the Dufferin District riddled with noise, dirt, vice, despair, and conflict. Its many brothels (which competed with open street prostitution), gambling establishments, and drug dens attracted disreputable "johns," dope peddlers, and gamblers (Shore, 1987, pp. 142–143). In line with the Chicago School theorists, Percy attributed the racial and ethnic tensions he observed to excessive cultural diversity, excessive stimulation, and the absence of institutions conducive to integration.

Halifax: Africville

> Of all the black communities in Nova Scotia the most well known—certainly the most notorious—was Africville. A black ghetto, Africville was an enclave or community, technically within the city of Halifax. In terms of city services, however, it was "in" but not "of" the city. (Clairmont & Magill, 1974, p. 30)

Clairmont and Magill's (1974) study of Africville is based on their observations of the forced relocation of its residents in the late 1960s and early 1970s. Africville was not situated in the centre of the city but otherwise shared the characteristics of an interstitial area. What had begun as an idyllic rural village was caught up in the expansion of Halifax. It was surrounded and divided by industrial enterprises and various institutions, including a prison, a hospital, and a sprawling open dump that was used for the disposal of night soil (sewage). Africville became a depressed shack town scheduled for future industrial and harbour development. It was home to people who had little education, low and uncertain incomes, and uncertain legal claim to the land on which they lived (Clairmont & Magill, 1974, pp. 19–20).

Africville was distinguished by its "elaborately exaggerated" reputation as a deviance service centre (p. 30). As a disorganized and poorly policed area, it had become identified as a place where Whites and Blacks alike went for bootleg booze, commercial sex, and unrestricted fun. Partly because of the neglect afforded it by the city government, Africville enjoyed "functional autonomy"; that is, residents had freedoms (such as the freedom to ignore building codes) that were not available in other parts of the city. This absence of external control was, in the beginning, compensated for by internal controls.

> ### Box 7.6 Social Disorganization in the Zone of Transition (cont.)
>
> Over the years, however, the small, once cohesive community lost its ability to unite and achieve community goals. From the 1930s on, a shifting kaleidoscope of Black and White drifters characterized the population, many attracted by the low rents, relative freedom, and deviant opportunities. High achievers and stable families began to move out, and the community's negative image scared off potential replacements. As Clairmont and Magill see it, the cycle of deterioration began with the encroachment of the city and the failure of city authorities to provide minimal services to the community. Allowing Africville to deteriorate to the point where its residents would accept relocation was, for the city at least, a convenient solution to the deviance problem.

FROM SOCIAL DISORGANIZATION TO DEVIANT TRADITION

EARLY SUBCULTURAL THEORY

By the end of the 1930s, the ideas of the Chicago School had begun to shift from an emphasis on how disorganization permits deviance to occur to an emphasis (which came to be known as "subcultural theory") on how deviant traditions in a community contribute to the maintenance of deviance in "delinquency areas." The new emphasis (partly a result of the aging of the transition zone and the slowing of immigration and migration) made one of its first appearances in Thrasher's (1927/1963) study of 1313 Chicago gangs. Thrasher begins *The Gang* in typical Chicago School style by noting the impact on society of immigration, urbanization, rationalization (secularization), social and geographical mobility, and industrialization. Along with prosperity and progress, these forces brought about gang delinquency, particularly in the zones of transition. Thrasher notes that when institutions are weakened by rapid social change, two main effects result. First, effective legitimate regulation disappears, leaving children and youths free to create their own (unconventional) forms of order. Second, weakened institutions in disorganized environments do not work effectively, which means they are not meeting basic needs. Together, these two effects set a favourable context for the emergence of delinquent gangs.

According to Thrasher, the gang begins with the playgroup. Although playgroups are a natural and spontaneous childhood phenomenon in all communities, those in organized and disorganized areas differ from each other. In organized areas, institutions are strong and the playgroups are supervised and channelled into legitimate activities such as sports. In disorganized areas, however, there are fewer opportunities for the kind of supervised play that integrates the participants into conventional social worlds. Thus, the playgroup in this area is likely to evolve in the direction of non-conformity. Because it is free, the unconventional playgroup is able to provide "the thrill and zest of participation in common interests, more especially corporate action, in hunting, capture, conflict, flight and escape" (pp. 32–33). As Thrasher puts it, "Gangs represent the spontaneous effort of boys to create a society for themselves where none adequate to their needs exists" (p. 32). There is no mention of girls. What distinguishes the nonconforming playgroup or "gang in embryo" from the delinquent gang is the presence of "tradition, unreflective internal structure, esprit de corps, solidarity, morale, group awareness, and attachment to territory" (pp. 32–33). What transforms the unconventional playgroup into the more organized, self-aware gang is conflict between the playgroup and the conventional social order, and between groups who battle for control of turf within the neighbourhood.

Thrasher related many of the differences between gangs to the degree of disorganization around them and to the kinds of opportunities for "action" that their communities offer them. For example, an area with poorly guarded rail yards might provide the delinquent gang with the opportunity for adventurous theft, followed by contact with local criminal elements, such as the fence, who will buy what they steal. Such contacts can draw the mischievous gang into a more criminal mode.

Clifford Shaw and Henry McKay, who between 1929 and 1942 published a series of massive studies in which they mapped and analyzed delinquent neighbourhoods in Chicago and in many other American cities, provided another example of early subcultural theory from the Chicago School. Shaw and McKay (1942/1969) used data from police and juvenile court records for the years between 1900 and 1940 to produce ecological maps. They found, as expected, that rates of crime showed a regular decrease as one moved from the centre of Chicago to its periphery. They also reported

- Areas characterized by low economic status tend to have high population turnover, heterogeneity (many groups), and poor self-regulation.

- Zones with high rates of juvenile delinquency also have high rates of adult crime.

- Recidivism (relapse into criminal behaviour) is highest in areas that have a high rate of delinquency.

- Each population group, regardless of racial or ethnic composition, experiences high rates of delinquency when it occupies areas of first settlement—rates that decline following a move to more stable areas.

- Patterns of behaviour characteristic of each zone maintain themselves even as different groups pass through them (communities with high delinquency rates in 1900 also had high delinquency rates in 1940, despite an almost complete transformation in ethnic composition).

Shaw and McKay went beyond the traditional focus of the Chicago School on the disorganized nature of the delinquency area to develop the "cultural transmission theory of delinquency." According to this theory, within a delinquency area, particular forms of vice, crime, or deviance become a tradition that is transmitted from one generation to the next. Youth in such neighbourhoods are not only pressured by their peers to engage in deviant activity, but also are in contact with older offenders who pass down the traditions of behaviour in the same way that language and other aspects of culture are transmitted from generation to generation (Fitzgerald, McLennan, & Pawson, 1981, p. 13; Shaw & McKay, 1931, p. 256). When they are successful in their criminal activities, older offenders often engage in extravagant displays of affluence and power and thereby become role models for youths living in areas with limited legitimate routes to wealth and influence. The cultural transmission theory thus explains delinquency not just in terms of social disorganization but also in terms of learning and culture.

THE CONTINUING ROLE OF SOCIAL DISORGANIZATION THEORY

By the 1950s, social disorganization was no longer the dominant explanation of socially undesirable behaviour, largely because the social forces that had driven it—rapid and uncontrolled industrialization, urbanization, and immigration—had become increasingly regulated and routine (Abbott, 1997).

However, social disorganization theory continues to play a role in the explanation of deviance (Esbensen & Huizinga, 1990; Handelman, 1995; Harries, 1980), and has even enjoyed a revival stimulated by the potential of new statistical techniques and new GIS computer mapping capabilities. Today's disorganization perspective work has five main directions. The first of these develops from Durkheim's position that such a thing as "just enough" deviance to keep a social system integrated exists. This can be described as the "defining deviance up or down" argument. The second thread is a continuation of the physical ecological and mapping concerns of the Chicago School. The third is found in "network" approaches, and the fourth is a spirited attempt to revive the idea of disorganization as a consequence of rapid change and disruption within communities. Finally, social disorganization has been incorporated in a variety of integrated theories that will be discussed in later chapters.

DEFINING DEVIANCY UP (OR DOWN)

This extension of Durkheim's work emphasizes the role of deviance in establishing the moral boundaries of society and the role of regulators in establishing just how much deviance is recorded and processed for this purpose. The first work along this path was Kai Erikson's *Wayward Puritans* (1966), which argued that the Puritan society experienced "crime waves" at times when moral boundaries were threatened by changes in the external environment or by development of new problems within the society. Erikson noted that the amount of crime recognized fit rather nicely with the supply of stocks and whipping posts, and it was just enough to serve the needs of the society for examples of defended morality. This number seemed only loosely connected with the actual numbers of people behaving in rule-violating ways. The Puritans were defining deviancy "up" to meet their needs for observable integration and regulation. Ben-Yehuda (1985) has used this idea to explain the role of witchcraft, the occult, science fiction, science hoaxes, and other forms of nonconformity as means of boundary management in society.

The definition theme was picked up again by U.S. Senator Daniel Patrick Moynihan (1993), who argued that in the United States, a similar process was occurring. This time, instead of raising the standards to produce higher crime rates, the agencies of social control were choosing *not* to notice behaviour that at other times would be regulated or punished. They were "defining deviancy down," according to Moynihan, because, by the older standards, more bad behaviour existed than would be good for society to recognize. Thus, the St. Valentine's Day Massacre of 1929 in which four gangsters killed seven gangsters was a major event, while similar and more deadly events that are now daily occurrences in many cities may garner little news coverage. According to Moynihan, we are "getting used to" a higher level of disorder. Moynihan also notes, however, that the United States is imprisoning an increasingly higher proportion of its population, and that more actions are "on the books" as deviant or criminal. What this may mean, then, is that more things are punishable but that a reduced proportion of people who do them face official punishment.

In 1996, James Hawdon put a new spin on the definition theme by observing that cycles of "actual" deviance (such as the use of cocaine) are *followed* by moral panics over the deviance. The panic occurs only once the behaviour itself is declining (Hawdon, 1996, p. 183). Hawdon argues that the variety of behaviour that goes unchallenged in society will increase during times of social change, especially when new groups are being accepted into the mainstream. Thus, during the years of heavy immigration, industrialization, and urbanization in the United States, the use of many kinds of now-illegal drugs increased dramatically. When the period of rapid change was over, this drug use began to decline. Just at this point, however, "moral entre-preneurs" began conducting successful campaigns to "demonize" and criminalize the drug user, creating more fear of this deviance than the numbers, and the direction of the numbers, warranted. This aspect of Chicago School ideas has been picked up and developed by functionalists (see Chapter 8) and interaction theorists (see Chapter 10).

ECOLOGICAL APPROACHES

The second modern extension of disorganization theory focuses on the ecological side of the Chicago School tradition. Canadian ecological research, which is often done by urban specialists rather than by sociologists, has tended to support the major contentions of Chicago School theory. Here, as in the United States, "there is evidence that blighted areas contribute disproportionately to a city's problems" (Boyd & Mozersky, 1975, p. 405). Not surprisingly, certain forms of subsidized or low-rental housing attract drug pushers, prostitutes, and others who take advantage of the absence of effective community controls to engage in deviant activities, and these people then provide role models and opportunities for the children of residents. It is also not surprising that such areas attract more of the kind of policing that results in high arrest rates and less of the kind that relies on strong police–community ties. Recent studies have developed the idea of "neighbourhood" disadvantage as a factor in distorted adolescent development (Elliott et al., 1996), and Chicago ethnography continues in many studies of inner city disorder (Jones, Newman, & Isay, 1997).

Criminologists have also developed the Chicago School ideas in the field of environmental criminology, which sees crime as occurring within a three-dimensional space in which a law, an offender, and a target meet (Brantingham & Brantingham, 1991, p. 2), and that can be affected by signs of disorder, such as "broken windows" (Kelling & Coles, 1996). These ideas have evolved into routine activities theory and criminal event theory, discussed in Chapter 11.

NETWORK APPROACHES

The third modern version of social disorganization theory, called "network theory," shares with Chicago School theory an emphasis on urban forms, only instead of ecological processes, it focuses on networks of relationships. Network theory looks at such issues as the breadth, depth, and strength of local networks, whether in the context of a residential neighbourhood or a particular company or industry (Bursik, 1988, p. 536). When networks are extensive and strong, members of the community are able to supervise and regulate one another's behaviour. When a neighbourhood is well integrated, children are more likely to be socialized into nondeviant roles and occupations. Greenberg, Rohe, & Williams (1982a, 1982b, 1985) identify the following three primary dimensions of local social control:

1. *Informal surveillance:* neighbours paying attention to what others are doing, while going about their own affairs.

2. *Movement-governing rules:* rules that identify certain parts of the city or the neighbourhood to be avoided, largely because they are unsafe.

3. *Direct intervention:* speaking to others, asking them their business, and admonishing adults or children who are engaged in unacceptable behaviour.

When the neighbourhood suffers from a high rate of population turnover or is characterized by the type of architectural and urban-planning design that tends to distance residents from one another, a greater proportion of community members feel alienated from their neighbours. Such people are often unwilling, or unable, to intervene effectively if they see disruptive deviant behaviour in their neighbourhood (Sampson, 1986, 1987; Simcha-Fagan & Schwartz, 1986). When offenders are released from prison into these disorganized neighbourhoods, they are more likely to get into trouble again (Gottfredson & Taylor, 1986).

SAMPSON AND GROVES: CHICAGO SCHOOL ONE MORE TIME?

Although almost eclipsed by other theories in the 1970s, social disorganization approaches never completely died out (Bordua, 1958; Chilton, 1964). The 1980s saw a revival of attention for social disorganization theories, mainly on the part of delinquency researchers (Bursik, 1986). An example of this is the work of Sampson and Groves (1989).

Sampson and Groves followed the logic, principles, and concepts of the Chicago School (derived mainly from the work of Shaw and McKay) to study British Crime Survey data, including self-report and victimization data, from 238 British neighbourhoods. They argue that structural community characteristics such as urbanization, residential mobility (turnover of population), ethnic heterogeneity, socioeconomic status, and family disruption diminish a community's ability to assert control over individuals' behaviour through formal and informal networks and organizations, and that this in turn is reflected in rates of criminal deviance such as drug use. What is new in such studies is not the ideas themselves but the availability of statistical data and data-processing programs, as well as advances in ecological mapping. Despite the power of such studies, this approach does not explain deviance well enough to exclude other approaches to the topic (Veysey & Messner, 1999).

INTEGRATED APPROACHES

Although Chicago School social disorganization no longer dominates the sociology of deviance, many of its ideas have been incorporated within symbolic interaction, and subcultural, functional, and conflict approaches, which we will discuss in other chapters of this textbook. Social disorganization approaches are found in combination with other theories as explanations of concentrations of undesirable factors in some areas rather than others. For example, we can identify the concentrations of welfare spending and low-birth-weight babies (Payne, 2000), the contexts of school disorders (Welsh, Stokes, & Green, 2000), juvenile delinquency and criminal opportunities (Ouimet, 2000), and calls to police (Warner & Pierce, 1993). Social disorganization theory is also used in explanations of urban–rural differences in helping behaviour (Amato, 1993), management of crime in race-segregated communities (Figueira-McDonough, 1995; Pattillo, 1998), and the effect of new forms of social disruption (such as that of new industry) on community life (Seydlitz & Laska, 1993).

SUMMARY

The original characteristics of Chicago School theory were rooted in the conditions of the time, which saw massive changes in migration, immigration, urbanization, and industrialization, along with the gradual separation of academic sociology from the more directly practical work being done by social workers and religious and political reformers.

The Chicago School emphasized an ecological metaphor for the study of social order and developed concepts and research tactics that exposed the natural areas and zones of the city. Whether the setting was Chicago's Gold Coast or Hobohemia, Montreal's Dufferin District, Halifax's Africville, or the deviant service centre of a company town, Chicago theory traced the origins of its deviant populations to community disorganization. Deviance occurred because Old World or rural values no longer held people together and they had not yet developed adequate alternatives.

By the 1950s, newer approaches overshadowed Chicago School sociology, but it did not die out entirely. Some of its ideas were absorbed into urban subcultural theories, interaction theories, and functionalist and conflict theories. Others entered into the work of city planners and criminologists. Although concern over the social impacts of immigration and urbanization has lost its former prominence, the integration and regulation of communities persist as important issues in sociological approaches to deviance.

STUDY QUESTIONS

1. How can criminal courts, legitimated by the assumptions of classical theory, deal with deviance such as that found in socially disorganized communities? Will specific or general deterrence work in such settings? (Refer to Chapter 4 for classical theories of deterrence.)

2. Looking ahead to conflict theory (Chapter 12), who is the real criminal when children are raised in conditions such as those at Grassy Narrows?

3. How has religion affected the study of deviance and in particular social disorganization studies?

4. How would Durkheim have explained the high suicide rate at Grassy Narrows?

5. Each deviance theory tends to focus on a different kind of deviance. Classical theory focused on crime. What kinds of deviance did Chicago School researchers study? What kinds were usually not dealt with? (Hint: deviance of the powerful.)

6. What was new about the University of Chicago, and how did this change the study of sociology there in the early twentieth century?

7. What was Hull House, and what role did it play with respect to the development of the Chicago School approach to deviance studies?

8. Who were the women of Hull House? How did they define their social role?

9. Looking ahead to Chapter 10, which concepts from the Chicago School became part of symbolic interaction theory?

10. What is the ecological fallacy, and how does it affect the value of having, or not having, a home address in a particular part of your hometown?

REFERENCES

Abbott, A. (1997). Of Time and Space: The Contemporary Relevance of the Chicago School. *Social Forces, 75*(4), 1149–1183.

Addams, J. (1909). *The Spirit of Youth and the City Streets*. Urbana, IL: University of Illinois Press.

———. (1913). If Men Were Seeking the Franchise. *Ladies Home Journal,* 104–107.

Adler, J. S. (1994). The Dynamite, Wreckage and Scum in Our Cities: The Social Construction of Deviance in Industrial America. *Justice Quarterly, 11*(1), 33–50.

Amato, P. R. (1993). Urban–Rural Differences in Helping Friends and Family. *Psychological Quarterly, 56*(4 December), 249–253.

Ames, H. B. (1972). *The City Below the Hill*. Toronto: University of Toronto Press. (Original work published in 1897)

Anderson, N. (1962). *The Hobo: The Sociology of the Homeless Man*. Chicago: University of Chicago Press. (Original work published in 1923)

Becker, H. S. (1999). The Chicago School, So-Called. *Qualitative Sociology, 22*(1 Spring), 3–12.

Ben-Yahuda, N. (1985). *Deviance and Moral Boundaries: Witchcraft, the Occult, Science Fiction, Deviant Sciences and Scientists*. Chicago: University of Chicago Press.

Bogue, D. J. (1949). *The Structure of the Metropolitan Community*. Ann Arbor, MI: Horace H. Rackham School of Graduate Studies, University of Michigan.

Bordua, D. J. (1958). Juvenile Delinquency and Anomie: An Attempt at Replication. *Social Problems, 6*, 230–238.

Boyd, M., & Mozersky, K. (1975). Cities: The Issue of Urbanization. In D. Forcese & S. Richer (Eds.), Issues in Canadian Society. Scarborough, ON: Prentice-Hall.

Brantingham, P., & Brantingham, P. (1984). *Patterns in Crime*. New York: Macmillan.

———. (Eds.). (1991). *Environmental Criminology* (rev. ed.). Prospect Heights, IL: Waveland Press.

Bulmer, M. (1984). *The Chicago School of Sociology: Institutionalization, Diversity, and the Rise of Sociological Research*. Chicago: University of Chicago Press.

Bulmer, M., Bales, K., & Sklar, K. K. (Eds.). (1991). *The Social Survey in Historical Perspective*. Cambridge, UK: Cambridge University Press.

Burgess, E. W. (1925). The Growth of the City. In R. E. Park, E. W. Burgess, & R. D. McKenzie (Eds.), *The City*. Chicago: University of Chicago Press.

Burgess, E. W., & Newcomb, C. (1931). *Census Data of the City of Chicago, 1920*. Chicago: University of Chicago Press.

Bursik, R. J., Jr. (1986). Ecological Stability and the Dynamics of Delinquency. In A. J. J. Reiss & M. H. Tonry (Eds.), *Crime and Community* (pp. 35–66). Chicago: University of Chicago Press.

———. (1988). Social Disorganization and Theories of Crime and Delinquency: Problems and Prospects. *Criminology, 26*(4), 519–551.

Campbell, D. F. (1983). *Beginnings: Essays on the History of Canadian Sociology*. Port Credit, ON: The Scribbler's Press.

Chilton, R. J. (1964). Continuities in Delinquency Area Research: A Comparison of Studies for Baltimore, Detroit and Indianapolis. *American Sociological Review, 29*, 71–83.

Christakes, G. (1978). *Albion W. Small*. Boston: Twayne.

Clairmont, D., & Magill, D. (1974). *Africville: The Life and Death of a Canadian Black Community*. Toronto: McClelland and Stewart.

Cortese, A. J. (1995). The Rise, Hegemony, and Decline of the Chicago School of Sociology 1892–1945. *Social Science Journal, 32*(3 July), 235–254.

Coser, L. (1977). *Masters of Sociological Thought: Ideas in Historical and Social Context*. New York: Harcourt Brace Jovanovich.

Deegan, M. J. (1990). *Jane Addams and the Men from the Chicago School 1892–1918*. New Brunswick, NJ: Transaction.

Delamont, S. (1992). Old Fogies and Intellectual Women: An Episode in Academic History. *Women's History Review, 1*(1), 39–61.

Downes, D., & Rock, P. (1981). *Understanding Deviance: A Guide to the Sociology of Crime and Rule-Breaking*. Oxford, UK: Clarendon Press.

Durkheim, É. (1951). *Suicide*. New York: Free Press. (Original work published in 1897)

———. (1961). *Moral Education: A Study in the Theory and Application of the Sociology of Education*. New York: Free Press.

Elliott, D., Wilson, W. J., Huizinga, D., Sampson, R. J., Elliott, A., & Rankin, B. (1996). The Effects of Neighborhood Disadvantage on Adolescent Development. *Journal of Research in Crime and Delinquency, 33*(4), 387–426.

Elshtain, J. B. (1998). Jane Addams: A Pilgrim's Progress. *The Journal of Religion, 78*(3), 339–361.

Erikson, K. T. (1966). *Wayward Puritans: A Study in the Sociology of Deviance*. New York: John Wiley.

Esbensen, F.-A., & Huizinga, D. (1990). Research Note: Community Structure and Drug Use: From a Social Disorganization Perspective. *Justice Quarterly, 7*(4), 691–709.

Figueira-McDonough, J. (1995). Community Organization and the Underclass: Exploring New Practice Dimensions. *Social Service Review, 69*(1 March), 57–86.

Fitzgerald, M., McLennan, G., & Pawson, J. (1981). *Crime and Society: Readings in History and Theory*. London, UK: Routledge and Keegan Paul.

Gill, O. (1977). *Luke Street: Housing Policy, Conflict and the Creation of the Delinquent Area*. New York: Holmes and Meier.

Glatzer, W., & Bos, M. (1998). Subjective Attendants of Unification and Transformation in Germany. *Social Indicators Research, 43*(1/2), 171–197.

Goodspeed, T. W. (1928). *William Rainey Harper*. Chicago: University of Chicago Press.

Gottfredson, M., & Taylor, R. B. (1986). Person–Environment Interactions in the Prediction of Recidivism. In R. Byrne James & M. Sampson (Eds.), *The Social Ecology of Crime*. New York: Springer-Verlag.

Grassy Narrows and Islington Indian Bands Mercury Pollution Claims Settlement Act (1986, c. 23). [On-Line]. Available: <http://laws.justice.gc.ca/en/G-11.4/text.html>.

Greenberg, S., Rohe, W. M., & Williams, J. R. (1982a). *The Relationship between Informal Social Control, Neighbourhood Crime, and Fear: A Synthesis and Assessment of Research*. Paper presented at the annual meeting of the American Society of Criminology, Toronto, ON.

———. (1982b). *Safe and Secure Neighbourhoods: Physical Characteristics and Informal Territorial Control in High and Low Crime Neighbourhoods.* Washington, DC: National Institute of Justice.

———. (1985). *Informal Citizen Action and Crime Prevention at the Neighborhood Level.* Washington, DC: National Institute of Justice.

Handelman, S. (1995). *Comrade Criminal: Russia's New Mafiya.* New Haven, CT: Yale University Press.

Hare, W., Hull, C., & Pritchard, D. (1999, May 13–26). *Report on* Christian Peacemaker Teams *(CPT) Fact-Finding Mission to Asubpeeschoseewagong Netum Anishnabek (Grassy Narrows First Nation)* [On-Line]. Available: <http://www.prairienet.org/cpt/archives/1999/may99/0017.html>.

Harries, K. D. (1980). *Crime and the Environment.* Springfield, IL: Charles C. Thomas.

Harris, C. D., & Ullman, E. L. (1945). The Nature of Cities. *Annals of the American Academy of Political and Social Science, 242*(November), 7–17.

Harvey, B. C. (1999). *Jane Addams: Nobel Prize Winner and Founder of Hull House.* Springfield, NJ: Enslow.

Hawdon, J. E. (1996). Cycles of Deviance: Structural Change, Moral Boundaries, and Drug Use, 1880–1900. *Sociological Spectrum, 16*(2), 183–207.

Helal, A. A., & Coston, C. T. M. (1991). Low Crime Rates in Bahrain: Islamic Social Control— Testing the Theory of Synnomie. *International Journal of Comparative and Applied Criminal Justice, 15*(1), 125–144.

Hoyt, H. (1939). *University of Chicago Press.* Washington, DC: Government Printing House.

Hughes, H. M. (1973). Maid of All Work or Departmental Sister-in-Law? The Faculty Wife Employed on Campus. *American Journal of Sociology, 78,* 5–10.

Jones, L., Newman, L., & Isay, D. (1997). *Our America: Life and Death on the South Side of Chicago.* New York: Scribner.

Kelling, G. L., & Coles, C. M. (1996). *Fixing Broken Windows: Restoring Order and Reducing Crime in Our Communities.* New York: Free Press.

Keys, C. B. (1987). Synergy, Prevention and the Chicago School of Sociology. *Prevention in the Human Services, 5,* 11–34.

Kobrin, S. (1955). The Chicago Area Project—25-Year Assessment. *Annals of the American Academy of Political and Social Science, 322,* 19–29.

Laumann, E. O., Gagnon, J. H., Michael, R. T., & Michaels, S. (1994). *The Social Organization of Sexuality: Sexual Practices in the United States.* Chicago: University of Chicago Press.

Lindner, R. (1996). *The Reportage of Urban Culture: Robert Park and the Chicago School.* Cambridge, UK: Cambridge University Press.

Madge, J. (1963). *The Origins of Scientific Sociology.* London, UK: Tavistock.

Matthews, F. H. (1977). *Quest for an American Sociology: Robert E. Park and the Chicago School.* Montreal: McGill-Queens University Press.

Moynihan, D. P. (1993). Defining Deviancy Down. *The American Scholar, 62*(1), 17–20.

Orcutt, J. (1996). Teaching in the Social Laboratory and the Mission of SSSP: Some Lessons from the Chicago School. *Social Problems, 43*(3), 235–245.

Ouimet, M. (2000). Aggregation Bias in Ecological Research: How Social Disorganization and Criminal Opportunities Shape the Spatial Distribution of Juvenile Delinquency in Montreal. *Canadian Journal of Criminology, 42*(2 April), 135–157.

Park, R. E. (1967). The City: Suggestions for the Investigation of Human Behavior in the Urban Environment. In R. E. Park & E. W. Burgess (Eds.), *Burgess*. Chicago: University of Chicago Press. (Original work published in 1916)

Pattillo, M. E. (1998). Sweet Mothers and Gangbangers: Managing Crime in a Black Community. *Social Forces, 76*(3 March), 747–775.

Payne, G. S. (2000). *The Influence of Social Stratification and Social Disorganization on Low Birthweight Babies: A Model of Structural Influences*. Unpublished doctoral dissertation, South Dakota University, Vermillion.

Pearson, G. (1975). *The Deviant Imagination*. London, UK: Macmillan.

Pfohl, S. (1985). *Images of Deviance and Social Control: A Sociological History*. New York: McGraw Hill.

Platt, J. (1994). The Chicago School and Firsthand Data. *History of the Human Sciences, 7*(1 February), 57–80.

Robinson, W. S. (1950). Ecological Correlation and the Behavior of Individuals. *American Sociological Review, 15*, 351–357.

Sampson, R. J. (1986). Neighborhood Family Structure and the Risk of Personal Victimization. In J. M. Byrne, & R. Sampson (Eds.), *The Social Ecology of Crime*. New York: Springer-Verlag.

———. (1987). Communities and Crime. In M. Gottfredson & T. Hirschi (Eds.), *Positive Criminology*. Beverley Hills, CA: Sage.

Sampson, R. J., & Groves, W. B. (1989). Community Structures and Crime: Testing Social Disorganization Theory. *American Journal of Sociology, 94*, 774–802.

Schuerman, L. A., & Kobrin, S. (1986). Community Careers in Crime. In A. J. J. Reiss & M. Tonry (Eds.), *Communities and Crime*. Chicago: University of Chicago Press.

Seeley, J. R. (1959). The Slum: Its Nature, Use and Users. *Journal of the American Institute of Planners, 25*, 7–14.

Seydlitz, R., & Laska, S. (1993). Development and Social Problems: The Impact of Offshore Oil Industry on Suicide and Homicide. *Rural Sociology, 93*(1 Spring), 93–112.

Shaw, C. R. (1930). *The Jack-Roller: A Delinquent Boy's Own Story*. Chicago: University of Chicago Press.

Shaw, C. R., & McKay, H. D. (1931). *Social Factors in Juvenile Delinquency* (Vol. 2). Washington, DC: U.S. Government Printing Office.

———. (1969). *Juvenile Delinquency and Urban Areas*. Chicago: University of Chicago Press. (Original work published in 1942)

Shkilnyk, A. M. (1985). *A Poison Stronger than Love: The Destruction of an Ojibwa Community*. New Haven, CT: Yale University Press.

Shore, M. (1987). *The Science of Social Redemption: McGill, the Chicago School, and the Origins of Social Research in Canada*. Toronto: University of Toronto Press.

Sibley, D. (1995). Gender, Science, Politics, and Geography of the City. *Gender Place and Culture: A Journal of Feminist Geography, 2*(1), 37–50.

Simcha-Fagan, O., & Schwartz, J. E. (1986). Neighborhood and Delinquency: An Assessment of Contextual Effects. *Neighborhood and Delinquency: An Assessment of Contextual Effects, 24,* 667–704.

Stokes, C. (1962). A Theory of Slums. *Land Economics, 48,* 187–197.

Suttles, G. D. (1972). *The Social Construction of Communities.* Chicago: University of Chicago Press.

Thomas, W. I., & Znaniecki, F. (1920). *The Polish Peasant in Europe and America.* Boston: Gorham Press.

Thrasher, F. (1963). *The Gang.* Chicago: University of Chicago Press. (Original work published in 1927)

Tobias, J. J. (1972). *Nineteenth-Century Crime: Prevention and Punishment.* Newton Abbot, UK: David & Charles.

Veysey, B. M., & Messner, S. E. (1999). Further Testing of Social Disorganization Theory. An Elaboration of Sampson and Groves's "Community Structure and Crime." *Journal of Research in Crime and Delinquency, 36*(2 May), 156–175.

Warner, B. D., & Pierce, G. L. (1993). Re-Examining Social Disorganization Theory Using Calls to the Police as a Measure of Crime. *Criminology, 31*(4 November), 493–518.

Welsh, W. N., Stokes, R., & Green, J. R. (2000). A Macro-Level Model of School Disorder. *Journal of Research in Crime and Delinquency, 37*(3 August), 243–284.

Zorbaugh, H. W. (1929). *The Gold Coast and the Slum.* Chicago: University of Chicago Press.

FUNCTIONALIST AND STRAIN PERSPECTIVES

By the 1950s, functionalism had become the dominant theory in North American sociology. More theoretical and less descriptive than Chicago School theory, the functionalist approach focuses on the interrelationships of parts of society with one another and with society as a whole and looks for unsuspected and unintended linkages between the parts. At the core of functionalism is the idea that deviance (both the actual behaviour of deviants and the image of deviance shared among people) is a natural product of the social order and may even have positive effects on the system. Any behaviour that persists in the face of strong disapproval must be contributing in some way to the survival of the system; otherwise, the process of cultural evolution would ensure that it would die out. If the purpose of the behaviour is not obvious, the perspective claims, we must simply be more persistent in our search for the social function it is fulfilling.

In the functionalist view, rules and rule enforcement are part of the processes that hold the social system together. Although they may vary widely from culture to culture and over time, rules are always related to one another and to the system as a whole. The fact that profit making may be illegal in one society (with a state-controlled market) and highly valued in another (within a capitalist system) is not arbitrary. The rules fit with everything else in the social order. Introducing market reform in places that are state controlled and have a black-market economy can precipitate painful changes in many other parts of the system. Unlike classical theory, functionalism has rarely focused on the subject of crime, and there has never been a substantial functionalist criminology.

STRUCTURAL FUNCTIONALISM

The mainstream functionalist approaches to deviance are emphatically structural; that is, they attempt to show that social conditions are frequently structured in such a way that they unintentionally produce deviance, just as a highway can be engineered with the unintended result that many accidents occur at particular points on it (Mann

& Lee, 1979). Chicago School theory blamed weak structure for *permitting* deviance to occur. Functionalists went beyond this by claiming that the structure produced structural strain that *caused* deviance.

If, for example, medical schools produce too many doctors who are all socialized to expect lives of affluence in major urban areas, the result will be strain. Too much competition will exist for too few legitimate medical needs in these areas. The urban health system may then suffer from various kinds of medical deviance such as unnecessary surgery, extra billing, and failure to report the misuse of health cards, while the hinterland areas suffer from overused or unavailable medical services. These problems of medical deviance are related to aspects of the system that are usually regarded as positive: competitive schooling, respect for science and medicine, the value of universal high-quality medical care, and so on. The issue here is that doctors are not just *allowed* to commit deviance by a lack of effective supervision and control in the occupation; they are also *pushed* toward deviance by the way in which cultural expectations and structural realities come together. The same pattern can be seen with many forms of deviance.

Often associated with functionalism is the idea of *subcultural solutions* to strain. Police officers, for example, are often placed in a situation of strain by the expectation that they will simultaneously serve, protect, and control. Keeping order, enforcing the law, and pleasing the public are not always compatible. For example, arresting someone for using drugs at a rock concert may precipitate life-threatening disorder. Similarly, maintaining order on the city's mean streets may not always be possible within the limits of official guidelines (Lee, 1981). At the same time, the police have more freedom than the average person does to use (or misuse) force. The combination of repeated strain and opportunity that police officers all have in common fosters a subculture that supports behaviour some might see as brutal or corrupt.

Strain-induced deviance may not always be supported by a subculture. The medical intern who endures long hours and stressful conditions in the emergency ward experiences strain between the demands of the hospital and the demands of the body. Interns may resolve such strain by using the readily available solution of drugs. The intern, however, is much less likely than the police officer to find others in the environment to culturally support a decision to obtain and use drugs illegally. Similarly, it has been argued that serial killers are ambitious people who have been thwarted in their drive toward acceptance in the class they aspire to join and who perceive their victims to be typical members of the class they feel has rejected them (Leyton, 1986). Although their problem (frustrated ambition) is common enough, they do not have the support of a serial killer subculture (see Figure 8.1).

ORGANIC AND CYBERNETIC MODELS

The early functionalists (Herbert Spencer, Émile Durkheim, Bronislaw Malinowski, and Alfred Reginald Radcliffe-Brown) shared with disorganization theorists a view of society as a kind of superorganism. Like a physical organism, each society acts to

Figure 8.1 Strain and Subcultural Models

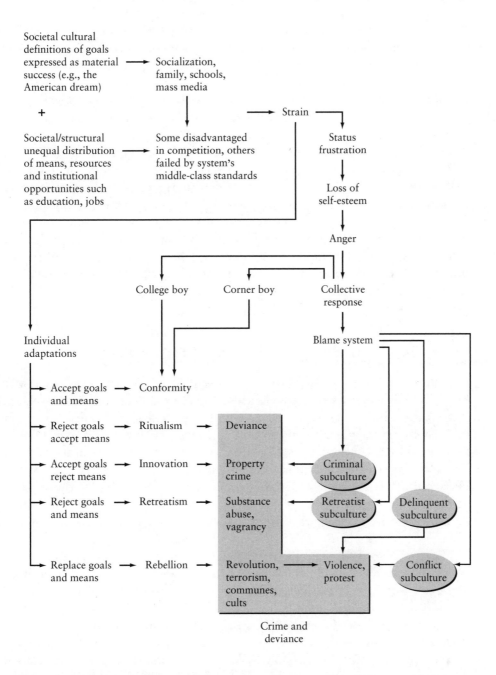

Crime and
deviance

Source: Stuart Henry and Dragan Milovanovic, *Constitutive Criminology: Beyond Postmodernism* (London: Sage, p. 140). Reprinted by permission of Sage Publications.

maintain itself in its environment. According to the organic model, if change occurs in that environment, the society responds adaptively to protect itself or even to improve its well-being. It may also evolve over time through internal development. Like the human body, society has a head (management functions) and circulation (communication, defence, and delivery functions), and the relationship of each part to every other part in the system is one of interdependence. Most parts perform some specialized function on behalf of the organism; those that no longer serve any purpose become vestigial and die out. In this view, deviance is much like illness. We need exposure to germs to maintain our immune systems, but some deviance, like some germs, may be too much.

Later functionalists like Harvard's Talcott Parsons shifted from the organic analogy toward a more mechanistic, cybernetic model of society. In this model, society is a homeostatic, self-regulating system that (as long as it is healthy) maintains a balance (equilibrium) of its internal parts in the face of a changing environment. A thermostat is an example of a homeostatic device. It turns on heating or cooling equipment whenever the temperature rises or falls beyond a preset comfort level. Deviance is a kind of excessive heat in the system that triggers a cooling off response (social control). When a system has too little deviance, it adjusts to create more. The relation between deviance and control is an endless feedback loop in a computer-like mechanical system.

STRATEGIC ASSUMPTIONS OF FUNCTIONALISM

Functionalist thinkers use two basic strategies in their approach to deviance. The first begins with assumptions about the functional requirements of system survival. Each social system, if it is to survive, must adapt to its external environment, meet some basic goals, maintain a minimum level of integration, and replace its members over time (Parsons & Smelser, 1956). Each society meets these needs in its own way. Deviance may emerge when the approved means are not quite adequate or are poorly integrated. Thus, individuals or groups may use amphetamines or cocaine in an attempt to live up to impossible standards in the workplace or use marijuana to "mellow out" in a sometimes terribly stressful world. Such drug use may actually serve the short-term needs of a society in a state of change.

Functionalism helps us understand the ambivalence and even inconsistency of social reactions to deviance. Our attitudes toward some kinds of behaviour change when the needs of society change. Homosexuality, for example, is less tolerated in wartime, when countries need more "cannon fodder" (soldiers) and a premium is placed on procreation. In functional terms, society naturally responds by regulating dysfunctional activities.

Functionalism can also explain why cults (nontraditional religious organizations) are seen as deviant by the wider society. The recruitment of other people's children is a necessary means of survival for these groups, at least until they have lasted long

Box 8.1 Functionalism and the Survival of Experimental Social Systems

In comparing nineteenth-century communes that survived over time with systems that did not, Kanter (1972) isolated the functional mechanisms that were characteristic only of the successful groups: continuance, cohesion, and control.

Continuance

The long-lasting groups had mechanisms to ensure that new members had a stake in the community. These mechanisms usually took the form of nonreturnable investments (time, money, goods), initiation rituals, or personal sacrifices such as a vow of abstinence from alcohol, meat, eggs, personal clothing, or sex.

Cohesion

Belonging was secured by processes that made members renounce personal relationships that might interfere with their full commitment to the group as a whole. Relationships with outsiders, including friends and family, and even sexual intercourse between group members was regarded as a distraction that might reduce loyalty to the group as a whole. Some groups regulated sexuality by physically separating the men from the women at all times (celibacy). Others solved the same problem by introducing a policy of free love and punishing those who were too selective. The functional equivalence of celibacy and free love might not be obvious, but it is shown by the fact that some groups experimented with both forms over the course of their existence. Imposing a commonality of experience on group members fostered cohesion. Systems of job rotation ensured that occupational differences would not interfere in this process. In addition, children were often raised communally and clothing was strictly regulated to avoid distinctiveness.

Control

Mortifying the group member's old social self and inducing a new transcendent identification with the group also fostered commitment. Mortification was often achieved through a process of group criticism or public self-criticism. Transcendent identity was cultivated through communal religious rituals and the development of a charismatic leadership.

The characteristics of successful communal societies are the very characteristics that make most outsiders uncomfortable with cults. Outsiders see new members giving up everything they own to the group; cutting their ties with family, friends, school, or jobs; living in places that are protected from outside intervention; engaging in unusual sexual arrangements; walking about in a liminal state of identity transformation; and treating their group's leader as a God-on-earth. The surrounding society is inclined to interpret these characteristics as some kind of exploitative plot, rather than as the survival mechanisms of a new religion. If the new group survives long enough to produce its own children as new members who can be raised in the faith, many of these mechanisms are no longer needed, and the group can move to a more respectable status in the wider social order.

enough for their own members to have children. This characteristic of cults, that they take young people from their families and turn them against their original faith, makes cults disreputable in the wider society but is essential to their long-term survival (Kanter, 1972).

A second basic strategy of functionalism is to look at deviance that has persisted and try to find out what effects it produces that would explain its contribution to the survival of the system. The notion that anything that persists must have a purpose is certainly debatable, but many functionalists proceed on this basis. This strategy has radical implications, for it suggests that the deviant is wrongfully punished for behaviour that not only is induced by the system but also serves its purposes. The idea that the deviant is produced by respectable society is an uncomfortable one.

THE CENTRAL CONCEPTS OF FUNCTIONALISM

FUNCTION

The concept of function is central to functionalist theory. A part or process of the social system is functional to the extent to which it contributes to the maintenance of the system. According to Merton (1949/1968, p. 24), "social function refers to observable objective consequences, and not to subjective dispositions (aims, motives, purposes)." What is positive for a particular system is any part or process (mechanism) that helps it survive. To say that a particular practice is functional, however, is not to say that it is a good thing (the treatment of deviants often helps to sustain political systems with little or no intrinsic value) nor is it even to claim that it is the best way of fulfilling the function. Often, functional alternatives (different ways of achieving the same end) exist. For example, society can discourage deviance either by penalizing it or by rewarding other kinds of behaviour.

MANIFEST AND LATENT FUNCTIONS

In Durkheim's work, intended functions were simply called "purposes," while the word "function" was reserved for the less obvious processes that were discoverable through a theoretical analysis of specific cases. In Merton's (1949/1968) version of functionalism, *manifest functions* are those with visible and comprehensible consequences, while *latent functions* are those whose consequences are less obvious and often unrecognized. Despite their hidden nature, our understanding of social life cannot progress without an appreciation of latent functions.

> The introduction of the concept of latent function in social research leads to conclusions which show that "social life is not as simple as it first seems." For as long as people confine themselves to *certain* consequences (e.g., manifest consequences), it is comparatively simple for them to pass moral judgements upon the practice or belief in question. Moral evalua-

tions, generally based on these manifest consequences, tend to be polarized in terms of black or white. But the perception of further (latent) consequences often complicates the picture. (Merton 1949/1968, p. 68, italics in original)

Jordan (1969) provides an example of a latent function when he notes that, although colonial slave codes were manifestly aimed at the slaves, they actually made little sense except as a means of imposing discipline on slave owners. By establishing guidelines for slave ownership, the slave codes introduced a conformity of practice that helped maintain the economic system. This example also shows the tendency of functionalism to justify behaviour that supports the system without providing an occasion or forum for questioning whether preserving the system is a worthy goal. Another example of latent function is the role of Judas in the final days of Jesus. The manifest consequences of Judas's betrayal are obvious, but it also had latent consequences that help explain the rise of Christianity and its endurance as a major religion.

Sometimes a function that is manifest at the outset of a practice gradually becomes latent. Compulsory schooling, for example, was introduced explicitly as a means of getting trouble-making children (whose parents were working in factories) off the streets and under control. Legislation against child labour had made street urchins a recognized social problem, just at a time when industrialists were demanding increasing numbers of workers who could read, do basic math, and be relied on. Thus, the public education system was deliberately designed to train working-class children in the knowledge, habits, and ethics that would make them good workers within the industrial capitalist order. Over time, this manifest function has been revised: public schools now share many of the educational ideals that originated in upper-class educational settings, and the original purpose of public schools has become less obvious.

DYSFUNCTION

Early functionalism tended to be Panglossian; that is, it assumed that if anything existed for a long time, it must have a good reason or purpose. Recognition that not everything conformed to this assumption came slowly and only partially. Robert Merton attempted to explain anomalies by introducing the concept of *dysfunction*. Dysfunction occurs when a part or process lessens the effective equilibrium of a system and contributes to stress or strain instead of the smooth operation of the whole. Dysfunctional elements, which can be manifest or latent, are analogous to serious bacterial or viral infections in the human body: they might stimulate the body's defence mechanisms and make it stronger, or they might overwhelm the defence mechanisms and weaken the body (Cuzzort & King, 1989, p. 154).

Consider an example of dysfunction taken from ancient times. When the Romans conquered the Greeks, they adopted many of their cultural habits, among them the use of lead-lined pots for cooking. Food cooked in such vessels became highly lead toxic. The lower classes, who cooked in earthenware pots, were spared, but those who moved up in the system and adopted upper-class ways experienced, along with the privileged, sterility, heavy child mortality, and mental impairment, all of which were caused by the unrecognized process of lead poisoning. This situation may well have contributed to the fall of Rome (Cuzzort & King, 1989, pp. 154–155).

THE FUNCTIONS OF DEVIANCE

Unlike the pathological approach, which treats deviance as bad and needing cure, functionalism challenges us to look for the latent positive consequences that may be an integral part of deviance. In examining prostitution, for instance, we may follow the pathologists and look for what is wrong with prostitutes, or we may consider the impact of their presence on the institutions of society and discover that, along with *dysfunctions* (harmful consequences), prostitutes also bring *eufunctions* (beneficial consequences) to the system as a whole (Cohen, 1966).

THE POSITIVE CONSEQUENCES OF DEVIANCE

According to the functionalist perspective, deviance has 10 major positive consequences.

1. *Clarification of rules.* Deviance may cause an unknown or unclear rule to be stated specifically and clearly. Rules are often only crude indicators or general understandings about the nature of relationships. Consider the recent explosion in sexual-harassment cases. Each case compels members of the group to attempt to specify the exact nature of sexual harassment and the extent to which it should be punished. In this and other cases, conflicting interpretations of social rules and prohibitions are worked out and become precedents for similar disputes in the future.

2. *Testing of rules.* Although every society needs some rules, it does not follow that all rules are good. Deviants may break rules to challenge them. The clearest example of this is the test case, in which an individual breaks a law, seeks to be convicted, and then appeals the case to the higher courts. If the law involved is ruled unconstitutional, the government will usually abandon or revise it. The test case is exemplified in Dr. Henry Morgentaler's career as a provider of (at the time) illegal abortions. Morgentaler would probably have been left alone had he not deliberately made his activities as public as possible, but he wanted to change the law, not just evade it. The person who tests the rules serves as guinea pig in the determination of which way the issues will be resolved. He or she may win and be vindicated, or lose and become another "prisoner of conscience."

3. *Alternative means of goal attainment.* Bell (1953) sees organized crime as a ladder out of the ghetto for people with few or no legitimate job opportunities.

4. *Safety valve.* A certain amount of deviance in each society serves as a kind of safety valve, a time-out from the demands of full conformity. The violence of a soccer match, the rowdiness of a hockey game, the street disorder of the Mardi Gras, or the alcoholic binge of New Year's Eve gives people a break from the strains of responsibility and propriety. Davis (1980), writing in 1937, argues that prostitution also performs a safety-valve function in providing a sexual outlet for clients who might otherwise be tempted to abandon their spouses. From this perspective, prostitution protects the stability of the family.

5. *Tension release and solidarity.* Dentler and Erikson (1959) suggest that groups characterized by high tension and stress regularly seem to find or produce at least one deviant member. In their study of Quaker work groups, they found that those in which at least one person acted, dressed, and spoke differently (and drew attention as a result) were more integrated and cohesive than those without such as person. They also concluded that the more extreme the deviant, the higher the group solidarity (see Box 8.2).

6. *Boundary maintenance.* Deviance may provoke a response that helps integrate the society (Coser, 1956). If the group unites to support the value that has been violated, the value will be reinforced and the integration of the community will be increased. The deviant becomes an external enemy against whom the rest of society can unite in opposition. The witch craze, discussed extensively in Chapter 3, is a good illustration of this process. The persecution of witches shored up the threatened authority of the Church and at the same time gave communities a united focus for action that reinforced their beliefs and values.

7. *Scapegoating.* An almost universal phenomenon in human societies is the search for scapegoats when things go wrong. In preliterate societies, if the rain did not come, it was believed that the gods had been provoked. The offenders were sought out and ceremonially punished in a manner intended to re-establish good relations with the powers of life and death (Sagarin & Montanino, 1977, p. 56). In Hitler's Germany, it was the Jews and the degenerates who were blamed for social ills. By attacking deviants, the authorities tried to make it appear as if they were solving Germany's problems.

8. *Raising the value of conformity.* When the deviant is punished, the value of conformity is enhanced. By identifying the failures, rule breakers, and unworthy, we simultaneously establish ourselves, relative to them, as successful, law-abiding, and worthy.

9. *Early warning system.* Deviance may serve as an early warning system for problems in the social order. For example, an outbreak of racist incidents may indicate the need for better multicultural education or for any number of other

changes to the system. A high dropout rate in a particular school may warn of the need for revised policies.

10. *Protection of vested interests.* Many vested interests are represented in our current patterns of naming and treating deviance. The criminal justice and mental health systems depend on the existence of deviance for their survival. Furthermore, the pattern of finding deviance in a society tends to preserve the balance of power in that most deviants are discovered among members of the lower socioeconomic class and other marginal groups. Bringing these groups under surveillance and control diverts attention from the actions of more powerful people. A company CEO, for example, may demand certain results, but it is the lower-level employees, not the CEO, who must cut corners legally and morally to achieve these results (or else lose their jobs). If the deviance is exposed, the CEO is rarely held responsible. Thus, looking for and exposing deviance at the lower level protects the interests of people at the higher levels, thereby helping to maintain the system.

Box 8.2   Axel: The Necessary Deviant

In one air force basic training group studied by Daniels and Daniels (1964) the deviant was a Protestant clergyman's son named Axel. This clumsy, bumbling, helpless, soft, offbeat person violated many of the norms of the group. Axel was always on the wrong foot, in the wrong place, or unprepared. Since the group was treated as a whole, his failures cost the group many privileges. Axel often received cruel teasing from the group, such as being locked out without his pants, or being given a GI shower (cold water and beating with stiff brushes). But over time, the flight marchers who ran the camp singled Axel out and used him as an object of humour. Axel became linked to the officers and men through a joking relationship. He became a kind of "licensed fool." Seeing Axel do everything wrong made others feel better about the demands being placed on them. Their laughter provided a much-needed release of tension. In later years, when the men gathered to talk about their military service, Axel was often remembered.

THE FUNCTIONS OF SOCIAL CONTROL

What about control? Just as functionalism can reveal the positive effects of deviance, it can also reveal the unrecognized negative effects of social control. Four ways in which control can have negative consequences follow:

1. Too much regulation may reduce the learning of self-control and may stifle creative responses to new situations.

2. Regulation means giving some people power over others, and this power can be abused. For example, in 1970, the War Measures Act was used to control the "apprehended insurrection" of Quebec separatists. This legislation was used by authorities in various parts of the country to arrest and detain people who had absolutely nothing to do with the FLQ Crisis, such as drug addicts and teenagers. Because of these abuses, the War Measures Act was replaced by the much more limited Emergencies Act.

3. Regulation intended to reduce one problem may lead to others. If people were forced to seek permission before having children, the number of children growing up in dysfunctional families might be reduced, but a wide sector of the population that failed to abide by the rules would be criminalized.

4. The treatment of deviants (imprisonment, avoidance) may actually reduce their motivation to return to conformity or even make it impossible. A criminal record is a bar to employment in many areas, and exclusion from polite society may encourage the individual to choose deviant friends.

Gary Marx (1993) lists many situations in which social control contributes to, or generates, rule-breaking behaviour. He argues, for example, that preemptive police actions, such as efforts to make a crowd move on, may actually create deviance such as resisting arrest or disorderly behaviour. He notes that police purchase of illegal drugs not only serves the manifest function of helping catch drug dealers but also serves latent dysfunctions in that it means more markets for drugs, more informers, and more homicides due to underworld control of informers.

DEVIANCE AT A DISTANCE: PARSONIAN FUNCTIONALISM

Davis (1975, p. 66) calls Talcott Parsons's American ivory tower version of functionalism "deviance at a distance" because of its focus on social patterns many levels above the participating actors. Indeed, Parsonian functionalism gives little consideration to "the disruptive, the deviant, the tension-producing, conflict-generating, and change-inducing forces" of human social life (Friedrichs, 1970, p. 145). When it does look at conflict and deviance, it tends to see them as problems for the social order, not, as Durkheimian sociology had done, as natural or even beneficial (Coser, 1956, p. 21).

Parsons (1947) argues that structural changes in the occupational system of society have affected the family in ways that tend to produce male delinquency. The modern economy takes the father out of the family for much of the day. The mother tends to raise both boys and girls, so that they come to regard being good and acting in terms of the expectations of the reasonable adult world as feminine traits (p. 172). When the boys reach manhood, they reject this model, and, in the absence of a male model to guide them, tend to behave in ways that reflect this rejection. Thus, boys are more likely than girls to engage in antisocial and destructive behaviour.

In discussing how aggressive tendencies are produced within systems, Parsons (1947) suggests that some systems suppress overt aggression, creating a large reservoir of aggressive impulses that may pose problems if a channel such as out-group hostility becomes available to them. Thus, in Parsonian terms, the Holocaust was a product of a faulty social system that suppressed natural aggression and then channelled its force against an out-group. It is the structure, not individual morality, that explains the behaviour.

FUNCTIONALIST THEORY APPLIED TO WOMEN

The best-known functionalist theorists were, to the very limited extent that they acknowledged gender at all, supporters of the idea that gender was a basis for a division of labour whereby men and women would be functionally interdependent based on gender-appropriate tasks.

Durkheim, for example, sometimes argued that women belonged in the realm of "asocial family functions," by which he meant "those natural, physical functions—reproduction, nourishment, cleanliness, etc.—that are universal biological imperatives" (Lehmann, 1994, p. 148). In contrast, men belonged in the "social" (cultured and productive) realms.

As a complex thinker, Durkheim's position on the point is not entirely consistent (Cladis, 1995, pp. 535–536), and this is true of Talcott Parsons's work as well. Nonetheless, the overall impact of functionalism has been to suggest that women who do not assume earth-mother roles may be unnatural, dysfunctional, and deviant, as are men who nurture and perform affective tasks instead of engaging in economic production (paid work) or external defence (such as politics and the military).

CLASSICAL STRAIN THEORY (CST): MERTON, COHEN, AND CLOWARD AND OHLIN

ROBERT MERTON: ANOMIE/ANOMIA

Robert Merton developed a version of functionalism as a middle-range alternative to the highly abstract "grand theory" of Talcott Parsons. Merton focused on specific, delimited forms of social behaviour: deviance, political crime, the social organization of science, propaganda, mass persuasion, and so forth (1938, 1946, 1949/1968, 1973). He did not try to integrate these separate interests into one overarching theory of social behaviour.

Merton is best known for his revision of the concept of anomie, sometimes Americanized as *anomia*. To Durkheim's concept of anomie he added the idea of strain, mainly the strain between aspirations and expectations in society. Anomia was the state of structural strain between the almost universal cultural goals of the American Dream and the much more restricted institutionalized means for achieving them. According to Kornhauser (1978, p. 143), "The charm of Merton's strain model consists one-third in its apparent simplicity, one-third in its seeming plausibility, and one-third in its virtual mandate to range sociologists squarely behind the poor."

However, Merton's strain theory does not challenge the desirability of the American Dream (supposedly the source of the strain that produces deviance), and, above all, it predicts that deviance will occur mainly among the poor. When we deal with conflict theories in Chapter 12, we will show that considerable evidence exists that advantaged classes commit their share (or more) of deviant acts, a reality that is hard to explain using Merton's approach.

In Merton's view, deviance is a form of adaptation to the strain that exists between "culturally prescribed aspirations and socially structured avenues for realizing these aspirations" (Merton, 1949/1968, p. 188). Merton's theory locates the primary cause of deviance as the socialization of individuals in all social classes to want what only those in privileged social strata can obtain by nondeviant means. If, for example, success is visualized as a suburban home with two late-model cars in the driveway, and 2.2 children who will take tennis and piano lessons and attend university, then many people in society will find themselves structurally blocked from reaching this goal in legitimate ways. In contrast, others will be born into families able to give them every opportunity. The structurally advantaged will fail only if they throw away the opportunity. Unlike Durkheim's anomie, Merton's is a condition of stress or tension, not one of disorganization.

Merton challenged Freud's idea that human needs are innate and incompatible with the social order. According to Merton, needs are socially created (via socialization to cultural norms), not inborn. As Merton expressed it, "If the Freudian notion is a variety of the 'original sin' doctrine, then the interpretation advanced in this paper is a doctrine of 'socially derived sin' " (quoted in Cullen, 1984, p. 76). In Merton's schema, five alternative modes of adaptation to the means/end relationship exist, modes that are largely determined by the availability of means in particular parts of the social structure (see Table 8.1). These five are conformity, innovation, ritualism, retreatism, and rebellion.

Table 8.1 Merton's Theory of Anomia: Models of Individual Adaptation

Modes	Cultural Goals	Means
1. Conformity	+	+
2. Innovation	+	−
3. Ritualism	−	+
4. Retreatism	−	−
5. Rebellion	+/−	+/−

Source: Adapted with permission from Robert K. Merton (1949/1968), *Social Theory and Social Structure* (New York: Free Press).

Conformity to the rules is the most likely adaptation when little strain exists between goals and means or few alternatives. In this view, upper-middle-class children who have caring parents are less likely to deviate from the rules than less advantaged children who have the same goals. Similarly, conformity is the most likely adaptation in a school or institution in which the competitive process is carefully supervised and offenders are given meaningful punishments.

Innovation covers behaviour such as cheating, stealing, or creative solutions. This response is to be expected when success is heavily emphasized but much less attention is given to the means used. Students know what happens when marks are important but no supervision of testing is provided. Professors may, like Sir Cyril Burt (discussed in Chapter 5), violate the "norms of science" (cheat) when they find themselves unable, otherwise, to reach the research recognition goals they have learned to value (Broad & Wade, 1982; Hackett, 1994).

Similarly, athletes find themselves in situations in which winning brings fabulous wealth and prestige, losing means loss both of funding and of the chance to compete again, and drug controls lack effective application (Cole, 2000). The findings of the Dubin Inquiry in the late 1980s, which brought Canadians a daily dose of stories about Ben Johnson, Charlie Francis, Dr. Jamie Astaphan, Angela Issajenko, and others, clearly showed that the problem of cheating in athletics is a serious and systemic one, not just the case of a few "bad apples" (Francis & Coplon, 1990). Finally, in many countries with controlled economies, legal markets do not always meet consumer needs, and many citizens innovate by participating in black markets. In Canada, the introduction of the GST was enough to provoke some people into joining the illegal "parallel" or "shadow" economy (Fleming, Roman, & Farrell, 2000; Muncie & McLaughlin, 1996). In some Western nations, this parallel economy constitutes more than one-third of the gross national product.

In Merton's view, any culture that places great emphasis on wealth, power, and prestige, but does not at the same time respect and emphasize the use of legitimate means to attain it, is likely to have many innovators. Some of these will find new and better ways of doing things, but many will simply take a criminal path.

Ritualism occurs when the means are accepted but in a manner that is disconnected from the declared goals. A professor at a prestigious university in Ontario once bragged at a party that he had all his lectures memorized. He had been teaching the same things in the same way for 20 years, despite the fact that his field had undergone many changes in that time. Such ritualist adaptation is favoured in institutions that pay little more than lip service to their ostensible goals. Similarly, bureaucratic red tape is often the product of conditions that produce ritualists; forms are filled in and filed, but little is accomplished.

Retreatism occurs when the standard social goals and institutionalized means are both rejected. Unlike the innovator, the retreatist does not bother to cheat, because the goals do not seem worth the trouble. Unlike the rebel, the retreatist has no alternative agenda. Retreatism is often associated with passive drug use and other forms of escapism (reading romance novels, vegetating in front of the TV all day). Merton has linked suicides, psychosis, and some artists and alcoholics to the retreatist mode.

Rebellion occurs when the goals and means established in the society come under attack. Minorities, for example, usually seek the kind of education that will enable them to compete for well-paying, responsible jobs. In this respect, they accept the goal and the means to achieve it. At the same time, however, they may want to change what is taught (or the way it is taught) so that it accommodates their culture and their needs. They may also want to see the end of privileged access to schools and jobs. The result can be a rebellious adaptation to the strain.

Although Merton's schema is often misinterpreted as an individualistic, social–psychological explanation for deviance, it actually is a structural explanation of the conditions under which a significant number of individuals find the adaptations to be the preferable choice. He does not predict that every person who experiences strain will respond with deviant actions. Merton's version of strain theory does not explicitly address individual differences in response to strain, nor does it focus on differences between males and females or on people from non-Western cultures.

ALBERT COHEN AND STATUS FRUSTRATION

In 1955, Albert Cohen expanded on Merton's idea of structural impediments to success (1955). He explained male, lower-class delinquency by showing that strain exists between the middle-class standards of the public school system and the resources and needs that lower-class boys bring into the classroom. Gang delinquency, in Cohen's view, is a group solution to status frustration. Cohen's (1955, pp. 24–31) theory has four basic assumptions:

1. Lower-socioeconomic-class youth tend to do poorly in school because of the use of middle-class (universalistic) standards of evaluation. This is not a question of different IQ levels or initial motivation but a reflection of such factors as the absence of books and quiet study space in the home, and the need to be hard and tough to survive on the street.
2. Poor school performance leads to gang formation, as those who have been rejected by the system join forces. As well, given the negative characteristics of the disadvantaged home, lower-socioeconomic-class youth tend to rely heavily on the peer group for guidance and on the street as a meeting place.
3. The function of the gang is to provide an alternative status system in which its members can enjoy acceptance and success.
4. The values of the delinquent gang are triumphantly and flagrantly oppositional to those that are taught in the schools. Overall, they are nonutilitarian (objects that are stolen may be destroyed or discarded, and violence may have no rational purpose); malicious (targeting smaller, innocent victims, as well as other people's weak spots); and negativistic (opposed to the values of the dominant classes).

They are characterized by "short-run hedonism," and by an emphasis on "autonomy of the gang."

Thus, according to Cohen, the gang does not just reject middle-class norms, it flouts them. Middle-class values such as long-range planning, preparation for gainful employment, postponement of gratification, acceptance of personal responsibility, cultivation of personableness, control of physical aggression, orientation toward success and achievement in the occupational world, and the virtual worship of possessions are rejected in favour of "free rogue" values (Cohen 1955, p. 104).

Cohen recognizes two other options or paths for lower-socioeconomic-class males. Some may be able to overcome their disadvantaged position and compete in the universalistic status system. These youths may become "college boys" instead of delinquents. Others who are not attracted to the aggressive gang may become "corner boys" (i.e., youths who enjoy "hanging around the corner" with their friends). They make the best of their situation and generally temporize with the middle-class world from which they will eventually seek working-class jobs (Cohen, 1955, pp. 128–130).

Lending support to Cohen's theory is Elliott and Voss's (1974) investigation of the correlation between school dropouts and arrests for delinquency. In a sample of 2000 students in California, they found that delinquency peaked just before dropout and subsequently declined. (The decline was particularly notable with respect to those who found jobs and were married.) Work by Willis (1977) and by Sullivan (1989) also supports the general link between despair caused by lack of opportunity to reach desired goals with delinquent and deviant outcomes. Willis and Sullivan indicate that there are two stages or phases in this process. The first phase is characterized by acting out against the school or social norms, often in humorous and "naughty" ways that bring status in an alternate status system. The second phase is despair as routes to real social status evaporate (Hagan, 1997).

Cohen's Strain Theory Applied to Women

Cohen shows a typical tendency to treat women's deviance as trivial and men's deviance as more worthy of interest and respect. Cohen sees the delinquent boy as an admirable specimen of "rogue male" whose untrammelled masculinity has a certain "aura of glamour and romance" (Cohen, 1955, p. 140). When Cohen discusses female delinquent styles, however, he sees a different pattern. According to Cohen girls have only one important goal, which is to have successful relationships and to marry well. Since such "masculine" interests as ambition, action, and mastery do not interest these girls, according to the theory, they do not experience strain in the same way that boys do. Failure in school does not lead to delinquency but failure in the dating game may. Cohen argues that the delinquent girl is mainly sexually promiscuous, and she acts this way because, for some reason, she is not able to succeed in personal relationships without "cheating" this way. Cohen provides virtually no data on this point and actually argues that the different focal concerns of the two sexes are "so obvious" that no further analysis is necessary (Cohen, 1955, p. 142).

RICHARD CLOWARD, LLOYD OHLIN, AND DIFFERENTIAL OPPORTUNITY THEORY

According to Richard Cloward and Lloyd Ohlin, learning environments and opportunities are not equally distributed in the social system (1960). A person's class, gender, ethnicity, and neighbourhood can make access to particular kinds of deviance or conformity easier or more difficult. Not only do slum children have less access to legitimate careers, but they also experience differential access to illegitimate careers. The neighbourhoods in which they grow up can influence whether they will be exposed to drug-trafficking careers, gangsterism, organized crime, disorganized vandalism, or none of these. Cloward and Ohlin thus extend Merton's anomia schema by introducing the concept of differential *illegitimate* opportunity.

Cloward and Ohlin's theory is intended to explain only those delinquencies that are "specifically provided and supported by delinquent subcultures" (Cloward & Ohlin, 1960, p. 9). In other words, they see delinquents as performing subcultural delinquent roles, not as expressing individual psychopathology or engaging in independent deviance (e.g., shoplifting) without the knowledge of their peers (Cloward & Ohlin, 1960, pp. 9–10).

Included in Cloward and Ohlin's theory are descriptions of three kinds of delinquent subcultures typically encountered among adolescent males in lower-class districts of large urban centres. These are the criminal, conflict, and retreatist subcultures.

A *criminal* pattern of gang behaviour is an economic response to strain. Criminal gangs seek monetary gain through crime. This pattern emerges when there is visible, successful adult criminal activity in the neighbourhood that allows boys to see a career path toward criminal success. Successful adult pimps, racketeers, bookies, or numbers runners may provide not only role models but also work opportunities for youths. The juvenile thief gains status by "pulling off a big score" and having money to spend. The apprentice in organized crime gains status by proving himself a "right guy" who can take the heat from police and rivals. Although the criminal gang breaks the law, it is not usually negativistic or disorderly. Destructive, purposeless behaviour would interfere with group success and is reined in, either by the gang itself or by the adult criminals with whom the gang deals.

When the neighbourhood lacks a stable pattern of adult criminal behaviour, or when youths do not mix with older criminals, the *conflict* form of gang behaviour emerges. Violence between gangs becomes a way of asserting control in a disorganized environment and earning a measure of status and success in the process. The street gang member attempts to achieve a reputation through violence and intimidation of others.

Whether neighbourhoods are dominated by either criminal or conflict gangs, some youths will be unable to take successful advantage of either legal or illegal opportunities. They are "double failures" who succeed neither at school nor in delinquency. These youths may form *retreatist* gangs that are dominated by escapist activities such as drug use (Cloward & Ohlin, 1960, p. 25).

Double failures are often rejects from conflict or criminal gangs. Despite this, they may adhere to a status system that provides a sense of success. "The drug addict wins deference for his mastery of the resources and knowledge for maintaining or increasing the esoteric experience of his 'kick' " (Cloward & Ohlin, 1960, p. 10). The "esoteric experience" that is sought may involve alcohol, marijuana, hard drugs, sexual experimentation, dance, music, or anything else that provides "out of this world pleasure" (Cloward & Ohlin, 1960, p. 26). Retreatist gang members may achieve a modicum of success through peddling drugs, acting as pimps, shoplifting, and minor hustling.

Cloward and Ohlin shared with Albert Cohen a belief that the middle-class offender (whether in a gang or not) is more amenable to individualized forms of control or therapy, which parents or community can provide. In contrast, the lower-class gang offender cannot readily be reached by individualistic solutions. He (or the rare she) needs to be uprooted from the culture to be "cured."

Spergel (1964) partially tested Cloward and Ohlin's ideas. In what he called the Racket Neighbourhood, Spergel found that juvenile delinquency was linked to organized crime through such operations as loan-sharking. Youths participated at lower levels and gradually worked their way up to more "responsible" positions within the criminal organization. This neighbourhood had little gang conflict and little drug use. In Slumtown, a disorganized neighbourhood that lacked an organized crime presence, fighting gangs dominated the scene. In Haulburg, a theft neighbourhood, teens participated in burglary and joyriding forms of car theft. Haulburg had little gang warfare and no organized property crime. Property crime was less organized than in Slumtown. Spergel did not find a retreatist pattern in these communities.

Cloward and Ohlin's theory provided the basis for a massive antipoverty program in the 1960s. Launched in New York City, the Mobilization for Youth Project attempted to alleviate strain in lower-class communities by improving education, creating work opportunities, and organizing for local improvements. This program unfortunately had little effect on serious delinquency, partly because it failed to cope well with turf wars among its participants (who gets to do what) and came up against some very powerful vested interests (Cazenave, 1999). Other programs with similarly good intentions have also failed to work, at least partly because none of them has been able to make a significant dent in the inequalities of opportunity that differentiate the privileged classes from those of lesser status (Adler & Laufer, 1995).

GENERAL STRAIN THEORY (GST): AGNEW

Beginning in the mid-1980s, Robert Agnew made popular a revised version of strain theory that includes, but also goes beyond, the Mertonian classical strain theory (Agnew, 1985, 1989, 1992, 1995). Rather than Merton's single source of strain (the disjuncture between cultural goals and structured means to them), Agnew proposes three forms of strain. Strain occurs not only when we fail to achieve goals, but also when others take away from us valued "stimuli" (either property or respect) or when we are confronted with unpleasant circumstances ("aversive stimuli"). Thus, Agnew's research includes questions about peer group, teacher, and parent–adolescent "hassles." Rather than Merton's narrow attention to the middle-range structural level, Agnew provides a more individualized, social–psychological version of strain theory (Passas & Agnew, 1997). He argues that negative circumstances alone do not translate into deviant action. Deviance will occur only when the conditions of strain are coupled with a psychological state of "negative affect" (disappointment, anger). Thus, the individual may attempt to deal with his or her feelings by instrumental, retaliatory, or escapist behaviour. Adolescent theft, violence, and drug use can be the outcome when responses that are more positive are not available or not chosen (Agnew, 1992). Although some writers consider the move from a social structural explanation toward a personalized, individual social psychological one to be "unfortunate" (Wark & Unnithan, 1998), others feel that this makes a stronger explanation.

It has been suggested that general strain theory (GST) is superior to Cloward and Ohlin's classical strain theory (CST) in that GST includes a more sophisticated and testable model. Several authors, however, have suggested that it should be linked with social learning theory and social control theory (which we discuss in Chapters 9 and 11), rather than be developed on its own (Farnworth & Leiber, 1989; Paternoster & Mazerolle, 1994, p. 252). Agnew has conceded that his theory "shares many, perhaps most, of its independent variables" with social control and learning theories but argues that his version is superior in a variety of ways (Agnew, 1995, p. 373). One aspect that is more developed in this theory than in the competing theories is the element of affective responses such as hostility, anger, and anxiety to conditions of strain (Aseltine & Gore, 2000; Mazerolle & Burton, 2000).

GENERAL STRAIN THEORY AND WOMEN

Agnew does not agree with the Mertonian assumption that male and female deviance is equally well explained by the strain of achieving material success (Simmons, Miller, & Aigner, 1980). Nor does Agnew's work support Cohen's idea that women's deviance results from interpersonal social strain while men's is caused by economic strain (Cohen, 1955; Leonard, 1982). Agnew's female subjects scored much higher than males did on measures of strain, even though the measures are incomplete at present

(Broidy & Agnew, 1997, p. 277; Katz, 2000). Agnew suggests that interpersonal strain, when it occurs, is even more important among males than it is among females. It appears, for example, that males are more disturbed by poor peer relations than females but perhaps not for the same reasons and not with the same behavioural outcomes. At this point, researchers testing and developing general strain theory are investigating four ideas: that males and females (1) experience different kinds of strain, (2) have differing subjective interpretations of the strain they experience, (3) have differing emotional reactions to strain, and (4) may differ in their propensity to translate their feelings about strain into deviant actions (Broidy & Agnew, 1997, p. 289)

Lafree: An Application of Strain Theory

The idea of strain continues to be important in recent research, both as a theory in its own right and as a concept within integrated approaches. An example of this is Lafree's (1998) argument that the decline in crime rates (in Canada and the United States since the early 1990s) can be attributed to the increased legitimacy of social control institutions (such as the justice system), increased economic well-being, and growing acceptance of alternatives to the American Dream. Each of these features, to the extent that they can be proven, would help to reduce strain and thus the deviant consequences of strain.

SUMMARY

Functionalism and strain theory highlight the consequences of deviance. Functionalism has been particularly fruitful in its insistence that we look beyond the manifest purpose of things by examining their latent consequences. This perspective focuses attention on behaviour that despite its deviant status is almost universal. The latent meaning of such behaviour is often unrecognized by the people who condemn it. By emphasizing the conservative implications of their theories, at the expense of more radical possibilities, functionalists and strain theorists contributed to the control of those who were defined as deviant, and the perpetuation of traditional gender roles. Although functionalist and strain approaches can be traced back to the 1930s, they reached the height of their popularity in the 1950s. In the 1960s (despite the revival that occurred in the 1980s), they were overtaken by interaction theories, which will be discussed in Chapter 10.

STUDY QUESTIONS

1. American functionalism dominated social science during the 1950s, a time when, following World War II, the homemaker role was held out as the goal for women and the breadwinner was expected to be male. There was also great fear of communist subversion. How can these features of society help to explain the popularity of functionalist thought?

2. If something (such as prostitution) lasts over time and the system survives, does this mean that (a) it must be serving the system somehow and (b) it is systemic rather than individual in its origin?

3. What does the term "structural" mean, in the context of structural functionalism?

4. Using the organic model (or analogy), is deviance more like an in-grown toenail, the common cold, or a terminal illness in the body?

5. How does the functionalist view of the origins of subcultures differ from the views of social disorganization theorists?

6. How does Rosabeth Kanter's analysis of nineteenth-century communes help to explain the tactics used by new religious movements (NRMs), otherwise known as cults?

7. Functionalism, in its time, had conservative effects. Can this theory be treated as a radical critic of society?

8. Functionalism is very rarely even mentioned in criminal justice textbooks. Why are criminal justice people (those who teach people who will likely work in the criminal justice system) uncomfortable with the idea that deviance can be functional?

9. Strain theory predicts that deviance and crime will occur mainly in the lower socioeconomic classes because of their reduced access to the materialistic goals of the American Dream. Is the deviance of the lower classes greater, or just different, from that of the upper classes?

10. How does Agnew's general strain theory differ from Merton's classical version of strain theory?

REFERENCES

Adler, F., & Laufer, W. S. (1995). *The Legacy of Anomie Theory*. New Brunswick, NJ: Transaction.

Agnew, R. (1985). A Revised Strain Theory of Delinquency. *Social Forces, 64,* 151–167.

———. (1989). A Longitudinal Test of the Revised Strain Theory. *Journal of Quantitative Criminology, 5,* 373–387.

———. (1992). A Foundation for a General Strain Theory of Crime and Delinquency. *Criminology, 30,* 47–87.

———. (1995). Controlling Delinquency: Recommendations from General Strain Theory. In H. D. Barlow (Ed.), *Crime and Public Policy: Putting Theory to Work*, pp. 43–70. Boulder, CO: Westview.

Aseltine, J. R. H., & Gore, S. (2000). Life Stress, Anger and Anxiety, and Delinquency: An Empirical Test of General Strain Theory. *Journal of Health and Social Behavior,* 41(3 September), 256–276.

Bell, D. (1953, June). Crime as an American Way of Life. *Antioch Review,* pp. 131–154.

Broad, W., & Wade, N. (1982). *Betrayers of the Truth: Fraud and Deceit in Science.* Oxford, UK: Oxford University Press.

Broidy, L., & Agnew, R. (1997). Gender and Crime. A General Strain Theory Perspective. *Journal of Research in Crime and Delinquency,* 34(3 August), 275–307.

Cazenave, N. A. (1999). Ironies of Urban Reform. *Journal of Urban History,* 26(1), 22–44.

Cladis, M. S. (1995). Review of *Durkheim and Women,* by J. M. Lehmann, in *Philosophy of the Social Sciences, 25,* 535–540.

Cloward, R. A., & Ohlin, L. E. (1960). *Delinquency and Opportunity: A Theory of Delinquent Gangs.* New York: Free Press.

Cohen, A. J. (1955). *Delinquent Boys.* New York: Free Press.

———. (1966). *Deviance and Control.* Englewood Cliffs, NJ: Prentice-Hall.

Cole, C. L. (2000). Testing for Sex or Drugs. *Journal of Sport & Social Issues,* 24(4), 331–334.

Coser, L. A. (1956). *The Functions of Social Conflict.* New York: Free Press.

Cullen, F. T. (1984). *Rethinking Crime and Deviance: The Emergence of a Structuring Tradition.* Totowa, NJ: Rowman and Allanheld.

Cuzzort, R. P., & King, E. W. (1989). *Twentieth-Century Social Thought.* Fort Worth, TX: Holt, Rinehart and Winston.

Daniels, A. K., & Daniels, R. R. (1964). The Social Role of the Career Fool. *Psychiatry,* 27(August), 219–229.

Davis, K. (1980). The Sociology of Prostitution. In S. H. Traub & C. B. Little (Eds.), *Theories of Deviance.* Itasca, IL: F. E. Peacock.

Davis, N. J. (1975). *Sociological Constructions of Deviance: Perspectives and Issues in the Field.* Dubuque, IA: William C. Brown.

Dentler, R. A., & Erikson, K. T. (1959). The Functions of Deviance in Groups. *Social Problems, 7,* 98–107.

Elliott, D., & Voss, H. L. (1974). *Delinquency and Dropout.* Lexington, MA: D. C. Heath.

Farnworth, M., and Lieber, M. J. (1989). Strain Theory Revisited: Economic Goals, Educational Means, and Deliquency. *American Sociological Review, 54,* 263–274.

Fleming, M. H., Roman, J., & Farrell, G. (2000). The Shadow Economy. *Journal of International Affairs, 53*(2), 387–410.

Francis, C., & Coplon, J. (1990). *Speed Trap.* Toronto: Lester & Orpen Dennys.

Friedrichs, R. W. (1970). *A Sociology of Sociology.* New York: Free Press.

Hackett, E. J. (1994). A Social Control Perspective on Scientific Misconduct. *Journal of Higher Education, 65,* 242–260.

Hagan, J. (1997). Defiance and Despair: Subcultural and Structural Linkages. *Social Forces, 76*(1), 119–125.

Jordan, W. (1969). *White over Black: American Attitudes Toward the Negro, 1550–1812.* Chapel Hill, NC: University of North Carolina.

Kanter, R. (1972). *Commitment and Community: Communes and Utopias in Sociological Perspective*. Cambridge, MA: Harvard University Press.

Katz, R. (2000). Explaining Girls' and Women's Crime and Desistance in the Context of their Victimization Experiences: A Developmental Test of Revised Strain Theory and the Life Course Perspective. *Violence against Women, 6*(6 June), 633–661.

Kornhauser, R. (1978). *The Social Sources of Delinquency: An Appraisal of Analytic Models*. Chicago: University of Chicago Press.

Lafree, G. (1998). Social Institutions and the Crime "Bust" of the 1990s. *Journal of Criminal Law and Criminology, 88*(4), 1325–1353.

Lee, J. A. (1981). Some Structural Aspects of Police Deviance in Relations with Minority Groups. In C. Shearing (Ed.), *Organizational Police Deviance*. Toronto: Butterworths.

Lehmann, J. M. (1994). *Durkheim and Women*. Lincoln, NE: University of Nebraska Press.

Leonard, E. B. (1982). *Women, Crime and Society: A Critique of Theoretical Criminology*. New York: Longman.

Leyton, E. (1986). *Hunting Humans: The Rise of the Modern Multiple Murderer*. Toronto: McClelland and Stewart.

Mann, E., & Lee, J. A. (1979). *RCMP vs. The People: Inside Canada's Security Service*. Don Mills, ON: General Publishing.

Marx, G. (1993). Ironies of Social Control: Authorities as Contributors to Deviance through Escalation, Nonenforcement, and Covert Facilitation. In D. Kelly (Ed.), *Deviant Behavior: A Text-Reader in the Sociology of Deviance* (Vol. 4). New York: St. Martin's Press.

Mazerolle, P., & Burton, V. S. (2000). Strain, Anger and Delinquent Adaptations. *Journal of Criminal Justice, 28*(2 March/April), 89–102.

Merton, R. K. (1938). Social Structure and Anomie. *American Sociological Review, 3*, 672–682.

———. (1946). *Mass Persuasion: The Social Psychology of a War Bond Drive*. New York: Harper and Row.

———. (1968). *Social Theory and Social Structure*. New York: Free Press. (Original work published in 1949)

———. (1973). *The Sociology of Science*. Chicago: University of Chicago Press.

Muncie, J., & McLaughlin, E. (Eds.). (1996). *The Problem of Crime*. London, UK: Sage and Open University Press.

Parsons, T. (1947). Certain Primary Sources and Patterns of Aggression in the Social Structure of the Western World. *Psychiatry, 10*(May), 167–181.

Parsons, T., & Smelser, N. (1956). *Economy and Society*. New York: Free Press.

Passas, N., & Agnew, R. (Eds.). (1997). *The Future of Anomie Theory*. Boston: Northeastern University Press.

Paternoster, R., and Mazerolle, P. (1994). General Strain and Delinquency: A Replication and Extension. *Journal of Research in Crime and Delinquency, 31*, 235–263.

Sagarin, E., & Montanino, F. (1977). *Deviants: Voluntary Actors in a Hostile World*. Glenview, IL: Scott Foresman.

Simmons, R. L., Miller, M. G., & Aigner, S. M. (1980). Contemporary Theories of Deviance and Female Delinquency: An Empirical Test. *Journal of Research in Crime and Delinquency, 17*, 42–53.

Spergel, I. A. (1964). *Racketville, Slumtown, and Haulburg*. Chicago: University of Chicago.

Sullivan, M. (1989). *"Getting Paid": Youth Crime and Work in the Inner City*. Ithaca, NY: Cornell University Press.

Wark, R. L., & Unnithan, P. (1998). Review of "The Legacy of Anomie Theory" Edited by Freda Adler and William S. Laufer. *Social Science Journal, 35*(3), 462–466.

Willis, P. (1977). *Learning to Labor: How Working Class Kids Get Working Class Jobs*. New York: Columbia University Press.

SUBCULTURAL AND SOCIAL LEARNING THEORIES OF DEVIANCE

This chapter examines theories that explain deviance as behaviour or ideas that are produced by subcultures and transmitted by learning. Some of these theories focus on the characteristics that make particular subcultures more likely than others to produce deviance. Such theories blame deviance on the beliefs and patterns of the subculture, whether it is an ethnic, occupational, leisure, age-group, or class subculture. Other theories within the same paradigm focus on the process of learning (often the learning of cultural or subcultural beliefs and patterns of behaviour), arguing that deviance is learned behaviour (not biological or psychopathic). Most sociological learning theories take their lead from the work of Edwin Sutherland.

SUBCULTURES

Tyler (1871, p. 10) defines culture as "that complex whole which includes knowledge, belief, art, morals, law, custom and many and any other capabilities and habits acquired by man as a member of society." Essentially, culture is the composite of our learned ways of thinking and behaving. Although some cultures are dominant, with enough power to impose their norms and values on the majority of people in a society, others are subcultures that coexist with but differ from the mainstream.

Whether they result from a collective resolution of strain, are simply a product of differential history, or are defensive formations, subcultures often involve values and norms (outlined below) that are deviant from the perspective of the wider culture.

- *Argot.* The subculture is frequently characterized by the use of an insider language. This is particularly true when the subculture is an ethnic or an oppositional subculture, but it also applies to such mixed groups as the computer subculture, which includes nerds, cyberpunks, hackers, and hacker-trackers, some of whom are rebels (Sterling, 1992). Similarly, the English punks, mods, teds, and skinheads studied by Hebdige (1979) each shared a differentiating argot and mode of dress. Many dictionaries of criminal and drug-user argots exist (Abel,

1984). The invention of words unique to the group is both a sign of insider status and a way of keeping unfriendly outsiders from knowing the group's business.

• *Vocabularies of motive.* The subculture may include justifications and excuses for behaviour that serve to neutralize the demands of the dominant culture. The delinquent gang member often sees gang behaviour as brave, heroic, and honourable. The criminal in a white-collar conspiracy may believe that government regulations are ill advised and not worthy of compliance. The "poacher" uses a vocabulary that justifies the "folk crime" and leaves him (or her) with a sense of being an accepted insider (Eliason & Dodder, 2000; Forsyth, 1997).

• *Distinctive clothing and body language* often mark subcultures. The gay community in the 1970s used an elaborate code of signals. Colour-coded handkerchiefs placed in the left or right pocket served, as would an argot, to communicate one's sexual preferences to insiders without attracting the attention of hostile authorities (Miller, 1993, p. 260). When these markers were assimilated by the fashion industry (and its heterosexual clientele), new ones took their place.

Box 9.1   Prison Argot

Fish	new inmate, inexperienced
$13\frac{1}{2}$	the sum of 12 jurors, one judge, and half a chance
Life-25	a life sentence, with 25 years before chance of parole
The hole	solitary confinement
Attitude adjustment	use of discipline or force to induce compliance
Bug	a crazy person
Punk	a male inmate forced into a submissive, feminine role
Bus therapy	the practice of transferring disruptive prisoners
Skinner	child molester, sex offender
Screw	correctional officer
Doing hard time	having difficulty serving a sentence, doing it the hard way
SHU	security handling unit
Snitch or rat	an informant

The terms above were common in the institutions where the author did volunteer work, and they seem to be widespread. Prison argot in Canada is similar to prison argot in other countries. An article on Israeli prison argot highlights the variety of special words that convey the same aspects of prisoner status that produce a special argot in Canada (Einat & Einat, 2000). Is this inmate a "stand up" or "right" guy who can be relied on to be loyal and stay cool? Then he's *melech hata* (king of the castle). Or is this person a snitch? Then he's *antenna* or *wiseh*. The heightened need for secrecy surrounding drugs, sex, and violence helps foster new words: *mizvada* is an inmate who hides drugs anally; *kipa aduma* is Little Red Riding Hood, an ambush. Unflattering terms abound for police officers and prison staff: *wisach* (contaminated) or *sharshuchot* (prostitutes).

NTL

- Subcultures may be characterized by *beliefs and norms* that diverge from the mainstream. But, as in the mainstream, considerable variation may exist within a particular subculture. It would be incorrect to see every member of a subculture, even a cult-like one, as a mindless follower of its dictates. Culture is one among many factors that affect how people interpret their worlds and determine how they will behave.

- Subcultures are developed through repeated contacts and maintained in *mutually supporting networks*. It is difficult to "cure" a deviant whose deviance derives from participation in a subcultural group, since the punishment will most likely make the deviant even more dependent on the group for the satisfaction of physical, material, and psychological needs. The behaviour is not likely to change unless the group changes or the individual leaves the group.

BLAMING SUBCULTURES

ETHNIC AND RACIAL SUBCULTURES

To the extent that cultural differences are real, they can play a role in deviance. A difference, say, in drinking patterns may increase the likelihood that particular groups will get into trouble for drunk driving or end up in detoxification centres (Greeley, McCready, & Theisen, 1980; Ziebold & Mongeon, 1982). Such differences need to be recognized by authorities but not allowed to prevent awareness that limits to cultural explanations exist. Thus, although a particular group may have a higher rate of drug abuse than another, it is probable that most members of that group do not use drugs. Policies requiring this one group (but not others) to take urine tests would not only do little to control this kind of deviance but would also feed public prejudice against the group. Police in particular need to be aware of how subcultural differences will affect police–citizen interaction (Cryderman & O'Toole, 1986).

Stereotypes exaggerate cultural differences and treat whole groups as deviant. Over time, various groups in Canada have been targeted in this way for their *assumed* predilections for certain forms of deviance. Among these groups have been the Chinese (targeted for opium use and gambling); Amish, Hutterites, German-speaking Jews, Japanese, and Italians (as wartime enemy aliens and spies); Italians (organized crime); Portuguese (immigration scams); French Canadians (organized crime and terrorism); Irish (alcoholism, petty crime, and terrorism); Native peoples (alcoholism, family violence, and crime); Sikhs and Armenians (terrorism); and Doukhobors (arson, nudity, and terrorism). More recently, media attention has been given to Asian organized crime. In each case, the stereotypes are poor representations of the real behaviour of most members of the group. Furthermore, such stereotypes divert attention from the wrongdoings of people who are not part of the targeted group and make it harder for those who have been targeted to obtain a fair hearing.

Box 9.2   The Case of Donald Marshall

Racial and ethnic stereotypes have helped to convict innocent persons and to impede exposure and correction of the injustice. Nowhere is this better illustrated than in the case of Donald Marshall (Harris, 1986). Marshall, a 17-year-old Micmac native, was accused of the 1971 fatal stabbing of a Black youth named Sandy Seale. As a result of grossly improper police procedures, Marshall was convicted of murder and sentenced to life imprisonment. After he had served more than a decade in prison, Marshall was declared not guilty, and an older non-Native man, Roy Ebsary, was charged and convicted of manslaughter in the death of Sandy Seale.

A royal commission of inquiry into Marshall's case found that not only had a serious miscarriage of justice taken place with respect to Marshall as an individual but also that racism (the belief that Aboriginals were less valuable than Whites and more prone to criminal activity) had tainted the process up to the highest level. The commission concluded that police conduct in the case had been "inadequate, incompetent, and unprofessional" and found fault with the prosecution, the defence, the judge, and the judges of the appeal court for having dealt with Marshall in a manner that was not consonant with his right to equal justice before the law.

While in prison, Marshall had adapted to the brutal inmate code, with its subculture of drugs, alcohol, and intimidation. Since his release, he has had great difficulty returning to ordinary life.

YOUTH SUBCULTURES

In comparison with the huge volume and tradition of studies of British and Australian youths, little work has been done to identify and analyze Canadian youth subcultures (Baron, 1989; O'Bireck, 1996a, 1996b; Tanner, 1990, 2001; Wilson & Sparks, 1996; Wilson & White, 2001, p. 7). Youth subcultures may arise out of strain or simply out of the gathering together and segregation of large numbers of young people in schools and leisure activities. In Western societies, these subcultures share three common characteristics: (1) they are based on *leisure* more often than on work or family; (2) they tend to be organized around the *peer group* rather than around individual friends, family, or ethnic groups; and (3) they are usually focused more on *style* than on political or social ideology (Frith, 1984).

The youth subculture is divided by variations that are based on gender, class, ethnicity, nationality, region, location in the social structure, and differential opportunity in the environment (such as the presence of soccer hooligans, criminal gangs, or access to computer-hacker culture). Brake (1985, p. 23; 1993) divided youth cultures into four groups: *respectable youth, delinquent youth, cultural rebels,* and *politically militant youth*. Respectable youth, involved in socially approved activities, constitute a negative reference group for the other categories. Delinquent youth often participate in activities such as "tagging" and "piecing" (forms of graffiti) that express their subcultural identities (Krauss, 1996; Lachmann, 1988). Tagging is the writing of a stylized version of the individual's subcultural nickname or tag. It may also be the tag of the crew to which the individual belongs. Piecing is the painting of large murals on walls (Ferrell, 1993, pp. 74–77). There are significant variations within these categories. "Straightedge youth," for example, constitute a faction within the punk rock movement that is distinctive in its militant opposition to drug use and casual sex (Wood, 1998). Riot Grrrl is a subculture that combines feminist consciousness with punk politics and style (Garrison, 2000, p. 14).

Cross-cultural influences strongly affect youth subcultures. Motorcycle gangs developed in Tokyo and Moscow even under conditions in which only wealthy persons could obtain Harley-Davidson motorcycles—it was the style and attitude that counted (Reuters, 1995). A subcultural element that is a solution to a problem in one country or area may be adopted as a fashion statement or a consumer culture variant in another (Tait, 1999). Consider the differences between English and Canadian "punk" subcultures. In England, punk subculture appears to result from strain in the educational and employment systems. Educational streaming channels some young people toward boring, oversupervised, and poorly paid occupations (Brake, 1985, p. 62). Not surprisingly, some of these "deselected" youth are alienated from the mainstream. When they come together in the school system, they develop defiant, provoking subcultures that attract other alienated individuals. Punk fashion and behaviour can be seen at least in part as a statement: "You are treating us like garbage, so we will dramatize our status by wearing garbage."

In contrast, punk in Canada serves mainly as a fashion that links young people with similar interests. Although it is hardly pro-establishment, it does not make a weighty political statement. Brake (1985, p. 144–162) argues that the less clear-cut social-class delineation of youth status in Canada (when compared with status lines in Britain and income disparities in the United States) has made its youth subcultural forms more a matter of style and shared activities than a collective solution to status problems. It is not clear, though, why youth status deprivation in England produces a punk culture; meanwhile, in the United States, similar deselection conditions produce "street elite" fighting gangs (Anderson, 1994; Katz, 1988). Other youth cultures that beg for greater understanding are the rave culture (Hutson, 1999; Oh & Atherley, 2000) and gothic culture (Castles, 2001; Tait, 1999).

OCCUPATIONAL SUBCULTURES

Occupations such as prostitution, thieving, gambling, and drug trafficking all develop their own subcultures, which are in part a reaction to the dominant respectable culture and in part an expression of common problems and experiences that cannot be shared with outsiders. Prostitutes, for example, may, within their subculture, see their role as equal or even superior to that of women who marry for money and security. In this subculture, prostitution may be justified as a kind of social or psychotherapeutic service for men who might otherwise resort to rape or leave a string of broken homes in their search for sexual experience. The subculture also supports the view that prostitution is better work than the alternatives: low-paid, insecure jobs that often include sexual harassment and other indignities. From the subcultural perspective, prostitution is more honest and valuable than many legal occupations. Prostitutes' argot calls customers "johns" and work "turning tricks." This subcultural argot often overlaps with the language of the drug user and the criminal underworld, a fact that reflects the overlapping of disreputable worlds.

Even within mainstream occupations, subcultures may emerge and express points of view that would shock the average outsider. The jokes that doctors, police officers, and lawyers tell one another often reflect a "them and us" dichotomy. The root of the subculture is common experience that cannot be shared with outsiders. The doctor or police officer knows that keeping up to date professionally or going by the book is not always possible. Outsiders cannot be trusted with evidence of this, however. It is common for people in these occupations to protect colleagues guilty of dangerous or unethical misconduct because they, too, feel vulnerable to outsiders' misunderstandings. Among police, the practice is called the "blue wall of silence."

Mars (1982) provides a British perspective on the deviance of workers. He divides occupations into *hawk, donkey, wolf pack,* and *vulture* types, each of which has a distinctive ideology, set of attitudes, and view of the world. Hawks are found in occupations that emphasize individuality, corner-cutting autonomy, competition, innovation, and control over others, such as professionals and business entrepreneurs. Donkeys are found in jobs characterized by isolation and subordination (e.g., supermarket cashier). Their deviance is likely to take the form of excessive sickness and absenteeism, cheating people (or the company) at the cash register, or sabotage of equipment. Wolves are found mainly in more traditional working-class occupations (e.g., mining), where the work is organized into teams. Teamwork is vital to success and security, and the individual who refuses to participate in group pilfering may not survive in the job. Vultures are found among travelling sales representatives, driver-deliverers (couriers), and others who have considerable freedom and discretion during the workday. An example of a vulture "fiddle" is the practice of "dropping short" (giving less gas to the customer than was ordered) and selling the surplus privately, often to thieves who require the gas to power the equipment they use to cut up stolen cars.

Mars emphasizes that most of the deviance associated with each work type is not the anarchic behaviour of "bad apple" individuals but rather behaviour that is enforced by the workgroups themselves. A worker who steals too much, thereby endangering his or her colleagues in deviance, will provoke the enmity of the group.

LOWER-CLASS SUBCULTURES

Walter Miller (1958) argues that male juvenile gangs are a by-product of the lower socioeconomic class's core culture. Unlike the strain theorists discussed in Chapter 8, Miller does not see the delinquent subculture as an oppositional response to strain.

He argues that the lower-class culture is unique in boasting a "distinctive tradition many centuries old with an integrity of its own" (p. 19) and goes on to characterize this distinctive tradition by addressing six focal concerns: trouble, toughness, smartness, excitement, fate, and autonomy.

1. *Trouble.* Individuals in the lower-class milieu are evaluated in terms of their actual and potential involvement in troublemaking activity. Being able to handle oneself in a fight or a tight situation lends prestige, but getting caught and having to pay is attributed to foolishness and incompetence. Activities such as fighting, drinking, and sexual risk taking may lend themselves to the creation of trouble.

2. *Toughness.* In Miller's view, the lower class assigns great importance to physical prowess, skill, fearlessness, and daring. The lower-class male wants to be seen as emphatically masculine. Although sentimentality may be given a limited place (as exemplified by the stereotypical heart-shaped tattoo encircling the word "Mother"), the culture generally rejects weakness, ineptitude, effeminacy, caution, and overt emotionality. The maintenance of the macho image may involve seemingly irrational violence or intimidation of others. In this culture, women are treated as objects of conquest.

3. *Smartness.* The kind of smartness valued by the lower-class culture is not academic intelligence but rather street smarts, which includes the ability to control and manipulate others; to gain advantage through instinct, knowledge, and strategy; to avoid being outsmarted or shown up by others; and to achieve wealth without working hard for it.

4. *Excitement.* The fact that most lower-class work is exhausting, repetitive, and boring places a premium on thrill, risk taking, change, and action. This may result in run-ins with police or high-risk and high-reward projects involving theft.

5. *Fate.* In contrast to the middle-class emphasis on planning for the future, members of the lower class are more likely to see the future as a matter of fortune or luck.

6. *Autonomy.* Members of the lower-class subculture express ambivalent feelings toward autonomy. The omnipresent desire to say, "Take this job and shove it" is counterbalanced by the fact that lower-class males often choose to work in authoritarian environments such as the army. Self-discipline is rejected in favour of superordinate discipline. Lower-class males associate being externally controlled with being cared for and frequently test authority to see whether it is firm.

When lower-class youths form delinquent gangs, the focal concerns discussed above become part of their subculture. In the gang milieu, however, two additional focal concerns appear. The first of these is *belonging* (concern about maintaining group membership in good standing), and the second is *status* (concern about being respected).

THE SUBCULTURE OF VIOLENCE

Another variant of the subcultural theme argues that rates of violent crime, particularly homicide, will be high in regions where little value is given to human life and where the subculture sees many kinds of behaviour as requiring a violent response. Wolfgang (1958) and Wolfgang and Ferracuti (1967) use this interpretation to explain a continuing pattern that shows higher rates of homicide among visible minorities than among Whites, and higher rates in some nations, including Colombia, South America, and Sardinia, Italy. Other observers regard violence not as an inherent subcultural value but rather as an adaptive response: people who have experienced violence (war, oppression) learn to be violent (Silberman, 1978).

The subculture of violence approach has also been applied to particular sports. Colburn (1986) suggests that fistfights in hockey, which may sometimes constitute illegal violence, are in fact a part of cultural understandings that are shared by the players. Fights can be social rituals that express a subcultural version of honour, fairness, and respect for the opponent. The fight may be defined as good or dirty depending on the extent to which it conforms to subcultural norms that bear little relation to either the formal regulations of the game or the Criminal Code of Canada. Similar observations have been made with respect to fan-generated violence at soccer matches, rock concerts, and even cricket matches.

CANADIAN CULTURE VERSUS U.S. CULTURE

The United States and Canada differ substantially in their rates of gun-related crimes. Handgun homicide rates are roughly 15 times higher in the United States than they are in Canada (Canadian Firearms Centre, 2000). Canada also differs dramatically in the way in which criminal deviance is treated. For example, Canada imprisons roughly 100 citizens per hundred thousand, while the United States incarcerates 600 per hundred thousand (Solicitor General Canada, 2000). Such differences have been attributed to deeply entrenched cultural disparities that have their roots in history, economy, and degree of inner-city disorder in the larger urban areas of the two countries (Ouimet, 1999). Historically, Canada, unlike the United States, was a counterrevolutionary society. Its traditions have tended to reinforce respect for institutional forms of authority, even when this authority has been abused (Friedenburg, 1980). The U.S. constitution guarantees to each *individual* the inalienable right to life, liberty, and the pursuit of happiness, as well as the right to bear arms. The Canadian constitution, in contrast, promises peace, order, and good government and qualifies all individual rights with the *collective* restriction, "reasonable" with respect to the rights of the whole.

A good deal of Canada's economic history is the history of enterprises that required heavy capitalization and thus encouraged collective rather than individual endeavours. Major American industries were often initiated by robber barons who bent many rules on their way to fame and fortune (Josephson, 1962).

The relationship between the population as a whole and the police has been quite different in Canada from that in the United States. In Canada, police presence generally preceded rather than followed the path of settlement, whereas the reverse was true of the United States. In the Yukon, for example, American miners dealt out justice through extralegal "miners courts," while Canadians in virtually the same area, and under the same conditions, relied on the North West Mounted Police (Hatch, 1991, p. 27). Even now, Canadians have been willing to tolerate programs such as British Columbia's CounterAttack and Ontario's RIDE, in which police stop every vehicle that passes their checkpoint, looking for evidence of drunk driving. Such programs would be unconstitutional in the United States. Canada is also distinctive in having a police officer (the red-coated Mountie) as a national symbol. This does not mean that all Canadians are more conforming than Americans or less tolerant of deviants. Canada's stand on issues such as medical marijuana is much closer to the liberal European model than is true of most states in the United States.

THE TRANSMISSION OF CULTURE: LEARNING THEORIES

EDWIN SUTHERLAND AND DIFFERENTIAL ASSOCIATION

Edwin Sutherland (1883–1950) began his professional career at the University of Chicago, where he did his doctoral thesis on unemployment, using the mildly reformist approach characteristic of the Chicago School. Having become slightly disillusioned about mainstream sociology, he transferred his allegiance to the study of crime, especially (but not exclusively) corporate crime. His followers, however, have extended his ideas to wider contexts of rule violation such as drug abuse, homosexuality, prostitution, aggression, suicide, and mental illness.

Sutherland used the concept of *differential association* to explain why some people become criminals while others do not (see Figure 9.1). What is differentially associated is not people but definitions. Definitions are normative meanings that are assigned to behaviour. They define an action or a pattern of action as right or wrong (Akers, 1985, p. 49). Definitions may be favourable to actions that violate the laws (DFVL) or unfavourable to violation of the law (DUFVL) (Sutherland, 1947; Sutherland & Cressey, 1966). Definitions can be nonverbal expressions of approval or disapproval (Stevenson, 1999).

Most of us are exposed to both kinds of definitions. We see people praising and practising honesty, fairness, and good work; we also see people justifying all sorts of wrongdoing and behaving dishonestly and unfairly. We hear definitions about the appalling consequences of drug use, and we hear definitions that underline the ecstasy of a drug high and the right to experiment. We see the advantages of getting along with authorities, but we also respect people who stand up for themselves and their chosen way of life. According to Sutherland, we are shaped by the preponderance of one or the other kind of definition in our lives.

Figure 9.1   Differential Association: Ideas That Discourage or Justify Deviance

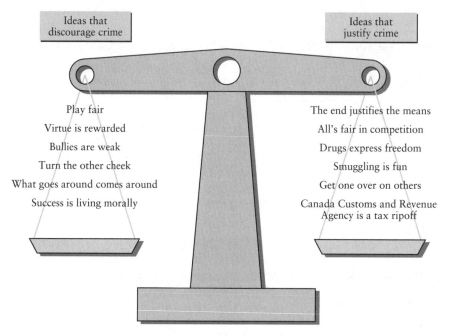

Source: Adapted with permission from E. Sutherland & D. Cressey (1978), *Criminology,* Tenth Edition (Philadelphia: J. B. Lippincott).

Sutherland presented his theory of differential association in a series of nine propositions that have strong associations with the idea of operant conditioning, despite his rejection of internal psychological theories such as behaviouralism (Jacoby, 1994; Sutherland, 1947, pp. 6–8):

1. *Criminal behaviour is learned.* Although this statement in itself may not be very striking, Sutherland uses it to negate all other explanations, whether biological or psychological. Every Oliver Twist needs his Fagan, which is to say every criminal needs teachers.

2. *An individual learns criminality through interaction and communication with others.* Criminality is not learned from reading trashy novels or watching violence on television, *unless* the reading or viewing is backed up by interaction with people who support its messages. The communication does not have to be verbal or a matter of conscious teaching. Our parents may not directly condone cheating on income taxes, avoiding customs duties, or speeding, but we may get these messages by the way they talk about these subjects. If we grow up in a family in which

"going on a bender" is the normal way to handle stress, we are far more likely to use alcohol in destructive ways (Brown, Creamer, & Stetson, 1987).

3. *The kind of interaction that matters most takes place within small, intimate groups.* Behaviour that is learned through intimate, face-to-face contact with significant others will be more firmly entrenched than ideas learned via formal contacts with the wider social system. Thus, for Sutherland, the fact that serial killer Paul Bernardo owned pornographic materials and books such as Bret Easton Ellis's *American Psycho* (which tells of a businessman who, like Bernardo, kidnaps and brutalizes young women) would not by itself explain Bernardo's behaviour.

   Differential association theory predicts that censorship, such as the use of "censorware" (computer software that blocks access to Internet sites that may contain pornography and violence but that also tends to block sites such as the official *Ally McBeal* Web site, the National Organization for Women, Planned Parenthood, and Amnesty International) (American Libraries, 2001; Kleiner, 2000), will do little to reduce children's deviance. This lack of effect would also apply to other censorship issues, such as removing from school libraries books that take a nonjudgmental or sympathetic stand on homosexual or lesbian sexuality, explain creationism, or present minorities in stereotypical ways, and to the denial of airplay to sexist, homophobic, or violent music (Ross & Saxe, 2001).

4. *What is learned in intimate interaction includes both the techniques of crime and the motives for crime.* The learning of *techniques of crime* is most obvious with respect to criminal "apprenticeships," in which more experienced criminals take on and train others in such activities as using drugs or weapons, picking a lock, hot-wiring a car, or running a confidence swindle. People also learn, as part of their upbringing, how and when to get mad about things (and how and when to talk themselves down from anger). The professional killer, for example, may use these skills to get "hot" enough to kill or "cold" enough to carry off a stress-producing plan (Dietz, 1983). Finally, the future criminal learns techniques for discovering the criminal potential in a situation. Criminal hustlers are dedicated to finding an edge that will allow them to cheat and manipulate others.

   Less obviously, criminals learn *motives for crime.* Subcultural values provide explanations, excuses, justifications, and rationalizations. Unlike the psychological concept of motive, which refers to a person's individual internal needs and desires, Sutherland's concept of motive refers to "vocabularies of motive" that we *learn* through interaction with others. Most of us learn through those vocabularies that violence is justified under certain conditions. In a Toronto criminal case, a man charged with assaulting his neighbour testified that just before the attack he had discovered that the neighbour had been sexually molesting his (the defendant's) nine-year-old daughter. The jury understood the "vocabulary of motive" invoked by the outraged father and acquitted him.

5. *"The specific direction of motives and drives is learned from definitions of the legal codes as favourable or unfavourable"* (Sutherland & Cressey, 1978, p. 87). Sutherland combines the idea of differential group organization (some groups have more criminal definitions than others) with differential association to explain that some subcultures evaluate violence, cheating, or general lawbreaking more positively than do others.

6. *The ratio of favourable to unfavourable "definitions" of the law as communicated within the group is a determinant of criminal behaviour.* This is the core of the theory. Criminals become criminal when an excess of definitions favourable to the violation of the law conditions them to engage in illegal activity. If DFVL is greater than DUFVL in the group environment, the group member will be criminal. Gangbanging norms, for example, include specification of the conditions for, and methods of, drive-by shootings, and the preponderance of such definitions in inner-city settings can overwhelm the messages learned through other sources of moral information.

7. *Certain variables affect the impact of favourable and unfavourable definitions.* These variables are frequency, duration, priority, and intensity. The dimensions of *frequency* and *duration* are self-explanatory. If we associate with a person or group frequently and for long periods, we are likely to be influenced by their ideas. *Priority* assumes that associations formed early in life are more funda-mental than those formed later in life. *Intensity* has to do with the strength of the association between the individual and the members of the group; we are more likely to be influenced by people we admire or care about. This proposition can be used to explain the failure of antidelinquency programs like Scared Straight! (discussed in Chapter 4). Spending three hours in a prison, where the inmates attempt to show just how awful it is, is simply not enough to undo a lifetime of reinforcement of criminal values and behaviour. The program lacks priority, fre-quency, and duration. It has a certain intensity, but not in the sense that those in the program have a close relationship with the inmates.

8. *Learning criminal behaviour is just like any other kind of learning.* The only dif-ference is *what* is learned, not *how* it is learned. Criminals are normal people who have learned the wrong lessons. Upper-class people learn criminality at work; lower-class people often learn it on the street. Both learn the same way. A person who is capable of learning criminal behaviour patterns is also capable of learning noncriminal behaviour patterns.

9. *The criminal is not exceptional in what he or she wants.* To say that prostitutes or thieves are "in it for the money" explains nothing because people in legal occu-pations are also in it for the money. Most of us would prefer to get what we want with less effort and less boredom, just as the criminal does. Criminals are excep-tional with respect to their means, not with respect to their goals. For Sutherland, the question about crime should be rephrased from "Why do they do it?" to

"Why do they do it in this particular way?" (Sutherland & Cressey, 1978, pp. 75–77).

Thus, for Sutherland, the explanation for deviance, especially white-collar criminal deviance, is found in what people learn, not in their biology or physiology, their psychopathology, or their material needs. Companies and their personnel do not violate laws because of their "Oedipus complex," "emotional instability," "lack of recreational facilities," or poverty. Participants see their actions as "just business" within a context that isolates them from definitions unfavourable to such violations (Sutherland, 1949, p. 247).

RONALD AKERS AND SOCIAL LEARNING THEORY

Many variants of Sutherland's learning theory have been proposed. One of these is Ronald Akers's social learning theory. Akers (1985, p. 46) argues that social behaviour is acquired through psychological processes of operant conditioning and through imitation and modelling. The specific process by which deviant behaviour (as opposed to conforming behaviour) becomes dominant in specific situations is *differential reinforcement*. The behaviour that is seen to be, or experienced as, most successful in securing the most desired payoff becomes dominant. The rewards and punishments can be social (praise, promotion, recognition, attention) or nonsocial (the physiological effects of drugs or food). This theory provides more scope for learning from vicarious experience and identification than is true of Sutherland's formulation but is otherwise consistent with Sutherland's approach. For example, Akers argues that the small, intimate groups in which learning takes place are important because people we like, respect, and spend time with control our most important supply of reinforcement.

In addressing the criticism that the differential association model fails to account for apparently spontaneous, senseless, or compulsive criminal behaviour, Akers cites the work of Frank Hartung to show that even the most spontaneous acts usually have roots in a long period of learning. Violent and aggressive people are often found to have had such behaviour reinforced either by their own experiences or by those of others. According to Hartung (1965, p. 140), when a person attacks another, it will normally be found that he or she (1) has experienced incidents of a similar nature that have been rewarding, (2) is not controlled by strong moral injunctions against violence, and (3) has learned violent patterns of thought and action.

Parents may unwittingly encourage and reward their children's violence by modelling the use of force (spanking or hitting the child) and by exposing the child to environments in which violence is a recommended means of defence or of attaining desired goals. The aggressive individual may not be conscious of the learning process because it has been more a matter of "out of awareness" conditioning than of formal, verbal teaching. One implication of this theory is that violent people can be taught to recognize and alter the thoughts that provoke their violent behaviour.

Like Sutherland, Akers developed a theory that has little to say (yet) about structured gender differences and their impact on the likelihood of exposure to definitions favourable to deviant choices (Morash, 1999).

GRESHAM SYKES, DAVID MATZA, AND NEUTRALIZATION THEORY

The theory of neutralization is one that informs Sutherland's fourth proposition about the learning of deviance, the importance of preexisting vocabularies of motive. We should note here that neutralization theory fits well in combination with learning theory but also fits well with interaction theory (Chapter 10) and control theory (Chapter 11). Sykes and Matza (1957) note that most delinquents are not deviant all the time. They participate along with nondelinquents in many conventional activities (school, religious observance, family life), and they often show respect for role models (outstanding teachers, sports figures, etc.). It is not accurate to say that they are delinquents (simply) because they are conforming to subcultural norms, since they do have attachments to the predominant norms of society (Matza, 1964). Delinquents, therefore, "drift" (Matza's word) between conventionality and deviance. How do they free themselves from conventional constraints to participate in delinquent activities? Sykes and Matza argue that they learn to use the following five neutralization techniques to justify or excuse their participation in the subterranean norms of the delinquent subculture:

1. *Denial of responsibility.* "I didn't mean to do it." "I couldn't help it." "I was sleepwalking."
2. *Denial of injury.* "We were just having fun." "I just borrowed it." "The insurance company will pay."
3. *Denial of or blaming the victim.* "She had it coming." "He was just a phony." "They shouldn't have been there."
4. *Condemnation of the condemners.* "The authorities are hypocrites." "Successful people cheat; they just don't get caught."
5. *Appeal to higher loyalties.* "I was protecting my family." "My friends needed me." "The gang comes first."

Scott and Lyman (1968) developed the notion of "neutralizations" in the idea of "accounts," which are the stories that we use to account for (excuse and justify) our deviant behaviour. Two categories of accounts exist: excuses and justifications. Excuses combine an admission that the action was wrong with a rejection of responsibility (I was drunk at the time; it was an accident). Justifications are claims that extenuating circumstances legitimate the behaviour (I was following orders; it was necessary; they deserved it). These ideas were tested by Scully and Marolla (see Box 9.3) and continue to inform recent work, such as David Shulman's (2000) study of the way in which private detectives account for a wide range of actions such as false billing, fraudulent evidence, illegal wiretapping, and selling confidential information

---

Box 9.3   Excuses and Justifications: Learned Vocabulary of Motive

Scully and Marolla (1984) studied imprisoned rapists to find out how they explained or justified their actions. They found a consistent pattern of excuses and justifications. Excuses involved blaming the behaviour on forces beyond the rapist's control (emotional problems, drug or alcohol intoxication), while justifications were attempts to make the behaviour seem acceptable (women as seducers who mean yes when they say no). Scully and Marolla were most interested in how the rapists used this vocabulary of motive after the fact to diminish responsibility and to negotiate a nondeviant identity. What these excuses and justifications share with Sykes and Matza's neutralizations is their status as culturally supported vocabularies of motive. In other words, the men in this study did not invent their excuses. Rather, they "used" them just as tools are used, to repair a "spoiled" identity. Although neutralizations for rape have come increasingly under attack in our society, these explanations are still recognized and given credence by some people.

Certain acts lack an acceptable vocabulary of motive in our culture. When we ask people why they committed fatal child abuse, for example, the most likely response is denial, concealment, or misrepresentation. When Margolin (1990) interviewed women who had killed their own babies, she found that few excuses or justifications were shared in the group. (Among the few given were sudden loss of control, accident, and psychosis.) By far the largest number of women in the sample responded with complete bewilderment (no explanation) or barefaced lies about how the child died.

---

to the other party; Joanna Higginson's (1999) study of how teen mothers excuse and justify the statutory rape (consensual but underage sex) that resulted in their pregnancies; and Teevan and Dryburgh's (2000) study of how Canadian youths explain their acts of delinquency.

Moshe Hazani (1991) expanded neutralization theory to include the idea that each subculture provides "symbols banks" that are used by deviants to formulate approved accounts. Hazani found that two groups of Israeli youths committed similar offences (car theft followed by reckless driving). The boys from the working class community of "Southem," most of them steadily employed as apprentice mechanics, stole cars from the wealthier "Northem" community. They called their joyriding *charaka* (an Arabic word meaning movement) and normally abandoned the cars after wrecking them. The boys from the upper-middle-class community of Northem stole cars to race them (called *racim*) or to impress friends with possession of a new BMW or Mercedes. The two groups used different vocabularies of motive to align their deviant actions with the dominant norms of Israeli society.

The Southem boys explained their thefts in three ways: first, as taking back what should have been theirs. The people in Northem were unfairly rich because of the big banks and the lawyers who kept the Southem residents poor. Second, they argued that *charaka* fed their physical craving (the inner worm = *dudah*) for excitement. Third, they argued that youth was a period in which young men should be showing off and venting excess energy, something most easily done with someone else's impressive car.

The Northem boys used five main explanations. First, they claimed that they only borrowed the cars. Second, even though these cars were often damaged and parts were stolen from them, the harm was not serious because the cars were insured. Third, the Northem boys argued that those who always obey the laws are losers. Fourth, those who were serving in Israel's elite combat units argued that they were owed the use of these cars. Finally, the Northem boys also referred to being in the stage of life at which they should take time out before assuming adult responsibilities. Thus, although the delinquencies of these youths were similar, each subculture drew on different vocabularies of motive to align their deviant actions with the dominant social norms.

Research suggests that neutralization theory is most effective when applied to middle-class, white-collar offenders than to most juvenile delinquents, at least with respect to neutralizations that conform to the theory by acting on behaviour *before* rather than after it occurs. Hindelang's (1970, p. 509) self-report study, for example, found that delinquents might resort to using these explanations in their dealings with authorities (i.e., after the fact) but generally not with one another (before the action). The "stand-up man" or "right guy" in the street or in jail is one who does not use excuses, does not justify the behaviour, and does not respect people who do. Alternatively, evidence shows that white-collar offenders employ techniques of neutralization to justify criminal acts they are about to commit (i.e., before the act). Cressey (1971), for example, studied embezzlers and came to the conclusion that they typically rationalized what they were doing as "just borrowing," "something the company deserved," or "a fairly common way of getting an entrepreneurial start." In the absence of such culturally approved (but subterranean) rationalizations, Cressey suggests, they would not have committed the prohibited acts. Cressey felt that companies could protect themselves by attacking the roots of such rationalizations.

SUMMARY

Subcultural theories of deviance may emphasize particular subcultures (ethnic or racial, youth, occupational, class), or they may stress the process of learning (differential association, differential identification and anticipation, social learning, and neutralization). Generally, these theories blame deviance on the values and beliefs that people learn in the company of others. From their perspective, deviance is normal to the groups in which it occurs; deviants are not fundamentally different from the rest of us, they have just learned different lessons; and, in many of these theories, "we are what we learn" and have little free choice in the matter.

STUDY QUESTIONS

1. Almost every group has some argot that is known to its insiders. (For academics, it is largely jargon, the specialized language of a discipline.) Think about the groups you participate in. Are there words that reflect group history and that are only understood within the group? What about wider groupings, such as participants in the rave subculture? How important is it that the group regards some outsiders as unfriendly to it?

2. Do excuses and justifications have their effect mainly before we commit offences (freeing us from our own conscience) or mainly after the offences (explaining ourselves to others)?

3. To what extent was Donald Marshall's trouble caused by Native youth subculture, and to what extent was it caused by the subculture of the Nova Scotia criminal justice system?

4. In Los Angeles, the practice of tagging is associated with gangs who steal their sprayers and sometimes kill members of other gangs. In Canada, tagging tends to be treated as vandalism and is less associated with criminal deviance. Why is tagging different in one place than in another?

5. Why do we tolerate advertising on buses but treat graffiti as vandalism?

6. Why do teen girls very rarely form their own gangs the way that many teen boys do?

7. What is the difference between punk in England and punk in Canada? What about other youth culture phenomena? What about gothic in Canada, the United States, Britain, and Australia? Does each national culture have an impact on its subcultures?

8. What kind of jobs do most students have? How would Gerald Mars classify these jobs?

9. Do you feel that hockey players who use violence should be taken to criminal court? Why do you feel that way?

10. To what extent does Canada's history affect recent Canadian rates for crime and social problems?

11. Can social learning be reversed by therapy and remedial programs? How important are intense, early experiences relative to what we learn in school and at work?

12. Do "slasher films" spawn trigger-happy teenagers?

13. In 1999, Paladin Press, publishers of a "breezy" manual on how to be a hit man (contract killer) agreed to a multimillion-dollar settlement to the relatives of three people gruesomely murdered by a killer who allegedly relied on the book, although he did not follow its instructions precisely (Castaneda & Wilson, 1999). Was this settlement justifiable?

14. What are Sykes and Matza's neutralizations? Try to think of some excuse or justification that doesn't fit into these categories.

REFERENCES

Abel, E. L. (1984). *A Dictionary of Drug Abuse Terms and Terminology*. Westport, CT: Greenwood Press.

Akers, R. L. (1985). *Deviant Behavior: A Social Learning Approach* (3rd ed.). Belmont, CA: Wadsworth.

American Libraries. (2001). Censorship Watch. *American Libraries, 32*(2), 19.

Anderson, E. (1994). The Code of the Streets. *Atlantic Monthly,* (May), 81–94.

Baron, S. (1989). The Canadian West Coast Punk Subculture: A Field Study. *Canadian Journal of Sociology, 14*(3), 289–316.

Brake, M. (1985). *Comparative Youth Culture: The Sociology of Youth Culture and Youth Subcultures in America, Britain and Canada*. London, UK: Routledge and Keegan Paul.

———. (1993). *Comparative Youth Culture* (2nd ed.). New York: Routledge.

Brown, S., Creamer, V., & Stetson, B. (1987). Adolescent Alcohol Expectancies in Relation to Personal and Parental Drinking Patterns. *Journal of Abnormal Psychology, 96,* 117–121.

Canadian Firearms Centre. (2000). *Firearms: Canada/United States Comparison*. Ottawa: Solicitor General of Canada.

Castaneda, R., & Wilson, S. (1999, May 22). "Hit Man" Publisher Settles Suit. *Washington Post*, p. A1.

Castles, S. (2001). Esprit de Corpse. *Newsweek (Bulletin), 118*(6255), 21–23.

Colburn, K., Jr. (1986). Honour, Ritual and Violence in Ice Hockey. In R. A. Silverman & J. J. Teevan (Eds.), *Crime in Canadian Society* (3rd ed.). Toronto: Butterworths.

Cressey, D. R. (1971). *Other People's Money: A Study in the Social Psychology of Embezzlement*. Belmont, CA: Wadsworth.

Cryderman, B., & O'Toole, C. N. (1986). *Chris N*. Toronto: Butterworths.

Dietz, M. L. (1983). *Killing for Profit: The Social Organization of Felony Homicide*. Chicago: Prentice-Hall.

Einat, T., & Einat, H. (2000). Inmate Argot as an Expression of Prison Subculture: The Israeli Case. *Prison Journal, 80*(3), 309–326.

Eliason, S. L., & Dodder, R. A. (2000). Neutralization among Deer Poachers. *Journal of Social Psychology, 140*(4 August), 536–539.

Ferrell, J. (1993). *Crimes of Style: Urban Graffiti and the Politics of Criminality.* New York: Garland.

Forsyth, A. (1997). Five Images of a Suburb: Perspectives on New Urban Development. *Journal of the American Planning Association, 1997,* 45–71.

Friedenberg, E. Z. (1980). *Deference to Authority: The Case of Canada.* Toronto: Random House of Canada.

Frith, S. (1984). *The Sociology of Youth.* Ormskirk, UK: Causeway Press.

Garrison, K. (2000). U.S. Feminism—Grrrl Style! Youth (Sub)Cultures and the Technologies of the Third Wave. *Feminist Studies, 26*(1), 141–171.

Greeley, A. M., McCready, W. C., & Theisen, G. (1980). *Ethnic Drinking Subcultures.* New York: Praeger.

Harris, M. (1986). *Justice Denied: The Law versus Donald Marshall.* Toronto: Macmillan.

Hartung, F. C. (1965). *Crime, Law and Society.* Detroit, MI: Wayne State University Press.

Hatch, A. J. (1991). Historical Legacies in Canadian Criminal Law and Justice. In M. A. Jackson & C. T. Griffiths (Eds.), *Canadian Criminology: Perspectives on Crime and Criminality.* Toronto: Harcourt Brace Jovanovich.

Hazani, M. (1991). Aligning Vocabulary, Symbols Banks, and Sociocultural Structure. *Journal of Contemporary Ethnography, 20*(2 July), 179–203.

Hebdige, D. (1979). *Subculture: The Meaning of Style.* New York: Routledge.

Higginson, J. G. (1999). Defining, Excusing, and Justifying Deviance: Teen Mother's Accounts for Statutory Rape. *Symbolic Interaction, 22*(1), 25–46.

Hindelang, M. (1970). The Commitment of Delinquents to Their Misdeeds: Do Delinquents Drift? *Social Problems, 17,* 509.

Hutson, S. R. (1999). Technoshamanism: Spiritual Healing in the Rave Subculture. *Popular Music and Society, 23*(3 Fall), 53–78.

Jacoby, J. (1994). *Classics of Criminology* (2nd ed.). Prospect Heights, IL: Waveland.

Josephson, M. (1962). *The Robber Barons (1934).* New York: Harcourt Brace Jovanovich.

Katz, J. (1988). *Seductions of Crime: Moral and Sensual Attractions in Doing Evil.* New York: Basic Books.

Kleiner, K. (2000). Watching the Detectives. *Mother Jones, 25*(4), 22–25.

Krauss, C. (1996, October 7). Evolution of Graffiti Spells Out Gang Crime. *The Globe and Mail,* p. A9.

Lachmann, R. (1988). Graffiti as Career and Ideology. *American Journal of Sociology, 94,* 229–250.

Margolin, L. (1990). When Vocabularies of Motive Fail: The Example of Fatal Child Abuse. *Qualitative Sociology, 4,* 373–385.

Mars, G. (1982). *Cheats at Work: An Anthropology of Workplace Crime.* London, UK: Unwin.

Matza, D. (1964). *Delinquency and Drift.* New York: John Wiley and Sons.

Miller, J. (1993). *The Passion of Michel Foucault.* New York: Simon and Schuster.

Miller, W. (1958). Lower-Class Culture as a Generating Milieu of Gang Delinquency. *Journal of Social Issues, 14,* 5–19.

Morash, M. (1999). A Consideration of Gender in Relation to Social Learning and Social Structure: A General Theory of Crime and Deviance. *Theoretical Criminology, 3*(4), 451–462.

O'Bireck, G. (1996a). Preppies and Heavies in Bigtown: Secondary School Experiences. In G. O'Bireck (Ed.), *Not a Kid Anymore: Canadian Youth, Crime and Subcultures* (pp. 247–281). Toronto: Nelson Canada.

O'Bireck, G. (Ed.). (1996b). *Not a Kid Anymore: Canadian Youth, Crime, and Subcultures.* Toronto: Nelson Canada.

Oh, S., & Atherley, R. (2000, April 24). Rave Fever. *Maclean's, 113*(17), pp. 38–44.

Ouimet, M. (1999). Crime in Canada and the United States. *Canadian Review of Sociology and Anthropology, 36*(3), 389–404.

Reuters. (1995). Some Russians Hunger to Hop on a Harley. *Christian Science Monitor, 87*(1999), 14.

Ross, S., & Saxe, F. (2001). Should Eminem Be Denied Airplay? *Billboard, 113*(8), pp. 75–77.

Scott, M. B., & Lyman, S. (1968). Accounts. *American Sociological Review, 33,* 46–62.

Scully, D., & Marolla, J. (1984). Convicted Rapists' Vocabulary of Motive: Excuses and Justifications. *Social Problems, 31*(June), 530–544.

Shulman, D. (2000). Professional's Accounts for Work-Related Deceptions. *Symbolic Interaction, 23*(3), 259–282.

Silberman, C. E. (1978). *Criminal Violence, Criminal Justice.* New York: Random House.

Solicitor General Canada. (2000). *Web Site.* [On-Line]. Available: <http://www.sgc.gc.ca>.

Sterling, B. (1992). *The Hacker Crackdown: Law and Disorder on the Electronic Frontier.* New York: Bantam.

Stevenson, C. L. (1999). The Influence of Nonverbal Symbols on the Meaning of Motive Talk. *Journal of Contemporary Ethnography, 28*(4 August), 364–389.

Sutherland, E. H. (1947). *Principles of Criminology.* Philadelphia, PA: J. B. Lippincott.

———. (1949). *White Collar Crime.* New York: Holt, Rinehart and Winston.

Sutherland, E. H., & Cressey, D. R. (1966). *Principles of Criminology.* Philadelphia, PA: J. B. Lippincott.

———. (1978). *Criminology* (10th ed.). Philadelphia, PA: J.B. Lippincott.

Sykes, G., & Matza, D. (1957). Techniques of Neutralization: A Theory of Delinquency. *American Sociological Review, 22,* 664–670.

Tait, G. (1999). Rethinking Youth Cultures: The Case of the Gothics. *Social Alternatives, 1999*(18 April), 15–21.

Tanner, J. (1990). Reluctant Rebels: A Case Study of Edmonton High-School Dropouts. *Canadian Review of Sociology and Anthropology, 21*(1), 79–94.

———. (2001). *Teenage Troubles: Youth and Deviance in Canada* (2nd ed.). Toronto: Nelson Thomson Learning.

Teevan, J. J., & Dryburgh, H. B. (2000). First Person Accounts and Sociological Explanations of Delinquency. *Canadian Review of Sociology and Anthropology, 37*(1), 77–94.

Tyler, E. B. (1871). *Primitive Culture.* London, UK: John Murray.

Wilson, B., & Sparks, R. (1996). "It's Gotta Be the Shoes": Youth, Race and Sneaker Commercials. *Sociology of Sport Journal, 13*(4), 398–427.

Wilson, B., & White, P. (2001). Tolerance Rules: Identity, Resistance and Negotiation in an Inner City Recreation/Drop-In Center. *Journal of Sport & Social Issues, 25*(1 February), 73–104.

Wood, R. T. (1999). Nailed to the X: A Lyrical History of the Straightedge Youth Subculture. *Journal of Youth Studies, 2*(2), 133–152.

Wolfgang, M. E. (1958). *Patterns in Criminal Homicide*. Philadelphia, PA: University of Philadelphia Press.

Wolfgang, M. E., & Ferracuti, F. (1967). *The Subculture of Violence: Toward an Integrated Theory in Criminology*. London, UK: Tavistock.

Ziebold, T. O., & Mongeon, J. E. (Eds.). (1982). *Alcoholism and Homosexuality*. New York: Haworth Press.

INTERACTION THEORIES*

A four-year-old refuses to dress herself. The reason may be one of the following:

1. She is not yet ready to do this for herself.
2. She is a brat and needs discipline.
3. She is "going through a phase" that will soon pass.
4. She is upset about a family member's death and is acting out because of it.

The same act may be interpreted in many ways according to the rules of the culture in which it occurs, the setting, and the characteristics of the people in the setting. Interpretation will play a role in how others, and even the child herself, respond to the act or, in this case, the apparent refusal to act. The parental interpretation, or construction of what the behaviour means, may in turn influence the future course of events, further interpretations, and outcomes. In this view, deviance is a human creation—a social construction that emerges out of interaction, becomes real, and affects subsequent events.

Interaction theories focus on the interpretation (social meaning) that is given to behaviour, and on the way such interpretation helps to construct the social world, the identities of people, and, ultimately, how they behave. For example, deviance labels can encourage commitment to deviant behaviour. A person who has been labelled a thief may have difficulty finding acceptance among former friends and thus seek friends who are disreputable. Legitimate work may be hard to find, especially in any responsible career, so that illegitimate work becomes more attractive. Along with the change in occupational status and friendship groups, a change in self-concept will likely occur, and this may lead to deviant thoughts and behaviour. Although this amplification of deviance does not always occur, it is a well-documented pattern.

---

* The use of the term "interaction theory" to describe a theory that interprets social behaviour follows custom, but it is somewhat arbitrary, since these theories do not all emphasize interaction. However, they do all emphasize *meaning and interpretation*, which ultimately emerge from interaction. Theories of interpretation or theories of (social) construction would be more accurate terms but are not commonly in use.

Interaction theories focus on the communication aspects of interaction, whether verbal or nonverbal. They often give more attention to the observers of behaviour than to the behaviour itself. Interaction theories have seven main characteristics.

1. *All interaction theories are concerned with the way in which meaning is constructed.* Infants do not see meaning in the surrounding environment but eventually learn to create meaning as part of their socialization. Although some interaction theories focus on meaning in the actor's life, others focus on meaning that is attributed to the actor by others.

2. *Most interaction theories pay little attention to norm-violating acts that are not remarked on by observers or treated by the deviant as a permanent part of his or her identity.* Primary (unnoticed) deviance is seen as transitory and virtually accidental; only as deviance is noticed and reacted to (secondary deviance) do these theories come into play.

3. *Interaction theories focus on organized, systematic deviance that is (or threatens to become) part of the deviant's social identity or role.* This role or identity may be forced on or chosen by the individual (or a combination thereof). Each interaction theory has central concepts that concern deviance that is structured or constructed into patterns of social expectations. Secondary deviance is an example of such a concept.

4. *All interaction theories are sequential. They deal with the social construction of deviance designations, their application, and their consequences.* These theories tend to use participant observation or rely on accounts given by the individuals observed because these techniques allow narrative unfolding of events and permit sequential analysis.

5. *All interaction theories deal implicitly or explicitly with the idea of stigma.* For most, stigma is a central metaphor that likens deviance to a contagious form of pollution, a sign of sickness or evil that right-minded people will avoid. The stigmatized individual has, to use Erving Goffman's (1963) term, a "spoiled identity." So-called respectable people are warned by the signs of spoiled identity (stigmata) to maintain social distance. People who associate with stigmatized individuals are also likely to be avoided in a process Goffman calls "courtesy stigma."

6. *Most theorists in the interaction paradigm engage in "underdog sociology."* They see themselves as giving a voice to those who are isolated from the mainstream. According to theorists like Edwin Lemert, underdog sociology distorts the subject matter of deviance by overemphasizing both the oppressive nature of social control agencies and the passivity and innocence of the exploited, degraded, or victimized deviant (Lemert, 1972, p. 16). Alternatively, Gouldner (1968) argues that by expressing the perspective of outsiders, the sociologist is helping the authorities to become even more effective in controlling them. Far from standing up for underdogs and helping them to achieve acceptance, the sociologist may be contributing to their oppression.

7. *Most interaction theorists are tacitly supportive of the deviants they study.* In Becker's (1963) world of dance musicians, there are "musicians" and there are "squares." The latter are ignorant and intolerant. And Wolf (1991), in his study of an outlaw motorcycle club, clearly identifies with the outlaw bikers' contempt for middle-class values and authority figures. He describes his participation in the club as a "reflection of my own dark side ... my own youthful rebellion and resentment" (Wolf, 1991, p. 10).

EARLY INTERACTION THEORY

CHARLES HORTON COOLEY (1864–1929)

The notion of the "looking-glass self" was central to Charles Horton Cooley's concept of identity. It consists of three elements: (1) how actors imagine they appear to others, (2) how actors believe others judge their appearance, and (3) how actors develop feelings of shame or pride, feelings that become an inner guide to behaviour (Cooley, 1902, p. 184). Cooley saw the social self as the root cause of social behaviour, whether deviant or conforming. Although Cooley's idea of shame remained underdeveloped in the work of his immediate followers, interest has recently revived in how shame can be a factor in deviance, even when the deviance remains (mainly) undetected by others (Hayes, 2000).

GEORGE HERBERT MEAD (1863–1931)

George Herbert Mead was a social philosopher closely associated with the Chicago School. Although his work did not focus on deviance as such, it provided a framework for understanding how the social self is created in interaction. In Mead's terms (1943) the social self is composed of an active "I" that is independent of particular situations and a receptive "me" that is situated and responsive. Although only one "I" exists (except possibly in the case of people with multiple personality disorder), the self can have many "me" parts: "me" as a parent, friend, con artist, or drug dealer.

The shape of the "me" is composed of the messages we receive by using others as mirrors of the self. A student who repeatedly receives negative messages about his or her academic performance is likely to incorporate these messages into the "me" part of the self (unless, of course, they are contradicted by some other valued source of information). When the "me" is affected this way, the "I" part of the self may become less assertive and successful, leading to increasing confirmation of the negative view, which then becomes part of the "me." The individual react in three ways: (1) accept the situation, (2) attempt to change the messages by presenting a new image to the world, (3) or challenge the reflection by questioning its accuracy.

Mead (1918) noted the interactional processes that produce designations of criminality and the power of the designation "criminal" to cut people off from the world.

In doing so, he foreshadowed some of the deviance theories that saw labelling as the source of confirmed criminal careers.

Only in the 1960s did interaction theory attract a critical mass of scholars who made the approach a significant one. In this period, many versions of interaction theory competed for attention and primacy. Among these were symbolic interaction, reaction, and labelling theories; dramaturgy; phenomenology/social construction, and ethnomethodology, all of which are addressed in the sections that follow. Each of these has some distinctive features but they overlap a great deal, and many of the theorists discussed here tried out several versions of interaction theory in the course of their careers.

SYMBOLIC INTERACTION THEORY

Symbolic interaction, the earliest, most general form of interaction theory, stems mainly from the work of George Herbert Mead. Symbolic interactionism emphasizes how meaning emerges in social interaction, how the social self is produced in socialization and influenced thereafter, how the way we appear affects how others see us, how we see ourselves mirrored in others' treatment of us, and how our interpretations of these realities can be revised. This theory is important to deviance studies mainly in that it is incorporated into later, more specific theories discussed immediately below.

SOCIETAL REACTION THEORY

The societal reaction perspective emphasizes when, under what circumstances, and how social responses are formulated and applied. Why do we sometimes jump to conclusions about people's social identities? Where do the categories we use for our eval-

---

Box 10.1   Three Central Concepts of Social Interaction Theory

1. *The social self* is the image that we present to others in interaction. Based in our interpretation of other people's reactions, it may be *authentic* (the self that is presented is the same as the self that is experienced), or it may be *inauthentic* (a false representation of the experienced self.)
2. *Significant others* are those who have particular influence in our lives. They often serve as role models.
3. *Generalized others* are those referred to in the cliché "What will people say?" By taking the role of the generalized other, we are able to participate in shared values and activities with people we do not know very well and to understand what behaviour will be viewed as deviant.

---

uations come from? In Kitsuse's (1987) view, deviance is the process whereby members of society *interpret* a behaviour as deviant, *define* people who engage in it (or seem to) as deviant, and, finally, *treat* them in whatever way they have deemed appropriate to that class of deviant.

An example cited by Kitsuse demonstrates this process: a 20-year-old student in a bar was engaged in conversation with a stranger. When the stranger showed interest in the fact that the student was studying homosexuality in his psychology class at university, the student suspected that the other fellow was a homosexual. When they got into an argument over psychology and the other fellow chose homosexuality to illustrate his point, the student left—a move he said he made because "by now I figured the guy was queer, so I got the hell out of there" (Kitsuse, 1987, p. 16). Kitsuse uses this example to show how assumptions about behaviours that *everyone knows* are indications of deviance are used in the process of interpretation and the assignment of meaning.

Societal reaction theorists also focus on the agencies of social control and on how factors such as vested interests, resources, alternative claims, and organizational needs may influence the issue of who is treated as a deviant and under what conditions. Although this idea is entirely consistent with symbolic interactionism, societal reaction theory focuses more explicitly on the views of those who react, not on the deviants who are defined this way.

A central concept of the societal reaction approach is *social distance*. The best-known measure of social distance is the Bogardus scale (Bogardus, 1933), which asks respondents whether they would willingly welcome someone with a particular ethnic, occupational, or behavioural characteristic into their family, workplace, community, and so forth. For some people, particular kinds of deviants are not welcome to share the same planet.

LABELLING THEORY

The name *labelling theory* originates in Howard Becker's statement that "deviance *is not* a quality of the act a person commits, but rather a consequence of the application by others of rules and sanctions to an 'offender.' The deviant is one to whom that label has successfully been applied; deviant behavior is behavior that people so label" (Becker, 1963, p. 9; italics in original).

Ironically, none of the major theorists discussed under this heading has laid claim to the description of labelling theory. Most of these theorists describe themselves as symbolic interactionists or interaction theorists. Nonetheless, other scholars use this term to describe their work. What they all have in common is an emphasis on the processes whereby labels are created and applied to people who may resist them or learn to live by them.

FRANK TANNENBAUM AND THE DRAMATIZATION OF EVIL

The foundation for the labelling perspective was laid by historian Frank Tannenbaum (Tannenbaum, 1938). Drawing on sources such as Frederic M. Thrasher's *The Gang*, Tannenbaum argued that although most young people engage in misconduct (e.g., cutting school, getting into fights, petty theft, and vandalism), only some are caught and treated as deviants. Those who are caught are more likely to go on to have long-term deviant careers. According to Tannenbaum (1938, pp. 19–20), "The making of the criminal ... is a process of tagging, defining, identifying, segregating, describing, emphasizing, making conscious and self-conscious; it becomes a way of stimulating, suggesting, emphasizing and evoking the very traits that are complained of."

Those who are treated as criminal are forced to associate with older criminals and more experienced young criminals in the correctional system. Here, they come to see themselves as true delinquents, without any hope for legitimate careers.

The challenge of Tannenbaum's work was not taken up immediately. Labelling theory remained largely undeveloped until the publication of Edwin Lemert's *Social Pathology* in 1951. According to Lemert (1951), early acts of deviance may be unnoticed by others and rationalized by the individuals who engage in them. Lemert calls these acts *primary deviance*. If the deviant acts attract a severe social reaction, then the individual may incorporate a deviant self-concept, into the "me" component of his or her social self, as well as engage in the activities associated with this concept. When this happens, *secondary deviance* has occurred. Some theorists also identify a third stage or type of deviance, *tertiary deviance*. In this phase, deviants stand up for their right to be different, often organizing with others and demanding respect and equality.

Like most later theorists, Lemert qualifies this view of the processes that give rise to deviant identities by recognizing that "individuals define themselves as deviant in their own terms and independent of specific societal reactions ... the interaction process seen in full organic reciprocity allows that individuals court, risk, even create conditions of their own deviance" (Lemert, 1972, p. 19). Thus, deviants are not empty organisms who simply respond to a label. The deviant is a participant in the sequence of events that leads to a confirmed deviant career.

HOWARD BECKER

The work of Howard Becker (1963, 1964, 1974) made labelling theory a major force in sociology and criminology, even though his main interests lay elsewhere (in studies of occupations, education, and the structure of the art world). Becker had studied under Everett Hughes at the University of Chicago in the late 1940s and early 1950s. From Hughes's studies on occupation, he took the ideas of "career" and "master status" and applied them not just to conventional occupational careers but also to outsider careers. Becker coined the key concept of "moral entrepreneur" to highlight the making and application of deviant designations in the creation of master statuses.

Becker's early work (as a graduate student) involved participant observation of the barroom musicians' social world at the Chicago tavern where he played piano (Martin, Mutchnick, & Austin, 1990). His insider position gave him access to information on jazz musicians, marijuana users, and other "deviants." His use of interactionist theory emphasizes the social process whereby the deviant discovers deviant behaviour and learns to participate in it. This process is one that unfolds over time, in sequential stages. The marijuana user is not escaping from social reality, he is accepting and participating in a subcultural form of that reality and in so doing he is acquiring a status, just as receiving a job promotion involves gaining a status. Public identity as a deviant is not just a label; it is a process and a status. As a master status that overrides other statuses held by the individual, deviant identity structures the course of social interaction. To be given a deviant status is to become an outsider in mainstream society.

CONSEQUENCES OF LABELLING

The Saints and the Roughnecks

In a study that is now regarded as a classic, William Chambliss (1987) describes two groups of youths he encountered in his high-school years. The Saints and the Roughnecks both committed serious acts of juvenile delinquency, but only the Roughnecks were labelled delinquent and treated as such. The Saints were young men of middle-class background who were willing and able to assume a "good boy" demeanour to deceive both teachers and police. They were careful to conduct most of their pranks, which included vandalism, drunk driving, and theft, away from their home community so that their image at home remained untarnished.

The Roughnecks, in contrast, did not assume a mask of civility in their dealings with authority figures. Nor did they restrict their brawls to inconspicuous places. All but one of the eight Saints finished college and found high-status positions in society. Two of the six Roughnecks made it to college on sports scholarships and ended up as teachers, one became a truck driver, and three confirmed the community opinion of them by becoming criminals. Of the criminals, two were convicted of murder and the third was involved in illegal gambling.

Labelling and the Blind Role

In another study on labelling, Scott (1969) argues that the disability associated with visual impairment is a learned social role, one in which the individual learns incapacity and dependency. Agencies created to support the blind use their control over services and information to back up their demand that the newly blind person be realistic and not fight the agencies' version of how the blind role should be played. Thus, in Scott's account, people who enter the agency perceiving themselves to have visual impairments of varying degrees come, over the course of their "rehabilitation," to view themselves as blind persons. Consistent with this perception, they adopt attitudes and behaviours that professional blindness workers think blind people should display (Scott, 1969, p. 119).

Assigning Labels

As we have seen, labelling theory emphasizes the way in which being labelled influences how others see us, how we see ourselves, and how we conduct ourselves as a result. Labels on people are just as necessary as labels on cans of soup. They are a convenient way of achieving a fairly high degree of predictability in social life, and thus of facilitating social cooperation. When we interact with others, we make initial assessments of them through the cues given by their appearance, by their background, or by what others have told us. As we interact with other people, we may revise our expectations concerning them. At both points, in our initial assessment and during interaction, we may assign labels to other people.

Labels are not just shorthand content summaries. The labels that we employ come from both personal experience and cultural traditions. Often we create or maintain labels that are useful to us, and revise or discard those whose usefulness has been exhausted. Unlike the label on the soup can, the label on a human being is likely to be at least partially wrong.

HARD LABELLING THEORY

Most interaction theorists follow Lemert and Becker in using labelling as a sensitizing concept within symbolic interactionism, rather than as a theory in and of itself. This is known as "soft labelling." It emphasizes the balance that exists between labellers and those they try to label, and the many possible outcomes of the process of labelling. Others use labelling as a full explanation of deviance. Thomas Scheff's (1984) theory of mental illness exemplifies this hard labelling in its deterministic position that the label causes the deviance. According to Scheff (1984, p. 189), mental illness is a residual category (residual deviance) that explains behaviour when all other explanations fail. The person enters the career of mental illness because this definition is successfully imposed as the only one conceivable in the culture or because he individual has been unsuccessful in escaping it by use of influence or power.

Labelling Women Deviant

Edwin Schur is one of the few interactionist theorists to specifically focus on what interaction theory means for women. He theorizes that North American women are trapped by the dominant evaluation of male role characteristics as "good" but inappropriate (deviant) when attained by women (Schur, 1983). Women will be deviant because they are not male (since male is the standard) or deviant because they are not conforming to the expected role-appropriate (female) conforming behaviour. Thus, the woman who works outside the home and the woman who is "just a homemaker" will both experience stigma. The women who is uninterested in sports or politics and

Box 10.2 The Five Central Concepts of Labelling Theory

1. *Career deviance* refers to a sequence of stages through which the actor passes. One sequence might begin with public identification as a deviant, progress to increasing contact with others similarly identified, and conclude with acceptance of the identity. Another sequence might involve being labelled "sick," receiving secondary gains such as support and sympathy, developing dependency on these things, failing to take every possible route toward minimizing the condition, and becoming a permanent "invalid."

2. *Master status* is a status that overrides all others. For example, the status of an axe-murderer would tend to overwhelm any other statuses a person might have. In contrast, hockey fan or bus passenger would not.

3. *Moral entrepreneurs* actively participate in forming and enforcing rules, and often profit (socially or financially) by doing so. People who promote the idea that cults are highly dangerous and who then make a living kidnapping and deprogramming cult recruits are examples of moral entrepreneurs. Although moral entrepreneurship is most often undertaken by groups or organizations, some forceful individuals have performed this role. For example, Harry Anslinger, head of the United States Bureau of Narcotics, launched a propaganda campaign about marijuana in which truth was sacrificed but the Bureau was enlarged.

3. *Moral crusades* are social movements that are aimed at producing changes in the rules or in the ways in which they are enforced. Moral crusades may be led by moral entrepreneurs.

4. *Moral panic* refers to overreaction to some form of deviance. It may be triggered when, say, drug users or child molesters are portrayed in the media as being greater in number and much more powerful than the evidence suggests. Moral panics may be used by politicians and others to create a common enemy.

5. *Labelling contests (also known as stigma contests)* may ensue when the attempt to assign a negative label to a person or group meets with resistance. A stigma contest of long standing has been fought by abortion activists on both sides of the issue; each side attempts to apply deviance labels to the other. Such contests are risky: the person who tries to apply a deviant label may have the tables turned on them. For example, in 1977, Anita Bryant, a well-known actress and former Miss America runner-up, campaigned (successfully) against legislation that would make it illegal to discriminate based on sexual orientation. It was an expensive victory, however. She lost her job as a representative for wholesome Florida Orange Juice and found herself permanently ostracized within the acting community. Such reversals are far from rare.

the one who becomes a professional athlete or politician will be considered deviant from the ideal. In addition, interaction theory helps to predict that women who are careless about their physical appearance and deference to others will pay a heavier penalty for it, on the whole, than men who do the same.

SEEKING STIGMA

Some groups or individuals may seek out and cultivate a stigmatized identity. Daniel Wolf, who radically altered his physical appearance to gain admission into an outlaw motorcycle club called the Rebels, discovered that his fellow cyclists admired and identified with the "one percenters" (Wolf, 1991). One percenters are the 1 percent of cyclists who give the activity a bad name. They do not belong to respectable cycle clubs such as the Canadian Motorcycle Association (CMA) or its American counterpart, the American Motorcyclists Association (AMA); nor are they "registered societies" with state or provincial authorities. The term "outlaw clubs" arose following a riot that took place in 1947, in Hollister, California. A group of 500 bikers (about 1 percent of the cyclists present at what was an AMA-sponsored tour and competition) cycled through bars and restaurants, urinated in the streets, and generally engaged in exceptionally rowdy behaviour ("Fat Men," 1997). Later events have linked outlaw cycle clubs with organized crime activities, including drug manufacture and distribution, trafficking, prostitution, gunrunning, fencing, and white-collar crime.

Although the biker identity is in part a response to negative social reactions (Wolf recounts being run off the road by "respectable" citizens and hassled by police based on his appearance), bikers clearly see themselves as makers of their own image. They deliberately seek out an identity that will shock respectable people and encourage them to keep their distance.

The Outsider's Dilemma

In another example of stigma-seeking, French author Jean Genet (1910–86) cultivated an image that was defiantly negative (White, 1993). Illegitimate, abandoned by his mother, he was raised first in an orphanage and then in a cold adoptive home. Genet responded to rejection by resorting to theft and male prostitution. At the age of 10 he was sent to a reformatory for theft and spent most of the next 30 years in some of the toughest prisons in Europe. In *The Thief's Journal* (1949/1965), Genet writes of the effort it took to rid himself of such encumbrances as remorse in order to develop into the most vile, satanic kind of person he could imagine. In so doing, he transformed himself into a nightmare of the respectable middle class that had initially rejected him.

According to Shoham (1970), Genet's relationship with society was characterized by what he calls "the outsider's dilemma." Genet wanted *acceptance* for his critique of the norms, his honesty about himself, and his suffering. Instead, his repeated violations brought him rejection. Having submissively accepted (even welcomed) the labels put on him and having fulfilled to the best of his ability the expectations of others that he would turn out badly, Genet resented the fact that society did not accord him the respect to which he felt entitled. His quest for acceptance as an outsider was an oxymoron, an attempt to reconcile antithetical goals.

STIGMA AND REINTEGRATIVE SHAMING

A major implication of theories of interaction is that a society that wants to control a particular form of deviance needs to communicate disapproval of the behaviour but risks confirming a deviant career. Braithwaite's (1989, 1999) theory of "reintegrative shaming" attempts to cut through this gordian knot.

Reintegrative shaming treats the offender with respect, as a good person who has done a bad deed, in contrast with stigmatization, which treats the offender as having demonstrated a basically flawed identity. The theory predicts that societies that degrade, humiliate, and exclude their deviants will have higher rates of deviance. The ideas of reintegrative shaming parallel the forms of social control found in many Aboriginal communities and religious communities, and in countries such as Japan (Braithwaite, 2000). Contemporary Western societies are comparatively stigmatic and experience very high rates of troublesome deviance (Sherman, 1993). This theory helps to explain why the currently evolving use of "drug courts" specifically designated to meet the needs of addicted offenders has not had a positive effect on recidivism (repeat offending). It appears that, as currently constituted, these courts are more stigmatizing than regular criminal courts and not sufficiently integrating. The result is higher recidivism, despite the objective advantages of such courts (Miethe, Lu, & Reese, 2000).

DRAMATURGICAL THEORY

Another version of interactionist theory is dramaturgical theory. Its central metaphor is "improvised drama." Dramaturgical theory makes use of concepts that parallel those of stage performances: roles, props, scenes, foreground, background, and so on. People project images of themselves on the social stage to be seen (and see themselves) in particular ways and to achieve particular ends. Such performances are achievements, often precarious, and always liable to breaches of front that can be embarrassing or discrediting. This is not just true of the "undercover operative," such as the secret agent (Jacobs, 1992). We are all, at least much of the time, imposters (inauthentic social selves) who assume social roles that only partly fit us, hoping that the repertoires that we possess will be enough to support a convincing performance.

The performer may be a person with a "Teflon identity," which can repel stigma, or may have a spoiled identity that needs to be managed. The shoplifter, the con artist, the impersonator, and the person who wants to be a lover but does not actually love are all consciously engaged in "performance" as they maintain the appearance of normalcy. Generally, they do this by using their knowledge of how "normal" people behave.

Alternatively, the individual may deliberately stage a performance of toughness, meanness, and inhumanity (alienness) to achieve notoriety or inspire awe in others, especially if he or she is living among other dangerous people (Katz, 1988). Another kind of performer is the student who works at conveying to professors an image of responsibility, intellectual strength, and diligence, while simultaneously presenting a very different social self in the nearest bar or pool hall. We all play contradictory roles to some extent, sometimes as sincere actors and sometimes as deliberate phonies. Without such performances, social order would fail.

Dramaturgical theory also highlights the way in which specific interaction becomes a drama representing wider issues and conflicts. The staged spectacle of the courtroom or public hearing becomes a theatre in which the individual actors represent forces beyond themselves. Thus, the trial of O. J. Simpson, the attempted impeachment of U.S. President Bill Clinton, or the moral narratives of Japanese *manga* comics can be interpreted in many ways through the lenses of dramaturgical concepts (Shapiro & Soss, 1999).

ERVING GOFFMAN

Dramaturgy is most closely associated with Canadian-born Erving Goffman (1913–1982), whose many books covered a spectrum from dramaturgical to social constructionist to ethnomethodological approaches (1959, 1961, 1963, 1967, 1979) and others. Goffman coined many of the concepts that dominate this perspective.

Goffman taught deviance at the University of California, Berkeley, from 1960 to 1966.

> Part of [Goffman's] appeal to students was his communication of the thrill and pleasure of intellectual discovery, his sensitivity to the perceptions of his audience, his naturalistic approach, which focused on micro factors, and his interpretive methodology. His fascination with secrecy and disjunctive scenes, and his cool personal style and ability to push limits and say what others knew but could not.... His subtle wit and sarcasm, facility with words, mysterious and mercurial character, ability to show role distance and manipulate the conventions of interaction, and example of having fun while doing research demonstrated that one could find occupational success without becoming an organization man. (Marx, 1984, p. 649)

DRAMATURGY AND THE MANAGEMENT OF STRAINED INTERACTION

Fred Davis (1962, 1963) uses a dramaturgical approach to look at the effect of potentially stigmatizing physical disabilities and disfigurements on social interactions. Much of his focus is on the way in which those who are potentially stigmatized manage interaction so as to achieve normalization of their status, or at least a semblance of this. The person with the disability or disfigurement is faced with a variety of choices in adjusting the presentation of self to allow reasonably normal interaction.

One management technique involves taking advantage of the "elastic fictions of normalcy and acceptance" that are part of the cultural equipment of all civilized

Box 10.3   The Seven Central Concepts of Dramaturgy

1. *Stigma* is a discrediting stereotype that implies moral pollution or danger and that creates a spoiled identity. Stigma is roughly the opposite of prestige in that it signals the presence of something shameful. The revelation of the stigmatizing characteristic can reduce the person's status instantly from "whole and usual" to "tainted" (Goffman, 1963, pp. 2–3). Goffman identifies three stigma types: physical monsters like the Elephant Man, moral monsters (cannibalistic serial killers like Jeffrey Dahmer), and out-groups that are regarded as less than fully human (Native peoples during the early settlement periods in North America and Australia).

2. *Stigmatic signs* are symbols that mark a deviant. Greek stigmatics were individuals with brand marks that identified them as runaway slaves. In the Middle Ages, a yellow cross signalled a person judged to be a heretic, and a thief might well be branded with a letter T on the forehead or the back of the hand. In Nathaniel Hawthorne's *The Scarlet Letter*, the stigmatic sign is a red letter A that stands for adultery. Under Adolf Hitler, the Nazis forced Jewish people to wear a yellow Star of David symbol.

3. *Management of identity or "identity work"* is undertaken to deal with or prevent stigmatization. Professionals must seem to be competent, even if they are presented with something beyond the scope of their training. The Christian who is born again illustrates one way of leaving a spoiled identity behind, but the new identity will require "work." Tattoos are often part of the "identity work" practised by gang members, prison inmates, and other outsider groups (Phelan & Hunt, 1998).

4. *Deviance disavowal* is a repudiation or denial of the stigma that is attached to a person and is often achieved with the use of *identifiers* (to indicate a respectable identity) and *disidentifiers* (which are incompatible with the unwanted identity). Thus, someone who wanted to unload a reputation of being poor and unkempt might disavow deviance through a public performance of that demonstrated wealth and cleanliness.

5. *Symptomatic action* is distinguished by Goffman (1959) from the content of a performance. The professor who mumbles and shakes in front of the class may be a brilliant scholar, while the person who inspires the trust of others may be a con artist or imposter. Mumbling and shaking are symptomatic actions that detract from the intended performance.

6. *Total institutions,* which include prisons, psychiatric hospitals, monasteries, boarding schools, and military camps, are places in which people live 24 hours a day under a particular authority. Practices in these institutions tend to be directed toward transforming the social self of the inmate or recruit in such a way that it comes to fit the needs of the institution (Paterniti, 2000). In army boot camps, for example, new recruits are deprived of most of the identifiers that support their prior sense of self and their links to civilian life; they are expected to wear a uniform and respond in terms of rank.

| **Box 10.3   The Seven Central Concepts of Dramaturgy (cont.)** |

7. *Moral career* is a concept that refers to a sequence of identity transformations that involve entry into—and possible exit from—a state of spoiled identity. The moral career of the mental patient, as outlined by Erving Goffman (1963), moves from a stage in which the individual is presumed sane but eccentric and is accorded respect as a citizen, to a stage in which the individual is considered mentally aberrant and treated as a patient. This stage may be followed by partial restoration of respectable status as the individual becomes an ex-patient.

people. Most of us have been taught to overlook the mistakes and problems of others, usually by looking away while they repair their image. The rule of "studied inattention" sometimes conflicts with the equally strong expectation that we look at the people with whom we are talking. One solution to this strain on interaction is to focus attention on a distracting object or topic. People with visual disabilities who have guide dogs often find that others focus on the dog rather than on them. This can interfere with the dog's training, but it does facilitate a kind of normalized interaction.

Another strategy, which sometimes has tragic results, involves the attempt to force the body to be "normal." An individual may resort to plastic surgery for cosmetic purposes or psychosurgery for a neurological condition. Many cures for "deviant" conditions are experimental and risky. Examples of this can be found in "cures" for obesity, such as liposuction, jaw-wiring, stapled stomachs, and taking potentially dangerous and addicting diet pills. Partly as a result of dieting, some people develop life-threatening eating disorders like bulimia and anorexia.

In recent years, people with various stigmatizing conditions have joined forces, not only to give one another support but also to engage in political action designed to educate the rest of society by debunking the myths and stereotypes that surround these conditions.

PHENOMENOLOGY AND SOCIAL CONSTRUCTION THEORIES

Phenomenology encourages us to look more carefully at the nature and ownership of commonsense constructs of meaning that make society available to consciousness. It also encourages us to recognize the deep rules that operate in social situations. A student, for example, follows superficial rules by arriving at the right classroom, properly prepared and on time; he or she follows deep rules by constituting the role of student in a way that is readily apparent to students, teachers, and college staff.

For many phenomenologists, the social order is a fragile human accomplishment resting on deep rules that maintain a sense of order and meaning in the face of chaos or meaninglessness. From this perspective, the reality of society emerges out of a kind of conspiracy in which most of us agree that certain things are real and true and that others are not. Persons who diverge from or challenge this ordering of society do more than just break rules; they threaten us with the possibility that none of it is concretely real, even though it (or something like it) is necessary.

One of the earliest presentations of the idea of social construction appeared in Peter Berger and Thomas Luckman's *The Social Construction of Reality* (1967), in which the authors combined phenomenology (mainly following Schütz, 1960, and Kuhn, 1970) with Marxian conceptions of "false consciousness" and "hegemony" (see Chapter 12) to produce a perspective that highlighted the way in which social categories are constructed and made real in their effect. This perspective stimulated studies of such phenomena as the construction of various psychiatric conditions (schizophrenia, ADHD), alcoholism, race, environmental destruction, and, well, just about everything (Coulter, 2001). These studies show that constructed categories are given a spuriously concrete interpretation. Their concreteness can be deconstructed when we look at how they were created by us in efforts such as the DSM (psychiatric diagnosis), discussed in Chapter 6.

Robert Scott (1972, p. 24) takes a phenomenological point of view when he argues that "deviance is inevitable because any attempt to impose order on the untidy phenomena of human existence will inevitably result in a certain amount of matter being left out of place." Anomalies will always exist, and society must develop mechanisms to protect its symbolic universe. Deviance is a property conferred on behaviour, appearance, or events that transgress the boundaries of the agreed-on symbolic universe that makes our existence ordered and meaningful.

According to Scott, these boundaries may or may not be clear. The person who experiences a bad LSD trip and leaves the symbolic universe is a clear anomaly on whom we can unambiguously confer the label deviant. Sometimes, however, when the situation is not clear, deviance becomes a property invoked to create and mark boundaries. The witch craze, for example, served to strengthen the religious world view by demonizing many of its anomalies. In either case, universe-maintaining mechanisms help to set apart the property of deviance so that it does not threaten the dominant conception of the socially constructed universe (Berger & Luckmann, 1967, pp. 104–116). Mythology, theology, philosophy, and science have all served as such mechanisms.

Behaviour that violates socially constructed reality may produce a variety of responses that help to maintain a sense of order (Scott, 1972). The deviance may be (1) *unnoticed,* as when the teacher fails to observe the cheating student; (2) *denied, debunked, or normalized,* as when we assume that people who claim UFO experiences are hoaxers or else deluded; (3) *excluded,* as when we commit people to a psychiatric hospital or throw them out of our club; (4) subjected to *annihilation,* as when we treat someone as an outsider and, therefore, of no consequence; or (5) *incorporated,* as when we change the rules to include the deviance.

Jack Katz (1988) engages in a relatively concrete exercise in phenomenological analysis applied to the deviance of shoplifters, killers, and the ghetto elites (gang members). His theorizing is based on the "foreground" part of crime: the action itself and the actor's experience of it. Indeed, Katz feels that background factors such as class, age, and opportunity are likely to cause the theorist to miss the point entirely. Katz's position is that criminals actively construct their criminal worlds. Instead of simply taking over existing role models or following subcultural norms, they invent and reinvent these as they go about doing whatever it is they want to do, which is mostly identity-building.

Much of the crime that is perpetrated by delinquents and killers, in Katz's view, results from the desire of criminals to construct a social identity that is hard, mean, and alien, as well as from their very effective manipulation of their image and environment to support this identity. Crime, Katz asserts, has a sensual, magical, creative, gamelike appeal that is lacking in most conventional law-abiding ways of confirming public identity. Criminality seems to have more creative authenticity than conformity, since it involves actively remaking the world instead of following preset rules. It seems more "righteous" than capitulation to the forces of respectability, in addition to which it uplifts, excites, and "purifies" the self.

Relatively little direct work on deviance has been done from this perspective. In fact, Berger and Luckmann argue that the need to have a theory of deviance at all is merely a by-product of the fact that official definitions of reality do not cover what actually happens. They point out that, if we lived in a world where homosexuality in the military was institutionalized and regarded as essential to virility and fighting efficacy, it would be the heterosexual soldier who required explanation and therapy (Berger & Luckmann, 1967). Given this view of the radical relativity of deviance, theories of deviance seem contrived and ultimately unimportant.

ETHNOMETHODOLOGY

Leiter (1980, p. 25) defines ethnomethodology as "the study of the methods people use to generate and maintain their experience of the world as a factual object." The term is composed of three parts: *ethno,* meaning people or culture; *method,* meaning producing practices; and *ology,* or the study of. Although ethnomethodology is an offshoot of phenomenology, it stresses contexts of interaction (courts, families, and other social settings) rather than the consciousness of individuals. Ethnomethodology does not deny that real causes for things may exist, but it shifts focus from the question "What causes behaviour?" to the question "How do people come to see forces like norms, values, social classes, and institutions as objectively real and as the cause of behaviour?" (Leiter, 1980, p. 25).

Ethnomethodology focuses on those everyday things that we think we already know but that look different when we treat them as problematic instead of as obvious. Although other theories may assume that we all share competence with respect to social meanings and that this does not change much from one context to another, ethnomethodology treats these methods and contexts as matters for investigation. It takes seriously, for example, the question of how members of a social group go about assessing the moral identity of other members. How is a person's past identity reconstructed by others when it is revealed that he has molested young children? What interpretive "work" produces the new identity that the person now owns? What happens if this identity turns out to have been based on false information?

Although similar to social interactionism, ethnomethodology goes further in examining the processes and contexts associated with the construction of meaning. It does not assume, as social interaction theory does, that the member of the social group is a cultural dupe who simply follows the traditions and expectations of other members.

HAROLD GARFINKEL

Harold Garfinkel coined the term ethnomethodology and was its first and most prolific representative. Garfinkel drew on Talcott Parsons's emphasis on the subjective reality of the actor as the connection between the actor and the social order, and Alfred Schütz's (1960; Wagner, 1970) phenomenological position that multiple possible realities exist that are dependent on the actor's work of interpretation.

However, rather than accept Parsons's assumptions about socialized actors as generally rule-abiding across situations, Garfinkel chose to see the nature of rule use (see Box 10.4, item 9) as problematic and linked to the context of interaction. Rather than repeat Schütz's emphasis on the consciousness of the actor, he focused instead on what the actor does to construct intersubjective meaning. Garfinkel's primary emphasis was on those aspects of social life that are taken for granted and are not questioned. He sought to understand the "members' methods" whereby we minimize our doubts about the reality of the social order so that we might participate in it.

Transgression as a Research Tool

One way to study members' methods is to disrupt or to not go along with the usual order (Garfinkel, 1972). As reported by Garfinkel, students were sometimes assigned the exercise of behaving at home as strangers, as though they were unfamiliar with the common understandings and expectations of daily life. Through this exercise, students came to appreciate the extent to which our use of "members' methods" transforms the reality that we see and to which we respond. It also showed them the considerable extent to which our perception of the world is based on trust in the unspoken, taken-for-granted constitutive rules of social life (not to mention how quickly people who do not use the expected methods are questioned about their sanity or their motives).

Box 10.4   Ten Key Concepts of Ethnomethodology

1. *Members* are those who participate in a shared stock of knowledge about the world. Student–teacher interactions are largely problem-free because each party makes correct assumptions about taken-for-granted things. When a student comes from a culture with dramatically different assumptions (e.g., about bribing teachers or treating them as servants), the shared assumptions are violated and work has to be done to repair them.

2. *Members' methods* are used by people to minimize their doubts about the reality of the social order so that they might participate in it. Ethnomethodology looks for recurring members' methods primarily by analyzing transcribed records of everyday conversations.

3. *Recipe knowledge* refers to the presuppositions that are generated in particular settings. The trained social worker, nurse, or teacher has recipe knowledge concerning how the people who come under his or her supervision should be categorized and treated. Actors in the criminal justice system develop recipe knowledge about such things as whether an arrest is a good one or what kind of deals will expedite a case through the system.

4. *Typifications* are constructs that are based on experience and that distil what seems typical or common about routinely encountered people or situations.

5. *Folk typifications* refer to the common stereotypes people use, regardless of their level of education or occupational training. The most studied typifications have been those that emerge in occupational socialization. These tend to reflect not only the distillation of experience and traditions but also the needs of the organization for efficiency and accountability. For example, Lundman (1980) found that police tend to classify situations into two general categories: those requiring "real" police work and involving substantial threat to persons or property, and those that are "bullshit." (There are also two main categories of citizens, "good folks" and "assholes.") Folk typifications are a major part of what passes as "common sense" of the people.

6. *Status degradation ceremony* refers to the interpretive work that transforms a person's status and identity to something lower. The process whereby we move from the status of upright citizen to alleged murderer to murderer is a process of status degradation. Harold Garfinkel (1956) outlines this process in the transformation of Senator Joseph McCarthy from an anticommunist hero of the American people to a discredited, dishonest, former bully who ended his life in an institution.

7. *Retrospective interpretation* refers to the reinterpretation of signs from a person's past as signalling "what they really were, all along." Elements of personal history suddenly take on new meaning as stages on the path to disrepute. Conversely, someone who has been regarded as disreputable may be revealed to be something else. For example, a man who has been labelled a drug addict may turn out to be an undercover police officer, or a thief may become a born-again person with very high standards of morality. When this happens, people tend to say that this characteristic was there all along.

Box 10.4   Ten Key Concepts of Ethnomethodology (cont.)

8. *Indexicality* refers to the idea that members' meanings are contextual; that is, they are dependent on the immediate social context in which the members work out common understanding of the situation. Like the pronouns "I," "you," and "she," the categories of murderer, child molester, forger, or transsexual change with the context. Is the woman standing on the corner a prostitute or not? How you figure this out involves the use of your member's meanings as applied to the current context.

9. *Rule using* in ethnomethodology is conceptualized as something the member undertakes to accomplish his or her ends. We are essentially rule-using beings, not rule-governed ones. Cognitive rules are used in organizing information to construct social reality. Consistency refers to the way in which subsequent conceptions fit. For example, if in the past, or in the talked-about experience of friends and family, males who hold hands with males are homosexual, then a man holding hands with another is homosexual. No attempt is made to test the assumption with other information, such as a different culture or special circumstances.

10. *Reflexivity* refers to the role of the observer in creating the phenomenon being observed. Part of the interpretive meaning of a good person or a bad one resides permanently in the categories that exist in the mind of the observer. This is also true for the ways in which teachers evaluate students.

The Case of "Agnes": A Double Deception

The case of Agnes became the basis of a chapter and an appendix in Garfinkel's *Studies in Ethnomethodology* (1967). Agnes first appeared at the department of psychiatry of the University of California as someone seeking to qualify for a sex-change operation. She presented herself as a female who had male genitalia. Since she had strongly feminine characteristics, including 38–25–38 measurements, soft skin, and no facial hair, she was able to convince the doctors that hers was a case of "testicular feminization syndrome," and that the surgery she wanted was appropriate.

Agnes had been living as a female for two years and at the time had a boyfriend who knew nothing of her abnormality. In those two years, she had undergone a process of learning the signs by which women demonstrate their gender and unlearning those signs that had been appropriate for the first 17 years of her life. She had to learn consciously how to move, how to sit, and how to use social space as most women do. Agnes's painful learning process, as recorded by Garfinkel, brought to the fore many taken-for-granted aspects of gender differences, including the assumption that the whole world is divided into just two legitimate genders.

Agnes received her operation, married, and moved away. Eight years later it was discovered that she had never been a genuinely (i.e., biologically established) intersexed person. She had used hormone pills (beginning at age 12) and made use of medical knowledge to convince the doctors and achieve her ends. This discovery added a whole new layer to the issue of how Agnes had manipulated common understandings of the experts to achieve a new gender status. She had convinced doctors that she was genuinely intersexed while simultaneously convincing the world that she was a woman. In both roles, she made use of common understandings to evoke from others the response she desired.

D. L. WIEDER AND THE CONVICT CODE

The uniqueness of ethnomethodology can be illustrated by its approach to the convict code, an informal (unwritten, unofficial) set of norms that is commonly found in prisons and other total institutions. The convict code specifies the appropriate forms of behaviour for inmates among themselves and in their relationships with staff. The rules outlined in the code (e.g., "Don't snitch on others") are often in conflict with official rules of the institution, as well as with its rehabilitative or educational goals.

A standard sociological interpretation of the code would blame the uncooperative, "tough-guy" behaviour of inmates on the rules that make up the code. The ethnomethodologist would instead look at the interaction of inmates with one another, and with the staff, in those contexts in which the convict code is mentioned. D. L. Wieder (1974) analyzed a California halfway house for paroled prisoners using this approach. He discovered that the code served as an "interpretive scheme" that was selectively used by both staff and inmates, particularly in instances of tension. It was complained about, joked about, and invoked in some circumstances but not in others. When an inmate referred to the "Don't snitch" part of the code, it was often to justify a failure to report wrongdoing or to express solidarity with other inmates. When staff members referred to the code, it was often to excuse their failure to know what was going on or to answer inmate complaints. Both inmates and staff used the idea of the code to make sense of and impose order on a particular pattern of events.

Although Wieder did not generalize his findings, the use of codes may be found in many other contexts. Teenagers and their parents, for example, may employ mutually recognizable codes when tensions make them useful.

RICHARD V. ERICSON AND MAKING CRIME

A social constructionist application of phenomenology that owes a great deal to ethnomethodology can be found in the work of Richard V. Ericson. Ericson has written several works that focus on the way in which the criminal justice system transforms accused persons into criminals. In *Making Crime: A Study of Detective Work* (1981), Ericson describes how police detectives, because of their training and the contingencies of the work setting, operate in an environment of specialized knowledge, low accountability, and high information control. He shows how a police detective uses the rules set by the Criminal Code and the Police Act as resources with which to make their actions meaningful and justifiable. In Ericson's view, detectives are constantly faced with the problem of meeting their mandate to discover and prosecute criminals while at the same time "covering their asses" with respect to the bureaucratic rules and the norms of the public.

The result is a system in which police reports and statistics on crime phenomena are constructs that meet organizational goals as much as (or more than) they are accurate descriptions of events or social realities (Meehan, 2000). Similarly, the criminal whose file appears in the records is a typified construct that bears some relation to the individual who committed an infraction but (again) reflects the contingencies of a system designed to produce convictions.

Although some observers have pronounced the death of ethnomethodology (Obershall, 2000), others perceive Erving Goffman as one of the most influential figures in post–World War II sociology and point to the continued use of ethnomethodological concepts and methods, often combined with other interactionist perspectives (Chriss, 1996).

SUMMARY

Symbolic interactionism, societal reaction theory, labelling theory, dramaturgy, phenomenology and social construction, and ethnomethodology all treat deviance as a form of meaning that emerges out of social interaction. On the whole, these are sequential theories that emphasize the reactions of the social audience far more than the nature of the offending behaviour. They tend to see the deviant as an underdog, a relatively innocent victim of oppressive social controls that sustain other people's interests or the social universe. Interaction theories enjoyed strong support in the 1960s, when they helped displace functionalism. By the 1970s, however, they had, in turn, been displaced by—or partially absorbed by—conflict and control theories, while many of their adherents moved on into postmodernist perspectives. Interaction remains a popular perspective on deviance.

STUDY QUESTIONS

1. Many television sitcoms (and similar entertainment) "work" on the way in which we can misinterpret other people's signals and behave badly as a result. Watch your favourite sitcom and figure out the cues, clues, and impression management in constructing the interpretations you see.

2. Children who are bullied in school often suffer academically and in sports as well. Which comes first?

3. Which is more important to you: feedback from a mirror about your appearance, or feedback from those close to you? Is the mirror image "just itself," or do you see it (in imagination) through the eyes of others?

4. Theory usually suggests that significant others are more important to us than the "generalized other." Are there times when you have been more concerned about "what people might say" than about the feedback of close friends? What were the special conditions for this?

5. Becker has joined others in saying that he is an interaction theorist, not a labelling theorist. Could Scheff make this claim too?

6. To what extent were the Saints and the Roughnecks sinners and heretics? Why were the Roughnecks subjected to much more discipline? Do you think the Roughnecks had less achievement mainly because they were seen as low achievers?

7. What is the "outsider's dilemma"?

8. How can shame help in rehabilitation? What else has to happen?

9. Which of Goffman's many concepts do you find most and least interesting? Why?

10. What did Agnes manipulate to get what she wanted?

11. What does Wieder's take on the convict code show about social norms? Does this apply to the case of Alexander Hamilton, described in Chapter 1?

REFERENCES

Becker, H. S. (1963). *Outsiders*. New York: Free Press.

———. (1964). *The Other Side: Perspectives on Deviance*. New York: Free Press.

———. (1974). Labelling Theory Reconsidered. In P. Rock & M. McIntosh (Eds.), *Deviance and Social Control*. London, UK: Tavistock.

Berger, P. L., & Luckmann, T. (1967). *The Social Construction of Reality*. Garden City, NY: Doubleday.

Bogardus, E. (1933). A Social Distance Scale. *Sociology and Social Research, 17*, 265–271.

Braithwaite, J. (1989). *Crime, Shame and Reintegration*. Cambridge, UK: Cambridge University Press.

———. (1999). Restorative Justice: Assessing the Optimistic and Pessimistic Accounts. In M. Tonry (Ed.), *Crime and Justice: A Review of Research*. Chicago: University of Chicago Press.

———. (2000). Shame and Criminal Justice. *Canadian Journal of Criminology, 42*(3 July), 281–294.

Chambliss, W. J. (1987). The Saints and the Roughnecks. In E. Rubington & M. S. Weinberg (Eds.), *Deviance: The Interactionist Perspective* (5th ed.). New York: Macmillan.

Chriss, J. (1996). Toward an Interparadigmatic Dialogue on Goffman. *Sociological Perspectives, 39*(3 Fall), 333–340.

Cooley, C. H. (1902). *Human Nature and the Social Order*. New York: Scribners.

Coulter, J. (2001). Ian Hacking on Constructionism: Review of "The Social Construction of What?" by Ian Hacking (1999). *Science, Technology and Human Values, 26*(1 Winter), 82–87.

Davis, F. (1962). Deviance Disavowal. *Social Problems, 9*(Fall), 25–33.

———. (1963). *Passage through Crisis*. Indianapolis, IN: Bobbs-Merrill.

Ericson, R. V. (1981). *Making Crime: A Study of Detective Work*. Toronto: Butterworths.

Fat Men on Bikes. (1997, December 7). *The Economist, 344,* pp. 25–27.

Garfinkel, H. (1956). Conditions of Successful Degradation Ceremonies. *American Journal of Sociology, 61*(March), 420–424.

———. (1967). *Studies in Ethnomethodology*. Englewood Cliffs, NJ: Prentice-Hall.

———. (1972). Studies in the Routine Grounds of Everyday Activities. In D. Sudnow (Ed.), *Studies in Interaction*. New York: Free Press.

Genet, J. (1965). *The Thief's Journal* (B. Frechtman, Trans.). London, UK: Anthony Bland. (Original work published in 1949)

Goffman, E. (1959). *The Presentation of Self in Everyday Life*. Garden City, NY: Doubleday.

———. (1961). *Asylums*. Garden City, NY: Doubleday.

———. (1963). *Stigma: Notes on the Management of Spoiled Identity*. Englewood Cliffs, NJ: Prentice-Hall.

———. (1967). *Interaction Ritual: Essays on Face-to-Face Behavior*. Chicago: Aldine.

———. (1979). *Gender Advertisements*. Cambridge, MA: Harvard University Press.

Gouldner, A. W. (1968). The Sociologist as Partisan: Sociology and the Welfare State. *The American Sociologist,* (May), 103–116.

Hayes, T. A. (2000). Stigmatizing Indebtedness: Implications for Labeling Theory. *Symbolic Interaction, 23*(1), 29–47.

Jacobs, B. A. (1992). Undercover Deception. *Journal of Contemporary Ethnography, 21*(2 July), 2000–2226.

Katz, J. (1988). *Seductions of Crime: Moral and Sensual Attractions in Doing Evil*. New York: Basic Books.

Kitsuse, J. I. (1987). Societal Reaction to Deviant Behavior: Problems of Theory and Method. In E. Rubington & W. M. S. (Eds.), *Deviance: The Interactionist Perspective*. New York: Macmillan.

Kuhn, T. (1970). *The Structure of Revolutions*. Chicago: University of Chicago Press.

Leiter, K. (1980). *A Primer on Ethnomethodology*. New York: Oxford University Press.

Lemert, E. (1951). *Social Pathology*. New York: McGraw-Hill.

Lemert, E. M. (1972). *Human Deviance, Social Problems and Social Control* (2nd ed.). Englewood Cliffs, NJ: Prentice-Hall.

Lundman, R. J. (1980). *Police and Policing: An Introduction*. New York: Holt, Rinehart and Winston.

Martin, R., Mutchnick, R. J., & Austin, T. W. (1990). *Criminological Thought: Pioneers Past and Present*. New York: Macmillan.

Marx, G. T. (1984). Role Models and Role Distance: A Remembrance of Erving Goffman. *Theory and Society, 13*(5 September), 649–662, Abstract, p. 649, as reported in *Sociological Abstracts 1984*. Accession #8505903.

Mead, G. H. (1918). The Psychology of Punitive Justice. *American Journal of Sociology, 23,* 577–602.

———. (1943). *Mind, Self and Society.* Chicago: University of Chicago Press.

Meehan, A. J. (2000). The Organizational Career of Gang Statistics. *Sociological Quarterly, 41*(3 Summer), 337–371.

Miethe, T. D., Lu, H., & Reese, E. (2000). Reintegrative Shaming and Recidivism Risks in Drug Court: Explanations for Some Unexpected Findings. *Crime and Delinquency, 46*(4 October), 522–542.

Obershall, A. (2000). Book Reviews: Theory and Progress in Social Science by James Rule (1997). *Social Forces, 78*(3 March), 1188–1191.

Paterniti, D. A. (2000). The Micropolitics of Identity in Adverse Circumstances. *Journal of Contemporary Ethnography, 29*(1 February), 93–120.

Phelan, M. P., & Hunt, S. A. (1998). Prison Gang Member's Tattoos as Identity Work: The Visual Communication of Moral Careers. *Symbolic Interaction, 21*(3), 277–299.

Scheff, T. (1984). *Being Mentally Ill: A Sociological Theory.* New York: Aldine.

Schur, E. M. (1983). *Labeling Women Deviant: Gender Stigma and Social Control.* New York: McGraw-Hill.

Schütz, A. (1960). The Social World and the Theory of Social Action. *Social Research, 27*(Summer), 203–221.

Scott, R. A. (1969). *The Making of Blind Men.* New York: Russell Sage.

———. (1972). A Proposed Framework for Analysing Deviance as a Property of Social Order. In R. A. Scott & J. Douglas (Eds.), *Theoretical Perspectives in Deviance.* New York: Basic Books.

Shapiro, V., & Soss, J. (1999). Spectacular Politics, Dramatic Interpretations: Multiple Meanings in the Thomas/Hill Hearings. *Political Communication, 16*(3), 285–315.

Sherman, L. (1993). Defiance, Deterrence and Irrelevance: A Theory of the Criminal Sanction. *Journal of Research in Crime and Delinquency, 30,* 445–473.

Shoham, S. (1970). *The Mark of Cain: The Stigma Theory of Crime and Social Deviation.* New York: Oceana Publications.

Tannenbaum, F. (1938). *Crime and Community.* New York: Ginn.

Thrasher, F. (1927/1963). *The Gang.* Chicago: University of Chicago Press.

Wagner, H. R. (Ed.). (1970). *Alfred Schütz on Phenomenology and Social Relations: Selected Writings.* Chicago: University of Chicago Press.

White, E. (1993). *Genet: A Biography.* New York: Random House (Vintage).

Wieder, D. L. (1974). *Language and Social Reality: The Case of Telling the Convict Code.* The Hague: Netherlands Mouton Press.

Wolf, D. R. (1991). *The Rebels: A Brotherhood of Outlaw Bikers.* Toronto: University of Toronto Press.

SOCIAL CONTROL THEORIES

Why are you not a criminal? When Joseph Rogers asked this question of his students, they were astounded at first and then produced lists that included such explanations as "My mom would kill me," "I wouldn't want to lose my teacher's respect," "I would lose the chance of being successful," and "I would feel ashamed." Rogers sees these explanations as the opposite side of Sykes and Matza's neutralizations. For him, they are *affirmations of connectedness, conscience, and respect for the rules* (Rogers, 1970).

Social control theories do not ask why deviants commit deviant acts, at least not directly. They deem it self-evident that many kinds of deviance are alluring, exciting, and relatively easy routes to fun and profit. Further, we are all born deviants. When toddlers wander from the safety of their own backyard, we do not ask why they did it—we ask why fences, training, and supervision did not stop them. The fact that children will wander if allowed to do so is assumed. When social control works, it creates conformity; when it fails, it does not cause deviance but simply allows the individual to choose the deviant path. This approach is compatible with biological and psychiatric explanations, since these theories assume that people will have drives and needs that must be restrained if civilization is to be maintained (as discussed in Chapter 5), but in control theory the emphasis is on barriers (or the lack of them), rather than the nature of the drives and needs.

Although control theories have their primary roots in disorganization theory (Durkheim, Chicago School), classical theory (Beccaria, Hobbes), and neutralization theory (Sykes and Matza), they place greater stress on the way in which socialization and supervision hold people to conventional paths.

With social control theories, we are back in the realm of positivism, that is, the tools of objective empirical science take precedence over the tools of interpretative understanding.

The main research technique used in control theories has been the statistical analysis of self-report data from large nonrandom samples of high-school or undergraduate students (Kempf, 1993, p. 152). Respondents are asked to fill out relatively simple questionnaires concerning their involvement with family, peers, school, and delinquent and deviant acts. Questions typically range from "Have you ever taken little things worth less than $2 that did not belong to you?" to "taken a car belonging to someone you didn't know for a ride without first asking the owner's permission?" to "used marijuana?" to "tried to have sex with someone against their will?"(Alarid, Burton, & Cullen, 2000; Hindelang, Hirschi, & Weis, 1981). Reliance on these checklists provides very little scope for interpretive analysis. An admission of assault, for example, could be in reference to a shoving incident or a fistfight. The full meaning of the encounter is lost in a simple yes or no answer. Similarly, this approach tends to make the measurement of background variables such as social class into a matter of where the respondent lives, family income, or occupational titles. The *experience* of social class is lost in such objective measures. Thus, although control theory has achieved status as a systematic scientific approach and remains one of the leading explanations of delinquent deviance, it has sometimes done so at a cost to the depth of its contribution to the understanding of deviance as a whole.

WALTER RECKLESS AND CONTAINMENT THEORY

Containment theory was an early version of the social control perspective. Walter Reckless, who was among the first generation of Chicago School graduate students, developed the theory. Reckless and his colleagues focused on the inner and outer factors that "contained" the average person but were absent or weakened in deviants (Reckless, Dinitz, & Murray, 1966; Reckless, 1973). They were particularly interested in the phenomenon of the "good boy" who lived in a high-delinquency neighbourhood. How was such a person inoculated against criminality?

INNER CONTROLS

According to containment theory, the individual experiences, in varying degrees, feelings of inferiority, hostility, anger, rebellion, and even organically based urges toward deviant gratifications. If these inner pressures toward deviance are uncontrolled, deviance will occur. Inner controls may be direct or indirect. *Direct* inner control is evidenced by the ability to feel guilt and shame and not to respond to this with neutralizations (Costello, 2000), while *indirect* inner control is based on the individual's rational interest in maintaining a "stake in conformity" (Toby, 1957). Both of these controls involve the presence of a strong, healthy self-concept that is inconsistent with deviant choices. The healthy self is conforming and conventional, goal-directed in a realistic and flexible way, and able to tolerate frustration and defer gratification (Reckless & Dinitz, 1967).

OUTER CONTROLS

Paralleling his view of the inner life, Reckless felt that the external world provided both pressures toward deviance and "fences" to prevent it. External factors such as poverty, relative deprivation, adversity, insecurity, deviant companions, and deviant opportunities can make deviance more likely unless contained by controls.

Like inner controls, outer controls may be direct or indirect. *Direct* outer controls are external to the individual and usually carry with them the threat of sanctions. A security camera in a store is a kind of external control. Direct outer controls are most effective when they are consistent across institutional settings, so that the individual faces a consistent moral front. *Indirect* outer controls are mainly relational—control derives from the need to maintain role relationships. This kind of control is most effective when conforming others hold the power to reward or punish, and when role networks overlap such that indiscretion in one area will be detected in many, thus multiplying its costs. If you work in a legitimate business owned by your family, you will very likely experience extensive indirect external controls.

TRAVIS HIRSCHI AND SOCIAL BONDING

Since publication of Travis Hirschi's *Causes of Delinquency* in 1969, social bond theory has evolved as one of the leading explanations of delinquency, and by extension to other forms of deviance (Hawdon, 1999; Hirschi, 1969). Hirschi's answer to the question "Why do most of us behave so well?" is that we obey rules because we form a strong bond to conventional society (see Figure 11.1). This bond comprises four distinct but overlapping elements: attachment, commitment, involvement, and belief. The theory has been an extremely influential one, continuing to find support even though Hirschi has moved on to develop different ideas. Kempf identified no less than 71 empirical tests of bond theory in the research literature between 1970 and 1991 (Kempf, 1993, p. 148). These studies extended the theory to company executives, rural youth, females, minority youths, and to a variety of kinds of deviance, including drug and alcohol abuse, adult crime, sexual behaviour, and mental health disorders (Durkin, Wolfe, & Clark, 1999).

ATTACHMENT

Attachment is a combination of caring and supervision. Being attached means having in our lives both significant others and "reference others" (people we use as standards for our own behaviour). When young people have strong attachment (emotional ties, effective communication) to family and school, the authority of those institutions will be strong and their social control will likely be effective (Leonard & Decker, 1994).

In Hirschi's work, attachment is measured by the nature of the bond between children and their parents and by the degree of parental supervision. A typical

Figure 11.1 Elements of the Social Bond Theory

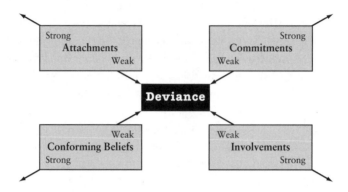

Source: Adapted with permission from T. Hirschi (1969), "Elements of Social Bond Theory," from *Causes of Delinquency* (Berkeley, CA: University of California Press).

question about supervision would be "Does your mother (father) know where you are when you are away from home?" while a question about the quality of family relations might be, "Do you share your thoughts and feelings with your mother or father?" (Kempf, 1993, p. 154). An extreme lack of attachment is characteristic of the psychopath, who neither cares how others feel nor welcomes their attention (supervision). But many people who deviate less extremely experience attachment as confining and resent the idea that others should have a say in their lives. Although not all unattached people become delinquents, lack of family attachment makes some youths available for gang participation. The deviant gang does not attract youths who have strong attachment to conventional (significant or reference) others.

Hirschi argued that any strong attachment, whether to family or peer group, would tend to lead to conformity. Hirschi argues that "we are moral beings to the extent that we are social beings" (Hirschi, 1969, p. 82). Members of conventional peer groups may have strong attachments, but delinquents are socially disabled people who are unable to form close attachments to anyone and who do not know what real friendship is (Brownfield & Thompson, 1991; Hirschi, 1969).

Indeed, many studies show that delinquent youths tend to have instrumental (utilitarian) rather than affective (emotional) attitudes in interpersonal relationships (Hansell & Wiatrowski, 1981), but strong support also exists for the position that when youths have a stronger attachment to an originally nondelinquent peer group than they have to the family or school, delinquent behaviour is more likely to occur (Massey & Krohn, 1986).

Although Hirschi emphasized family attachment over other attachments, some of his followers have given considerable attention to the school as a bonding agent, particularly for youths who have disturbed family backgrounds or who belong to disadvantaged ethnic or racial groups (Wiatrowski & Anderson, 1987). Although Hirschi's original formulation of "school attachment" emphasized the student's grades, this has not proven useful in later studies (Kempf, 1993, p. 158). Boocock (1980, pp. 212–236) found that the most important aspect of school attachment as an insulator against deviance is integration into the social system of the school; that is, acceptance by one's peers is a more important bond than academic success.

COMMITMENT

Toby (1957) calls commitment "a stake in conformity." The idea behind commitment is that the more people have to lose by violating norms, the less likely they are to risk it. Among those who are employed, those who see their work as "career employment" are less likely to engage in workplace misconduct than those who are in "survival jobs" (Huiras, 2000).

Hirschi measured commitment largely in terms of occupational aspirations, judging people who had higher aspirations to be more committed than others. Thus, Hirschi would rank a job requiring university education over a trade profession in terms of its degree of commitment. Later research has shown, however, that commitment toward lower-status positions can be just as intense (Wiatrowski & Anderson, 1987). Many researchers have suggested that religiosity—"an earnest regard for religion" (Cochran & Akers, 1989)—is a commitment that should insulate people from deviance, but the evidence is far from conclusive (Johnson et al., 2001).

INVOLVEMENT

Involvement, when voluntary, is frequently a consequence of commitment. People deeply committed to conventional lines of action are likely to devote much of their time and energy to conventional activities. Students who fall into this category will immerse themselves in productive activities such as homework and organized sports, while youths who lack such involvement are free to engage in nonproductive activities like drug or alcohol use. One study found that the relationship between "involvement" and delinquency was strong, while two others found it to be conditional or unimportant (Kempf, 1993, p. 169; Macdonald, 1989).

BELIEF

Belief is the element of bonding that most closely corresponds to Reckless's inner control. In Hirschi's (1969) theory, belief is the acceptance of the dominant value system of society and focuses mainly on values such as respect for the police and concern for teachers' opinions. People who are bonded in this way believe in respecting police, obeying the law, and staying out of trouble. They do not share the neutralizing beliefs that police are oppressors, rules are unreasonable, and law evasion is clever. Although one would expect participants in established religious groups to be the people most likely to have these beliefs and, therefore, the least likely to be involved in deviance and crime, the record is far from consistent on this point (Bainbridge, 1989, p. 288). According to Hirschi, people from all parts of society share the same basic conventional beliefs and differ only in the extent to which they support or neglect them.

Box 11.1   Questioning Hirschi: Control Theory's Negative Cases

Giordano (1987) reports her findings from a study of control theory's negative cases. A negative case occurs whenever a person in the research sample provides a pattern of responses that does not fit with the predictions generated from the theory. The most important part of Hirschi's control theory—the bond of attachment—predicts that youths with poor attachment to their families will report more delinquency than youths who are closer to their parents; by the same token, youths with strong family attachments will report less delinquency. Thus, negative cases would be indicated by (1) youths with low attachment who are not delinquent, and (2) youths with high attachment who are delinquent. In Giordano's sample of 197 respondents, 150 were classified as consistent with control theory in that they had high attachment and low delinquency, while another 5 were consistent with the theory in that they had low attachment and high delinquency. The remainder were not strictly consistent with the theory, and Giordano chose to study this group.

When attachment was low and so was delinquency, often a great deal of non-delinquent deviance existed or the presence of another very strong bond did. Girls with low attachment, for example, had repeated unwanted pregnancies and eating disorders. Among boys, the pattern of low attachment and low delinquency was often mediated by an intense commitment to an activity such as getting sports scholarships or getting into college or the Air Force.

High attachment and high delinquency cases also occurred. Many of these youths had high attachment to families that did not oppose delinquency or even expected it. Giordano noted that for most of these "exceptions" to the theory, a nondeviant self-concept, despite reports of extensive misbehaviour, existed. That is, they defined their deviance as "just having fun."

Thus, despite the apparent contradiction of negative cases, Giordano found that these cases did not invalidate the theory as a whole.

Giordano's study does suggest several areas in which the theory needs to be adjusted to accommodate the kind of negative cases she reported. Most important is the need for a clearer conceptualization of the dependent variable. Delinquency may be an important part of what happens when social controls are weak, but it is not the only form of problem behaviour that may emerge. The concept of delinquency used in most social control studies is one that is appropriate to survey self-report methodology. It includes theft, joy riding, underage drinking, assault, drug dealing, and sometimes rape. It does not include psychosomatic illness, sexual promiscuity, or paraphilias (sexual disorders).

Hirschi's formulation, therefore, does not give weight to the presence of subcultures that are characterized by alternative beliefs (Gottfredson, 1999; Hirschi, 1996).

Bond theory has been extended by other theorists in directions that Hirschi did not anticipate and (given Hirschi's distain for subcultural and differential association theory and his opposition to theoretical integration) is unlikely to approve (Hirschi & Gottfredson, 1986; Hirschi, 1969). For example, Jeffrey Ulmer has argued persuasively that the theory would be stronger if it recognized the possibility that structural, moral, and personal commitment and investment contingencies (mainly the consequences of labelling) can entrench people in deviant career paths (Ulmer, 2000). That is, the availability of certain paths and not others, an individual's moral consciousness, and the attractiveness of particular choices may result in choices that become irretrievable commitments. Learning to be a successful upper-level drug dealer, for example, is a choice that may make subsequent conformist choices unattractive (Adler & Adler, 1983), while making self-employment one of the few viable alternatives. Alarid and her associates also find that attachment to delinquent friends is correlated with delinquency, suggesting that control theory needs to incorporate elements of differential association theory (Alarid et al., 2000).

ROUTINE ACTIVITIES: A SITUATIONAL ANALYSIS

In 1979, Cohen and Felson introduced a variant of control theory that evolved from but went beyond Hirschi's concept of "involvement" (Cohen & Felson, 1979; Osgood et al., 1996, p. 639) and further developed the ecological thread of the Chicago School approach, which was discussed in more detail in Chapter 7.

Routine activities theory was formulated to explain the ecological patterns of victimization in urban areas, and it is a powerful explanation of the phenomenon of repeat victimization (Wittebrod & Nieuwbeerta, 2000). Felson and Cohen argue that the probability of a crime incident increases when there is a convergence in time and space of three distinct elements: motivated offenders, suitable target(s), and the absence of capable guardians (see Figure 11.2).

According to routine activities theory, the three-sided convergence depends for its existence less on the particular aspects of the community than on the lifestyle—the routine activities—of the potential victims. The person who is unmarried and young, for example, is more likely to be victimized than is an elderly married person, mainly because victimization coincides with activities in which young singles are more likely to engage (e.g., attending sports events, patronizing restaurants or bars, going to work, or simply being away from home). Homes are more likely to be burglarized in areas where both spouses are working so that the home is empty and undefended during the day. Kennedy and Forde (1990, pp. 137–151) found that Canadian data support this interpretation. However, the idea that the victim is somehow responsible for the victimization (other than being in the wrong place at the wrong time) is not well supported. In studies of sexual harassment in the workplace, for example, the personal

Figure 11.2 Routine Activities Theory

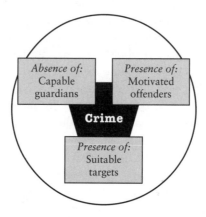

Source: L. E. Cohen & M. Felson (1979), "Social Change and Crime Rate Trends: A Routine Activities Approach," *American Sociological Review, 44,* 588–608. Reprinted by permission.

characteristics of the victim that make him or her a suitable target are often little more than gender, age, or newness on the job (De Coster, Estes, & Mueller, 1999).

The routine activities formulation can be extended to include other forms of deviant behaviour simply by substituting "opportunity" for "victim" (Osgood et al., 1996, p. 636). Osgood and his colleagues used this approach to explain the distribution of activities such as heavy alcohol use, illicit drug use, and dangerous driving among young people. Their data support their argument that unstructured socializing activities with peers in the absence of authority figures is an important aspect of deviant behaviour outcomes. By unstructured activities, Osgood and his colleagues mean those that are not structured by rules—for example, those concerning dating or participation in sports. They argue that lack of structure allows time for deviance, the presence of peers makes deviant acts easier and more rewarding, and the absence of authorities such as parents reduces the likelihood of negative reactions (Osgood et al., 1996, p. 651).

HIRSCHI, GOTTFREDSON, AND LOW SELF-CONTROL

In the 1990s, Travis Hirschi and his colleague Michael Gottfredson began to argue for a radically different version of control theory, known as the "low self-control theory" or, more ambitiously, "the general theory of crime" (Gottfredson & Hirschi, 1990). In part, this radical change came in response to criticism that Hirschi's bond theory deals with individual personality characteristics only by assuming them to be nonexistent or unimportant (Wilson & Herrnstein, 1985). This theory was originally presented as part of the analysis of a 1994 cross-sectional survey of approximately 2000

Edmonton, Alberta, high-school students. It focuses almost exclusively on inner controls, specifically the regulation provided by the individual's capacity to defer gratification and control impulses (Hirschi & Gottfredson, 1994). Even more than the original control theory, and very much like earlier forms of positivism, this theory locates the source of deviance within the deviant (his or her lack of control). Hirschi and Gottfredson argue that self- control is a stable personality trait. The person with low self-control will tend to be a career deviant—repeatedly breaking the rules for impulsive, opportunistic reasons—while the person with high self-control will not. Gottfredson and Hirschi define the repeat offender according to whether he or she typically uses force or fraud to achieve short-term gains (Gottfredson & Hirschi, 1990, p. 959). They also extend their theory to include nonfraudulent, nonviolent, but risky behaviour such as smoking and alcohol abuse, which are, in this view, "analogous" to crime (Reed & Yeager, 1996, p. 360).

Gottfredson and Hirschi begin with several assumptions about risky deviant behaviour. These assumptions apply best to street crimes and drug misuse and to intimate interpersonal violence, not to carefully planned and executed crimes (Sellers, 1999). First, crime is assumed to provide more *immediate* gratification of desires than does noncriminal behaviour. Second, criminal acts provide *easy* or *simple* paths to gratification. Stealing is much easier than earning a paycheque. Fighting is considerably more direct (both faster and easier) than suing. Thus, "diligence, tenacity, or persistence in a course of action" is not required of the criminal (Gottfredson & Hirschi, 1990, p. 89).

Third, criminal acts are *exciting, risky,* or *thrilling* when compared with conventional (cautious, cognitive, and verbal) lines of action. The criminal can rely on unreflective speed, agility, or stealth. Fourth, crime (or at least the street crime addressed by Gottfredson and Hirschi) provides *few* or *meagre long-term benefits*. Criminal activities interfere with potentially more profitable long-term commitments to work, family, and friends. Criminals do not have to be stable and reliable. Their low self-control results in unstable marriages, friendships, and employment records.

Fifth, most crimes require *little skill* or *planning*. They do not require extensive cognitive, academic, or even above-average manual skills. Apprenticeship is short and easy or unnecessary. Finally, crimes often result in *pain* or *discomfort for the victim*. Criminals are self-centred individuals who are unable to empathize with the suffering of others. Whatever charm and generosity they display is utilitarian and unrelated to deep feelings.

CHILDREARING AND SELF-CONTROL

According to Gottfredson and Hirschi, the above characteristics are indicative of low self-control. Where does low self-control come from? Gottfredson and Hirschi locate the origins of low self-control in the family, arguing that it is the result of ineffective childrearing. The low self-control personality emerges naturally when there is an absence of discipline, supervision, and affection in the home.

If self-control is to become part of a child's personality, three conditions must be met. First, at least one person must monitor the child's behaviour. Second, the monitor must recognize deviant behaviour when it occurs. Parents who do not recognize the signs that their child is a bully, thief, or drug user will be ineffective in training him or her. Third, once aware of the deviant behaviour, the supervising person must punish it—not necessarily physically, Gottfredson and Hirschi emphasize, but in a straightforward fashion (e.g., a clear statement of disapproval). Obviously, some families are better able than others to provide these three conditions. It is also probable that these conditions are met for females to a greater degree than they are for males (LaGrange & Silverman, 1999; Nakhaie, Silverman, & Lagrange, 2000).

Gottfredson and Hirschi present their theory of low self-control as a "general theory of crime," and their intent is clearly to produce a theory that covers all kinds of crime and most deviance ("analogous imprudent behaviors") as well (Evans et al., 1997, p. 475). The theory has not faired well, however, with respect to organizational or corporate offending that is typical of big business and multinational corporations. Despite the assumptions of this theory, the use of force and fraud are obviously not restricted to undisciplined individuals (Reed & Yeager, 1996, pp. 357–359).

CONTROL BALANCE: ANOTHER GENERAL THEORY?

In 1995, Charles Tittle published his manifesto on control balance as a general theory of deviance (Tittle, 1995). This theory "tries to bring together a large number of earlier theories into one coherent account" and is, at this point, "complex" (Tittle & Paternoster, 2000, p. 549). Tittle proposes that the individual's motivation toward deviance is a function of his or her balance of being controlled (either by others or by situational constraints) or being in control. The degree of control to which the individual is subjected relative to the control that he or she can exercise is the *control ratio*. For Tittle, deviance can be understood as "a manoeuvre to alter control imbalances" to overcome feelings of humiliation provoked by any reminder of one's unbalanced control ratio (Tittle & Paternoster, 2000, p. 557).

The theory claims that the desire to avoid being controlled and "to exercise more control than one is subject to" is "the major compelling force for human motivation" (Tittle & Paternoster, 2000, p. 550). Tittle divides behaviour into three types: conformity, submission, and deviance. The deviance category includes five types, differentiated mainly by their seriousness as defined by the probability that a deviant act will activate countercontrolling responses. Thus, deviance includes *predation* (e.g., theft, rape, sexual harassment), *exploitation* (corporate fixing of prices, contract killings), *defiance* (vandalism, unconventional lifestyles), *plunder* (the plunderer takes or uses without regard to how this self-serving action affects others), and *decadence* (impulsive acts, with no consistent organization)(Tittle & Paternoster, 2000, p. 553). Tittle's category of *submission* can also be seen as deviance. Submission is defined as "complete obedience marked by *an inability to imagine alternatives* and includes such behaviour as eating excrement on command" (Tittle & Paternoster, 2000, p. 554, italics in original).

Tittle argues that an individual with a control deficit (more controlled than controlling) will be motivated toward predatory or defiant behaviour. He gives the example of a teen sitting in a shopping mall who is asked by mall security (in a demeaning way) to leave. Other control features may curtail the motivation toward a defiant response, but it will likely be present. Tittle calls this kind of deviance motivation *repressive* (p. 562) in contrast with the *autonomous* deviance committed by those with a control balance surplus, who are more likely to commit exploitation, plunder, or decadent deviance. Control balance theory may be useful in explaining the decline of officially recorded deviance during times when oppression is lessened. Karstedt (2000, p. 21) has observed that this theory (like power-control theory, discussed below) may provide insight into the changing statistics concerning women's crime and problem behaviours.

Although this theory has received considerable attention in the recent theoretical literature, it is not fully developed and has undergone limited testing (Piquero & Hickman, 1999).

POWER-CONTROL THEORY

Power-control theory is a variant of control theory that emphasizes differences in power among potential deviants, and, by extension, the importance of social class and gender. People with power have greater opportunity to avoid surveillance and discipline at work and in their neighbourhoods, and more opportunities to avoid being held responsible for their actions, either because no one knows, or because they can access the best (legal) protection available. The presence of power and absence of control create conditions of freedom for unconventional behaviour (Hagan, Gillis, & Simpson, 1993, p. 1174).

John Hagan's power-control theory is one of the best known and most controversial of this kind of control theory. Although more established than control-balance theory, it too is "an evolving theory with an associated program of research" (Meier, 1987, p. 11). Power-control theory combines elements of bond theory with neo-Marxian conflict theory (as outlined in the next chapter). As an approach, it differs from the previously discussed versions of control theory in proposing an explanation of crime and deviance that is structural rather than individual.

Power-control theory work has, to date, focused mainly on how the gendered social class structure is reproduced in the childrearing practices of families and how these practices in turn influence the likelihood that girls will be more risk-avoidant and more conforming than boys. The following six assumptions drive this theory:

1. The social class system establishes the ranking of individuals in terms of power. At the top of the system are "owners," who are in positions of authority. Below them are "managers," who are subject to authority and who can exercise it over others. At the bottom are *employees,* who are subject to authority and exercise none themselves.

2. The class position of a parent in the occupational sphere is reflected in his or her relative power in the family (Hagan, 1989, p. 145). Because the social class system is patriarchal (hierarchical and male dominated), the typical family structure is also patriarchal. A significant minority of families can be classified as egalitarian, however, because both parents work at the same class level, because neither is employed, or because the family is headed by a single parent (Hagan, Simpson, & Gillis, 1987). Some women who do not work outside the home nonetheless have considerable influence within the family, based on other forms of power, such as inherited wealth (Hagan & Alberto, 1990). Women's power in the family is more evident in the upper classes than in the lower ones.

3. The family in which the husband has a command position at work while the wife is restricted to the home and domestic responsibilities (including childrearing) is likely to be strongly patriarchal. The mother in this family exercises more control over her daughters than over her sons. Girls experience a higher degree of relational controls (working alongside the mother, identifying with the housekeeping role), as well as more informal controls. Boys are relatively free of domestic supervision and control.

4. The difference between the supervision of girls and boys has an effect on their propensity for risk taking. Because encouragement and freedom for risk taking is severely curbed, girls become relatively risk-averse. Boys learn to appreciate the excitement and fun of risk, which also prepares them for risk-taking positions in the workplace comparable to the ones held by their fathers. Thus, the patriarchal class structure is reproduced in the family.

5. Because boys raised in patriarchal families are both less supervised and less risk-averse than girls, they are more likely to take delinquent risks and, therefore, come into contact with formal social control systems (child welfare agencies, the school, and police). Boys consistently have higher rates of official delinquency than girls (Hagan, 1989, p. 146).

6. In the egalitarian families referred to earlier, girls are less likely to be encouraged in paths of risk-averse domesticity. In these families, boys and girls receive more comparable amounts of supervision and control (or lack thereof), and their rates of risk taking and actual delinquency are much more similar (Hagan & Kay, 1990).

Hagan's version of power-control theory constitutes an attempt to bridge two major theoretical traditions, namely control theory and conflict theory. The individualizing tendencies of control theory and the radical tendencies of neo-Marxian conflict theory and modern feminism (see Chapters 12 and 13) find an uneasy coexistence

---

Box 11.2   A Test of Power-Control Theory: Delinquency in the Great Depression

The Great Depression of the 1930s changed the organization of many traditional families, as men and women alike became part of the working unemployed. As predicted by power-control theory, this circumstance would produce (1) greater equality between parents and (2) increased childrearing responsibilities on the part of fathers, particularly with respect to sons. Based on these changes, power-control theory would also predict a greater reduction of male delinquency than female delinquency during the Depression years.

McCarthy and Hagan (1987) used the records of Toronto Family Court to measure male and female delinquency rates during three five-year periods: 1924 to 1928 (before the Depression), 1929 to 1933 (during the Depression), and 1934 to 1938 (subsequent to the Depression). They found that before and after the Depression, delinquency rates for boys and girls rose and fell together, with the boys' rates consistently above those of the girls. During the Depression years, however, the rates diverged, with male delinquency mainly declining. Girls' rates were less consistent, but the delinquency rate for those aged 13 to 14 increased.

Although variables such as referral practices, changes in the law, and changes in social services may have influenced the absolute amount of reported juvenile delinquency, McCarthy and Hagan conclude that only power-control theory can explain changes in the distribution of delinquency by gender during the Depression years.

---

here. The tensions produced by the attempt to combine different theoretical perspectives appear most notably in power-control theory's conceptualization of delinquency. As a control theory, power-control gives us an image of delinquency as real behaviour that is risky and fun. Delinquency is seen as the result of unsupervised activities and socialization into the risk-taking values of capitalism. As a conflict or feminist theory, however, power-control also sees delinquency as a construction imposed on those with less power. In this perspective, delinquency is a category produced by the control apparatus of the patriarchal, industrial-capitalist system. This inconsistent conceptualization (real behaviour or construct) runs through power-control theory (Hagan & Alberto, 1990). Overall, however, power-control theory emphasizes common forms of delinquency such as theft, joyriding, and vandalism and does not examine the constructed categories of state-defined delinquency and deviance. Like the studies by Hirschi and other control theorists, Hagan and his colleagues have focused on relatively trivial forms of delinquency. They explicitly deny that the theory is formulated to explain serious delinquency or adult crime (Hagan et al., 1993, p. 394). Other authors have attempted to extend the theory to include a wide variety of risk-taking activities (Grasmick, Blackwell, & Bursik, 1993).

An interesting variation on this emphasis on common delinquency is Hagan's (1989, ch. 9) study of women's "deviant role-exits." This study sees women, especially those within patriarchally structured families, as being so controlled in their selection of roles that their main paths to freedom, resistance, or expression of repressed inclinations are to leave home (run away), develop a psychosomatic illness or depression, or attempt suicide. Like control theory, and unlike most conflict and feminist theory, power-control theory documents these issues, but does not envisage political action to encourage change.

Despite these problems of integration, power-control theory has several advantages over earlier approaches to deviance. These include (1) its ability to pinpoint the actual, as opposed to officially recognized, class and gender location of deviance and (2) its use of alternative methods, such as the use of time-series data. A more detailed explanation of these two advantages follows:

1. *The class and gender location of deviance.* Power-control theory points to the members of the upper classes rather than to the lower classes as people who are free from supervision and from regulation by others at work and in the neighbourhood, and who have greater opportunities to commit deviant acts (Winslow & Gay, 1993). High-consensus crimes (ones most of us agree are bad), such as strong-arm robbery or murder, may not fit the power-control theory predictions quite as well as lower-consensus deviance. Nonetheless, power-control theory argues that official records, which show longer criminal careers for the lower classes, are misleading, since they reflect more policing of the lower classes, rather than more offences in that group (McCarthy & Hagan, 1987). Power-control theory stresses the "poverty of a classless criminology" (Hagan, 1992).

   Power-control theory also locates deviance by gender in a unique way. Most theories of women's crime imply that women are simply less deviant, overall, than men (Jenson, 1993), but this is inconsistent with records that show that women's crime rates have varied a great deal over the years (Hagan et al., 1993; Steffensmeier & Allan, 1996, p. 468). For example, in the first half of the eighteenth century, women constituted up to 40 percent of all defendants in London's Old Bailey Court, but sank to only 10 percent in the twentieth century (Feeley & Little, 1991). Power-control theory relates these changes across historical settings mainly to the separation of the workplace from the home in the early years of industrialization. In industrialization, women's roles were increasingly restricted to a "cult of domesticity" in the home and family, where their deviance would result in "reintegrative shaming" rather than formal court processes (Braithwaite, 1990, p. 93; Hagan et al., 1993, p. 386). Presumably, the rise in women's criminal convictions during the twentieth century from negligible numbers to about 15 percent for serious crimes and up to 43 percent for minor property crimes reflects the loosening of this domestic sphere (Steffensmeier & Allan, 1996, p. 463).

2. *The use of historical time-series data to test the theory.* The work of Boritch and Hagan (1990) can be used to illustrate how power-control theorists have used historical records innovatively. In this work, Boritch and Hagan examine the records of male and female arrests in Toronto between 1859 and 1955. In particular, they

focus on the initial effect on the city of the sudden increase in female labour force participation in the mid-nineteenth century. No longer regulated by family ties, and often living on subsistence-level wages, women's rates of "public order" offences (drunkenness, prostitution, begging) became a recognized social problem, which was heightened by moral panic over its consequences for women's "true calling" as mothers and guardians of virtue and faith. Eventually, panic subsided and newly created institutions like the YWCA residences constrained women within an informal system of social controls. As a result, officially recorded offences by women declined dramatically by the late nineteenth century. Boritch and Hagan extend this time-series analysis to encompass many of the current interpretations of women's changing gender roles and their involvement in crime, including those proposed by Adler (1975) and Smart (1978).

HAGAN'S POWER-CONTROL THEORY AND FEMINIST THEORY

Power-control theory, and the research based on it, has helped to correct the false impression that women's rates of deviance would climb dramatically (becoming more like men's rates) as they entered the labour force and achieved greater freedom (Adler, 1975). Power-control theory predicts the documented slight rise and then levelling off of female crime and the reduction of deviant role-exits from oppressive conditions. Women who have experienced greater emancipation have lower crime rates and lower rates of alcohol and drug addiction, mental disorders, and suicides (Karstedt, 2000, p. 21; Steffensmeier, 2001, pp. 191–192). Power-control theory can also combine with feminist theories that emphasize the continuing strain produced by women's economic marginalization (Naffine, 1987). Acts of fraud (bad cheques) and larceny (shoplifting) continue to dominate the kinds of crimes committed by women, not armed robbery and sexual assaults. Increasing liberation has not led to any demonstrable increase in "masculinized" women criminals, although, as in the past, the occasional exception is given a disproportionate amount of attention.

SUMMARY

The dominant assumptions of control theory are that deviance is an inherent human tendency and that it is conformity, rather, that requires explanation. As defined by Walter Reckless, the "good boy" in a high-delinquency area has strong inner controls. Travis Hirschi's early version of control theory focuses on the relative strength of social bonding as a means of keeping people on conforming paths. His later version places greater emphasis on self-control and its sources in childrearing practices. Relatively recent additions to control perspectives, power-control theory, and control balance theory provide a structural view of deviance that permits consideration of potential theoretical integration of conflict, feminist, and control theories.

STUDY QUESTIONS

1. Why aren't *you* a criminal? How do your answers to this question compare with inner and outer controls, social bonds, and self-control theory? Which theory seems to work best?

2. What are the limitations of checklist questionnaires in measuring how often people commit deviant acts? Does reliance on this technique affect the validity of control theory?

3. Which of Hirschi's bonds corresponds most with Reckless's inner controls? Is self-control theory more compatible with this?

4. Hirschi highlights attachment as an important bond. How does this correspond to Durkheim's ideas (Chapter 1, Chapter 7) about regulation and integration? Is attachment a better concept than anomie?

5. Hirschi claims that "we are all moral beings to the extent that we are social." If we interpret this to mean that those who deviate from the dominant morality aren't social, is it accurate?

6. What are negative cases? Do negative cases invalidate a theory?

7. Is low self-control theory a "general theory of crime"? Does it explain all kinds of crime? (What about carefully planned crime?)

8. To what extent does the concept of low self-control correspond to the concept of psychopathy discussed in Chapter 6?

9. How does power-control theory define deviance?

10. Power-control theory uses concepts from Marxist theory. Is it more of a Marxist theory or more of a control theory? (See Chapter 12 for Marxist theories.)

REFERENCES

Adler, F. (1975). *Sisters in Crime*. New York: McGraw-Hill.

Adler, P., & Adler, P. (1983). Relations between Dealers: The Social Organization of Illicit Drug Transactions. *Sociology and Social Research, 67*, 260–278.

Alarid, L. F., Burton, J. V. S., & Cullen, F. T. (2000). Gender and Crime among Felony Offenders: Assessing the Generality of Social Control and Differential Association Theories. *Journal of Research in Crime and Delinquency, 37*(2 May), 171–201.

Bainbridge, W. S. (1989). The Religious Ecology of Deviance. *American Sociological Review, 54*, 288–295.

Boocock, S. S. (1980). *Sociology of Education: An Introduction*. Boston: Houghton Mifflin.

Boritch, H., & Hagan, J. (1990). A Century of Crime in Toronto: Gender, Class, and Patterns of Social Control, 1859–1955. *Criminology, 28*(4), 567–599.

Braithwaite, J. (1990). *Crime, Shame and Reintegration.* Cambridge, UK: Cambridge University Press.

Brownfield, D., & Thompson, K. (1991). Attachment to Peers and Delinquent Behaviour. *Canadian Journal of Criminology, 33*(1), 45–60.

Cochran, J. K., & Akers, R. L. (1989). Beyond Hellfire: An Exploration of the Variable Effects of Religiosity on Adolescent Marijuana and Alcohol Use. *Journal of Research in Crime and Delinquency, 26,* 198–225.

Cohen, L. E., & Felson, M. (1979). Social Change and Crime Rate Trends: A Routine Activities Approach. *American Sociological Review, 44,* 588–608.

Costello, B. (2000). Techniques of Neutralization and Self-Esteem: A Critical Test of Social Control and Neutralization Theory. *Deviant Behavior: An Interdisciplinary Journal, 21*(4 July/August), 307–329.

De Coster, S., Estes, S. B., & Mueller, C. W. (1999). Routine Activities and Sexual Harassment in the Workplace. *Work and Occupations, 26*(1 February), 21–50.

Durkin, K., Wolfe, T. W., & Clark, G. (1999). Social Bond Theory and Binge Drinking among College Students. *College Student Journal, 33*(3 September), 450–462.

Evans, T. D., Cullen, F. T., Burton, J. V. S., Dunaway, R. G., & Benson, M. L. (1997). The Social Consequences of Self-Control: Testing the General Theory of Crime. *Criminology, 35*(3 August), 475–504.

Feeley, M., & Little, D. (1991, June). *The Vanishing Female: The Decline of Women in the Criminal Process, 1687–1912.* Paper presented at the annual meeting of the Law and Society Association, Amsterdam.

Giordano, P. C. (1987). *Confronting Control Theory's Negative Cases.* Conference paper in *Theoretical Integration in the Study of Deviance and Crime: Problems and Prospects.* The Albany Conference. Department of Sociology at New York State University, Albany, NY.

Gottfredson, M. (1999). Review of "Social Learning and Social Structure," by Ronald Akers. *American Journal of Sociology, 105,* 283–284.

Gottfredson, M., & Hirschi, T. (1990). *A General Theory of Crime.* Stanford, CA: Stanford University Press.

Grasmick, H. G., Blackwell, B. S., & Bursik, R. J., Jr. (1993). Changes in the Sex Patterning of Perceived Threats of Sanctions. *Law and Society Review, 27,* 679–705.

Hagan, J. (1989). *Structural Criminology.* New Brunswick, NJ: Rutgers University Press.

———. (1992). The Poverty of a Classless Criminology—The American Society of Criminology 1991 Presidential Address. *Criminology, 30*(1), 1–19.

Hagan, J., & Alberto, P. (1990). The Social Reproduction of a Criminal Class in Working-Class London, circa 1950–1980. *American Journal of Sociology, 961*(2), 265–299.

Hagan, J., Gillis, A. R., & Simpson, J. (1993). The Power of Control in Sociological Theories of Delinquency. In F. Adler & W. S. Adler (Eds.), *New Directions in Criminological Theory. Advances in Criminological Theory* (Vol. 4, pp. 381–397). New Brunswick, NJ: Transaction.

Hagan, J., & Kay, F. (1990). Gender and Delinquency in White Collar Families: A Power-Control Perspective. *Crime and Delinquency, 36,* 391–407.

Hagan, J., Simpson, J., & Gillis, A. R. (1987). Class in the Household: A Power-Control Theory of Gender and Delinquency. *American Journal of Sociology, 92,* 788–816.

Hansell, S., & Wiatrowski, M. (1981). Competing Conceptions of Delinquent Peer Relations. In G. Jensen (Ed.), *Sociology of Delinquency.* Beverly Hills, CA: Sage.

Hawdon, J. E. (1999). Daily Routines and Crime: Using Routine Activities as Measures of Hirschi's Involvement. *Youth & Society, 30*(4 June), 395–415.

Hindelang, M., Hirschi, T., & Weis, J. (1981). *Measuring Delinquency.* Beverly Hills, CA: Sage.

Hirschi, T. (1996). Theory without Ideas: Reply to Akers. *Criminology, 34*(2), 249–256.

Hirschi, T. C. (1969). *Causes of Delinquency.* Berkeley, CA: University of California Press.

Hirschi, T., & Gottfredson, M. (1986). The Distinction between Crime and Criminality. In T. F. Hartnagel & R. A. Silverman (Eds.), *Critique and Explanation: Essays in Honor of Gwynne Nettler.* New Brunswick, NJ: Transaction.

Hirschi, T., & Gottfredson, M. R. (1994). *The Generality of Deviance.* New Brunswick, NJ: Transaction.

Huiras, J. (2000). Career Jobs, Survival Jobs and Employee Deviance. *Sociological Quarterly, 41*(2 Spring), 245–264.

Jenson, G. F. (1993). Power-Control vs. Social Control Theories of Common Delinquency: A Comparative Analysis. In F. Adler & W. S. Adler (Eds.), *New Directions in Criminological Theory. Advances in Criminological Theory* (Vol. 4, pp. 363–398). New Brunswick, NJ: Transaction.

Johnson, B. R., Jang, S. J., Larson, D. B., & De Li, S. (2001). Does Adolescent Religious Commitment Matter? A Re-examination of the Effects of Religiosity on Delinquency. *Journal of Research in Crime and Delinquency, 38*(1 February), 22–45.

Karstedt, S. (2000). Emancipation, Crime and Problem Behavior of Women: A Perspective from Germany. *Gender Issues, 18*(3), 21–59.

Kempf, K. L. (1993). The Empirical Status of Hirschi's Control Theory. In F. Adler & W. S. Adler (Eds.), *New Directions in Criminological Theory. Advances in Criminological Theory* (Vol. 4, pp. 143–185.). New Brunswick, NJ: Transaction.

Kennedy, L. W., & Forde, D. R. (1990). Routine Activities and Crime: An Analysis of Victimization in Canada. *Criminology, 28*(1), 101–115.

LaGrange, T. C., & Silverman, R. A. (1999). Low Self-Control and Opportunity: Testing the General Theory of Crime as an Explanation for Gender Differences in Delinquency. *Criminology, 37*(1), 41–72.

Leonard, K. K., & Decker, S. H. (1994). The Theory of Social Control: Does It Apply to the Very Young? *Journal of Criminal Justice, 22,* 89–105.

Macdonald, P. T. (1989). Competing Theoretical Explanations of Cocaine Use: Differential Association versus Control Theory. *Journal of Contemporary Criminal Justice, 5*(2), 73–88.

Massey, J., & Krohn, M. (1986). A Longitudinal Examination of an Integrated Social Process Model of Deviant Behavior. *Social Forces, 65,* 106–134.

McCarthy, B., & Hagan, J. (1987). Gender, Delinquency and the Great Depression: A Test for Power-Control Theory. *Canadian Review of Sociology and Anthropology, 24*(2), 153–177.

Meier, R. F. (1987). *Deviance and Differentiation.* Conference paper presented in *Theoretical Integration in the Study of Deviance and Crime: Problems and Prospects.* The Albany Conference. Department of Sociology at New York State University, Albany, NY.

Naffine, N. (1987). *Female Crime: The Construction of Women in Criminology*. Sydney, Australia: Allen and Unwin.

Nakhaie, M. R., Silverman, R. A., & Lagrange, T. (2000). Self-Control and Resistance to School. *Canadian Review of Sociology and Anthropology, 37*(4), 443–461.

Osgood, D. W., Wilson, J. K., O'Malley, P. M., Bachman, J. G., & Johnston, L. D. (1996). Routine Activities and Individual Deviant Behavior. *American Sociological Review, 614,* 635–655.

Piquero, A. R., & Hickman, M. (1999). An Empirical Test of Tittle's Control Balance Theory. *Criminology, 37*(2), 319–342.

Reckless, W. C. (1973). *The Crime Problem* (5th ed.). New York: Appleton-Century-Crofts.

Reckless, W. C., & Dinitz, S. P. (1967). Pioneering with Self-Concept as a Vulnerability Factor in Delinquency. *Journal of Criminal Law, Criminology and Police Science, 58,* 515–523.

Reckless, W. C., Dinitz, S., & Murray, E. (1966). Self-Concept as an Insulator against Delinquency. *American Sociological Review, 21*(December), 744–746.

Reed, G. E., & Yeager, P. C. (1996). Organizational Offending and Neoclassical Criminology. Challenging the Reach of a General Theory of Crime. *Criminology, 34*(3), 357–382.

Rogers, J. (1970). *Why Are You Not a Criminal?* Englewood Cliffs, NJ: Prentice-Hall.

Sellers, C. (1999). Self-Control and Intimate Violence: An Examination of the Scope and Specification of the General Theory of Crime. *Criminology, 37*(2 May), 375–404.

Smart, C. W. (1978). *Women, Crime and Criminology*. London, UK: Routledge and Keegan Paul.

Steffensmeier, D. (2001). Female Crime Trends, 1960–1995. In C. M. Renzetti & L. Goodstein (Eds.), *Women, Crime and Criminal Justice* (pp. 191–211). Los Angeles: Roxbury.

Steffensmeier, D., & Allan, E. (1996). Gender and Crime: Toward a Gendered Theory of Female Offending. *Annual Review of Sociology, 22,* 459–487.

Tittle, C. R. (1995). *Control Balance: Toward a General Theory of Deviance*. Boulder, CO: Westview Press.

Tittle, C. R., & Paternoster, R. (2000). *Social Deviance and Crime: An Organizational and Theoretical Approach*. Los Angeles: Roxbury.

Toby, J. (1957). Social Disorganization and Stake in Conformity: Complementary Factors in the Predatory Behavior of Young Hoodlums. *Journal of Criminal Law, Criminology and Police Science, 48,* 12–17.

Ulmer, J. (2000). Commitment, Deviance and Social Control. *Sociological Quarterly, 41*(3 Summer), 315–337.

Wiatrowski, M., & Anderson, K. L. (1987). The Dimensionality of the Social Bond. *Journal of Quantitative Criminology, 3*(1), 65–79.

Wilson, J. Q., & Herrnstein, R. J. (1985). *Crime and Human Nature*. New York: Simon and Schuster.

Winslow, R. W., & Gay, P. T. (1993). The Moral Minorities: A Self-Report Study of Low-Consensus Deviance. *International Journal of Offender Therapy and Comparative Criminology, 37*(1), 17–27.

Wittebrod, K., & Nieuwbeerta, P. (2000). Criminal Victimization during One's Life Course: The Effects of Previous Victimization and Patterns of Routine Activities. *Journal of Research in Crime and Delinquency, 37*(1 February), 91–123.

CONFLICT, CRITICAL, AND POSTMODERNIST THEORIES

An article that appeared in the *Edmonton Journal* in April 2000 (Simons, 2000) describes the case of 17-year-old Adam Laboucan from Quesnel, British Columbia, who sexually assaulted a three-month-old baby, injuring the child enough to require reparative surgery. Laboucan confessed to having beaten and drowned a three-year-old boy four years before this—he had been interviewed about the death but released. The courts, operating on neoclassical principles, declared him to be a dangerous offender and sentenced him to imprisonment that will very likely last until he dies. Laboucan has a recorded IQ of 70, possibly due to Fetal Alcohol Syndrome or to serious brain damage from a car accident that occurred before his assaults. His mother reports that he is sexually confused, having since age three shown a tendency to want to be female, and he engages serious levels of self-mutilation, eating at his own body. But other realities exist here.

His White father, an illiterate oil-field worker who never played a role in Laboucan's life, had abandoned Laboucan's Native mother. She had many boyfriends during Laboucan's childhood, one of whom tortured him by butting out lighted cigarettes on his body. Laboucan was sexually assaulted not only by a male friend of his mother's but also, possibly, by a female friend. On the night he molested the baby, Laboucan's mother had sent him to the pawnshop for money so that she could play bingo. She told Laboucan that she would pay him for babysitting her friend's child while they went to bingo but only if she won. The attack on the child came after she called from the bingo hall to say that she was losing.

The theories that we have looked at thus far would most likely locate the cause of Laboucan's behaviour in moral evil, lack of deterrence, community disorder, psychiatric disorder or brain damage, racial origins, or the labelling of youths with mental disabilities. Demonic theory would claim he was possessed or evil. Classical theory might say the laws (or the rules of his environment) were not severe enough or not well enough enforced. Constitutional theories would look at his inadequate superego, his sexual compulsions, or his resentment. Some of them might call his genetic background degenerate. The Chicago School would lay some blame on his disrupted family, the kind of neighbourhood his mother was living in, and the absence of community support for single mothers. Functionalism might point to the utility of Laboucan as a scapegoat whose punishment reassures the community that its boundaries are intact. Interaction theory would recognize that Laboucan had lost the battle for a respectable self-image. The control theories would see him as inadequately socialized and without effective supervision.

Conflict theories, however, would pose different questions and suggest different conclusions. They might ask, for example, how is it possible that a modern, industrial-urban society, which can conduct space exploration and provide huge sports arenas with retractable roofs, has children growing up the way Laboucan did? How does the economic and political system work so that Laboucan's incapable mother remained his sole protector, even when she was clearly unable to give him the basic securities of life? Why was his situation ignored when he was strongly suspected in the earlier drowning death? Why is blame not attached to the people who, over the years, saw and did nothing? Why does government spend more on entertainment than it does on Fetal Alcohol Syndrome prevention programs? (See Table 12.1 for a comparison of social control and conflict theories.)

Like interpretive theories, but much more openly, conflict theories tend to take the side of the underdog, but they go further in denouncing the conditions that produce underdogs and keep them under. The ignorance, poverty, greed, and selfishness that produced Laboucan's life course can be seen as by-products of a competitive capitalist system. There are elements of systemic injustices, including systemic racism, in his story as well.

In *The Red Lily* (1894), novelist Anatole France observed that the law forbids both rich and poor "to sleep under bridges, to beg in the streets and to steal bread." Implicit in this brief statement are several insights relevant to the conflict approach to deviance. First, the rules (whether legal or customary) are made by the powerful and, even when framed in "universalistic" ways, tend to regulate the conduct of the powerless. The law that forbids begging is egalitarian in its formulation (everyone is

Table 12.1 Comparison of Modern Sociological Theories

	Social Control	Conflict
Conception of deviance	Natural	Constructed as excuse for control
Explanation	Failure of internal and external controls	Criminalization serves capitalist interest
Remedies	Strengthen family, civil religion, and other institutions	Modify or overthrow capitalism

equally forbidden to beg), but it is not egalitarian in its effect, since it restricts only those people for whom begging is a necessary or preferred source of income.

Second, the rules are part of a system that preserves the preferred way of life for the powerful even when it is harmful for others or channels them (like Adam Laboucan) into criminal or deviant roles. A criminal's perceptive perspective on the system is summarized in the title of bank robber Micky McArthur's memoirs *I'd Rather Be Wanted Than Had* (1990). McArthur clearly feels that playing the game the way it is set up (obeying the law) is letting others steal from you.

Third, people who break the rules do so either out of need, in protest against a system that oppresses them, or because they are so damaged by the system that conformity is nearly impossible. People may sleep under bridges because they have no other options, because they resent the controls imposed by missions and agencies for the poor, or because they are not acceptable even in shelters. The auto dealer may engage in price gouging because it is the only way to stay in business given the current structure of the marketplace (Leonard & Weber, 1991). The company engineer who cuts corners on safety, resulting in maiming or death in the workplace or on the highway, may do so because continued employment depends on meeting the unrealistic goals set by upper management (Dowie, 1991).

Although many conflict theorists take the position that upper-level crime is motivated by boundless greed, most see the upper-level deviant as a participant in a system that rewards cheating and discourages or penalizes honesty whenever it jeopardizes profit margins. Underclass deviance is often motivated by despair or protest. Conflict theory's deviants, whether high or low status, are not sick, undercontrolled, or perverse; they are simply individuals who are attempting to make the best of unequal opportunities, either from within the system or outside it.

Conflict theory is also characterized by six other propositions:

1. *Power is the most important explanatory variable.* The fact that some people have more power than others and use it to maintain or improve their position at the expense of others is the fundamental cause of social problems, including deviance, racism, sexism, war, and environmental degradation.

2. *Groups with clashing interests and values, and with unequal resources, compete with one another, thereby producing winners and losers.* Conflicts do not necessarily or even usually benefit society as a whole. Rather, they benefit some groups at the expense of others and often at the expense of the whole.

3. *Groups struggle to have their own definitions of right and wrong established as part of the status quo and even made into law.* The imposition of these definitions and laws serves to constrain their competitors, whose customs are made illegal, deviant, or irrelevant.

4. *Definitions of crime and deviance are weapons in the struggle between groups for a share of power in the system.* Successful competitors see their rules enforced and other people's rules marginalized as subcultures. Any law or rule

can be understood by posing the question "Who gains?" and by tracing the path back to the interests of those in power.

5. *Deviance is neither normal nor inevitable.* People break rules because something is wrong with the way in which society is structured.

6. *The source of deviance does not reside in the body or mind of the individual but rather in the unequal relationships between people.* Individualistic explanations of deviance and crime are ideological tools used by those in power to justify the state's use of "therapeutic" intervention (i.e., treating noncomformists with mood-modifying drugs, psychotherapy, psychosurgery, and other mind-altering techniques).

VALUE NEUTRALITY AND PRAXIS

Early pluralist conflict theorists followed the lead of Max Weber and tried to emulate scientific detachment (see Box 12.1). They attempted to separate their roles as theorists and researchers from their role as concerned citizens. In their quest for Weber's "value neutrality," they sought to study current realities and future possibilities in strictly empirical terms and to avoid emotional involvement with the issues of their research. Just as medical researchers would be regarded as having stepped outside their role if they were to give lectures on the perniciousness of a particular disease (instead of studying its origin and how it spreads), so the social researcher given to making political judgments would be seen as having strayed outside professional boundaries.

Later conflict theorists, particularly those following in the path of Karl Marx, have argued that it is not only impossible but also immoral to separate the "is" from the "ought to be." From their perspective, the responsibility of the researcher is to engage in either short-term or long-term praxis. *Praxis* means combining knowledge and activism to challenge oppressive ideologies or structures. Praxiological research is aimed at the analysis of oppressive social structures and is in itself both academic and political (Edwards & Scullion, 1982; Harvey, 1990, pp. 22–23).

According to praxiological thinkers, the social scientist should study the "real" nature of society to expose its structures of domination and undermine the pervasive legitimating ideologies that sustain them. We might, for example, study civil rights litigation in prison contexts to reveal and document the role of law as an instrument of class oppression. But we should not study it in order to help officials make the oppression more effective or efficient (Collins, 1984, p. 1; Thomas, 1984). Similarly, a conflict approach to social work would attempt to reveal the ways in which social workers are expected to control and contain disadvantaged groups to keep the dominant system from being inconvenienced by them. A conflict theorist would try to find ways to transform social workers into agents of change who would empower the disadvantaged.

MARXIST THEORIES

KARL MARX

For Marx (1818–83), crime and deviance were relatively unimportant by-products of the division of capitalist society into owners of the means of production (the *bourgeoisie*), wage earners (the *proletariat*), and those whose survival depends on crime or welfare (the *lumpenproletariat*). Marxism is a structural theory that emphasizes the system (conflict, competition) over personal characteristics (such as greed) as the driving force behind social action. Workers are exploited largely because employers who do not exploit them will soon be displaced, through competition, by those who will.

Factories and workplaces in which workers experience conditions of alienation, whereby neither the process of work nor the ultimate product has meaning for them, characterize the system of industrial capitalism. The extreme case of this is the assembly line, in which each worker is little more than a cog in a machine that produces machines (Spencer, 2000). Alienation is assumed to lead to many kinds of deviance, such as sabotage, that express the human need for meaningful activity and personal significance.

The needs of successful capitalist enterprise are often at odds with the interests of other groups in society, not just those of employees. The expropriation of lands for commercial purposes (part of early industrial capitalism) helped create a disenfranchised class composed of "beggars, robbers [and] vagabonds," who were treated by the law as willful criminals, even though much of their behaviour was based on need or protest (Marx, 1867/1987, p. 734).

Marx was ambivalent about the lumpenproletariat of his day, considering a large proportion of them to be social parasites who weakened the ranks of labour (Taylor, Walton, & Young, 1973). His colleague, Friedrich Engels, came to the conclusion (now categorized as left idealism) that crime by the poor was a form of political protest. Many Marxists feel that Marxism cannot be applied to crime and deviance without producing serious distortions (revisionism). As in power-control theory, tension exists between the feeling that crime is *real* and the theory's revelation that it is *constructed* (Hirst, 1972, p. 29; Mugford, 1974, p. 595).

MARXISM AND DEVIANCE: WILLEM BONGER

According to Willem Bonger (1876–1940), capitalism produces harmful deviance because it makes everyone in the system selfish (Bonger, 1916). Only by taking the means of production out of the hands of the few and distributing resources based on need would it be possible to avoid the greed-driven (but unrecognized) predation by the rich and the officially recognized deviance of the poor. Bonger felt that if the structurally induced forms of crime were eliminated, all that would remain would be a small residue of psychopathic forms.

INSTRUMENTAL AND STRUCTURAL MARXISM

Early Marxism took two main forms, instrumental and structural. According to instrumental Marxism, the state (which includes government, military, and law enforcement institutions) is, crudely and directly, a tool of the ruling class. Definitions of crime and deviance are made by the state in the interests of the propertied classes. Miliband (1969) provides support for this characterization by documenting the strong ideological and social connections between economic and political elites and the rules that we live by. The instrumentalist position can also be illustrated by Richard Quinney's early work *Class, State, and Crime* (1977). In it, Quinney sees crime and deviance as products of the need of the ruling class to control the proletariat. In his view, the criminal law is an instrument of the state and the ruling class in that it is formulated by the state to serve the interests of the owners of the means of production (see Figure 12.1)

Quinney (1977) attributes the growth of proletariat and "surplus" populations to the crises that afflict capitalism in its later stages. Competition, particularly in periods of recession, continually depletes the ranks of the owners. By joining the ranks of salaried employees, these displaced capitalists contribute to the growth of the proletariat. At the same time, however, technological advances render an increasing number of wage earners redundant and unemployable, since their type of work no longer exists. Thus, the surplus population also grows. According to Quinney, two increasingly coercive state institutions perform the control of both populations: crim-

Figure 12.1   A Neo-Marxist Model

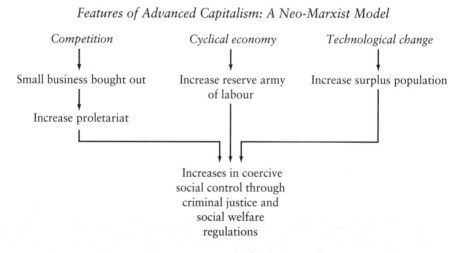

Features of Advanced Capitalism: A Neo-Marxist Model

Source: Adapted from R. Quinney (1977), *Class, State, and Crime* (New York: McKay).

inal justice and social welfare. Those subjected to these institutional controls are assigned negative labels that justify their loss of autonomy.

Structural Marxism argues that the state does not act solely to represent the interests of a monolithic ruling class (Chambliss & Seidman, 1982). The state preserves itself by protecting the capitalist system but not necessarily by protecting all capitalists. Although the interests of the system and its primary beneficiaries normally coincide, in some areas they do not. For example, capitalism requires competition, yet many capitalists do everything in their power to drive competitors out of the market or to create price-fixing arrangements that make competition unnecessary (Snider, 1992). If their actions threaten the system, individual capitalists may be criminalized or marginalized. Some may be punished to maintain the appearance that injustices are controlled. Smaller marginal companies are much more likely to be successfully prosecuted on pollution and safety charges than are their larger and more deviant counterparts (Snider, 1992). Similarly, structural Marxism recognizes that the government may on occasion put its specific interests (such as getting re-elected) before those of the ruling class (Chambliss & Seidman, 1982).

PLURALIST CONFLICT THEORIES

Pluralist (liberal) conflict theory traces its roots back to the work of Max Weber (1864–1920). Much of Weber's work can be viewed as an argument with the theories of Karl Marx. Weber felt that the economy was not the only determinant of conflict in society, or not always the most important one. His successors developed pluralist views of conflict according to which society is characterized by the competition among many different groups, each of which has access to certain power-relevant resources. Groups may variously have many members with education, expertise, wealth, or connections with power holders.

Conflict between groups results in winners and losers, most of whom remain in the field. Since social change improves the resources of some and depletes the resources of others, the contest is never entirely over. Pluralist conflict theory allows groups to improve their position in the whole and to force others to live by their standards, at least in the short term. Deviance definitions are just one weapon powerful groups use to weaken and control competitors who are not strong enough to cast them off. The relevance of pluralist conflict theory for deviance lies in the relationship between winning in the conflict between groups and being able to establish rules that give the winner more freedom and the loser more constraints. People labelled as deviant are disproportionately drawn from the losers.

Vold's (1958) theory of group conflict is regarded by many as a classic statement of pluralist conflict theory. In Vold's view, politically organized groups who seek the assistance of government in their efforts to defend their rights and protect their interests produce laws and rules. When successful, new rules and laws tend to limit the rights of others and hamper their interests. Thus, crime is a form of political resistance against the rules that are set by other groups; only a very small proportion of it is meaningless or pathological.

CRITICAL THEORIES

NEO-MARXIST CRITICAL THEORY: THE FRANKFURT SCHOOL

Felix Weil established the Frankfurt School in the early 1920s. Among its first generation were Theodor W. Adorno, Max Horkheimer, Herbert Marcuse, Friedrich Pollock, Leo Lowenthal, and Walter Benjamin. Not surprisingly, given its exile to New York during the Nazi period, the school focused much of its research on such issues as the social production of the "authoritarian personality" and the inculcation of "false consciousness" that led people to support regimes that oppressed and dominated them. The school disbanded in the late 1960s, just as its traditions were beginning to take hold in North America (Agger, 1991; Lynch, 1999).

The initial issue addressed by the Frankfurt School was why the revolution prophesied by Marx had not occurred when and where the theory would have predicted. Revolutionary Russia had not been a highly capitalistic country, while capitalistic Western European countries seemed far from the point of revolutionary upheaval. In the school's view, Marx had been correct about the increasingly serious internal contradictions of capitalism; however, he had underestimated the extent to which *false consciousness* could be fostered and exploited such that, despite periodic crises, the majority of the people saw the existing system as inevitable, rational, and unchangeable. The domination of society by the state was a combination of external exploitation (which contributed to powerlessness) and ideological indoctrination, which constituted "discipline from the inside" or "*surplus repression*" (Marcuse, 1965, pp. 32–34).

The Frankfurt School theorists also challenged the ideas of positivism (including Marxist positivism), which they saw as a technique for producing passivity and fatalism. Instead of studying the status quo as an inevitable condition of life, they treated "social facts" as historical products that can and should be questioned and changed. The critical school theorists generally rejected the scientific method. Their goal was "emancipation and enlightenment" through the revelation of hidden coercion and the discovery of "real" interests (Geuss, 1981, p. 55).

ANTONIO GRAMSCI AND HEGEMONY

Neo-Marxists working outside the Frankfurt School have also developed theories that stress the connection between power and truth, and the way in which manipulation of truth is controlling. Antonio Gramsci (1891–1937), who was imprisoned under Mussolini's fascist regime, argued that Marx's theory needed to be expanded to include not only the economic base but also the repressive and ideological apparatuses of the state (Gramsci, 1971).

Box 12.1   Richard Quinney and the Social Reality of Crime

In *The Social Reality of Crime* (1970), Richard Quinney outlines a pluralistic conflict position in six propositions:

1. *Crime is a definition of behaviour that is made by authorized agents in the political process.* As such, it is not a product of individual psychopathology or immorality. It follows from this that an increase in the number of criminal definitions will be answered by a corresponding increase in the amount of crime.

2. *Criminal definitions reflect the fact that the desires, values, and interests of the most powerful groups (i.e., those with the greatest influence on rule making) often conflict with the interests of less powerful groups.* These interests may change over time, especially if the composition of the dominant groups changes. More conflict and change in society means more rules being formulated and applied, and hence, more crime.

3. *The manner in which the rules are enforced depends on the extent to which authorities see particular infractions as a threat to their interests.* Criminal definitions are applied most vigorously to behaviour that is most conspicuously opposed to the interests of the powerful.

4. *The behaviour of people in less powerful segments of society has a greater likelihood of being defined as criminal and may be partly structured in response to the criminal definitions that are applied to it.* The pattern that is established by the rule breakers and the rule enforcers may become reciprocally reinforcing, as each group acts in terms of its self-concept and its definition of the other.

5. *The media and other communications institutions play a major role in constructing and disseminating images of crime.* Their influence is such that people in all segments of society tend to agree that particular actions presented in the media are deviant or criminal.

6. *The social reality of crime is constructed by the formulation and application of definitions made by those who have influence over the rule-making (political) process, by the development of behavioural patterns in response to these definitions, and by the dissemination of conceptions of crime, by way of social communications media.*

Quinney later dismissed the pluralistic conflict position presented in *The Social Reality of Crime* as a "bourgeois academic exercise," and by 1977 had (temporarily) taken up the neo-Marxist instrumental position described elsewhere in this chapter.

Gramsci's concept of *hegemony* has been particularly important in the study of deviance. Hegemony refers to a world view so dominant that people are unable to conceive of alternative possibilities. It is the "common sense" of society, the fund of definitions and descriptions of social situations and social needs that normally is understood. Hegemony emerges out of the combination of dominance that is inherent in hierarchical structures (the opinions of employers are more important than those of employees) and the manufacture of consent facilitated by the media, educational institutions, and religion. Thus, hegemony is ideological and cultural authority that represents the perspective of the dominant groups in the society.

Gramsci argued that hegemony was never entirely complete or uncontested, because it competed with the awareness that was produced in the daily experience of people who were oppressed by it. The working class possessed a "dual consciousness" that could be the basis for the development of a revolutionary consciousness. Kinsman (1987) uses the concept of hegemony to raise consciousness with respect to the world view that supports heterosexuality over every other sexual reality. Similarly, feminists point to the hegemonic characteristics of patriarchy. Although finding its roots in the Marxian concept of false consciousness, the concept of hegemony foreshadowed the postmodern conception of discourse theory, discussed below (Morera, 2000).

CRITICAL CRIMINOLOGY AND DEVIANCE STUDIES

Critical criminology emerged from the turmoil of conflict theories during the 1970s and is not strictly distinct from conflict theories or postmodern approaches. The boundaries remain both fuzzy and contested, while individual theorists move from one variation to another as they explore different possibilities. An example of this is the work of Richard Quinney, as outlined in his retrospective *Bearing Witness to Crime and Social Justice* (2000). Nonetheless, critical conflict theory has some distinctive emergent characteristics that make it a valuable addition to deviance theory.

Critical criminology recognizes that our belief in the reality of race, class, gender, religion, and other differences helps to structure the social reality in which we live. In this sense, it is a structural conflict approach and much of what we have said about conflict theories could be repeated here—for example, that competition is structural rather than individual but leads to individual greed and violence, that deviance designation (labelling) is controlled by those with power and applied to control those who have less power regardless of their actual actions, that "suite crime" and patriarchal abuses are protected, while less harmful practices are not, that deviance can be a form of protest, and that the distinctions between groups are part of the mystification that provides a basis for patterns of domination and differential privilege.

Critical criminology highlights the importance of human agency, even though structural forces are not denied. Society is seen as a product of human action that can be changed by human action, rather than (as in most Marxist societies) as part of a history that follows some immutable path that leaders can only discover, not change. The overall goal of critical criminology is not only to expose the way in which presumed differences are exploited in ways that perpetuate social injustice but also to participate, along with others, in forms of human action that can bring about a more just society. Critical criminological theory is (not surprisingly, given its name) mainly focused on crime and the criminal justice system but sees these categories as part of the mystification process. In critical terms, the so-called criminal justice system needs to be deconstructed to show that "criminal" is not a term that refers to those who harm but is often a term that harms, and "justice" is not the outcome of most courts and prisons. Critical theorists argue that the capitalist, patriarchal, and racist order of society affects all aspects of life, not just those elements that fall within criminology.

THE NEW CRIMINOLOGY

One of the earliest theories that is usually included in the "critical theory" category is the "new criminology" introduced in the 1970s by criminologists who were working in both Britain and Canada. Among the founders of the new criminology were Ian Taylor, Paul Walton, and Jock Young (1973, 1975). Their deviancy theory combined social interactionism, Marxist concepts and categories, and radical attitudes that supported the elimination of capitalist oppression.

According to the new criminology, systems of control are inherently unjust because their real goals are self-perpetuation and self-aggrandizement. The law is a system that reflects workplace morality as conceived by the upper class as a guide for the lower class, not for itself. Deviance is resistance on the part of those who are being had by the system. In this view, it is capitalism that is criminally deviant, not only in the sense that it causes crime but also in the sense that it oppresses, exploits, and degrades human bodies while distorting and constraining human minds.

New criminology theorists argued, as did the anarchist theorists, that deviance and crime were nothing more than the result of capitalism, and that correctionalism (crime control) was simply a tool of that system. The new deviancy theory strove for a social order in which the "facts of human diversity" would not be "subject to the power to criminalize" (Taylor et al., 1973, p. 282). In the idealized society, no one would be a criminal, regardless of his or her actions. Not surprisingly, this view came to fit under the rubric of "left idealism" since it rendered deviance and crime in idyllic terms. Rock (1979, p. 80) was not alone in seeing this as a "drift into otherworldliness," especially when its view of deviants as misunderstood, oppressed freedom seekers was contrasted with the realities of murder assault, and child abuse. Indeed, new criminology theorists tended to focus their attention on issues like soft drug use (Young, 1971) and moral panics about hooligans (Cohen, 1971), avoiding "left realist" issues like crimes against women, Blacks, and the working class (Jary & Jary, 1991, p. 330). Left realism, established in England and Canada in the 1980s by Jock Young, Roger Mathews, John Lea, and Brian MacLean, argued that however much the ultimate origins of crime were located in the capitalist system, it was necessary to control crime in the interests of all citizens. This perspective is seen in the work of Walter DeKeseredy (DeKeseredy & Schwartz, 1991), who writes extensively on the problem of violence against women in Canada (2000; DeKeseredy, Alvi, & Ellis, 1993). It is notable that, in the course of studying the empirical reality of crime and crime control, most advocates of this perspective came to adopt less idealistic positions.

Although itself short-lived, the new criminology stimulated a number of new directions in deviance studies. Three of these are (1) human rights theory, which emphasizes

Box 12.2   Left Realism: Crime Really Is a Problem

Crime is not an activity of latter-day Robin Hoods—the vast majority of working-class crime is directed within the working class. It is intra-class, not inter-class in nature. Similarly, despite the mass media predilection for focusing on inter-racial crime, it is overwhelmingly intra-racial. Crimes of violence, for example, are by and large one poor person hitting another poor person—and in almost half of these instances it is a man hitting his wife.

This is not to deny the impact of crimes of the powerful or indeed of the social problems created by capitalism which are perfectly legal. Rather, left realism notes that the working class is a victim of crime from all directions. It notes that the more vulnerable a person is economically and socially the more likely it is that *both* working-class and white-collar crime will occur against them.... Realism is not empiricism. Crime and deviance are prime sites of moral anxiety and tension in a society which is fraught with real inequalities and injustices. Criminals can quite easily become folk devils onto which are projected such feelings of unfairness. But there is a rational core to the fear of crime, just as there is a rational core to the anxieties which distort it. Realism argues with popular consciousness in its attempts to sepa-rate out reality from fantasy. But it does not deny that crime is a problem.

Source: Jock Young, "The Failure of Criminology," in R. Matthews and J. Young (eds.), *Confronting Crime* (London: Sage, 1986), 23–24. Reprinted with permission of Sage Publishing Ltd.

using existing human rights codes as the standards by which behaviour should be judged (Galliher, 1991); (2) peacemaking theory, which combines elements of Marxian and Gandhian humanism with a religious base to criticize the violence of social control and argue for a system expressing compassion, forgiveness, and love (Pepinsky & Quinney, 1991, p. ix); and (3) anarchist criminology, which calls for a total dismantling of repres-sive justice (especially state forms of justice) and its replacement with forms of tolerant mutual aid, such as restorative justice (Ferrell, 1993; Ferrell & Sanders, 1995; Tifft & Sullivan, 1980). Constitutive criminology (described below, under "Beyond Postmodernism") can also be considered a form of critical criminology theory, distinct from other postmodern forms in its insistence on the importance of human agency in con-structing the world, not just deconstructing it (Henry, 1999; Henry & Milovanovic, 1999).

DISCOURSE THEORIES: STRUCTURALISM, POSTSTRUCTURALISM, AND POSTMODERNISM

Discourse is talk. Discourses are modes of making meaning in society. They provide the modes of expression that shape what can be said and thought. Scientific discourse, for example, was not available to people who lived before C.E. 1700, so that other understandings dominated. In many parts of the world, religious discourses still pre-dominate and may even be gaining strength. In the Western world, the discourses of medicine, psychology, sociology, criminology, and technology tend to dominate the ways in which deviance and crime are understood. Michel Foucault, for example, argued that the Enlightenment gave rise to discourses that restricted the development of knowledge to those paths that supported increasing control over the individual. Although knowledge in the Renaissance could be characterized as an open field within which science and alchemy coexisted, knowledge in the age of reason was defined, enclosed, and "tamed" (Foucault, 1970; Lemert & Gillan, 1982, p. 19).

Discourse theories attempt to deconstruct these ways of making meaning, showing how they have been formed and highlighting the ways in which they channel thoughts so that the dominant power holders of their time are supported. For example, one study of the discourses used by police in constructing gay men showed that there were three police discourses: one highlighting effeminate characteristics, one highlighting pedophilia and promiscuity, and one of "conditional acceptance," roughly equivalent to "don't ask, don't tell." None of these discourses can be construed as conducive to acceptance of gays as police officers (Praat & Tuffin, 1996). In another postmodernist account, Charles Acland focuses on the cultural phenomenon of "youth in crisis" (Acland, 1995). The focus is not on the youth as such, but on the way in which the understandings of youth are created and used in a cultural politics

Box 12.3   The Intellectual Climate of Discourse Theories

Discourse theories have tended to be popularized by intellectually charismatic figures such as Jacques Derrida, Jean Baudrillard, and Michel Foucault, who are surrounded by acolytes and disciples. Although the source of the ideas behind the theories can be traced to the German philosophical tradition, their focus centres on Paris, where the intellectual environment has encouraged scholarship that is showy but often deliberately provocative, opaque, and labyrinthine. Discourse theory is full of flashy neologisms and startling statements along the lines of the "God is dead" controversy. The successful lecture is one that plays a game with the listeners. It produces a good deal of discussion about what the theory really means in itself and in relation to the ideas of competing savants. Intellectuals play a role not unlike that of celebrity movie stars or sports figures and must be "new" all the time to retain the attention and loyalty of their followers. It does not pay to be too easily understood or too clear about the methods used to create stunning, artistic, and deeply philosophical observations. The writings of these intellectuals are often bestsellers in the book market, left on coffee tables to show social status. Discourse theorists, especially Michel Foucault, have been expected to be at the forefront of various political actions, such as the uprisings of students and workers in France in 1968, and have participated in campaigns for all kinds of oppressed groups (Miller, 1993, p. 15). Given this atmosphere, it is somewhat surprising that this type of thought has contributed a great deal to the understanding of deviance and control.

that helps to maintain the very systems that produce youth problems. Acland acknowledges that there is real violence and real victimization in the lives of youths, but that is not the focus of his interest.

The impact of discourse may occur through the things that are said, in words, print, or pictures; it may also be through what does *not* appear. Dominant discourses silence or marginalize alternative views, demonize them, or render them invisible. Consider, for example, how the dominant conception of male and female gender roles has, until recently, almost totally suppressed the voices and even recognition of cross-gendered and alternative sexualities (Burrington, 1994).

Although discourse theories may take some inspiration from Marxism, and on occasion draw on its concepts, they ultimately reject Marxist ideology and method. Discourse theories are critical conflict theories in the sense that they see the dominant discourses of our time (science, medicine, capitalist economics) as forces that produce docile, limited human beings who are disciplined into conformity with the political economy of their time and who lack the emancipatory discourses (ways of thought) with which to liberate themselves.

The word "structuralism" as it is used in discourse theories differs from the usual sociological concept of structure as the constellation of roles and the relations among them, which together constitute a social order. The structure sought by the structuralist inheres in the hidden reality that lies behind the production of meanings in the social order, and this is intimately bound up with the nature of language.

Structuralists like Ferdinand de Saussure and Jacques Derrida are distinguished by their conviction that the basis of the social order resides in the structure of language. Poststructuralists (Mikhail Bakhtin, Michel Foucault, Pierre Bourdieu) reject this, arguing that discourses (meaning-constellations) are pragmatically constructed in processes of social communication in particular historical contexts. They are made and remade, and can be challenged by practices that "transgress" their rules—practices that are usually interpreted as deviance *because* they transgress these rules. An example of this can be found in Stanley's (1995, p. 91) analysis of adolescent joyriding, raving, and hacking as transgressive activities that produce a "wild zone" of unregulated activity that "tactically subverts rationalised space."

The methodology of the structuralist and poststructuralist is generally either *hermeneutic* (interpretive) or *deconstructionist* (taking apart and examining the work that has created a social reality). The early study of hermeneutics involved trying to uncover the authentic version of the Bible, when handwritten copies often contained errors, and trying to create a coherent theory of what the Bible really meant when, for example, it was important to know whether Christ meant for his followers (the Church) to remain poor. (As seen in Chapter 3, the losers in these interpretive battles became heretics and were often persecuted.) The theory and methodology of hermeneutics were later applied to the study of all kinds of "texts" and even used to "read" art, landscape, and culture as kinds of text.

POSTMODERNISM

Given the importance of communication to postmodernist discourse theory, it is ironic that so much of what is written is difficult to read or decode without a lengthy apprenticeship. Postmodernist writing is often a kind of transgression of the grammatical—an attempt to escape from the restrictions of grammatical and lexical rules to express understandings that escape those regulated forms. In addition to problems of communication, postmodernism sometimes seems to fall into an endless regression of deconstruction, leaving a residue that is so relativistic that it amounts to nihilism (Melichar, 1988; Schwartz, 1991). Why work so hard to show that there is nothing there? For those who *can* follow, postmodern writing can be liberating, funny, and intensely serious.

The terms "postmodernist" and "poststructuralist" often include the same authors and very similar kinds of work. Modernism refers to the culture of the first half of the twentieth century, expressed, for example, in the highly functional glass and steel towers of buildings such as New York's Seagram Building, completed in 1958 and contemporaneous with a society based on rationality and science. With postmodernism, however, form no longer closely follows function or any fixed rules. Postmodernism, if it "copies" modernism, does so ironically, comically, with a deliberate avoidance of fixed rules such as functionality or conformity. Postmodern writers give highest value to nonlinear thought (overturning conventions of linguistic order) and to overturning, through deconstruction, the "master narratives" of White-male-Western-middle-class claims to knowledge. Some postmodernists are deeply cynical about all systems of meaning, tending to see the whole world as caught up in the "hyperreal" fantasy-reality of mass-consumerism and media images (Baudrillard, 1995).

Box 12.4   Death at the Parasite Café

"Hear me out. To be a *power-reflexive* reader you must risk the vulnerability of entering an uncannily feared situation with eyes/ "I"s crossed doubly and to drift for a time indeterminate and disturbing. After that, perhaps you will be able to more rigorously and more generously theorize the material dynamics of power as the fateful medium of exchange cuts into and across the bodies of those it (dis)positions. This might be your last chance to masquerade yourself in such a way as to strategically perform a ritual series of difficult to dance but nevertheless possible (social) movements that might allow you to both critically distance yourself from the scenes and screens to which you yourself seem most given over to in relations of power, while at the same time unlearning enough about yourself to risk an altered intimacy with others, including those others you keep locked like shadows in the back of your mind...." Having spoken those words, Black Madonna Durkheim drove me to the front door of what appeared to be an abandoned state institution....

Source: From Stephen Pfohl, *Death at the Parasite Café: Social Science (Fictions) and the Postmodern* (New York: St. Martin's Press, 1992). Reprinted with permission.

Many of the issues of great significance to discourse theorists are of little direct concern to deviance theorists. A good deal of discourse theory centres on disputes over whether the human being is the ultimate basis of reality (the centred subject of traditional theory), or whether text and culture is more real than the individual (the decentred subject of structuralist theory), or whether there is no basis of reality in either individuals or words (the limitlessness of poststructuralist theory). Unfortunately, it is almost impossible to draw out the implications of these disputes for deviance without at the same time doing some damage to the work as a whole. Efforts to turn the postmodernist and poststructuralist writer Michel Foucault into a sociologist run the risk of distorting and trivializing his contribution. Nevertheless, it is important to recognize the way in which his work on marginalized people and the changing forms of social control has entered into the language of deviance theory.

MICHEL FOUCAULT

Michel Foucault (1926–84) exerted a powerful influence over academic and cultural life in France and America during the 1980s. A prominent criminologist has written that to write about punishment and control today without referring to Foucault would be "like talking about the unconscious without Freud" (Cohen, 1985, p. 10). Foucault was often challenged and vilified, both for his ideas, which challenged and undercut the dominant ideas of established experts of his time (in history, medical science, literature, and economics), and for his lifestyle (Danaher, Shirato, & Webb, 2000, pp. 2–3).

Foucault's concepts enable us to study the way in which both overtly coercive institutions such as prisons and "helping" institutions such as education, health, and social welfare have a disciplinary (control) function. All of them are increasingly involved in treating their clientele as objects to be contained and controlled. Foucault analyzed these processes to uncover alternative paths, paths that might lead away from objectification and control to "subjectification" and resistance. Subjectification, in Foucault's work, means a procedure whereby people are enabled to constitute themselves as their own masters, reclaiming the subjective, active dimension of the self (Lacombe, 1996, p. 350).

Foucault's most important contribution to the understanding of deviance and control lies in his assumption that knowledge cannot be disentangled from power relations. To know something is to delimit it, to place a value on it, and to displace other ways of knowing. An épistème (an historically bounded way of knowing) codifies, classifies, and straitjackets us by controlling our perceptions and our sense of what is possible and what is not. As Foucault (1979, p. 272) expresses it, "power and knowledge directly imply one another.... there is no power relation without the correlative constitution of a field of knowledge, nor any knowledge that does not presuppose and constitute at the same time power relations."

The concept of power and knowledge as inextricably bound is one thread that runs through Foucault's many publications; another thread is his concept of "limit-experiences," which he deliberately sought for himself and which ultimately led to his death.

Insanity, Sadomasochism, and the Limit-Experience

Foucault believed that traditional conceptions of reality need to be challenged and opposed; one technique for doing this is to seek out the *limit-experience*. The limit-experience is a kind of "edgework" that tests the boundaries of ordered reality (Lyng, 1990). The madman is thus a hero of sorts, someone who has (perhaps involuntarily) risked everything to experience alternative worlds. Foucault himself often balanced on the edge of what others might call insanity, deliberately pushing his mind and body to the breaking point. By stretching human experience to its outermost limits, Foucault hoped to arrive at a reality that transcended the conventional dichotomies of consciousness and unconsciousness, life and death, reason and madness, pleasure and pain, and truth and fiction (Irwin, 1970).

Foucault was not oblivious to the potential dangers that awaited those who defied the rule of rationality. Transgression is not always liberating. In Foucault's terms, a sexually predatory deviant such as the Marquis de Sade evades the "Castle of Conscience" only to find himself in the "Castle of Murders," an equally confining space. De Sade was caught up in an endless cycle of transgression, confinement, and "repeated non-existence of gratification" (Foucault, 1962, pp. 247, 504). In this, as in all his written work, Foucault exposes the "asylums" of our lives without handing us any key.

Foucault and Panoptical Discipline

In *Discipline and Punish* (1979), Foucault documents the historical transition from punishment by means of public torture and execution to punishment by means of imprisonment. Although the prison was ostensibly a product of rational humanitarianism (more kindness and respect, less pain), Foucault sees it as a form of coercion all the more insidious for its apparent benevolence. The terror of preclassical coercion

---

Box 12.5 Foucault, Madness, and the Enlightenment

In *Madness and Civilization* (1962), Foucault traces the history of mental illness in European society. In the Middle Ages, up to about 1500, people with mental illnesses were neglected but free from the constraints of rationality and civilization. After 1500, they were increasingly placed in asylums, where they were "cared for" but also contained and constrained. Although the confinement of people with mental illnesses continued and was seen by the time of the eighteenth century as a humane application of scientific knowledge, from Foucault's perspective, the ideology of rationality that characterized this period simply represented a different and more insidious form of social control through which people were snatched from the free chaos of insanity and dropped into the "enclosed anguish of responsibility" (Foucault, 1962, pp. 247, 504). Foucault's view of Enlightenment rationality as a psychological straitjacket is a pervasive theme in the work of anti-psychiatrists like R. D. Laing, David Cooper, and Thomas Szasz.

---

was replaced by a mechanism of power that produced discipline rather than reform. What it also produced was the criminal, a pathologized individual requiring (so authorities believed) increased surveillance and control (Foucault, 1979, p. 277).

According to Foucault, the prison was only one institution that reflected the dominant coercion of rationality. All major institutions of society exhibited parallel processes of panoptical (as conceived by Bentham) discipline. Authorities in schools, factories, and army barracks established panoptical rules and regulations concerning efficient use of time, attention to tasks, proper deference, dress, cleanliness, and sexual decency. Panoptical discipline produced "docile bodies," obedient people drained of creative energy (Miller, 1993, pp. 15, 222).

A History of Sexuality and the Limit-Experience

In his unfinished *A History of Sexuality* (1978), Foucault argues that although the discipline associated with social control (the panopticon model) drives pleasure out of our "docile bodies," it cannot prevent it from reappearing "transmogrified" in fantasies where it can feed new ways of self-creation. *A History of Sexuality* also addresses the way in which the regulation of sexuality masks more insidious forms of social control. Foucault points out, for example, how antimasturbation campaigns, although doomed to failure vis-à-vis their ostensible goal of eradicating masturbation, succeeded in achieving their actual goal of increased surveillance of children (Foucault, 1978, p. 42).

Box 12.6   The Transgressions of Pierre Rivière

I, Pierre Rivière, Having Slaughtered My Mother, My Sister, and My Brother is a book Foucault compiled for use in his class (Foucault, 1975). Most of the book consists of Rivière's own account of his life and what his actions meant to him, but it also includes medical testimony, newspaper articles, witness accounts, legal testimony, and judges' opinions. In 1835, Rivière killed his pregnant mother, his sister, and his brother in an orgy of violence and mutilation. He then welcomed his own execution as expiation for his sins and a release from his resentments. The court, however, judged him insane, and commuted his death sentence to life in prison. Five years later he managed to hang himself.

Foucault saw this man as a "tragic hero" who faced the abyss between living within the restrictions of normalcy and taking the leap into the terrifying chaos of unregulated use of power. Rivière represented, within Foucault's interpretation, a person whose transgression illuminated the ambiguousness of the line between the permissible and the outlawed, and the connection among repression, transgression, sacrifice, and ordained punishment (Miller, 1993, p. 228). *I, Pierre Rivière ...* reproduces the conflicting discourses produced by Rivière, the medical experts, the legal experts, the media, and finally, Foucault himself, as each of these discourses attempt to make sense of Rivière's actions. For Foucault, Rivière's account does not explain his behaviour but is in fact part of the crime (Foucault, 1975, p. 83).

Foucault and the Gay Community

Members of the gay community have looked in vain to Foucault's work for support that would link being gay to some kind of essentialist position or link it with important people of the past who engaged in what are now considered gay practices. Foucault believed that biological interpretations of "gay" existence were merely another form of the discourse of positive science, which, by naming and knowing the homosexual, turns this person into an object of power. For Foucault, sexuality is something that individuals create in their everyday experimentation with sex and pleasure. It is not a reality to be found in the body or in some physical sign. It can be a means of self-creation and resistance.

Foucault also felt that each historical period was a separate reality, such that Plato, Michelangelo, or Sappho, for example, is not an ancestor of today's gay. Thus, although Foucault often participated in activities that helped homosexuals who had become entangled with the law, and did not deny his homosexual activities, he was reluctant to call himself a gay person or to work for gay organizations (this issue is covered at length throughout Miller's 1993 biography and is also discussed from a slightly different point of view in Gallagher and Wilson [1987]). Although very much concerned with the nature of ethical conduct, Foucault regarded all ethical standards as spuriously grounded in the "modernist enterprise" and saw them as dangerous in their potential for repression. Foucault did not offer an alternative, other than the reality of the experience of the moment or the dream (Bernauer & Mahon, 1994, p. 142).

BEYOND POSTMODERNISM: DANGERIZATION

AND DEVIANCE

Recent work by Stuart Henry and Dragan Milovanovic (1996, 1999) ventures beyond Foucault and other postmodernists. This approach agrees with the postmodernists that modernism (exemplified by positivism and control theory, for example) is too committed to the views and interests of power holders. It also accepts the postmodernist position that deconstruction can be used to undo modernist thought and reveal its contradictions and assumptions. Henry and Milovanovic, however, argue that the knowledge that humans coproduce the world they live in does not have to be an endless regression of skeptical deconstruction. They argue for an affirmative position: if we understand how the harmful reality is created, we can find ways to replace it.

In *Constitutive Criminology*, Henry and Milovanovic suggest the development of "replacement discourses" (Henry & Milovanovic, 1996, pp. x–xi), whereby deviance and crime are transformed from violations of the norms (the modernist position) to objectively discernable uses of power in ways that harm, impair, or destroy others. Examples of replacement discourse might be found, for example, with respect to transgendered people, who now have a discourse of liberation to free them from the pathologized place made for them in the modern period (Finn & Dell, 1999).

Similarly, childless women now have access to recognized discourses of radical feminine identity that can potentially free them from the modernist discourses that conflate femininity with motherhood (Gillespie, 2000).

We can also see how replacement discourses among Blacks, Aboriginals, and other marginalized populations can displace the discourses that deviantize and even criminalize their resistance to the hegemonic dominance of White, middle-class, and (often) patriarchal forms (Clarke, 2000). Other examples cited by Henry and Milovanovic are Barak's *newsmaking criminology* (the practice of using criminology to subvert the dominant media images of crime and deviance) and the practice of *narrative therapy* as a way to encourage those involved in dysfunctional families to reconstitute themselves by constructing liberating life narratives (Lanier & Henry, 1998, pp. 284–285).

Replacement discourse may be threatening to the established realities, and it may potentially become a new kind of problematic discourse. An example of this can be found in John Fekete's best-selling *Moral Panic: Biopolitics Rising* (1995), in which he argues that the biopolitical discourse over violence against women has reached the status of moral panic at Canadian universities and is fostering a harmful suppression of thought and speech (Fekete, 1995). Whether political correctness is empowerment or repression may depend on the standpoint of the observer.

THE RISK SOCIETY: DANGERIZATION AND EXCLUSION

The term "risk society" entered the sociological language through the work of Ulrich Beck (1987, 1992a, 1992b, 1997, 1999) and Beck, Giddens, & Lash (1994). For Beck, late modernity (that is, the present time) is characterized by new forms of threat and empowerment that are having a profound effect on the way in which we evaluate and respond to the possibility of harm. Although the foundational phases of capitalism were mainly concerned with the distribution of goods to the top of society, little concern was shown for the massive costs and risks borne by the voiceless multitudes at the bottom. There was little discourse on the subject of uncontrolled or uncontrollable risks. All that has changed. Environmental pollution, workplace hazards, and criminal violence may still disproportionately affect those who are at the bottom, but now the risks are more evenly distributed. Risk is no longer an acceptable cost of doing business.

Occurring along with these changes has been a change in the popular understanding of the role of elites and experts. Experts cannot reassure us, because we do not really believe them—we rely more on our feelings, intuitions, and media infotainment. This, in turn, is heavy on dramatic and untypical extreme cases and uses experts only as 20-second sound bites. Political leaders are now more like "instructed delegates" who use experts to find out what the public will believe and support (Brodeur,

1999; Wood & Shearing, 1999), not what will be most beneficial to society (Flanagan, 1987, pp. 403–443; Rosenau, 1992).

Beck seems to welcome the challenge posed by a distrustful, disrespectful citizenry when it is directed at experts' opinions about environmental dangers or at unaccountable politicians, but he does not consider the negative effect that such "risk angst" (Rigakos, 1999) may have. Overall, are more alert to dangers such as pedophiles and predators than previous generations were, and we unrealistically want these risks reduced to zero. Michalis Lianos and Mary Douglas (2000) speak of the resulting "dangerization" as meaning the "end of deviance." By this, they mean that deviance (moral) is replaced by risk (probability). We are increasingly seeking security by "systems, strategies and tactics based on suspicion and backed by [risk] probabilities" that, in effect, divide our world into safe and unsafe contexts. Society relies increasingly on automated systems of access. Social control in society is based on auditing principles (like those used by insurance companies) that help us to decide whom to trust and how much. The result is the deepening of segregation, avoidance, and self-restriction that increases our fear of those people whom we have made strangers.

Just as was true for Foucault's work, the correctional system is a model for dangerization. There, we see an increasing reliance on "the new penology," which groups inmates by their abstract risk-assessment measures and results in a well-run system that no longer worries much about justice, rehabilitation, or human values. This notion of safety is paradoxical. The more excluding systems we create, the less safe we feel, and, the less safe we feel, the more we engage in social exclusion (Young, 1999).

NOT IN MY BACK YARD

One area in which the fears of the risk society are clearly visible is in the not in my back yard (NIMBY) responses of all but the most anomic communities to LULUs (locally unwanted land uses). The NIMBY response is framed in a discourse that, varying little between one community and another or between one threat and another, treats marginalized people as uniquely, factually, and permanently dangerous. It treats the siting of any service for the homeless, criminals, troubled youths, people with AIDS, the psychiatrized, or even different racial groups as an unacceptable risk to neighbourhood security, property values, social status, and lifestyles or an inequitable imposition on powerless communities and an unwarranted extension of human rights to people who do not deserve them (Balin, 1999; Takahashi, 1999; Woo, 1997). NIMBY discourse finds no reassurance in "probabilistic risk analysis," the language of science and experts (Bier, 1999; Slovic, 1999). Instead, it favours worst-case scenario possibilities, anecdotal evidence, and moral exclusion. It defines community in an exclusionary, privatized way (Champlin, 1998).

NIMBY discourse justifies categorical exclusion of "people like them" from "decent" residential spaces. Overall, the NIMBY literature documents the repeated re-creation of the NIMBY arguments with respect to risk and equity in social loads

(Lake, 1994; Takahashi, 1999) and quality of life, focusing on moral and physical hazards to children and effects on community self-image and prestige (Belkin, 1999; Benzby-Miller, 1988).

For at least four reasons, we can expect this conflict over acceptable siting to intensify (Deutschmann, 2000), as will the problems of exclusion-generated deviance (Finer & Nellis, 1998). First, increasing numbers of stigmatized persons have substantial needs for supervision and support. We cannot go back to relying on the extended family and community to help these people, backed by the infrequent use of custodial measures—there are too few families and communities capable of this and far too many people needing them. This increase is fed by the use of criminalizaton and related stigmatizing tools to deal with all sorts of social problems, including homelessness, mental illness, and cultural divergence (Fischer, 1992; Taylor, 1997).

Second, greater public cynicism exists about rehabilitation (Martinson, 1974), unwarranted though it may be (Gendreau, 1981), and zero-tolerance anti-crime and anti-disorder initiatives have more support, even though research has shown these initiatives to be ineffective unless coupled with strong reintegrative support. Offenders and people with mental illnesses are increasingly constructed in the public mind as incurable moral monsters (Sloop, 1996). Those who have been constructed as criminals and deviants become the human toxic waste that no community wants. With respect to ex-offenders, this construction of danger is exacerbated by highly inflammatory community notification policies (Bedarf, 1995; Earl-Hubbard, 1996). When coupled with the "attrition of parole" (Brodeur, 1990), such practices make re-entry more, rather than less, problematic.

Third, the rising cost of even temporary warehousing in large institutions is an incentive to increasing deinstitutionalization. Finally, an increasing number of services, such as landfills, toxic waste sites, nuclear energy plants, airport runways, and homes for addicts, refugees, AIDS victims, and others are considered LULUs.

In skeptical postmodern critical theory (Baudrillard, Foucault), the gap between NIMBY and other ways of understanding siting conflicts is irresolvable, since there is no way out of the spiral of relativism that renders every set of ideas equal to every other, so that truth claims based on experience carry no more weight than truth claims based on wild guesses, fear, or cynical political strategy. Skeptical postmodernism accepts the presence of conflicting, irreconcilable, or incommensurable discourses but provides no footing from which to construct any higher-level alternative. Constitutive criminology's affirmative postmodernism allows for the possibility of developing humanistic replacement discourses that have a real effect in the world, even if they, too, could be subjected to ongoing deconstruction and reformulation.

Box 12.7 Not in *My* Back Yard: The Fortress Society

In response to the heightened awareness of danger in the "risk society," emulation of "privatopias" and a "fortressing" of communities is increasing. Less social space is seen as public and more is private (Blakely & Snyder, 1997). Within gated communities, a Durkheimian escalation of deviance occurs, whereby dandelions on the lawn or cars parked in the driveway become unacceptable violations of the rules (Whwang, 2000). Wexford Plantation on Hilton Head Island allows no one in who is not accompanied by a property owner, has closed circuit monitoring of all its roads, and, like the six other Hilton Head Plantations that comprise the Island, has its own gun-carrying deputized officers. In Las Colinas (near Dallas) the entire town is privatized and the town square is a privately owned mall (Owens, 1997). Hidden Hills, formerly a suburb of Los Angeles, became the first U.S. gated city when, in 1961, it incorporated itself but left its gates and private homeowners association in place. City Hall stands outside the gates, partly so that outsiders will not have an excuse to enter the city. "If people could get into town just by saying 'we're going to city hall,' " explains city attorney Amanda Susskind, "then the residents of Hidden Hills would have no security" (Stark, 1998). If security rests, as Giddens (1990, pp. 35–36) claims, "on a balance of trust and acceptable risk," this balance has been increasingly lost. Thus, we can predict that the conflict between the current practice of siting social services in neighbourhoods will continue to produce vigorous NIMBY resistance.

SUMMARY

The theories discussed in this chapter differ from other theories in stressing the role of differential power in the establishment of the categories of deviance and their application to disadvantaged groups. These theories raise the question of whose interests are served by the existence and use of deviance labels, and their answers often suggest that it is the social order rather than the deviant that needs to be transformed. Some of these theories are more optimistic than others in assessing the prospects for a non-hierarchical social order—one in which one group does not have its own interests served at the expense of other groups. By extension, conflict, critical, and postmodern theories as a whole are ambivalent about the possibility of either a world without deviance or a world in which deviance definitions are no longer wielded as a weapon of power. No recent theorists have claimed that the solution to this use of power will be as simple as a political revolution led by or on behalf of the "textual outlaw."

Change in the processes of deviantization will require a fundamental transformation of social consciousness. It seems appropriate to observe here that, until the postmodernists begin to write in more accessible language, the average citizen will unlikely even be aware of this challenge to common beliefs and understandings. In the meantime, Marilyn Porter's (1995, p. 430) observation that "unlike Marxism or feminism, postmodernism is *not* rooted in involvement outside the academy and it is manifestly *not* informed by commitment or passion" poses the serious challenge to postmodernists that they should link their critiques to a constructive program. In the meantime, many social processes that lead to "dangerization" in replacement for deviance are changing the nature of modern life.

STUDY QUESTIONS

1. Conflict theory, like functionalism, is theory posed at a structural level. It looks at the influence of social structure (the arrangement of social roles, emphasizing inequality). To what extent is a structural theory compatible with a micro-level theory such as symbolic interaction? Can you imagine integrating these approaches?

2. Do you find conflict theory upsetting? Can you explain why some people find that it makes them angry?

3. What is the difference between "value neutrality" and "praxis"? Is it possible to do both?

4. How did Willem Bonger connect Marxist economic theory to the issues of crime and deviance in society?

5. How does structural Marxism differ from instrumental Marxism? Which of these Marxist variations can explain why some corporations and some white-collar offenders are disciplined for their cheating and exploitation?

6. What does hegemony mean? Which represents hegemony better, the civics class that teaches about obedience and loyalty or the armed police at a public demonstration?

7. Richard Quinney, like John Hagan (Chapter 11), has developed many different theoretical variations of conflict theory. Is it better to develop one theory as far as it will go, or is it better to test different perspectives?

8. In what sense was the early "new criminology" too idealistic? How does left realism correct for this?

9. What is "discursive analysis" (analysis of discourse)? How do hermeneutics and deconstruction assist in this?

10. Is discourse always verbal?

11. How does the sociological analysis of structure differ from the linguistic analysis of structure (semiotics)?

12. Why is postmodern writing intriguing but hard to understand?

13. How does Foucault's idea of panopticon differ from Bentham's original proposal?

14. Why should we be concerned about increasing fortification of the "exclusive society"?

REFERENCES

Acland, C. R. (1995). *Youth, Murder, Spectacle: The Cultural Politics of "Youth in Crisis."* Boulder, CO: Westview.

Agger, B. (1991). Critical Theory, Poststructuralism and Postmodernism: Their Sociological Relevance. *Annual Review of Sociology, 17,* 105–131.

Balin, J. (1999). *A Neighborhood Divided: Community Resistance to an AIDS Care Facility.* Ithaca, NY: Cornell University Press.

Baudrillard, J. (1995). The Gulf War Did Not Take Place. Translated by P. Patton. Bloomington, IN: Indiana University Press.

Beck, U. (1987). The Anthropological Shock: Chernobyl and the Counters of the Risk Society. *Berkeley Journal of Sociology, 32,* 153–165.

———. (1992a). Modern Society as Risk Society. In N. Stehr & R. Ericson (Eds.), *The Culture and Power of Knowledge: Inquiries into Contemporary Societies* (pp. 199–214).

———. (1992b). *The Risk Society.* London, UK: Sage.

———. (1997). *The Reinvention of Politics: Rethinking Modernity in the Global Social Order* (M. Ritter, Trans.). Cambridge, UK: Polity Press.

———. (1999). *World Risk Society.* Cambridge, UK: Polity Press.

Beck, U., Giddens, A., & Lash, S. (1994). *Reflexive Modernization: Politics, Tradition and Aesthetics in the Modern Social Order.* Cambridge, UK: Polity Press.

Bedarf, A. (1995). Examining Sex Offender Community Notification Laws. *California Law Review, 83,* 884–923.

Belkin, L. (1999). *Show Me a Hero.* Boston: Little, Brown.

Benzby-Miller, S. (1990). Community Corrections and the NIMBY Syndrome. *Forum on Corrections Research.* [On-Line]. Available: <www.csc.scc.gc.ca/text/pblct/forum/index_e>.

Bernauer, J. W., & Mahon, M. (1994). The Ethics of Michel Foucault. In G. Gutting (Ed.), *The Cambridge Companion to Foucault.* Cambridge, UK: Cambridge University Press.

Bier, V. M. (1999). Challenges to the Acceptance of Probabilistic Risk Analysis. *Risk Analysis, 19*(4), 703–710.

Blakely, E., & Snyder, M. G. (1997). *Fortress America: Gated Communities in the United States.* Washington, DC: Brookings Institution Press.

Bonger, W. (1916). *Criminality and Economic Conditions.* Boston: Little, Brown.

Brodeur, J.-P. (1990). The Attrition of Parole. *Canadian Journal of Criminology,* (July), 503–510.

———. (1999). Disenchanted Criminology. *Canadian Journal of Criminology, 41*(2), 131–136.

Burrington, D. (1994). Constructing the Outlaw, Outing the Law, and Throwing Out the Law. *Utah Law Review, 2,* 255–267.

Chambliss, W., & Seidman, R. (1982). *Law, Order and Power* (2nd ed.). Reading, MA: Addison-Wesley.

Champlin, D. (1998). The Privatization of Community: Implications for Urban Policy. *Journal of Economic Issues, 32,* 595–604.

Clarke, P. D. (2000). Land of the East Wind: Mise en Forme d'une Mémoire Mi'qmaq (Formation of a Mi'qmaq Memory). *Canadian Review of Sociology and Anthropology, 37*(2 May), 167–195.

Cohen, S. (Ed.). (1971). *Images of Deviance*. Harmondsworth, UK: Penguin.

———. (1985). *Visions of Social Control: Crime, Punishment and Classification*. Cambridge, UK: Polity Press.

Collins, H. (1984). *Marxism and Law*. New York: Oxford University Press.

Danaher, G., Shirato, T., & Webb, J. (2000). *Understanding Foucault*. London, UK: Sage.

DeKeseredy, W. (2000). *Women, Crime and the Canadian Criminal Justice System*. Cincinnati, OH: Anderson.

DeKeseredy, W., Alvi, S., & Ellis, D. (1993). *Contemporary Social Problems in North America*. Toronto: Addison Wesley Longman.

DeKeseredy, W., & Schwartz, M. D. (1991). British Left Realism on the Abuse of Women: A Critical Appraisal. In R. Quinney & H. Pepinsky (Eds.), *Criminology as Peace Making* (154–171). Bloomington, IN: Indiana University Press.

Deutschmann, L. (2000, November). *Not in My Back Yard and the Reintegration of Offenders: Discourses of Rejection and Inclusion in the Risk Society*. Paper presented at the conference of the American Society of Criminology, San Francisco, CA.

Dowie, M. (1991). *"Pinto Madness." Deviant Behavior and Human Rights*. Englewood Cliffs, NJ: Prentice-Hall.

Earl-Hubbard, M. (1996). The Child Sex Offender Registration Laws: The Punishment, Liberty, Deprivation and Unintended Results Associated with the Scarlet Letter Laws of the 1990s. *Northwestern University Law Review, 90*(2), 788–862.

Edwards, P. K., & Scullion, H. (1982). Deviancy Theory and Industrial Praxis: A Study of Discipline and Social Control in an Industrial Setting. *Sociology, 16*(3 August), 322–340.

Fekete, J. (1995). *Moral Panic: Biopolitics Rising (Food for Thought)* (2nd ed.). Montreal: Robert Davies.

Ferrell, J. (1993). *Crimes of Style, Urban Graffiti and the Politics of Criminality*. New York: Garland.

Ferrell, J. & Sanders, C. R. (1995). *Cultural Criminology*. Boston: Northeastern University Press.

Finer, C. J., & Nellis, M. (Eds.). (1998). *Crime and Social Exclusion*. Oxford, UK: Blackwell.

Finn, M., & Dell, P. (1999). Practices of Body Management: Transgenderism and Embodiment. *Journal of Community and Applied Social Psychology, 9*(6 November–December), 463–476.

Fischer, P. (1992). The Criminalization of the Homeless. In M. J. Robertson & M. Greenblatt (Eds.), *Homelessness: A National Perspective*. New York: Plenum.

Flanagan, S. C. (1987). Value Change in Industrial Society. *American Political Science Review, 81,* 1303–1319.

Foucault, M. (1962). *Madness and Civilization*. New York: Pantheon.

———. (1970). *The Order of Things*. London, UK: Tavistock.

———. (1975). *I, Pierre Rivière, Having Slaughtered My Mother, My Sister, and My Brother* (F. Jellinek, Trans.). Lincoln, NE: University of Nebraska Press.

———. (1978). *A History of Sexuality: An Introduction*. London, UK: Allen Lane.

———. (1979). *Discipline and Punish*. New York: Vintage.

Gallagher, B., & Wilson, A. (1987). Sex and the Politics of Identity: An Interview with Michel Foucault. In M. Thompson (Ed.), *Gay Spirit: Myth and Meaning*. New York: St. Martin's Press, Stonewall Inn Editions.

Galliher, J. F. (1991). *Deviant Behavior and Human Rights*. Englewood Cliffs, NJ: Prentice-Hall.

Gendreau, P. (1981). Treatment in Corrections: Martinson Was Wrong. *Canadian Psychology, 22,* 332–338.

Geuss, R. (1981). *The Idea of a Critical Theory: Habermas and the Frankfurt School*. Cambridge, UK: Cambridge University Press.

Gillespie, R. (2000). When No Means No: Disbelief, Disregard and Deviance as Discourses of Voluntary Childlessness. *Women's Studies International Forum, 23*(2), 223–234.

Gramsci, A. (1971). *Selections from the Prison Notebooks of Antonio Gramsci*. New York: International Publishers.

Harvey, L. (1990). *Critical Social Research*. Englewood Cliffs, NJ: Prentice-Hall.

Henry, S. (1999). Constitutive Criminology. *Criminology, 29*(2), 293–316.

Henry, S., & Milovanovic, D. (1996). *Constitutive Criminology: Beyond Postmodernism*. Thousand Oaks, CA: Sage.

———. (Eds.). (1999). *Constitutive Criminology at Work*. Albany, NY: State University of New York.

Hirst, P. Q. (1972). Marx and Engels on Law, Crime and Morality. *Economy and Society, 1*(February), 25–56.

Irwin, J. (1970). *The Felon*. Englewood Cliffs, NJ: Prentice Hall.

Jary, D., & Jary, J. (1991). *The HarperCollins Dictionary of Sociology*. New York: HarperCollins.

Kinsman, G. (1987). *The Regulation of Desire: Sexuality in Canada*. Montreal: Black Rose.

Lacombe, D. (1996). Reforming Foucault: A Critique of the Social Control Thesis. *The British Journal of Sociology, 47*(2), 332–352.

Lake, R. W. (1994). Negotiating Local Autonomy. *Political Geography, 13*(5), 423–442.

Lanier, M., & Henry, S. (1998). *Essential Criminology*. Boulder, CO: Westview Press.

Lemert, C. C., & Gillan, G. (1982). *Michel Foucault: Social Theory and Transgression*. New York: Columbia University Press.

Leonard, W. N., & Weber, M. G. (1991). Automakers and Dealers: A Study of Criminogenic Market Forces. *Law and Society Review, 4*(February), 407–424.

Lianos, M., & Douglas, M. (2000). Dangerization and the End of Deviance. *British Journal of Criminology, 40*(2 Spring), 261–278.

Lynch, M. J. (1999). Working Together: Towards an Integrative Critical Criminological Model for Social Justice. *Humanity and Society, 23*(1 February), 68–78.

Lyng, S. (1990). Edgework: A Social Psychological Analysis of Voluntary Risk Taking. *American Journal of Sociology, 95*(4 January), 851–886.

McArthur, M. (1990). *I'd Rather Be Wanted Than Had.* Toronto: Stoddart.

Marcuse, H. (1965). Repressive Tolerance. In R. P. Wolff, B. Moore, Jr., and H. Marcuse (Eds.), *A Critique of Pure Tolerance.* Boston: Beacon Press.

Martinson, R. M. (1974). What Works? Questions and Answers about Prison Reform. *The Public Interest, 35,* 22–54.

Marx, K. (1987). *Capital: A Critique of Political Economy.* New York: International Publishers. (Original work published in 1867)

Melichar, K. E. (1988). Deconstruction: Critical Theory or an Ideology of Despair? *Humanity and Society, 12,* 366–385.

Miliband, R. (1969). *The State in Capitalist Society.* London, UK: Wiedenfeld and Nicholson.

Miller, J. (1993). *The Passion of Michel Foucault.* New York: Simon and Schuster.

Morera, E. (2000). Gramsci's Critical Modernity. *Rethinking Marxism, 12*(1 Spring), 16–46.

Mugford, S. K. (1974). Marxism and Criminology: A Comment on the Symposium Review. *Sociological Quarterly, 15*(Autumn), 591–596.

Owens, J. B. (1997). Westec Story: Gated Communities and the Fourth Amendment. *American Criminal Law Review, 34*(3 Spring), 1127–1160.

Pepinsky, H., & Quinney, R. (Eds.). (1991). *Criminology as Peacemaking.* Bloomington, IN: Indiana University Press.

Pfohl, S. (1992). *Death at the Parasite Café: Social Science (Fictions) and the Postmodern.* New York: St. Martin's.

Porter, M. (1995). Call Yourself a Sociologist—And You've Never Been Arrested?! *Canadian Review of Sociology and Anthropology, 32*(4), 415–437.

Praat, A. C., & Tuffin, K. F. (1996). Police Discourses of Homosexual Men in New Zealand. *Journal of Homosexuality, 31*(4), 57–73.

Quinney, R. (1970). *The Social Reality of Crime.* Boston: Little, Brown.

———. (1977). *Class, State, and Crime.* New York: McKay.

———. (2000). *Bearing Witness to Crime and Social Justice.* Series in Deviance and Social Control. Albany, NY: State University of New York Press.

Rigakos, G. S. (1999). Risk Society and Actuarial Criminology: Prospects for a Critical Discourse. *Canadian Journal of Criminology, 41*(2), 137+.

Rock, P. E. (1979). The Sociology of Crime, Symbolic Interactionism and Some Problematic Qualities of Radical Criminology. In D. Downes & P. Rock (Eds.), *Deviance and Social Control.* London, UK: Martin Robertson.

Rosenau, J. (1992). The Relocation of Authority in a Shrinking World. *Comparative Politics, 24*(3), 253–271.

Schwartz, M. D. (1991). The Future of Criminology. In B. McLean & D. Milovanovic (Eds.), *New Directions in Critical Criminology.* Vancouver: Collective Press.

Simons, P. (2000, April 23). We Still Need Our Scapegoats, It Seems. *Edmonton Journal,* p. E16.

Sloop, J. M. (1996). *The Cultural Prison: Discourse, Prisoners and Punishment.* Tuscaloosa, AL: University of Alabama Press.

Slovic, P. (1999). Trust, Emotion, Sex, Politics, and Science: Surveying the Risk-Assessment Battlefield. *Risk Analysis, 19*(4), 689–701.

Snider, L. (1992). Commercial Crime. In V. Sacco (Ed.), *Deviance: Conformity and Control in Canadian Society.* Scarborough, ON: Prentice-Hall.

Spencer, D. A. (2000). Braverman and the Contribution of Labor Process Analysis to the Critique of Capitalist Production: Twenty-Five Years On. *Work, Unemployment and Society, 14*(2 June), 223–243.

Stanley, C. (1995). Teenage Kicks: Urban Narratives of Dissent Not Deviance. *Crime, Law and Social Change, 2,* 91–119.

Stark, A. (1998). America, the Gated? *Wilson Quarterly, 22,* 58–80.

Takahashi, L. M. (1999). *Homelessness, AIDS and Stigmatization: The NIMBY Syndrome in the United States at the End of the Twentieth Century.* Oxford, UK: Clarendon Press.

Taylor, D. (1997). Social Control of Marginalized Populations: The Los Angeles Aggressive Panhandling Ordinance. *Criminology, Law and Society* (Winter).

Taylor, I., Walton, P., & Young, J. (1973). *The New Criminology: For a Social Theory of Deviance.* London, UK: Routledge and Keegan Paul.

———. (1975). *Critical Criminology.* London, UK: Routledge and Keegan Paul.

Thomas, J. (1984). Law and Social Praxis: Prisoner Civil Rights Litigation and Structural Mediations. *Research in Law, Deviance and Social Control, 6,* 141–170.

Tifft, L. & Sullivan, D. (1980). *The Struggle to Be Human: Crime, Criminology and Anarchism.* Orkney, UK: Cienfuegos Press.

Vold, G. (1958). *Theoretical Criminality.* New York: Oxford University Press.

Whwang, S. (2000, October 15). The Nouveau Web Riche/Silicon Valley: Lifestyles Out of Synch in Some Communities. *Houston Chronicle,* p. 5.

Woo, K. (1997, April 21). Examining the Issues Behind NIMBY Positions: Society. *Los Angeles Times,* p. 1.

Wood, J., & Shearing, C. (1999). Reinventing Intellectuals. *Canadian Journal of Criminology, 41*(2), 311+.

Young, J. (1971). *The Drugtakers: The Social Meaning of Drug Use.* London, UK: MacGibbon and Kee/Paladin.

———. (1999). *The Exclusive Society: Social Exclusion, Crime and Difference in Late Modernity.* Thousand Oaks, CA: Sage.

THE TRICKSTER THEME: FEMINISTS AND OTHER CREATIVE OR CHAOTIC SUBVERSIVES

In this chapter, we will revisit the materials we have viewed so far, not in the spirit of summary and completion, but in the spirit of examining what have we learned and how can we make the best use of it. At the end of the chapter, we will conclude by bringing the trickster (first discussed in Chapter 3) back in to show that all of this has been an exploration of order and chaos, good and evil, and reality constructed in the interests of the powerful.

Feminist writers (writers who, male or female, take the standpoint of women's interests in their work) have often complained that, in deviance texts, the chapters on women tend to be placed at or near the end, a placement that suggests their lack of importance (Daly, 1997; Young, 1996, p. 34). This complaint may be exaggerated, but evidence for it exists (Gelsthorpe & Morris, 1994). Other "outsiders"—the excluded and deviantized—may well have an even more justified complaint, but here we focus mainly on women. Throughout this book, the places where women's contributions have been ignored, underestimated, or even plagiarized by men (as in the Chicago School of the 1920s) have been documented, but like other groups, women have remained in the margins. The main story has been that of the dominant theories and themes about men and usually by men.

PREFEMINIST, FEMINIST, AND POSTFEMINIST THINKING ABOUT DEVIANT WOMEN

Traditionally, prefeminist theories of deviance have treated women mainly in two ways. In the first, they have assumed that what is true of men is either also true of women or else does not matter (Mark & Lesieur, 1992). In the second, females have been discussed in ways that emphasize individual moral, biological, or psychological abnormality (relative to men), and ignore the influence of gendered social conditions (Smith, 1995, pp. 113–114).

In prescientific theories, misogyny painted women as madonnas or witches, or ignored them as outside the "rational man" of classical thought. In early positivist theories, either female deviants are "normal" women, incapacitated by maternity and hormones, or they are "abnormal" women, masculinized and doubly deviant. In this material, women's deviance is associated with unsupported assumptions about feminine wiles, sexuality, irrationality, and low intelligence (Konopka, 1966). Functionalists praised the functionality of a sexist division of labour, seeing the pattern of the 1950s female homemaker and male breadwinner as a natural and effective form of social organization that defended itself by defining working women, single parents, and others as deviants. When interactionist theorists looked at women, most of them failed to recognize the power behind the constructed, predominantly male conception of normality (Schur, 1984). In labelling theories, women who behave and appear in ways that contravene social expectations are labelled deviant while those who accept these social expectations are regarded as inferior.

Through all of these theories, the image of women's deviance became increasingly depressing and "anemic." As Millman (1975, p. 251) expresses it, mainstream [modernist] theories of deviance

> have come to associate women with the dullest, most oppressive aspects
> of society, or else to view their deviance in narrowly sex-typed (and unap-
> pealing) terms, yet to see in our male deviants the expression of creativity
> and courage to stand up to society's hypocrisies.

Both early feminism and control theory propose that as women move out of domestic servitude, their crime and deviance will become more like men's. In particular, their rates of serious criminal activity will climb (Adler, 1975; Hagan & Kay, 1990; Simon, 1976). There is very little empirical evidence to support this. In power-control theory, women can either remain in the home and raise risk-averse daughters who will follow their example and commit themselves to the domestic role, or they can seek jobs with authority and raise risk-taking girls who will be judged delinquent for doing what their brothers do. Feminist thinkers, discussed below, are more likely to see the deviance of women as a product not of their emancipation but of their economic marginalization, continuing dependency, and increasing public presence where any deviance may be observed. Women in Canadian prisons are very rarely emancipated women—they are much more likely to have histories of violent victimization, sexual abuse, and actions taken to protect and support their men and their children (Austin, Bloom, & Donahue, 1992; Carlen, 1988).

Conflict theories have provided an arsenal of concepts that have helped illuminate women's position and potential in society. Although these concepts have greatly enriched feminist analyses, the overall treatment of women by many (noncritical) conflict theorists has been just as myopic as was true of earlier theorists. When conflict theories actually address the subject, it is usually only to express notions about women's lesser corruption due to their nonparticipation in the economy and their meagre abilities relative to those of men (Bonger, 1916, pp. 59–64). The new criminology included not a single word about women (Leonard, 1982, p. 176). The currently fashionable structuralism of Jacques Lacan posits a phallocentric universe that is immutable, thus providing no basis for women to challenge its hegemony (Fraser, 1992). The poststructuralism of Foucault demonstrates the power of *men* to construct their own reality but says nothing about women.

FEMINISM(S) AND CONFLICT THEORIES

Most feminist theories fall into categories that parallel "masculinist" (patriarchal) versions of conflict theory or postmodernist theory. Marxist conflict theories have provided the basis for Marxist feminist theories; pluralist conflict theories relate to liberal conflict feminist theories; and social constructionist and poststructuralist discourse theories correspond, at least in part, to radical feminist theories. Queer theory (explanation from the standpoint of gays, lesbians, and sometimes bisexuals and transsexuals) parallels the feminist branches of conflict theory (hooks, 1994; Seidman, 1994).

Box 13.1   Common Characteristics of Feminist Theories

Kathleen Daly and Meda Chesney-Lind (1988) outline five common characteristics of feminist theory:

1. *Gender is related to biological sex differences, but it is not simply derived from them.* Rather, gender is a complex social, historical, and cultural product. Feminists differ in the extent to which they feel that gender is related to essential differences between men and women as opposed to constructed differences.
2. *Gender relations are fundamental to the organization of social life and social institutions.* Any change in gender relations will necessitate change in many other aspects of life. Men will not inevitably lose if women gain, since the changes may improve life for men as well. For example, if women are freed from the need to be emotional, men may be freed from the need to deny their emotions.
3. *The present organization of gender roles does not reflect a symmetrical division of labour.* Gender relations constitute a hierarchical ordering in which men's roles are dominant and more highly rewarded than women's roles.
4. *The systems of knowledge we have inherited are those of men who held dominant positions in the social order.* Some theorists look behind this reality to uncover the ways in which inherited knowledge controls men even as it privileges them over women.
5. *Women should not be peripheral, invisible, or mere appendages to men in the development of knowledge.* In fact, they should be at the centre of intellectual inquiry. For some feminists, this means that women should no longer be marginalized in the academic world; for others it means that they should be given privileged places within it.

MARXIST FEMINIST THEORIES

Although they diverge in many ways, Marxists and Marxist feminists have in common a belief that social class (economic position), as a variable, is more fundamental than gender (Simpson & Elis, 1994). Gender relations, Marxist feminists feel, will be resolved once the central issue of class relations is resolved. From their perspective, women's position in society is a consequence of the hierarchical power relations of capitalism. These relations objectify women by assigning them social roles that serve dominant male interests (interests that are themselves created and maintained by the system).

In the Marxist view, female deviance and crime (and the deviance of youths raised by single mothers) result from women's marginalized economic position within both the legitimate world and the world of crime. Women in a capitalist-patriarchal system are less criminal because, in such a system, the most serious crimes are those that reinforce male dominance and privilege via aggression (Messerschmidt, 1986). When men are freed from oppressive capitalist relations, women, the doubly oppressed, will also be freed. Marxist feminists use the Marxist paradigm to argue for revolutionary changes in the political economy of nations and to combat what they view as the "false consciousness" of groups like Real Women that enshrine the traditional female role and support the patriarchal hegemony that sustains the capitalist system.

LIBERAL CONFLICT FEMINIST THEORIES

Liberal conflict feminists see gender as one among many valid, competing categories in society, others of which are class, ethnicity, and race. This approach parallels pluralist conflict theory. Containing and balancing these overlapping interests can and does at times give rise to intense stress within this part of the feminist movement. Such was the case when a women's hostel in Toronto was rocked by a political coup staged by women of colour within the organization. In the resulting media frenzy, the reputations of many people were shredded by charges of racism, lesbianism, emotional instability, greed, and ingratitude. Similar strains have emerged over issues like pornography and prostitution, which have different meanings for women at different levels in the economic system—for some, participation in these activities is seen as a choice and a way of making a living, while for others, pornography and prostitution are seen as the worst sort of capitulation to exploitation and oppression (Bell, 1987).

Liberal conflict feminists are further characterized by their support for initiatives designed to improve women's position within the existing structure rather than to overthrow the system. Thus, they advocate "fixes" such as employment equity (job quotas), provision of daycare for working mothers, better education for women, and less streaming of women into domesticity or caring professions. This form of feminism tends to attract moderates who target specific injustices and practices for remediation (e.g., laws that punish prostitutes but not their customers and the differential treatment of girls in sports) but who do not challenge the system as a whole and often reject the label "feminist."

RADICAL FEMINIST THEORIES

Radical theories and postmodernist theories raise the possibility of liberating understandings of deviance and control but also go beyond what is tested and clearly attainable.

Non-Marxist radical feminists share in common with postmodernism their emphasis on the importance of language in constructing differences between men and women. These theorists tend to challenge the rules, especially those that define appropriate gender roles. On a small scale, Carolyn Heilbrun challenges the stereotype of the "good girl" through her fiction when she has her detective heroine engage in a number of vices (Heilbrun, 1988, p. 122).

Mary Daly (1978) has gone much further than this in developing not only a radical feminist philosophy but also a completely new language (with its own dictionary) in which to express it. You may note some similarities between Daly's work and the passage quoted from Stephen Pfohl in Chapter 12. The need to tell a new story using the old grammatical and semiotic forms creates a tension in the work. In her autobiographical book, *Outercourse* (1992, p. 1), Daly describes her many battles with the omnipresent powers of patriarchal authority.

> As I Re-member my own intellectual voyage as a Radical Feminist Philosopher, I am intensely aware of the struggle to stay on my True Course, despite under mining by demons of distraction that have seemed always to be attempting to pull me off course. These I eventually Discovered and Named as agents and institutions of patriarchy, whose intent was to keep me—and indeed all living be-ings—within a stranglehold of the foreground, that is, fatherland. My True Course was and is Outercourse moving beyond the imprisoning mental, physical, emotional, spiritual walls of patriarchy, the State of Possession. Insofar as I am focused

Box 13.2   Coming Out

When Queen Victoria affixed her signature in 1885 to a law prohibiting homosexuality between men, she brooked no suggestion that it be expanded to include females. Women, she said flatly, simply did not do such things.

They did, of course, but laws weren't needed to render them invisible. Sexual and social mores did that, and, to a large extent, still do....

A lot of young, politicized lesbians wonder where the payback is for their participation in the women's movement. Where are the feminists when gay bookstores are targeted by Canada Customs, raided by police, and lesbian pornography—made by, with, and for women—is ruled obscene.

"Feminists accuse us of copying males in our porn," says Toronto writer Sue Campbell. "But if we don't have our own images, we'll never have our own freedom."

Source: From Lynda Hurst, "Coming Out," *The Toronto Star,* June 26, 1993, p. D1. Reprinted with permission—The Toronto Star Syndicate.

on Outercoursing, naturally I am surrounded and aided by the benevolent forces of the Background.

In Daly's vocabulary, "foreground" is a "male-centred and monodimensional arena where fabrication, objectification, and alienation take place; zone of fixed feelings, perceptions, behaviours; the elementary world: FLATLAND." This in turn refers to yet more definitions that express the vision that is not expressible within the language as it exists. Background, on the other hand, refers to "the Realm of Wild Reality: the Homeland of women's Selves and of all other Others; the Time/Space where auras of plants, planets, stars, animals and all Other animate beings interconnect" (Daly, 1992, p. 1). Like Dorothy Smith, Daly believes that there is a deviantized "woman's standpoint" and that this standpoint is more inclusive and, therefore, superior to the male standpoint that excludes and demeans it (Smith, 1973).

POSTMODERNISM AND FEMINISM: IS THERE A POSTFEMINIST POSITION?

Premodern and modern theories tended to place everything into dualistic categories of good/bad, male/female, science/nature, normal/abnormal, order/chaos, and so on, with each duality dominated by the first element in the pair (Martinez, 1994; Smith, 1973). When faced with the entirely subversive enterprise of postmodernist deconstruction, these fixed categories are revealed as controlling and absurd (Jervis, 1999). Postmodernism, like the trickster, appeals to us with humour and play, frightens us with the possibility of chaos, and shakes up our fixed opinions about nearly everything.

Postmodernism, by exposing the imposing "canon" of patriarchal modernist approaches and highlighting its exclusions and distortions, has fit well with the deconstructionist part of the feminist agenda. Feminists have been quick to seize, for example, on the deconstruction of biological discourse, even though the pioneers of this approach, such as Foucault, were not interested in its application to women. Postmodernism challenges the long-held assumptions (from Lombroso through to Polk and Freud) that women's biology makes them unfit for full inclusion in the public world, that men seek status and women seek men, that men must be freed from capitalism before women can be free, and so on.

Postmodern deconstruction allowed recognition that the dominant modernist theories distorted and demeaned the experience of excluded or subordinated lives: the lives of women (largely), and the lives of Aboriginals, Blacks, gays, and others. An example of this distortion is Kohlberg's theory of moral development (see Chapter 6), whereby the woman who reaches the phase that includes both the *ethic of responsibility* and the *ethic of rights* achieves the same "high" moral rank as the male who achieves only the latter (Gilligan, 1982). By showing the direction that a full inclusion of subordinated themes might take, we can begin to imagine what a noncanonical, liberating study of deviance might look like. At the same time, we should not underestimate the difficulty of achieving a fully integrative discipline.

The main problem of postmodernism, though, as shown in the work of Foucault, is that it is very good at deconstructing but has (thus far) no mechanism for the production of alternative (replacement) discourses that would be less damaging or more liberating. When postmodern writers challenge the "essentialist" idea that women are fundamentally different in inherent ways, they seem to undermine the very principle on which feminist organizing is done. As Hrdy (1981, p. 190) notes, if there are in fact

> no important differences between males and females in intelligence, initiative, or administrative and political capacities ... [then] the feminist ideal of a sex less egotistical, less competitive by nature, less interested in dominance, a sex that will lead us back to "the golden age of queendoms, when peace and justice prevailed on earth," is a dream that may not be well founded.

Ultimately, we need understandings of behaviour that are not just versions of patriarchy or any other system of dominance. These may take the form of a new "replacement discourse" based on a universalistic notion of "justice," based on the "person" apart from such details as gender, race, and culture (Lyman, 1995, p. 225) or find some other basis that cannot be deconstructed as a biased form of power manipulation.

THE TRICKSTER HAS THE LAST WORD

Trickster discourse has been recognized, mainly in postmodern works, as a way of illuminating or disrupting our ideas about fundamental aspects of life: the nature of human identity (the trickster is a shape-shifter, embodying many aspects of other beings while remaining itself), gender (the trickster is often superficially male but also disconcertingly female; neither and both), respectability (the trickster is a god and a fool, powerful and clumsy, greedy and sexual, never respectable), and above all, rationality (the trickster is rational only when this is unexpected).

As noted by (lesbian) writer Shane Phelan (1996, pp. 130–131), the strength of postmodernist theory lies in its "coyoteness." It is not surprising then, that the trickster appears, in one form or another, in much of the feminist, lesbian, gay/queer, Aboriginal, and Black literature that is increasingly penetrating the mainstream— bringing with it its chaotic and creative force for change. For example, H. L. Gates (1989) describes the Black literary tradition as a trickster discourse that is contestatory, multivocal, mulilayered, and ironic. This is exemplified in the work of Audre Lorde (1982). The Aboriginal tradition has been revived in the works of Vizenor (1993), King (1993), and others (Lowe, 1996; C. Smith, 1997), including artists (Ryan, 1999) who use the trickster as an indigenously based way to challenge the forces of assimilation and dominance. Other "ethnic outsiders" have also found voice this way (J. R. Smith, 1997).

Within feminism, trickster discourse not only subverts patriarchy but also helps to challenge the forces that would create a "feminist thought police" to enforce some sort of orthodoxy among feminists. Among gender outlaws (bisexuals, transsexuals, and others), it opens up other ways of being whole and supports resistance to being labelled, categorized, and objectified.

It is not necessary to belong to an outsider category to find the trickster idea a form for creativity and liberation. This can be seen in the plays and writings of Joyce, Becket, and Orton (Rusinko, 1995). These cultural representations of the trickster in life do not focus on deviance as such, but it is clear that the trickster is the archetypical deviant. Coyote is scorned as a pest but survives. Deviance is scorned and reviled, and dangerous to embrace, but it shakes us up and allows us to experience a fuller life.

SUMMARY

At the beginning of this book, we visited with the idea of the trickster. Often embodied as Coyote, Raven, or Rabbit, the trickster is subversive, disrespectful, and completely unimpressed by things being the way that they are. Deviance studies have, in the main, represented dominant ideologies, premodern and modern, which excluded and devalued perspectives other than that of middle-class White Western males.

Biological determinist explanations of deviance dominated much longer and more fully with respect to women than with respect to men. Attempts to move beyond the unwarranted emphasis on women's biology, appearance, and dependent roles toward a fully sociological or political picture of women's deviance have not yet drowned out the discourse of pathology.

Most of the newer work in the field of women's deviance is being done by men and women who take one of the many versions of the feminist perspective. Some are liberals who seek to reform society, so that women's roles will no longer hinder them. Some are Marxists who seek to change the economic system, so that neither men nor women are oppressed and exploited. Some are radicals who seek a much deeper structural and ideological overhaul of the discourses that guide us, so that women are no longer trapped in categories that they have not made for themselves.

Postmodernist thought has provided an example and a methodology for deconstructing the images and theories that have imprisoned the bodies and minds of "others" in multitudes of deviant attributions and categories. Postmodernism has shown the possibility of a different kind of freedom in a society without fixed standpoints and rigid truths. Although much of this material is utopian, and some of it merely replaces male dominance with female dominance, it has helped us to see that other worlds are possible, just as an earlier period moved beyond the ignorance of demonic superstition and fear. Whether ideas such as replacement discourse can help us find a meaningful integration of the theories discussed in this book remains to be seen, but the prospect of breakthrough has never been closer.

STUDY QUESTIONS

1. How much order, and what kind, do we need in order to have society? Must there be dominance and exclusion? How might a functionalist answer this? What is the radical answer?

2. Is it possible to liberate minorities and excluded categories without, for example, permitting the sexual exploitation of children? How might a liberating replacement discourse based in human rights help to accomplish this?

3. How can postmodernist thinking deconstruct the ideas of functionalism with respect to the need for deviance (and hence the need for exclusion)?

4. What kinds of thought are best classified as "prefeminist," "feminist," or "postfeminist"?

5. Why does feminism have difficulty coping with women's other identities as Blacks, Aboriginals, third world or first world, mothers, workers, and so on?

6. What do power-control theory (Hagan) and labelling theory (Schur) have in common with respect to their recognition of women's place in society? Why do radical feminists regard this as "not enough"?

7. The closest Foucault came to discussing women's issues was his publication of the memoirs of a nineteenth-century French hermaphrodite (Foucault, 1980). Does this mean that his theory can be dismissed as incomplete?

8. What are the common characteristics of feminist theories, according to Daly and Chesney-Lind?

9. How do writers such as Daly justify the invention of dictionaries of new words? Is this need for new words similar to the development of academic jargon or criminal argot?

10. Why are so many women reluctant to accept the label of "feminist"? Is this rejection of the label similar to Foucault's rejection of the label of homosexual?

11. Why do many feminist organizers express discomfort over postmodernist feminism? What are the implications of postfeminism for essentialist feminism (i.e., feminism based on the idea that women are intrinsically different from men)?

REFERENCES

Adler, F. (1975). *Sisters in Crime*. New York: McGraw-Hill.

Austin, J., Bloom, B., & Donahue, T. (1992). Female Offenders in the Community: An Analysis of Innovative Strategies and Programs, Part 6 of 8. *Contemporary Women's Database: Infonautics Corp, 09*(01), 46–57.

Bell, L. (Ed.). (1987). *Good Girls/Bad Girls: Sex Trade Workers and Feminists Face to Face*. Toronto: Women's Press.

Bonger, W. (1916). *Criminality and Economic Conditions*. Boston: Little, Brown.

Carlen, P. (1988). *Women Crime and Poverty*. Milton Keyes, UK: Open University Press.

Daly, K. (1997). Different Ways of Conceptualizing Sex/Gender in Feminist Theory and Their Implications for Criminology. *Theoretical Criminology, 1*(1), 25–52.

Daly, K., & Chesney-Lind, M. (1988). Feminism and Criminology. *Justice Quarterly, 5*(4), 497–538.

Daly, M. (1978). *Gyn/Ecology: The Metaethics of Radical Feminism*. Toronto: Fitzhenry and Whiteside.

———. (1992). *Outercourse: The Be-Dazzling Voyage*. San Francisco, CA: Harper.

Foucault, M. (1980). *Herculine Barbin* (R. McDougal, Trans.). New York: Pantheon.

Fraser, N. (1992). The Uses and Abuses of French Discourse Theories for Feminist Politics. In M. Featherstone (Ed.), *Cultural Theory and Cultural Change*. London, UK: Sage.

Gates, H. L. J. (1989). *The Signifying Monkey: A Theory of African-American Literary Criticism*. New York: Oxford University Press.

Gelsthorpe, L., & Morris, A. (Eds.). (1994). *Feminist Perspectives in Criminology*. Milton Keynes, UK: Open University Press.

Giddens, A. (1990). *The Consequences of Modernity*. Cambridge, UK: Polity.

Gilligan, C. (1982). *In a Different Voice*. Cambridge, MA: Harvard University Press.

Hagan, J., & Kay, F. (1990). Gender and Delinquency in White Collar Families: A Power-Control Perspective. *Crime and Delinquency, 36*, 391–407.

Heilbrun, C. (1988). *Writing a Woman's Life*. New York: Ballantine.

hooks, b. (1994). *Teaching to Transgress: Education as the Practice of Freedom*. New York: Routledge.

Hrdy, S. B. (1981). *The Woman That Never Evolved*. Cambridge, MA: Rowman and Allanheld.

Jervis, J. (1999). *Transgressing the Modern*. Oxford, UK: Blackwell.

King, T. (1993). *Green Grass, Running Water*. Boston: Houghton Mifflin.

Konopka, G. (1966). *The Adolescent Girl in Conflict*. Englewood Cliffs, NJ: Prentice-Hall.

Leonard, E. B. (1982). *Women, Crime and Society: A Critique of Theoretical Criminology*. New York: Longman.

Lorde, A. (1982). *Zami: A New Spelling of My Name*. Trumansburg, NY: Crossing.

Lowe, J. (1996). Monkey Kings and Mojo: Postmodern Ethnic Humor in Kingston, Reed, and Vizenor. *Melus, 21*(4), 103–127.

Lyman, S. M. (1995). Without Morals or Mores: Deviance in Postmodern Social Theory. *International Journal of Politics, Culture and Society, 9*(2), 197–236.

Mark, M., & Lesieur, H. R. (1992). Commentary: A Feminist Critique of Problem Gambling Research. *British Journal of Addiction, 87,* 549–565.

Martinez, T. (1994). Embracing the Outlaws: Deviance at the Intersection of Race, Class and Gender. *Utah Law Review, 1,* 193–207.

Messerschmidt, J. (1986). *Capitalism, Patriarchy and Crime: Toward a Socialist Feminist Criminology.* Totawa, NY: Rowman and Littlefield.

Millman, M. (1975). She Did It All for Love: A Feminist View of the Sociology of Deviance. In M. Millman & R. Kanter (Eds.), *Another Voice: Feminist Perspectives on Social Life and Social Science.* New York: Doubleday.

Phelan, S. (1996). Coyote Politics: Trickster Tales and Feminist Futures. *Hypatia, 11,* 130–150.

Rusinko, S. (1995). *Joe Orton.* Englewood Cliffs, NJ: Prentice-Hall.

Ryan, A. J. (1999). *The Trickster Shift: Humor and Irony in Contemporary Native Art.* Vancouver: University of British Columbia Press.

Schur, E. M. (1984). *Labelling Women Deviant: Gender, Stigma, and Social Control.* Philadelphia: Temple University Press.

Seidman, S. (1994). Queer Theory/Sociology: A Dialogue. *Sociological Theory, 12*(2), 166–177.

Simon, R. J. (1976). American Women and Crime. *Annals of the American Academy of Political and Social Science, 423,* 31–46.

Simpson, S. S., & Elis, L. (1994). Is Gender Subordinate to Class? An Empirical Assessment of Colvin and Pauly's Structural Marxist Theory of Delinquency. *Journal of Criminal Law and Criminology, 85*(2), 453–480.

Smith, C. (1997). Coyote, Contingency and Community: Thomas King's *Green Grass, Running Water* and the Postmodern Trickster. *American Indian Quarterly, 21*(3), 515–535.

Smith, D. (1973). Women's Perspective as a Radical Critique of Sociology. *Sociological Inquiry, 44*(1), 7–13.

———. (1995). *Criminology for Social Work.* Houndsmills, UK: Macmillan.

Smith, J. R. (1997). *Writing Tricksters: Mythic Gambols in American Ethnic Fiction.* Los Angeles: University of California Press.

Vizenor, G. (Ed.). (1993). *Narrative Chance: Postmodern Discourse on Native American Literatures.* Norman, OK: University of Oklahoma Press.

Young, A. (1996). *Imaging Crime.* London, UK: Sage.

COPYRIGHT ACKNOWLEDGMENTS

Grateful acknowledgment is made to the copyright holders who granted permission to reprint previously published material.

Box 1.2 (Deviance and the Media). Block quotation from *Black Swine in the Sewers of Hamptead,* by Thomas Boyle, copyright © 1989 by Thomas Boyle. Used by permission of Viking Penguin, a division of Penguin Putnam.

Figure 2.2. "The Crime Funnel" reproduced from *Juristat,* Catalogue No. 85-002, volume 10, July 1990. Statistics Canada information is used with the permission of the Minister of Industry, as Minister responsible for Statistics Canada. Information on the availability of the wide range of data from Statistics Canada can be obtained from Statistics Canada's Regional Offices, its World Wide Web site, at http://www.statcan.ca, and its toll-free access number, 1-800-263-1136.

Box 2.2 (Validity of Information). From "The Lupollo Family" from *A Family Business: Kinship and Social Control in Organized Crime,* by Francis A. Ianni. Reprinted with permission.

Page 55. Block quotation from *Hustlers, Beats and Others,* by Ned Polsky, 1967 edition. Reprinted by special arrangement with The Lyons Press.

Figure 2.4. "An Example of the Use of Uniform Crime Reporting Data in Combination with Other Sources of Information," created from Statistics Canada's CANSIM database, Matrix Nos. 3302 and 3309; and "Sentencing in Adult Provincial Courts: A Study of Nine Jurisdictions, 1993–1994," Catalogue No. 85-513. Statistics Canada information is used with the permission of the Minister of Industry, as Minister responsible for Statistics Canada. Information on the availability of the wide range of data from Statistics Canada can be obtained from Statistics Canada's Regional Offices, its World Wide Web site, at http://www.statcan.ca, and its toll-free access number, 1-800-263-1136.

Figure 3.1. From *Struwwelpeter: In English Translation,* by Heinrich Hoffman.

Page 77. Block quotation from *The Women's Encyclopedia of Myths and Secrets,* by Barbara G. Walker. Copyright © 1983 by Barbara G. Walker. Reprinted by permission of HarperCollins Publishers, Inc.

Figure 3.3. "Heretics about to Be Burned," from Mary Evans Picture Library. Reprinted with permission.

INDEX